Rituals of Self-Revelation:
Shishōsetsu as Literary Genre
and Socio-Cultural Phenomenon

Harvard East Asian Monographs
164

Rituals of Self-Revelation:
Shishōsetsu as Literary Genre and Socio-Cultural Phenomenon

Irmela Hijiya-Kirschnereit

Published by the Council on East Asian Studies, Harvard University;
and distributed by Harvard University Press,
Cambridge (Massachusetts) and London   1996

Copyright © 1996 by the President and Fellows of Harvard College
Printed in the United States of America

© 1981 of the original German edition by Franz Steiner Verlag Weisbaden
GmbH, Sitz Stuttgart, P.O.B. 101061, D-70009 Stuttgart, Germany

The Council on East Asian Studies at Harvard University publishes a monograph series and, through the Fairbank Center for East Asian Research and the Reischauer Institute of Japanese Studies, administers research projects designed to further scholarly understanding of China, Japan, Korea, Vietnam, Inner Asia, and adjacent areas.

Library of Congress Cataloging-in-Publication Data

Hijiya-Kirschnereit, Irmela.
  [Selbstentblössungsrituale. English]
  Rituals of self-revelation : shishōsetsu as literary genre and
socio-cultural phenomenon / Irmela Hijiya-Kirschnereit.
    p. cm. — (Harvard East Asian monographs ; 164)
  Includes bibliographical references and index.
    ISBN 0-674-77319-5
  1. Autobiographical fiction, Japanese—History and criticism.
  2. Japanese fiction—20th century—History and criticism.
    I. Title.   II. Series.
PL747.67.A85H5513 1996
895.6'3009—dc20   95-43358
                            CIP

Contents

Preface ix

Abbreviations Used in the Notes and Bibliography xxi

Preliminary Remarks on Procedures xxiii

Introduction 1

PART ONE: CONTEXT AND ORIGINS 11

1 HISTORICAL AND CULTURAL CONTEXT 13

2 *SHIZENSHUGI*—JAPANESE NATURALISM 21

3 TAYAMA KATAI—A JAPANESE NATURALIST 31
The Question of "Influence" 35
West-East Elective Affinities 36
"Misunderstandings" 37
Innovation as Renovation 39

4 "FUTON" 43
Autobiographical Elements 44
The Influence of Hauptmann 46
The Genealogy of the Work 48
"Reinforcements" in Contemporary Literature 50

5 THE "THEORETICAL" RECEPTION OF "FUTON"—REVIEWS AND ESSAYS 57

6   THE "PRACTICAL" RECEPTION OF "FUTON"—
    IMITATIONS AND PARODIES   63

PART TWO: SHISHŌSETSU RESEARCH   71

7   GENERAL OBSERVATIONS ON THE STATE OF RESEARCH   73

8   THE "CLASSICS" OF SHISHŌSETSU RESEARCH   79
    Kobayashi Hideo: "Watakushishōsetsuron"   79
    Itō Sei: *Shōsetsu no hōhō*   83
    Nakamura Mitsuo: *Fūzoku shōsetsuron*   86
    Hirano Ken: *Geijutsu to jisseikatsu*   89

9   A SURVEY OF SHISHŌSETSU RESEARCH   95
    History of Shishōsetsu and of Shishōsetsu Theory   95
    Shishōsetsu Authors and Works   100
    Special Aspects of Shishōsetsu   108
    Recent Trends in Shishōsetsu Research, 1979–1988   115

PART THREE: GENRE THEORY   129

10   HISTORY OF THE TERM   131
    Predecessors of Shishōsetsu   132
    Theoretical Premises   136
    The Origins of the Term *Watakushishōsetsu*   138

11   THE LITERARY DEBATE SURROUNDING SHISHŌSETSU   147
    The Context of the Discussion   147
    The Dispute over Shishōsetsu   150

12   CONVENTIONAL DEFINITIONS OF SHISHŌSETSU   161

13   GENRE THEORY IN JAPAN   165

14   SHISHŌSETSU—AN ATTEMPT TO DEFINE THE GENRE   169
    Preliminary Thoughts   169
    Outline of a Structural Model   174

PART FOUR: TRANSFORMATIONS IN SHISHŌSETSU   195

15   LITERARY EVOLUTION—AN OUTLINE   197

16   SHISHŌSETSU—EXAMPLES AND ANALYSES   201
    Iwano Hōmei: "Tandeki" (1909)   201
    Chikamatsu Shūkō: "Giwaku" (1913)   208
    Shiga Naoya: "Wakai" (1917)   212
    Kasai Zenzō: "Ko o tsurete" (1918)   220

Kikuchi Kan: "Tomo to tomo to no aida" (1918)   223
Hayashi Fumiko: *Hōrōki* (1928–1930)   230
Dazai Osamu: *Ningen shikkaku* (1948)   237
Miura Tetsuo: "Shinobugawa" (1960)   247

PART FIVE: SHISHŌSETSU WITHIN THE SYSTEM OF LITERARY COMMUNICATION   261

17   INTRODUCTORY REMARKS   263

18   SHISHŌSETSU'S COMMUNICATIVE FUNCTION   269
　　　The Author of Shishōsetsu   269
　　　The Hero in Shishōsetsu   278
　　　The Shishōsetsu Reader   285

19   ASPECTS OF TRADITIONALISM   297
　　　Diaries and Miscellany Literature   297
　　　"Lyricism"   300
　　　Nature Mysticism   302

20   THE CULTURAL CODE   307
　　　The *Makoto* Principle   307
　　　Empiricism   310
　　　The Myth of Immediacy   312
　　　Irrationalism and Fatalism   314

21   SHISHŌSETSU—A CRITICAL ASSESSMENT   321

Bibliography   329

Appendix to the Bibliography   351

Index of Persons and Works   357

Subject Index   367

Preface

Why shishōsetsu? When I began working on this topic in the second half of the seventies, my interest was first of all directed at exploring an important prose genre in modern Japanese literature; but at the same time I was convinced that by studying shishōsetsu, I could obtain valuable clues as to a specific understanding of literature and its role for readers, authors, and a society as a whole. It was, however, a time when shishōsetsu was still suffering from the effects of the severe criticism during the immediate postwar period in the late forties and early fifties. As a consequence, literary studies hardly dealt with the topic, and critical essays and other materials were sparse and scattered. The only publication in book form then known to me was Yamamoto Kenkichi's *Watakushi-shōsetsu sakkaron,* which was first published in 1943, and, in an extended version, in 1966; this study, however, did not focus on the genre as such but on a number of its authors. There was another book length study, Nishida Masayoshi's *Shishōsetsu saihakken* of 1973, but I only learned of it long after I had completed my own manuscript in 1979, publishing my book in the original German version in 1981.[1] Since the late seventies, the history of shishōsetsu research has indeed taken a new turn, and it is at this turning point where, significantly, my own study is situated.

In retrospect, we can see clearly that it was in the second half of the seventies that Japanese writers and readers took a new interest in matters of shishōsetsu, and this development was reflected in the field of literary study which has since produced a larger number of books on the topic than it did during half of the century preceding it. Indicative of this new trend at about the turn of the decade is Japanese literary criticism as it is documented, for example, in *Bungei nenkan,* the Literary Yearbooks. A closer reading reveals that shishōsetsu is increasingly used as a kind of measuring device. Thus, the question as to whether a certain work is shishōsetsu or not gains relevance as a criterion, and what is moreover remarkable is the fact that an affinity towards shishōsetsu no longer automatically leads to a negative evaluation.[2] In this context, we may also discover that it is by no means clear what is meant by shishōsetsu or a shishōsetsu-like style of writing, and so we may well come across odd statements such as that Tsushima Yūko's cycle of stories "Hikari no ryōbun" (Sphere of Light) is probably not shishōsetsu, but "extremely shishōsetsu-like" (*kiwamete shishōsetsuteki*),[3] or that Toyoda Minoru's Naoki prize-winning "Nagaragawa" (The River Nagara) is a "shishōsetsu-like shishōsetsu without being shishōsetsu" (*shishōsetsu de wa nai shishōsetsutekina shishōsetsu*).[4] In round-table talks and discussions of major critics, shishōsetsu begins to feature prominently from the early eighties[5] onwards, and one critic, Ueda Miyoji, confesses in one of these talks that he would rather refrain from using the term any more in his current critical articles (*bungei jihyō*), precisely because almost anything published these days was shishōsetsu-like anyway (. . . *tsukurarete iru sakuhin ga, hotondo to itte ii kurai shishōsetsuteki de aru kara nan desu ne*).[6] According to this rather extreme viewpoint, shishōsetsu practically coincides with artistic prose or so-called "pure literature" (*junbungaku*).

Admittedly, we will also encounter scholars of literature who take a strongly critical stance towards shishōsetsu such as Shinoda Hajime, whose *Nihon no gendai shōsetsu* (Contemporary Japanese Prose) of 1980 abounds with critical invectives against representatives of the genre, which he rejects for aesthetic reasons such as its lack of structure. On the whole, however, shishōsetsu encounters a generally more positive attitude, which is apparent not only from the increasing number of scholarly studies on the topic, but also from collections of material such as a popular selection of works under the heading of *Shishōsetsu meisakusen* (Collection of Famous Shishōsetsu), edited by the PEN center and selected by Nakamura Mitsuo in 1980, as well as from many others which will be introduced later in the research report in Chapter 9 of this study.[7]

It is interesting to note that even those authors of literature who were not automatically associated with the genre previously no longer feel the need to distance themselves from shishōsetsu. They may even deliberately admit a certain closeness which is all the more astonishing in the case of Endō Shūsaku's historical novel *Samurai* of 1980, which is described in the book's inset/supplement by the author as his "own kind of shishōsetsu" (. . . *kono shōsetsu wa boku no shishōsetsu mitaina mono nan da yo,* p. 8). Also the example of Ōe Kenzaburō comes to mind; his works, since his 1982 *'Rein tsurī' o kiku onnatachi* (Women Who Listen to the Rain Tree), have frequently provoked comparisons with the genre, going so far as to the effect that in 1991, critic Matsubara Shin'ichi felt obliged to stress explicitly the non-shishōsetsu quality in an article about his literature.[8] Yet it is not only the well-established authors of the postwar generation but countless writers having since entered the literary stage who have—in a surprisingly straightforward manner—been categorized as contributing to this much-abused genre.[9]

Other authors employ the genre's name in a playful way: for example, Nosaka Akiyuki's 1979 collection of stories is titled *Shishōsetsu,* the first character, denoting "death," being homonymous with the first element of the genre's name, Sino-Japanese "I" (*shi*). Another example is Setouchi Harumi's novel of 1985, *Watakushishōsetsu,* while another female author, Hayashi Mariko, instructs the readers of her 1988 story written with the characters to read them "Shishōsetsu," one more coquettish reference to an all too familiar pattern. Remarkably, the latter is not a typical example of the genre, but the author nevertheless plays with typical shishōsetsu reading habits.[10]

As these random samples of playing with the popularity of shishōsetsu conventions suggest, the genre appears to be as vitally alive as ever, in spite of critics such as Isoda Kōichi, who, in his *Sengoshi no kūkan* (The Space of Postwar History, 1983) diagnosed its increasing anachronism. On the contrary, new generations with an unbroken curiosity in the genre emerge among writers, afflicted with what Hayashi, in the story mentioned before, named a "writing disease" (*kakitagaru byō*)—thereby using the same expression as Akutagawa did more than half a century earlier to describe the irresistible impulse to confess. And on the part of the readership, the appetite for these self-disclosures has not waned either. It will be one of the tasks of this study to identify reasons for the popularity of shishōsetsu among Japanese readers.

When asked for the reasons for this obvious revaluation of the genre in recent years, one can only speculate. Yet it seems certain that a variety of factors has to be taken into account. As a general trend, the growing interest since the seventies in matters of national culture and identity, manifested, among others, in the *Nihonjinron* boom, could form one framework. The renewed interest in matters deemed "typically Japanese" is another expression of this motivation, and as the Introduction to this work will show, shishōsetsu is counted among such matters. In the wake of this re-awakened interest follows a revalorization drawing a much more positive picture of the genre than in the preceding decades. This development may have been fostered by a generational change in Japanese literary criticism marked by the death of Kobayashi Hideo, the towering father figure of Japanese criticism, in 1983. At the same time, however, we observe that literary research in Japan increasingly turns to more recent topics which, although this was never explicitly stated, had somehow been regarded as less serious objects of research before. This greater openness to new themes and approaches, indicated, for example, by the special edition themes of literary and semi-academic journals with wide circulation, may also be responsible for the growing research interest in shishōsetsu. And last but not least, literary life itself, or, what I have termed elsewhere the "stubborn persistence of a much-abused genre,"[11] may have inspired research after all.

In academia outside of Japan, or, to be more precise, in North America and Western Europe, the topic of shishōsetsu is likewise viewed in a more favorable light. This can be traced back to two main tendencies. One of them is an obvious curiosity about topics traditionally deemed particularly "Japanese" and therefore difficult to tackle. Since the late seventies, the younger generation of American and European Japanologists have turned to translations and critical studies of hitherto widely neglected authors such as Shiga Naoya, Kajii Motojirō, Ozaki Kazuo, Dazai Osamu, Shimao Toshio and others who happen to be exponents of shishōsetsu. Often, translations are combined with critical commentary or interpretive essays attempting to unravel the seemingly hermetic material.

The other important tendency in the study of Japanese literature on both sides of the Atlantic is its rapprochement with strands of mainstream criticism in the eighties which prompted new perspective and approaches. In the case of shishōsetsu research, the application of narratological theory inspired by Tzvetan Todorov or Gérard Genette has proven particularly fruitful. Edward Fowler's *Rhetoric of Confession* of 1988, while also contributing to the history of the genre, testifies to this new narratological interest. Moreover, post-structuralism or deconstructivism as well as psychoanalytical, feminist and new historicist criticism have since entered the study of Japanese literature. In this context, critical inquiry into modern Japanese fiction has opened up new horizons. Against the background of a discourse analysis inspired by Foucault, Bakhtin, Bourdieu and others, research interest has shifted and constituted new agendas. One observes these phenomena *in nuce* in relation to one of the central notions associated with the genre of shishōsetsu, that ominous "modern self" or *kindai jiga* which, as a new notion of a modern, liberated individual, is said to have formed, albeit on a more or less subconscious level, a major driving force in the formation of shishōsetsu as a genre. It seems, though, that the *kindai jiga* has much of the nature of a fata morgana, while shishōsetsu developed its vitality largely unrelated to concepts born out of the wishful thinking of a rather flat modernization theory.

Still, since the genre is regarded as an expression of a particular subjectivity, shishōsetsu research finds itself within the maelstrom of a fundamental questioning of the nature of subjectivity, be it from the angle of linguistic theory and Lacan's assertion that "the ego is a function or effect of a subject which is always dispersed, never identical with itself, strung out along the chains of the discourses which constitute it,"[12] or be it in the form of Althusser's "decentred" function of several social determinants. In the field of modern Japanese literary history, James Fujii, among others, has most radically interrogated "the positive, empiricist, and commonsensical conception of the subject that has anchored the Western humanist tradition and expressed itself through realist literary conventions."[13]

While these studies which insist on the power of the discourse over the subject certainly open up new horizons in our inquiry and constitute new awareness and knowledge, their epistemologies do not automatically render other perspectives obsolete. On the contrary, we may observe that for those interested in establishing causalities, or genealogies, a Foucaultian approach which focuses on discourse analysis will not provide satisfying answers. Or, to take the example of an earlier and most challenging study, Karatani, who in the only article I consulted for the original version of this study still called himself Yukihito instead of the now common reading Kōjin, appeared to be as disappointing in providing a "genealogy" of shishōsetsu as he is fascinating in his reading of crucial paradigms in modern literary history, as developed by him in his *Origins of Modern Japanese Literature,* first published in 1980.[14]

In the light of this and many other Japanese and Western studies on modern literature, much of what I sketched as a "background" to the emergence of shishōsetsu may sound outdated or cry for precision or modification. But the same holds true for other periods in Japanese literary history. Looking back over the past fifteen years makes one aware that in all established fields, the study of Japanese literature has developed considerably, making my considerations concerning the relationship of shishōsetsu with traditional genres such as *zuihitsu* and *nikki* sound badly in need of sophistication. Certainly, they would have greatly profited from what we now know about the borderlines between and interrelatedness of poetry and prose. But intended as a preliminary sketch for a new, "historicized" assessment of the genre, I present them for further inquiry as the rough material that they are.

As a matter of fact, the whole study would certainly look quite different were I to write on shishōsetsu now. Undoubtedly, much would have been rephrased or rearranged in the light of new findings. It seems wise, however, to resist the temptation to rewrite this study in parts or to incorporate new materials, for this could only result in an unfelicitous hybrid version. Instead, I present the study in its original shape. The only addition is the last part of the research report, "Recent Trends in Shishōsetsu Research, 1979–1988." Apart from an updating of some data such as the years of death of authors still alive in 1981 and a few minor modifications, the text and footnotes present the study as it was completed in 1979 and went into print in 1981.

It was a time when, in German Japanology, not much research was done on twentieth century literature since this was regarded, as in Japan, to be intrinsically more lightweight than "classical" material. Japanology, though, was a tiny island (or ivory tower) within a bubbling sea of new theories and methodologies in the German academia of the seventies, and it was therefore Germanic, Slavic, Romanic and Anglo-American literature and language studies as well as sociology and philosophy which were an inspiration to my attempt at applying "methods" to the study of modern Japanese literature. One of my first publications, an article titled "Critical Remarks on Japanese Literary Criticism," published in 1974, bespeaks the will to criticize the hidden assumptions of Japanese criticism in the light of a more "advanced," "enlightened" theory,[15] and it is no wonder that it was completely ignored in German Japanology as was my doctoral dissertation, published in 1976, on a contemporary topic, namely "Mishima Yukio's novel 'Kyōko no ie'—An Attempt at an Intratextual Analysis."[16] This isolation within Japanology and orientation along theories and concepts then prevalent in German academia in the field of literary history and genre theory, mostly of structuralist and reception theory origin, spiced with critical theory, semiotics, communication theory and psychoanalysis, characterizes the present study. Readers from other scientific communities will perceive that the reception of theories and methodologies may differ from country to country, not only in the weight given or denied to a certain approach but also in the point of time and order of its reception. In Western Europe, however, this observation seems commonplace, as we are very much aware of fairly different "discursive worlds," even in neighboring countries. That these differences should be reflected in the study of Japanese literature is therefore only to be expected.[17]

Meanwhile, German Japanology has also experienced a certain development, even though the relatively small number of researchers does not facilitate a dialogue within the field. Yet it may be more than symbolic that among the youngest generation of Japanologists, we also encounter a fundamental critique of the epistemology of shishōsetsu research from the point of view of Habermas' *Theory of Communicative Action,* taking the form of a polarization between a decontextualized rationalism and a relativistic and tendentially reactionary contextualism.[18]

We hope that the present study will, after all, not be completely outdated by the time of its publication in English. The Japanese version which appeared in 1992 was surprisingly well received, judging from more than a dozen reviews.[19] It seems that it served to stimulate a new debate on the genre. To speak of the present book as presenting the study in its "original shape" amounts, however, to a gross simplification. Thus, it was a fascinating experience to all of us who tackled the task of reworking an English version of the text to be confronted with the resistance of English to this kind of discursive German prose, and the work on the English manuscript was also a fascinating lesson in the ambiguity of natural languages and in the distance between "neighboring" languages. Even the title posed unexpected difficulties, for the German *Selbstentblößung* implies all—self-revelation, disclosure, and denudation.

Some idiosyncrasies of the German version indicative of a particular understanding of key terms had to be resolved such as the consistent use of quotation marks in order to make readers aware that "novel," "story," and "short story" were nothing more than auxiliary devices to render the Japanese *chōhen, chūhen,* and *tanpen shōsetsu* comprehensible without necessarily implying that they shared constitutive features of the Western genres. Meanwhile, the incongruity between Western and Japanese genres has been pointed out by a number of authors, including Masao Miyoshi and Janet Walker. One of the consequences of the lack of alternatives for a constant "distancing" of Western and Japanese genre names was that I tried to avoid them altogether wherever possible, although the problem is thus by no means solved. One solution would have been to retain the Japanese terms, but this runs counter to a general practice which practically all studies on Japanese literature have employed so far.

Other terminological alterations are hard to assess. The German version, for example, distinguishes between hero and protagonist, the latter being a more recent and more neutral designation which is therefore applied in most cases in the book. For reasons of style, however, the English version substitutes "hero" for "protagonist," so that the difference is no longer perceptible.

Different academic conventions and publishing practices, along with the constrictions of style, were responsible for a restructuring of the table of contents and layout to the effect that the study now possesses a different architecture—the German format favors differentiation and transparency of structure, as reflected in an elaborate hierarchy of chapters and subchapters, while the present version comes closer to a horizontal arrangement of different aspects. Also, I learned that in American studies within the humanities, abbreviated forms of quotation, giving only the author's name and the year of publication plus page number, a practice which we favor for its convenience, are not acceptable. As a consequence, the research report had to be reworded in many parts to avoid awkward redundancies in the text. While the required change of format affected the style and content of the study to a greater degree than anticipated, this was certainly not a major problem in the complicated history of the present version.

Here a word may be in order on the long and ever delayed history of the English version. Some of the reviewers of the original version, above all Richard Bowring, had proposed a translation; and it was Katō Shūichi, reviewer of my *Selbstentblößungsrituale* in vol. 10 of the *Journal of Japanese Studies,* who took the initiative to propose a Japanese version. In the States, one University Press had shown a keen interest in the manuscript for a long period before it changed its policy, and it was at this point of time that the Council on East Asian Studies at Harvard University, upon recommendation by Howard Hibbett, took over. The problem was, however, to come up with a translation at a point in time when, in the context of Japanese Studies, there seemed to me hardly anyone available who was versed in the vocabulary of theories employed. Moreover one was not likely at the time to encounter concepts and expressions such as "defamiliarize," "problematic," or "affective schema" in studies of Japanese literature in English. The result was that in the first draft translation made by Caroline Busse, herself a specialist in European history, much of the technical terminology as well as the more specific lines of argument were lost. Nevertheless, the draft translation completed by the mid-eighties was the basis for the courageous decision of the Council on East Asian Studies at Harvard to publish the book. It took several years until an edited version reached me, a result of meticulous editing by Florence Trefethen, then Executive Editor at the Council. Unfortunately, I was then in the midst of negotiations with several universities, and when in 1991 I decided to move from Trier, where I had been appointed a Professor in 1986 and built up the Department of Japanese Studies, to Berlin, settling here was more work than I had anticipated, so that work on the edited manuscript was postponed again and again and I almost gave up the idea of having the translation published. Meanwhile, however, the Japanese version appeared in April 1992, and it was the unexpectedly positive response in Japan as well as the equally unexpected renewal of a translation grant by the German Inter Nationes Fund (the contract for which had expired) that made me reconsider completing the task. I was also encouraged by Dr. Katherine Keenum, successor to Florence Trefethen, to go ahead with preparing the book. In the summer of 1993, then, Matthias Hoop, a doctoral candidate in Japanese literature, began to retype and restructure the whole edited manuscript according to this publisher's rules. The next step was that we both went back to the original once more and tried to restore as much of its original stylistic flow and nuances of meaning and to find adequate vocabulary for the technical terms, a process which involved checking the text again word for word, line for line. Nadeem Niazi, a native speaker of English and graduate student of Yale and the Free University in comparative literature, was the next to check our English against the original. Finally, Lee Ann Best, Assistant Editor at the Council, took pains to edit and refine once more the latest English version in a final checkup. The present synthetic version is therefore the result of extensive teamwork on both sides of the Atlantic, and I am deeply grateful to everyone involved in this painstaking process: the work could not have been completed without their help.

I also remember with special gratitude Janet Walker's constant encouragement over the years with this project which she had supported from the very beginning, as well as Carol Gluck's sympathy and advice. Carol also introduced Winnie Olson to me who, with the rare capacities of being a Japan specialist, well-versed in German and an excellent stylist, agreed to edit the manuscript. Undoubtedly, this book would have profited greatly from her commitment, and it was only the complication of communicating between New York and Trier that eventually forced us to give up the idea.

Thanks to the energy, toil, and encouragement of so many persons, the present English version will now, hopefully, help to bridge the gap between scientific communities on both sides of the Atlantic. It is the Council on East Asian Studies at Harvard University as well as the Inter Nationes Fund in Bonn, Germany, whom I would like to thank for their patience and interest.

---

1. Works which had not been accessible to me when writing the book as well as titles which have appeared since 1981 are listed in the Appendix. It is hoped that this comprehensive list of references concerning shishōsetsu, including the asterisked titles in the main bibliography, will facilitate further research.
2. Cf., e.g., Nakajima Makoto in *Bungei nenkan* 1980, pp. 61f. and 64, Akiyama Shun in *Bungei nenkan* 1981, p. 97, Akiyama Shun in *Bungei nenkan* 1982, pp. 59, 77, 88f., 116 etc.
3. Ueda Miyoji in Saeki Shōichi et al., "Kyōdō tōgi 'Shishōsetsu,'" p. 149.
4. Ōmori Morikazu, "Dai rokujūyonkai: Nagaragawa—Toyoda Minoru," *Naoki-shō jiten. KKK* (enlarged special ed.), June 1977, p. 370.
5. Cf. the round-table talk cited in note 3, but also Shinoda Hajime et al., "Nihon bungaku no genzai (kyōdō tōgi)," 1982.
6. Ueda Miyoji in Saeki Shōichi et al., "Kyōdō tōgi 'Shishōsetsu,'" p. 149.
7. The most recent book-length study on shishōsetsu is Andō Hiroshi, *Jiishiki no Shōwa bungaku: Genshō to shite no "watakushi"* (Tokyo: Shibundō, 1994).
8. Matsubara Shin'ichi, "Ōe Kenzaburō no bungaku," *Nishi Nihon shinbun,* 23 October 1991, p. 19.
9. To take one recent example: 1991 Mishima Yukio prize winner Saeki Kazumi published a collection of stories, *Ki no ichizoku,* in 1994, which is announced in the catalog of new titles *Kore kara deru hon* (no. 5, March 1994, p. 19) as a collection of an author who "continues to write shishōsetsu."
10. I have described the narrative strategies and allusions to the shishōsetsu pattern of reception of this story in an essay titled "Erzählte Erfahrung und literarischer Markt," in *Japanische Literatur der Gegenwart,* ed. Siegfried Schaarschmidt and Michiko Mae (Munich: Hanser, 1990).
11. Cf. my 1984 essay listed in the Appendix to the Bibliography.
12. Terry Eagleton, *Literary Theory: An Introduction* (London: Basil Blackwell, 1983), p. 169.
13. James Fujii, *Complicit Fictions: The Subject in the Modern Japanese Prose Narrative* (Berkeley: University of California Press, 1993), p. 2.
14. Cf. Karatani Kōjin, *Kindai bungaku no kigen* (Tokyo: Kōdansha, 1980).
15. Cf. my "Kritische Bemerkungen zur japanischen Literaturkritik."
16. There were only Japanese reviews of the book. The earlier essay, however, was reviewed by Marián Gálik, who began his review of the present book by stating: "When reading Dr. Hijiya-Kirschnereit's first work entitled 'Kritische Bemerkungen zur japanischen Literaturkritik' from the year 1974, the present reviewer remarked that it was 'truly a

remarkable' study. The same could be asserted about the book under review." Cf. the review of the German version in *Asian and African Studies* (Bratislava, London) 20 (1984), pp. 211–214.

17. Cf. *Othernesses of Japan: Historical and Cultural Influences on Japanese Studies in Ten Countries,* ed. Harumi Befu and Josef Kreiner (Monographien aus dem Deutschen Institut für Japan-Studien der Philipp-Franz-von-Siebold-Stiftung, vol. I; Munich: Iudicium, 1992). My contribution in the volume deals with "Japanologie and its 'Teutonicisms': Reflections on a 'National' Approach in Japanese Studies."

18. Cf. the forthcoming M.A. thesis by Rainer Weihs at the Free University of Berlin.

19. Under the title *Shishōsetsu: Jiko bakuro no gishiki* (Tokyo: Heibonsha, 1992).

Abbreviations Used in the Notes and Bibliography

GBRT	*Gendai bungakuron taikei*
GNBD	*Gendai Nihon bungaku daijiten*
GNBR	*Gendai Nihon bungaku ronsōshi*
GNBT	*Gendai Nihon bungaku taikei*
HJAS	*Harvard Journal of Asiatic Studies*
JJS	*The Journal of Japanese Studies*
JQ	*Japan Quarterly*
KBG	*Kokubungaku: Kaishaku to kyōzai no kenkyū*
KBHT	*Kindai bungaku hyōron taikei*
KBYJ	*Yōrei ni miru kindai bungakushi yōgo jiten*
KGJ	*Kokugogaku jiten*
KKK	*Kokubungaku: Kaishaku to kanshō*
MBZ	*Meiji bungaku zenshū*
MN	*Monumenta Nipponica*
NBD	*Zōho kaitei Nihon bungaku daijiten*
NBS	*Shinchō Nihon bungaku shōjiten*
NKBT	*Nihon koten bungaku taikei*
NKBZ	*Nihon koten bungaku zenshū*
NKiBT	*Nihon kindai bungaku taikei*
NOAG	*Nachrichten der Gesellschaft für Natur- und Völkerkunde Ostasiens*

Preliminary Remarks on Procedures

READINGS OF JAPANESE NAMES

In general, the readings given in the respective texts were observed. In cases where they were missing or diverging, the reading given in *Shinchō Nihon bungaku shōjiten* was taken as a rule.

SOURCE REFERENCES

Wherever possible, original sources were cited. In other cases, quotations were taken from the Collected Works (*zenshū*). If they were not existent or accessible, another collection of texts was used instead. See the List of Abbreviations.

PAGE REFERENCES WITHIN THE TEXT

Where literary works were summarized and synopses of relevant theoretical debates were provided, page numbers set in parentheses refer to the work under discussion.

DATES

On first mention of an author's name, biographical dates are given. The dates given for a literary work refer to the first publication. Serialized newspaper novels thus date before their publication in book form. In cases of closer analysis, the month is added.

READING THE GENRE NAME IN JAPANESE TITLES

If the reading is not given or titles to be ascertained in reference works are well-known, the reading *shishōsetsu* instead of *watakushishōsetsu* is employed.

Introduction

> Each new treatise on the "autobiographical" novel results in a further complication of the problem.

This warning from Kobayashi Hideo,[1] the long-standing Nestor of Japanese literary criticism, arouses our curiosity. What are the problems and what does he mean by complication?

The problems arise at the outset with the naming of this study, or, to be more precise, with the designation of its subject matter, the literary genre denoted by the characters that mean "I," and "novel."[2] Two readings are possible, the purely Sino-Japanese *shishōsetsu* or a Japanese-Sino-Japanese hybrid (*yutōyomi*) *watakushishōsetsu*. According to the standard dictionary, *Kōjien,* a possible first recourse in cases of doubt, *shishōsetsu* is correct. The second reading is, however, most common in literary reference works and, until now, it has not been considered necessary to make a single reading mandatory, doubtless because in Japan the problem arises only in the spoken language, since both pronunciations are based on the same written form. On the other hand, many literary critics insist on the reading *watakushishōsetsu*, although they can give no compelling reason for that choice. Even in personal conversations with a number of researchers, I have been unable to discover their motivation. The majority seems to share the opinion of their colleague Usui Yoshimi: "*Shishōsetsu* is strange. It must surely be *watakushishōsetsu.*"[3]

If, however, being "strange" (*okashii*) is to be a criterion, it ought to apply to the other reading, for statistics indicate that a pure Sino-Japanese reading is much more frequent, not to mention the fact that it is more pleasant to pronounce than a hybrid. Nevertheless, to avoid appearing just as arbitrary in my own choice, I add these reasons:

If one relies, in addition to the previous arguments based on general language usage, on a semantic differentiation, it seems to me that, in *watakushishōsetsu,* there is an emphasis on the "I" in the sense of a first-person narrator. It will be one purpose of this study, however, to show that this emphasis on the "I" is by no means an essential characteristic of the genre; some of the best-known examples are written in the third-person form. *Shishōsetsu* is, therefore, more suitable, since the "I" in it can be readily interpreted to indicate, on a more abstract level, the central author-hero in the novel, and this, we will learn, is indeed a significant characteristic of the genre.

Furthermore, we will consider a historical aspect. *Watakushishōsetsu* was the ad hoc name created by writers to designate a group of works written in the first-person form. When this term was adopted in general discussion and began to stand for the genre as a whole, the reading *shishōsetsu* won out.[4]

A scholar of Western literature might shake his head at problems as absurd as this. But one must try to prevent inaccurate inferences; shishōsetsu is not a shadowy, generally neglected term in Japanese literature, but

> a genre that has remained highly important in Japanese literature down to the present day.[5]

> Whether we like it or not—since [the beginning of] the modern age, shishōsetsu has continuously been the dominant mode of Japanese literature, that is, it possesses as it were archetypal (*genkei*) rank and importance.[6]

> There are really no contemporary writers who have not written shishōsetsu.[7]

There is no dearth of such remarks from historians of Japanese literature. On the contrary, there is absolute agreement on the centrality of this genre in this century's literature. Hirano Ken, for example, writes:

> Our modern Japanese literary history was forced to condense and assimilate the history of several centuries of European literature in the space of less than seventy years. At this hectic pace, the [rapid] rise and fall of a multiplicity of literary currents (*bungei shichō*) was inevitable. In the midst of this bewildering series of different "isms" (*shugi shuchō*), shishōsetsu has now existed for more than forty years and still exists today. This is certainly reason enough to consider it a mature literary tradition. It would be impossible to say any-

thing coherent about the internal logic that runs throughout modern Japanese literature if one were to ignore this shishōsetsu tradition.[8]

The genre does indeed form a focal point, for almost all of the theoretical and practical questions that arose in Japan's literary world since the later Meiji days can be exemplified through shishōsetsu. This will become clear as soon as we take a look at its origin and history.

Shishōsetsu developed at the beginning of the century from *shizenshugi,* a literary current that took its orientation from European naturalism and declared its dedication to truth and "straightforward description." *Shizenshugi,* however, achieved general recognition only after the insistence on unconditional and value-free description was reinterpreted in favor of unsparing personal testimony. The origins of shishōsetsu are to be found in this change of direction, when the private and privatistic became a subject for literature and when the mainstream of *shizenshugi* shifted to confessional literature whose aesthetic value began to be judged according to the sincerity of the confession.

One glimpses already the knot this book will attempt to untangle. The question of European influence on Japanese literature, of the conditions necessary for receptivity to this influence, the "misunderstandings," and the conversion of theory into practice are daunting problems that have not yet been clearly resolved in research up to this time. Yet no examination of the origins of shishōsetsu can ignore the question of Western influence.

Scarcely more is known about the non-literary factors that favored the birth of the new genre. It is impossible to identify and catalogue neatly the relevant historical influences; yet one is not justified in letting this mistrust lead to a purely formalist or biographical approach, as is the case in Japanese shishōsetsu research.

Such problems relating to the genre will be considered in the first part of this book, "Context and Origins." A general picture of the historical and intellectual-historical context is followed by a socio-cultural and literary characterization of *shizenshugi,* and then by an examination of one paradigmatic figure. The pivotal point of this section is formed by the examination of the short story "Futon," regarded in Japan as both the first and a representative example of shishōsetsu. This is followed by a delineation of the development which led to the present shape of the work, of its "buttresses" in the literature of the period, a discussion of Western influences, and of the reactions of contemporaries to it—in short, this section tries to give a picture of the historical situation, of the horizon of expectation of the period, and of the specific characteristics that led contemporary reception to consider "Futon" a sensational innovation to the extent that it is considered a turning point in Japanese literary history.[9]

The slight interest that Japanese literary studies have shown in shishōsetsu up to the present stands in sharp contrast to its generally accepted significance. Apart from four monographs, all of them comprising individual essays on various shishōsetsu writers, no systematic study has been published on the subject. There has been no bibliography nor any research report. Shishōsetsu research, if that term can be used, is formed by an almost incalculable number of essays and short articles in a variety of publications, as well as sections in literary histories. The work of finding, collating, and evaluating this material has proved so large that it seemed advisable to spare future scholars the task by presenting a brief research report as Part Two of this book. Needless to say, that report is also essential to the present study insofar as it helps clarify previous results, is a point of departure for my own considerations, and provides criteria for the assessment of the present study.

Although Japanese critics and literary specialists neglected the shishōsetsu phenomenon after the end of World War II, there has recently been a marked increase of interest in the subject, especially since the completion of this study in German in January 1979. Inspired by recent developments in contemporary literature, shishōsetsu research attained additional currency and interest. The publications that have become available since have been subsequently worked into the book.[10] More than anything, they form strong evidence that the subject has since gained importance as a field of research.

Having posed the question of "What?" it would be naive and unprofessional not to ask "How?" For in literary studies, too, we have come to accept the basic fact that method is what creates its topic. In our evaluation of previous research, we must therefore not only examine results but keep an equally watchful eye on methodological premises, epistemology and approach. In doing so, we will inevitably transcend the immediate area of concern, since it will become clear that the problems that arise in shishōsetsu research exemplify problems central to the study of modern Japanese literature, problems which up to now have widely been ignored by scholars of Japanese literature (*Nihon bungaku*) abroad. The intention is by no means to replace "old" methods with "new" ones, which would themselves inevitably have to be replaced by yet more "progressive" ones, but first of all to understand Japanese scholarship on the basis of its own criteria. This will result in acknowledging the fact that the Japanese understanding of scholarship, and its function in society as a whole, differs considerably from a Western context. Acknowledging this fact was crucial for determining the method employed in this study. Japanese research will continue to provide an important foundation but it must also be subjected to critical questioning. The obvious discrepancy between epistemologies should not be an impediment but will, it is hoped, exert a constructive influence on the present study.

It is the special situation of the discipline which also accounts for the peculiarity of this study that has been consciously developed as a textural blend of theory and practical analysis. In a Western philology, many of my comments on the approach adopted would doubtless be superfluous, but, given a "mother discipline"—Japanese philology—which tends to deny the relationship between theory and practice,[11] and given the situation of a study of Japanese literature abroad, neither firmly rooted in Japanese nor in Western methodologies, it may be useful after all to account for my own approach. Thus, metacritical comments were not relegated to a particular chapter devoted to "theory," even though they might at times appear as hindrances or digressions. Instead, they are placed in direct contact with practical problems where they can be put to the test. The fact that I have also included numerous quotations from Japanese literary studies serves a dual purpose in the context of my epistemological inquiry, conveying as much about their own approach as they disclose about shishōsetsu, their object—such information will be of use in many ways.

Genre theory is a neglected field of research in Japan; so it is not surprising that no attempt has been made in the secondary literature on shishōsetsu to define the genre and to develop criteria that distinguish it from other genres. However, since it is scarcely possible, according to a Western conception of scholarship, to do research on a subject without an approximate definition, one of the tasks in Part Three is the construction of a hypothetical structural model for the genre. According to my understanding, a genre will have to be conceived as a reality in the literary communication process, and not as an arbitrary cluster of texts.[12] My own definition of shishōsetsu will therefore have to be developed through orientation towards the Japanese context with its respective criteria, without, however, adapting the definitions of Japanese philology which, strictly speaking, cannot claim to be definitions at all.

To what extent does this book address genre-history? So far, no systematic study of the historical development of shishōsetsu has existed apart from a few, in some cases decidedly problematic, attempts to describe individual phases. In view of the present state of research, it would be hazardous indeed to attempt such a delineation. Instead, I have tried to address this complex topic which has not yet been placed within a historical framework under a variety of aspects. For this purpose, I have woven together the arguments of literary history and literary theory. Part One mainly presents, in varying depth, areas of literary history including the aspects of production and reception aesthetics. The emphasis is on a "close up" presentation, so to speak, of the historical moment at which shishōsetsu originated. Part Three includes a chapter presenting the "predecessors" of the genre in earlier Meiji literature, which should provide us with a better understanding of later developments. Part Four shows "Transformations in Shishōsetsu," considering in chronological order eight representative works. The analysis, replete with cross-references, also contains clues to their historical classification. Each work is considered under different systematic criteria. The objective of this procedure, which can be attained only by approximation, is to deal with the individual works—which sometimes included a closer study of prior research—and at the same time to verify the usefulness and descriptive value of the structural model presented. My ideal would have been a synthesis of genre theory and genre history. At the present stage, however, I can only deliver some preparatory work necessary to achieve that ideal.

Yet the genre of shishōsetsu is by no means of purely internal literary significance; in fact, it cannot be adequately understood and explained on the basis of a strictly formalist approach. A literary study that is satisfied merely to list phenomena without being able to interpret them is bound to be superficial. It is therefore important to include the cultural code, that is, the rules determining the semantic-semiotic field relevant to the text.[13] Part Five of this book deals with some of the elements of this code, the knowledge of which is essential for a deeper understanding of shishōsetsu. At the same time, it allows us to do much more than merely make a satisfactory and adequate interpretation of the genre. On the one hand, we can now grasp the relationship of shishōsetsu to literary tradition in a meaningful way, which we could not do in terms of an internal literary phenomenon. On the other hand, we obtain guidelines by which to measure the paradigmatic nature of shishōsetsu as a socio-psychological phenomenon; and this is the point which adds importance to the topic of this study far beyond literary history proper:

Since shishōsetsu is characteristically confined to the private and personal sphere and lacks the perspective of interpersonal communication, the genre illustrates the implications of Japan's "vertical society" (*tate shakai,* Nakane Chie) and the self-image of intellectuals in that society. It also sheds light on the prerequisites for the public response to the genre. Given the strong market-orientation of Japanese literature, such a response was essential to ensure the genre's continuity down to the present day.

The act of personal revelation in shishōsetsu runs according to strict rules; it is a ritual in which the author and the reader play an equal role. Elements of this ritual—gestures and attitudes—are also described in the fifth and last part of the book. The crucial role of extraliterary factors such as the cultural code and social organization for our understanding of the function of literature should become more than evident in the case of a genre such as that discussed here, since, even when the autobiographical subject declares him- or herself to be an outsider in society, he or she is still a product determined by it. According to Berger and Luckmann, "identity is produced by the combined effects of organism, individual awareness, and social structure."[14] A shishōsetsu researcher is continually forced to acknowledge these interrelationships. And while these cannot form the central concern in a literary study, they are clearly relevant for historical, political, cultural-anthropological and socio-psychological research on twentieth-century Japan.

Intuitively, this has obviously also been accepted in Japanese studies, as we can see from the frequency of statements to the effect that shishōsetsu is a "typically Japanese" genre, even a "form of thought" (*kangaekata*),[15] a "fatal Japanese reality,"[16] a "cultural necessity,"[17] and a "method with very close ties to the psychological tendencies of the Japanese people."[18] Thus, a study of shishōsetsu can also function as an example of the anthropological objectives of literary research. Understanding literature as a phenomenon of cultural anthropology leads, in the case of Japan, to the recognition that there is no, as it were, transcultural catalogue of criteria, a recognition that is bound to affect any research undertaken.

The present study does not meet the standards of advanced theory in every respect, nor was this possible, since basic research was lacking in almost every area concerned, be it Japanese literary history or the theory of literature in Japan. Each of the problems addressed in the areas of literary theory and practice had to be newly interpreted or defined. This was equally true for the terminology of modern philology, for traditional poetics and art theory, as well as for the question of literary influence and the role of tradition. Consequently, much of this was conceived in an all too rough manner and will need to be refined and modified in the future.

The book will, however, have fulfilled its purpose if it succeeds in sketching the significance of the shishōsetsu genre for twentieth-century literary history and if this stimulates further inquiry into the problems which could only be hinted at in this context. For "the problem of shishōsetsu extends over many areas of modern literary studies and is always the starting point and the conclusion of research; it is therefore impossible to explain the characteristics of modern Japanese literature without solving this cardinal problem."[19] In addition, this study is also meant to be a modest attempt at creating a synthesis of Japanese and Western literary studies, a synthesis that can be realized only on the basis of metacritical reflection.

---

1. Kobayashi Hideo, "Cartoons," p. 123. By the term *autobiographical novel* Kobayashi is clearly referring to shishōsetsu.
2. *Shōsetsu* was introduced as the translation for the European terms *Roman*, *novel*, and *roman* in the mid-1880s, which justifies my retranslation: "novel" for *shōsetsu* and *chōhen shōsetsu* (also "story" for *chûhen* and "short story" for *tanpen shōsetsu*). These terms, however, do not imply any identity with the Western genres but correspond to conventions that have developed with reference to Western terminology in Japan.
3. Usui Yoshimi, *Shōsetsu no ajiwaikata*, p. 130.
4. Cf. also "The Origins of the Term *Watakushishōsetsu*" (Chapter 10).
    A work title such as Fujieda Shizuo's (b. 1908) "Shi-shishōsetsu" also stands in favor of the reading *shishōsetsu*, as it is improbable that the reading *watakushi-watakushishōsetsu* was intended in view of the Japanese tendency to abbreviate long expressions. Since a mixed reading *watakushi-shishōsetsu* (and vice versa) is more or less out of the question, the most obvious reading would be *shi-shishōsetsu*, which would serve as an indication of the frequency of *shishōsetsu* in general language use.
5. Hisamatsu Sen'ichi, *The Biographical Dictionary of Japanese Literature*, p. 340.
6. Morikawa Tatsuya, "Bungaku wa hirakareru," p. 191.
7. Usui Yoshimi, *Shōsetsu*, p. 132.
8. Hirano Ken, *Geijutsu to jisseikatsu*, p. 16.
9. Cf. Nakamura Mitsuo, *Fūzoku shōsetsuron*, p. 29.
10. This happened in several stages: For the original German version of 1981, studies available until November 1980 were integrated. Subsequent studies up to 1988 were reviewed in the appendix to the research report in Chapter 9 ("Recent Trends in Shishōsetsu Research").
11. Further details on this in Irmela Hijiya-Kirschnereit, "Wissenschaft als Kunst."
12. Cf. Klaus W. Hempfer, *Tendenz und Ästhetik*, p. 18.
13. Cf. J. Schulte-Sasse and R. Werner, *Einführung in die Literaturwissenschaft*, p. 195. For greater detail cf. Umberto Eco, *Einführung in die Semiotik*, pp. 57ff., 112.

14. Peter L. Berger and Thomas Luckmann, *Die gesellschaftliche Konstruktion der Wirklichkeit,* p. 185.
15. Senuma Shigeki, "Shishōsetsuron no keifu," p. 25.
16. Inagaki Tatsurō, quoted in Kokubo Minoru, "Shishōsetsu no seiritsu 1," p. 49.
17. Takahashi Hideo, *Genso to shite no "watakushi,"* p. 97.
18. Ara Masahito, "Shishōsetsuron," p. 30.
19. Ariyama Mitsuhiro et al., *Meiji bungaku kara Shōwa bungaku made,* pp. 112f.

Part One
Context and Origins

1 · Historical and Cultural Context

In the Preface to his voluminous study on modern Japanese fiction Shinoda Hajime explains his approach: "I sought to make clear the appearance (*ariyō*) that modern Japanese literature has attained, by cutting it off from the everyday space and time, where it originated, and placing it in the realm of imagination, where it belongs to no particular person or time."[1] Although we may not often encounter statements as explicit as this one, the approach itself is very widespread indeed, not only in Japanese, but also, albeit to a lesser extent, in Western literary scholarship. Literature continues to be seen today, as it was in the past, as an autonomous creation lacking any recognizable connections to other, non-literary contexts. According to the view generally accepted in Japan, a work of art is self-explanatory and stands on its own, except for a possible reference to the artist's personality. On this basis there exists neither temporal nor spatial distance from it: "Reading a work of literature means directly confronting a stranger and developing a relationship with him or her."[2] This is not to deny that there have been attempts in Japan at relating literary to general history, but these have usually been limited to juxtaposing individual works or schools of literature with actual political events without attempting a closer description of the mutual effects suggested by the juxtaposition.

While the present state of research does not permit a systematic correlation of literature and history, the view that literature is an autonomous form of art created in a vacuum is clearly no longer tenable.

In Western scholarship, literature has come to be regarded as a complex semiotic system that cannot be understood by cutting it off from its various contexts. This is not, however, the place to repeat the more recent arguments in literary theory which already form the basic knowledge of much of non-Japanese philology.[3] A reference to these theories is necessary only to illustrate the limits of conventional Japanese attitudes and to explain the approach adopted in this study.[4]

All previous works on the shishōsetsu genre have used Tayama Katai's story "Futon" as both their starting point and focus of discussion. "Futon" is considered to be not only the first work of the genre but also a model. One should scrutinize such a viewpoint, and I will therefore examine in detail both the work itself and the historical moment in which it appeared. This serves to show the conventional understanding of the work and its role in shaping the genre, and it also provides the basic information necessary for the genre theory developed here. More importantly, I shall consider the point of intersection of this story with other lines of development (which has not until now received serious attention) so as to shed new light on the genre that emerged from it.

Having stated the importance of the intrinsic relationship between work and context, I have endeavored to examine the origins of both "Futon" and the genre in the light of numerous different—although not all conceivable—contexts. This approach contrasts with the accepted Japanese pattern of a monolinear explanation based on literary-intrinsic factors or, even more frequently—due to the popularity of biographical interpretation, or rather, "biographism"[5] in Japan—on the author's psyche. Political and intellectual history or Japanese naturalism, therefore, provided not merely the background against which the individual work was written and the shishōsetsu genre originated, but also the factors instrumental to its development. It is often difficult to determine the correct emphasis to place on a particular factor and its relative significance, because the essential factual and theoretical research has not yet been carried out. Nevertheless, the following discussion should allow us to understand and assess the appearance of this particular work and the development of the shishōsetsu genre in the context of its varied determining factors.

Attempts at tracing developments in modern Japan invariably explore the beginning of the Meiji period; and this book is no exception. In the middle of the nineteenth century, European powers and the United States exerted increasing pressure on Japan, forcing the Tokugawa Shogunate to abandon its policy of isolation and establish trade and political relations with the West; this external pressure coincided with a growing impulse within Japan toward political and spiritual renewal. The period between 1860 and the mid-1880s was one of extraordinary intellectual activity with Western ideas rapidly gaining currency, as can be seen from the growing number of works in European languages published in Japanese translation. The new government encouraged this activity in order to "enlighten" (*keimō*), that is, to inform and educate the people. Thus, the majority of the books translated were in the fields of politics, philosophy, or science and technology. Fiction was traditionally scorned in Japan,[6] which may explain why the epoch-making tract by the writer and scholar of English Tsubouchi Shōyō (1859–1935) on the *Essence of the Novel* (*Shōsetsu shinzui*, 1885–1886), the first theoretical discussion of the subject in modern Japan, was a necessary precursor to contemporary intellectuals' revaluation of prose literature. Tsubouchi argued for the intrinsic value of fiction as an artistic genre which provided insight into human emotions and actions by means of logically constructed plots and precise psychological characterization. His idealistic attitude is illustrated by his rejection of the conventional objectives *kanzen chōaku* (promotion of virtue and chastisement of vice), which had resulted in weak plot and description in the light narrative literature of the Edo period (*gesaku*). These weaknesses were both the cause and the result of the low regard in which narrative literature was held by intellectuals. Tsubouchi's insistence that fiction was a self-relevant artistic genre eventually led to major innovations in literature.

The sudden and massive confrontation with Western culture engendered insecurity among the educated classes, particularly among the former samurai and daimyo, who were forced to adopt completely new patterns of behavior. Even matters of everyday life were a source of bewilderment to the former feudal lords, who sought advice from the government on such problems as permission to enter a particular restaurant or visit the pleasure quarter.[7] The introduction of Western technology, the development of a modern system of traffic and communications, and the introduction in 1872 of compulsory education changed life for ordinary citizens as well. All areas of life, even dress and eating habits, were affected.[8]

However intense and broadly based, the adoption of Western ideas and achievements in the early Meiji period was not an indiscriminate or unplanned process. A "highly developed eclecticism"[9] determined the concentration on utilitarian, scientific, and technological aspects. The main objective, expressed in the slogan *fukoku kyōhei* (enrich the nation and strengthen the army), was a strong state able to withstand the challenge of the Western imperialist powers. The far-reaching changes, pursued under the banner of modernization (often considered to be practically synonymous with Westernization) resulted in a centralization of control which subordinated the good of the individual to that of the state and insisted on conformity,[10] ideas that were, however, by no means new in Japan.

The young men of the early Meiji period were hungry for knowledge. It was to be expected that they would not be satisfied with the officially approved scientific subjects but would move on to read Western literature and philosophy. One result of this interest was the movement to revaluate fiction (*shōsetsu*)[11] mentioned previously. Also giving impetus to change were the "enlightenment" writings of Fukuzawa Yukichi (1835–1901), who introduced basic ideas of Occidental culture in his *Encouragement of Learning* (*Gakumon no susume*, 1872–1876) and in his *Outline of Civilization* (*Bunmeiron no gairyaku*, 1875). He argued that since all people were born equal, the social differences between them were the result of education; hence his enthusiasm for a practical and critically applied science. He regarded the paternalistic, hierarchical attitudes of the past as a threat to the autonomy of the Japanese state and emphasized the importance of individual self-respect, as well as a sense of national independence and freedom.

The individualism he promoted so enthusiastically was developed theoretically and also practiced by the young generation of Meiji intellectuals. It was expressed in the idealization of behavior directed from within which disregarded traditional rules and norms. One typical representative of this generation was the writer Futabatei Shimei (1864–1909), who was obliged to leave school at the age of 15 as a result of a dispute with the headmaster—clearly outrageous behavior in the eyes of the average obedient citizen. He subsequently attended the Foreign-Language School in Tokyo but left, shortly before graduation, once again the result of trouble with the school's authorities.

In addition to being the author of *Ukigumo* (The Drifting Cloud, 1887–1889), considered to be Japan's first modern novel,[12] Futabatei was also an important figure in the early Meiji period in other ways. He originally intended to use his knowledge of the Russian language for diplomatic or military purposes, but his interest in Russian literature[13] and his friendship with Shōyō encouraged him to write novels. *Ukigumo* is considered to be the novel which, for the first time, largely fulfilled the requirements established by Shōyō. The novel's main character is based on the example of the "superfluous man" of Russian literature, and typifies the young intellectual of the Meiji period. The novel paints a portrait of a society in transition, describing in new and realistic ways the contrasts between town and country, between traditional values and imported ideas, between the "old" and the "new" type of person.[14] *Ukigumo* broke new ground in Japanese literature insofar as it incorporated many ideas outlined in *Shōsetsu shinzui*.

But most noteworthy of all, the novel was the first successful example of *genbun itchi* (unity of the spoken and written language) replacing the classical written language with a style approaching that of spoken language. Narrated from the point of view of the hero, an introspective "average" person, *Ukigumo* combined new forms and new subjects in literature, each of which influenced the other. Futabatei was thus far in advance of his contemporaries in psychological realism and style,[15] and the standards he established and the literary pattern he developed served as models for generations of writers to come.

The impulse to acquire Western culture and civilization as quickly and as thoroughly as possible, influenced by the belief that this was the only way to withstand pressures from the imperialist powers of the West, led the Japanese to scorn their own traditions. Things Japanese came to have a "shameful negative identity,"[16] while the foreign culture was positively valued. Thus it was believed that genuine "modernization" could not be achieved merely by adopting the products of Western technology and culture, but that it was also essential to absorb the spiritual and ethical underpinnings of those achievements. Therefore, after Christian missionaries were again admitted to Japan in 1873, the former samurai, who were now looked to as spiritual leaders, converted to Christianity. However, trouble soon arose: because the embrace of Western ideas had been too feverish, the upheavals in society too violent, and the rejection of Japan's own identity had continued for too long, a negative result was inevitable. In addition, those who had led the modernization movement became increasingly conservative with age, and they resigned in the face of the practical problems involved in implementing the social reforms they had advocated.[17] The range of often conflicting Western ideas, whether scientific or philosophical, with which the Japanese were confronted threw doubt on the credibility of all of them, including Christianity. Finally, the growth of individualism, Christianity and socialist thought were perceived as a threat to the power of the state.

An official hardening of attitudes and impatience with reform was signaled in 1889 with the promulgation of the Meiji Constitution, a conservative document embodying the notion of *kokutai*, which combined Shinto, Confucian and German theories of the State. It declared the Tenno to be the absolute, divine monarch and personification of the state, and the people, by virtue of their common ancestry, to be members, together with the Tenno, of a racial and spiritual family.[18] The Imperial Rescript on Education, issued in 1890, ensured the dissemination of these traditional attitudes.[19] A clear sign of the changed spiritual climate was the dismissal of Professor Uchimura Kanzō (1861–1930) from the First Higher School in 1891 following a public outcry at his refusal to bow to a picture of the Tenno because of his Christian beliefs.

Thus, in the late 1880s Japan entered a period of "reactive nationalism" (Herbert Passin)[20] which was to last until World War I. The intellectually curious, self-critical, and insecure Japan now became increasingly confident but less open; order and discipline were valued more highly than innovation. Japan's self-assurance grew with its diplomatic successes and, above all, its military victories in the wars with China (1894–1895) and Russia (1904–1905). These achievements were made possible by Japan's tremendous economic development following its abolition of the fiefdoms (1871) and other reforms.

As militarism, imperialism, and the mystification of the state as expressed in theocratic Shinto teachings became increasingly prevalent, the third decade of the Meiji period also saw the withdrawal of the intellectuals from matters of public interest. They turned instead to "the path that leads inwards." Young men, among them Kitamura Tōkoku (1868–1894), who originally intended to be politicians refused to become involved in public life because they were disappointed by the "dirty business" of politics; their own lofty ideals were apparently irreconcilable with harsh reality. Thus, the intellectual climate of the early third decade of the Meiji period was dominated by romanticism, inspired by writers such as Byron and Emerson and documented in the journal *Bungakukai,* which was founded in 1893 by Tōkoku, Shimazaki Tōson (1872–1943), and others; the neo-idealism of Eduard von Hartmann, introduced to Japan by Mori Ōgai (1862–1922); and the individualism, scepticism, and "instinctivism" of Tayama Chogyū (1871–1902), a student of Nietzsche's thought. The period also saw renewed interest in poetry as demonstrated in the publication of the first anthology of poetry in a new free style, *Shintaishi shō* (Selection of Poetry in the New Style) in 1882, and, much later, Tōson's *Wakanashū* (Seedlings' Collection) in 1897. Likewise, the epoch is marked by the nationalism of Kuga Katsunan (1857–1907) and Miyake Setsurei (1860–1945) and the "orientalism" of Okakura Tenshin (1863–1913).[21] Parallel to these movements was the attempt to revive old traditions in prose literature, above all the style of

Ihara Saikaku, the preeminent fiction writer of the eighteenth century, which was admired and imitated by the writers of the Ken'yūsha (Society of Friends of the Inkstone, founded in 1885). The evocative, rhythmical, lyrical passages of *Takekurabe* (Comparing Heights, 1895), by the first important woman writer of the Meiji period, Higuchi Ichiyō (1872–1896), are particularly reminiscent of Saikaku's style.[22] At the same time, her description of everyday life in Tokyo contains elements of the same social criticism which features prominently in the work of the socialist writer Kinoshita Naoe (1869–1937) or of Ozaki Kōyō (1868–1903), Tokutomi Roka (1868–1927), and others.

Socialist ideas gained wide currency among intellectuals as a response to the growing social problems resulting from Japan's stepped-up industrialization and militarization following its war with China. The intellectual climate at the turn of the century was characterized in particular by a combination of socialism and Christianity and by the romantic movement centered on the journal *Myōjō* (The Morning Star). However, this active involvement on the part of some Christian and socialist intellectuals, or the general interest aroused when the pollution caused by the Ashio copper mine was discovered in 1891, should not obscure the fact that the majority of writers were indifferent to social issues at the end of the nineteenth century and the beginning of the twentieth.

How then can the rise of naturalist literature in Japan be explained? This question will be considered in the following chapter.

---

1. Shinoda Hajime, *Nihon no gendai shōsetsu,* p. 8.
2. Sakagami Hiroichi, "Bungaku o ajiwau yomikata," p. 81.
3. In view of the profusion of theoretical works on the semantic status of literary texts I shall merely refer to some of the more important ones here: Umberto Eco, *Einführung in die Semiotik;* Jurij M. Lotman, *Die Struktur literarischer Texte;* Siegfried J. Schmidt, *Ästhetizität;* Tzvetan Todorov, *Poetik der Prosa.* The titles of other works I consulted are named in Chapter 14.
4. A comparison of the traditional Japanese concept of the work with more relevant concepts from Western studies can be found in Irmela Hijiya-Kirschnereit (hereafter I.H.-K.), "Kritische Bemerkungen zur japanischen Literaturkritik," p. 58.
5. Cf. I.H.-K., *Mishima Yukios Roman "Kyōko-no ie,"* pp. 17ff.
6. See below, "Theoretical Premises" (Chapter 10).
7. Cf. Marius B. Jansen, "The Meiji Restoration," pp. 6f.
8. Yanagida Kunio, *Japanese Manners and Customs in the Meiji Era,* includes a detailed description of changes in the way of life.
9. Hugh Borton, *Japan's Modern Century,* p. 188.
10. Ibid., p. 189.
11. The term *shōsetsu* was introduced by Tsubouchi Shōyō in his *Shōsetsu shinzui* as the

equivalent of the European novel and refers both to large epic and small forms. In accordance with the rule given in note 2 of the introduction I have adopted the terms given in Japanese works of reference (e.g. "short story" for *tanpen shōsetsu*).

12. Cf. Marleigh G. Ryan, *Japan's First Modern Novel.*
13. Cf. Bruno Lewin, *Futabatei Shimei in seinen Beziehungen zur russischen Literatur.*
14. Cf. Ryan, *Japan's First Modern Novel,* pp. 149ff. on Futabatei's realism.
15. Jürgen Berndt, "Einiges zur Problematik bei Betrachtungen der modernen japanischen Literatur," p. 395, remarks on this: "that in a certain way Futabatei takes up a special position with his first novel Ukigumo and stands outside Japanese literary development. . . . One will have to assume that this work is based less on an extremely brilliant recognition of the social problems of that time—being thereby nearly two decades ahead of Japan's literary development—but rather on exact knowledge of Russian literature and an astonishing ability to project himself into this literature."
16. Kenneth B. Pyle, *The New Generation in Meiji Japan,* p. 48.
17. Ibid., p. 187.
18. For example, cf. the quotation in Kōsaka Masaaki, *Japanese Thought in the Meiji Era,* pp. 380ff. on the "family state."
19. As an example of the presentation of these teachings cf. the quotation in John K. Fairbank et al., *East Asia,* p. 671.
20. Cited in William Caudill, "The Influence of Social Structure and Culture on Human Behaviour in Modern Japan," p. 247.
21. Cf. Pyle, pp. 74ff.
22. Richard Lane, *Japan's Modern Century,* pp. 117f. includes a comparison of the styles of Saikaku's *Shoen ōkagami* and Higuchi Ichiyō's *Takekurabe*.

2 · Shizenshugi— *Japanese Naturalism*

Whether Japanese naturalism really deserves to be called naturalism at all is a subject much discussed by Japanese scholars. That discussion will not be continued here,[1] since this is not the place for an extensive examination of the phenomenon which would, in any case, require much effort to clarify questions of terminology. That would in turn divert us from our main intention of giving a short introduction to the literary movement from which shishōsetsu originated.[2]

Although *shizenshugi* is held to be the Japanese translation of the European term—first used in 1889 by Mori Ōgai—it was originally applied vaguely and indiscriminately to various works by writers who were not necessarily followers of European naturalism. Therefore, by 1897, when the term *shizenshugi* or *shizenha* was used as a common denominator for writers such as Ozaki Kōyō, Higuchi Ichiyō, Futabatei Shimei, and others, it denoted "merely an objective, realistic tendency."[3] Only later would *shizenshugi* become the established term used to refer to the literary movement introduced from Europe and represented in particular by Zola, Flaubert, Maupassant, and the Goncourt brothers. Before this usage became established, however, some Japanese writers had already begun emulating their European idols, notably Kosugi Tengai (1865–1952), whose *Hatsusugata* (The New Year's Dress), modeled after Zola's *Nana,* was published in 1900. The theory of naturalism had been introduced to Japan as early as 1889 by Mori Ōgai,[4] and works of the writers mentioned became available in Japan, in the original, or in English or Japanese translation, in the 1890s.

At the beginning of this century, the time at last seemed ripe for Japanese naturalism: the forewords to Kosugi Tengai's *Hatsusugata* and his *Hayariuta* (The Popular Song), published two years later, are not only "famous as the first concrete examples of the influence of French naturalist theory on Japanese writers,"[5] but they also mark the beginning of what is called early naturalism (*zenki shizenshugi*) or Zolaism (*Zorashugi*).

We shall examine works by Kosugi Tengai a little closer in order to describe their naturalism and evaluate the extent to which they are based on Zola. In the foreword to *Hatsusugata,* Tengai repudiates the "culinary" aspect of literature. According to him, he neither writes to satisfy his own taste nor that of the critic or reader. He seeks to move the reader not by the unusual but by what is normal and average.[6] His rejection of the unusual could well be motivated by a criticism of the literature of his "romantic" and aestheticist contemporaries. The idea that it is the writer's task to give an account of life around him is at the same time an obvious reference to Zola's positivist-determinist conception of literature as developed in his *Roman expérimental* (1880). Tengai is even more explicit in his next work:

> Nature is nature. It is neither good nor bad, neither beautiful nor ugly. Good and bad, beautiful and ugly are merely arbitrary names given by a particular person in a particular country and a particular epoch to one part of nature.
>
> The novel, on the other hand, is nature in the field of the imagination. There is no reason to restrict it by feeling obliged to address good, bad, beautiful or ugly.
>
> It is quite sufficient if the reader is enabled to picture clearly the phenomena in the work, just as his senses comprehend the phenomena of nature.
>
> Whether the reader is moved or not is not a matter of concern to the poet. He should relate what he imagines just as it is, because what would happen if a portrait painter said, "Your nose is too big" and planed it off?
>
> When reproducing the imagined, not the least personal [element] may be added.[7]

Zola's influence is undeniable here. The author as medium, as the detached reporter refraining from any kind of evaluation, with the aim of achieving absolute objectivity in description—this is the naturalist concept Tengai tried to put into practice in his novels and stories.

Hatsusugata is the story of the geisha Koshun and her relationship with men of differing social strata. It is not so much the mode of presentation as the cast of characters, partial similarities in background as well as identical details that suggest the French model, although Yoshida

Seiichi points out that Tengai at times abandoned what was historically possible in order to remain close to the original novel, *Nana*.[8]

One and a half years later Tengai again used *Nana* as his model for the story *Hayariuta*. Here he came much closer to Zola's naturalism in describing the instrumental and fatal influence of heredity and environment. The story of the heroine, an inherent nymphomaniac whose adultery with a young doctor becomes the subject of a popular song, was the author's most successful work and therefore helped spread naturalist ideas.

Kosugi Tengai, however, was by no means the only writer who sought to adapt naturalism in theory and practice. Tayama Katai (1872–1930) also made his first attempts at naturalist writing at roughly the same time. As with Tengai, programmatic statements prevail in an earlier stage, while his literary practice only gradually came to live up to his revolutionary demands. In the preface to his story *No no hana* (The Flowers in the Field, 1901) he declared:

> And so to write down what I have been thinking recently, aren't we orientated too much towards success in today's literary world? . . . Maupassant's *Bel ami* and Flaubert's *Éducation sentimentale* are both works that contain any number of weaknesses as far as naturalism is concerned, and they are rather unhealthy; but, because they are not clouded by the author's irrelevant subjective impressions, nature's magnificent face can still be seen, and life's destiny is clearly shown. The literary world of the Meiji period should therefore not be so interested in success, and I wish that they would give a faithful and unhesitating account of life's secrets and the devil's insinuations. Then the face of nature would be reflected, albeit indistinctly, in the literature of the Meiji period.[9]

Katai's call for renewal in contemporary literature was concerned with style, with a mode of presentation that was as objective as possible, and with the subject matter, which should be the truthful portrayal of "nature." Nagai Kafū (1879–1959) placed even greater emphasis on the need to display the darker side of human life:

> There can be no doubt that a part of man is beast. Is not this physical side the explanation for carnal temptation? Or does the explanation lie in what we inherited from our ancestors who had descended from animals? However that may be, mankind has built up religion and moral concepts from customary practices and feelings, and at the end of a long cultural process we now refer to this dark side of man's nature as absolute sin. How will this dark, beastly nature develop under such predetermined conditions? In order to create perfect, ideal lives I believe we have to start by examining this dark

side. Is it not as essential as examining the evidence and details of a crime in court so that the light of justice may shine? That is why I will not hesitate to concentrate on presenting a true-to-life picture of dark subjects such as violence and carnal lust which are part of our heredity and environment.[10]

In this foreword to Kafū's story *Jigoku no hana* (Hell Flowers, 1902), the powerful influence of Zola's *Roman expérimental* is combined somewhat curiously with his own early idealism. His demands for an objective examination of human nature and particular interest in deviations, and his biological-deterministic view of human nature reflecting Darwin's influence on naturalism, are both naturalist in Zola's sense.

In the work itself, heredity as a determining factor plays no part. The story is about a young woman, an English teacher who falls in love with a reporter. He is in turn having an affair with the lady of the house where she teaches. After Sonoko, the heroine, is raped by the director of her school, she decides to start a new, unconventional life. Her counterpart is Tomiko, the daughter of the house, who is despised because of her loose lifestyle. Sonoko, however, wants to lead a moral life in spite of her degradation, while at the same time challenging society with her "back-to-nature" views.

The story contains many features of motif, plot pattern, and character that are characteristic of early Japanese naturalism. For example, the subject of adultery was popular with writers at the time and appeared again in Shimazaki Tōson's story *Kyūshujin* (The Former Husband, 1902),[11] published in the same year and inspired by Flaubert's *Madame Bovary*. Generally speaking, the eternal triangle is a source of endless inspiration to Japanese naturalists, from which we can draw two conclusions. The subject contains a reference to the immediate literary tradition, to the influences of the period and contemporary taste, since we can also find similar stories by the predecessors and literary adversaries of the *shizenshugi* writers. Probably the most famous examples of these are the serialized novel *Konjiki yasha* (The Golden Demon, 1897–1902) by Ozaki Kōyō—a representative work of the pre-naturalist Meiji period according to Kimura Ki[12]—and Tokutomi Roka's novel *Hototogisu* (The Cuckoo, 1898–1899) which was also published as a series of installments. Yet the large proportion of romances in *shizenshugi* literature is also an indication of the tendency to restrict oneself to private problems while ignoring matters of social concern. Elements of social criticism, where they had existed at all, dwindle, as subjectivism and sentimentality gradually come to characterize *shizenshugi* and lead to the emergence of the shishōsetsu genre.

In *Jigoku no hana,* Kafū introduces further subjects important to *shi-*

zenshugi literature:[13] the position of women in society, the conflict between traditional values and the new morality, and the social restrictions which forbid individual self-expression. *Jigoku no hana* documents among other things the search for an up-to-date image of women. For Kafū, the young teacher Sonoko combines the merits of a woman who is emancipated but willing to conform. Rebellious Tomiko, however, remains unacceptable because she is so radical that she places herself outside society. Thus *shizenshugi* literature does not transcend the limits set by the historical and social context in its portrayal of women. Still, the subject of women finds increasing attention, but, while "modern" women are cautiously idealized, the idealization is often revoked later. The same is true for the subject of feudalistic morality versus enlightened liberalism, frequently portrayed in terms of a generational conflict within the family. If describing these problems is seen as a sign of social criticism, then the same must be said of earlier works such as *Hototogisu,* the popular serialized novel mentioned previously. Here the author takes the part of a young woman married to a high-ranking civil servant who is sent back to her family when she develops tuberculosis—a story based on real events. In any case, *shizenshugi* writers have no monopoly on social criticism and it is, in fact, much more in evidence in so-called anti-naturalist literature.[15]

The one notable exception is Shimazaki Tōson's novel *Hakai* (The Broken Commandment), which, as Japanese literary historians agree, marked the beginning of Japanese naturalism proper in 1906. *Hakai* is about a young schoolteacher called Ushimatsu who belongs to the underprivileged Eta class and has to promise his father never to reveal his origins. In spite of secret feelings of sympathy for other Eta, he succeeds for a long time in resisting the urge to number himself among them, but he eventually decides to solve his inner conflict by revealing the truth. The story ends harmoniously with Ushimatsu emigrating to Texas.

This novel, modeled on European works, particularly Rousseau's *Confessions* and Dostoevski's *Crime and Punishment,* was immediately hailed as an epoch-making masterpiece equal to European naturalist novels.[16] However, *Hakai* illustrates the fact that Japanese naturalism had already reached a cross-roads, combining as it does two features which were subsequently to diverge again: the socio-critical and the confessional aspect. Due to the success, eighteen months later, of Tayama Katai's short story "Futon," the egocentric, private element became dominant and characterized the entire subsequent literary development of the genre—a change of direction that Nakamura Mitsuo records with deep regret.[17] "Futon" will be examined in detail in Chapter 4. Let us return now to the programmatic statements which formed the theoretical framework for *shizenshugi* in the early years of this century.

In the following years, and particularly in the period known as the major phase of Japanese naturalism from 1906 to 1911, naturalist ideas were taken up and expanded by many other writers. Phrases such as *rokotsunaru byōsha* (unvarnished description, Tayama Katai 1904),[18] *heimen byōsha* (flat description, Katai 1908),[19] *shasei* (reproduced true to nature, Shimazaki Tōson),[20] and *zettai mushinen* (complete absence of one's own ideas, Iwano Hōmei)[21] are evidence of a theoretical desire to establish an objective, unemotional, and value-free style of writing which was considered essential to naturalism.[22] The increasing number of theoretical statements towards the end of the decade are also proof of the diversity of *shizenshugi*.

The concepts expressed in the prefaces to stories or in reviews and essays hardly form a coherent theory; even the statements of one single writer lack systematic consistency. It may, therefore, seem questionable to count among the naturalists both Iwano Hōmei, with his "mystic semi-animalism" (*shinpiteki hanjūshugi*, 1906)[23] inspired by Swedenborg, Emerson, and Maeterlinck, and, at the same time, Kunikida Doppo, who referred to Wordsworth and Turgenev. To speak of *shizenshugi* is even more problematic as far as the works themselves are concerned, since they frequently seem to contradict their authors' theoretical ideas. However, this is no reason to reject the term itself. For as a technical term it has become well established since the early professions of loyalty to naturalism inspired by European literature; it refers to a number of writers—the most important being Kosugi Tengai, Nagai Kafū, Oguri Fūyō, Shimazaki Tōson, Tayama Katai, Hasegawa Tenkei, Shimamura Hōgetsu, Iwano Hōmei, Masamune Hakuchō, Tokuda Shūsei, and Mayama Seika—from the beginning of the century until about 1918. It would be foolish to reject a term that has been in use in Japanese literary studies up to the present day, particularly since we could hardly think of a better one to replace it.[24] Instead, it would be more useful to turn our attention to the peculiarities of the phenomenon known as *shizenshugi* in order to distinguish it from the equally imprecise European definition of naturalism and to see what those authors really had in common that could justify such a classification.

1. *Shizenshugi* was expressed first of all in theoretical form; it existed in statements and declarations of intention and only later did a style of writing develop that corresponded to the authors'—and our—expec-

tations of a naturalist style.²⁵ There is no doubt that those authors believed themselves to be naturalist writers even if they all had somewhat different ideas as to what naturalism was.

2. Japanese naturalists and their European predecessors both saw a definite break between themselves and previous literary forms which had tended toward "artistry" (*gikō*) and "gold plating" (*mekki*) (Tayama Katai in "Rokotsunaru byōsha," 1904).²⁶ The awareness that they embodied a new literature united these writers, even though their work in retrospect may not seem particularly revolutionary.

3. A further common feature was the reference these authors made to European literature, above all, of course, to the French, German, and Scandinavian naturalists. Yet Tolstoy, Dostoevski, Turgenev, Wordsworth, Nietzsche, and Rousseau, to name but a few, exerted at least an equally strong influence on various Japanese naturalists and we can agree with Dennis Keene that *shizenshugi* was initially nothing more than "a general absorption of nineteenth-century European literature" and the subsequent attempt to create a realistic style.²⁷

4. In its demand for realistic literature *shizenshugi* was part of the tradition that began with Tsubouchi Shōyō's *Shōsetsu shinzui* and which was established in practice with Futabatei Shimei's *Ukigumo*. However, *shizenshugi* differs from these beginnings of the modern novel in Japan in its broader-based reception of European literature practiced by a large circle of intellectuals who, on the basis of previous experiences, developed a deeper understanding of European theories. Needless to say, the early "realistic"²⁸ works also provided Japanese naturalists with a cognitive advantage.

5. In spite of individual differences, we are justified in speaking of *shizenshugi* as a literary movement because of the common background of those authors, largely of the same age,²⁹ who were considered to be the leading naturalists; without exception they all came from impoverished families in the provinces and were excluded from an elite education at the state universities.³⁰ Their literary origins lay in the romantic movement centered on the magazine *Bungakukai*. Shimazaki Tōson, Tayama Katai, Kunikida Doppo, and Iwano Hōmei were all originally known as romantic poets. The change from poetry to prose, or, to quote a phrase coined by one of the authors concerned, "from fantasy to reality" (*kūsō kara jijitsu e*), is an essential feature of *shizenshugi*.³¹ A further experience common to many naturalists is their former identification with Christianity, through which they were confronted with socialist ideas. Their highest objective, the liberation of

the individual, was based on Christianity and on Takayama Chogyū's cult of genius, which he derived from Nietzsche. This idealist trait links naturalism to the romantic movement. Their subsequent rejection of Christianity is another pattern shared by numerous naturalists. Kōsaka Masaaki even suggests a temporal and causal connection: He sees the break with Christianity as both a condition for, and at the same time, a result of the movement toward naturalism.[32]

6. Japanese naturalists and the intellectuals of the time shared a basic pessimism and a feeling of alienation because of the increasingly reactionary climate following the Sino-Japanese War and because of the burden of their continuous search for cultural identity. It is no coincidence that, from this time until the end of the Russo-Japanese War (1904–1905), the great Meiji writers such as Tsubouchi Shōyō, Futabatei Shimei, Mori Ōgai, Kōda Rohan, Yamada Bimyō, and Ozaki Kōyō all produced no new works.[33] It was a time when the poets were productive, while prose seemed to have reached a dead-end.[34] Then, from out of this silence, the *shizenshugi* writers raised their voices: they expressed their disillusionment and alienation and announced a new art form relevant to these experiences.[35]

7. Although Japanese naturalist writers considered the scientific basis of the new literature to be what was essentially innovative about it, reserving an important place for the scientific approach in their own concepts,[36] it is the very lack of analytic description and the relative neglect of heredity and environmental factors in *shizenshugi* works which distinguishes it markedly from European naturalism. Japanese writers intended *shizenshugi* to express their opposition to the all-powerful state and to feudal attitudes as well as their fight to emancipate the individual. However, in practice, the impetus towards emancipation was directed entirely towards the liberation of the author, who soon advanced to the status of essential subject matter to naturalism and who appeared to be the most accessible subject for precise, scientific observation. The naturalist novel acquired a confessional character, it rapidly developed into a genre in which the principle of absolute objectivity postulated for *shizenshugi* was replaced by the demand for absolute sincerity. Thus, shishōsetsu was born, and the turn towards the exclusively private (the "privatistic," I should like to call it) sphere meant the disappearance of social criticism in *shizenshugi,* which had, however, never been as significant as it was in European naturalism.

In trying to evaluate the importance of *shizenshugi*, we must first of all recognize that it included practically no criticism of contemporary issues, nor any socially revolutionary components. It took effect, however, within literature, where it laid the virtual foundation for modern Japanese literature by developing a realistic style of description and by opening up new areas of experience. In addition, the seriousness that naturalist writers devoted to the literary examination of their experiences did much to enhance the status of fiction in Japan. Narrative literature, which had at best been considered as ranking second to poetry due to the burden of a didactic function, won increased respect, as did the writers themselves who came to form a society within society, the "literary world" (*bundan*). Furthermore, one of the most profound effects of *shizenshugi*—if also the most elusive—may have been a shift in Japanese attitudes towards attaching greater importance to the individual and his or her emotional needs. Roughly speaking, this was a development from a feudal-traditional ideal of man whose identity was judged solely on the basis of the social group to which he belonged towards a more individualistic—although not Western!—understanding. *Shizenshugi* (and shishōsetsu, which developed from it) is without doubt only one of many factors in this process, but it is nevertheless of great significance.[37]

---

1. Dennis Keene, "Flaubert and Yokomitsu," p. 72 rejects this as "pointless," correctly, in my opinion. On the justification of the term *shizenshugi* see below.
2. Dennis Keene, "The Shinkankakuha," pp. 37f. comments on the problematic of the Japanese naturalism discussion.
3. Yoshida Seiichi, *Shizenshugi no kenkyū*, vol. 1, p. 233.
4. For details cf. ibid., pp. 130–135: "Zora no inyū: Ōgai o chūshin to shite" (The Introduction of Zola: With Particular Consideration of Mori Ōgai).
5. Nakamura Mitsuo, *Nihon no gendai shōsetsu*, p. 95.
6. "Hatsusugata (jo)" in *Kindai hyōronshū I, NKiBT,* LVII, 192.
7. "Hayariuta jo," ibid., p. 195.
8. Yoshida Seiichi, *Shizenshugi no kenkyū*, vol. I, p. 153.
9. "'No no hana' jo," *NKiBT,* LVII, 193.
10. "'Jigoku no hana' batsu," ibid., p. 196.
11. The work was banned on grounds of immorality shortly after publication since it was said to contain a topical background, cf. Joseph Roggendorf, "Shimazaki Tōson," p. 50.
12. Cf. Kimura Ki, "Kōyō, Rohan, Ichiyō no kyōtsūsei to idōsei," p. 14.
13. Kafū is associated with Zolaism only for a short period, i.e. from 1902 to 1903, cf. Edward Seidensticker, *Kafū the Scribbler,* p. 14.
14. Cf. also the discussion of Katai's "Futon," Chapter 4.
15. Cf. William F. Sibley, "Naturalism in Japanese Literature," p. 166.

16. Shimamura Hōgetsu: "'Hakai' o hyōsu" (May 1906 in *Waseda bungaku*), text in *NKiBT*, LVII, 258–260, here p. 258.
17. Cf. Nakamura Mitsuo, *Fūzoku shōsetsuron*, p. 9.
18. Yoshida Seiichi, *Shizenshugi no kenkyū*, vol. I, pp. 321ff.
19. Ibid., vol. II, p. 171.
20. Cf. the quotations in Arima Tatsuo, *The Failure of Freedom*, p. 93.
21. Ibid., pp. 94, 236.
22. Iwano Hōmei's concept of *ichigen byōsha*, of "one-dimensional description" (1917) also belongs in this context, cf. Yoshida Seiichi, *Shizenshugi no kenkyū*, vol. II, pp. 452ff.
23. Cf. "'Shinpiteki hanjūshugi' nōto" and "Hōmei to Nīche" (Hōmei and Nietzsche) in Ōkubo Tsuneo, *Iwano Hōmei no jidai*, pp. 115–118, 129–132.
24. It could be argued that it would be more suitable to do without such a categorization altogether. The following discussion shows, however, that we are dealing with a literary generation that was formed by common experiences, which fully justifies including them under one heading.
25. Cf. e.g., Tayama Katai's self-critical consideration of the years in which he wrote "sentimental, long-winded novels of longing," quoted in Oscar Benl, "Naturalism in Japanese Literature," p. 20.
26. Cf. *Kindai hyōronshū I, NKiBT*, LVII, 198f.
27. Dennis Keene, "Shinkankakuha," p. 38.
28. The term *realism* (*shajitsushugi, rearisumu, riarizumu*) is not as sharply defined as *shizenshugi* and can therefore be compared with it only with some reservations.
29. Hōgetsu and Doppo were born in 1871, Katai, Shūsei, and Tōson in 1872 and Hōmei in 1873.
30. Details in Arima, *Failure of Freedom*, pp. 84ff.
31. Nakamura Mitsuo, *Nihon no kindai shōsetsu*, p. 122.
32. Cf. Kōsaka, *Japanese Thought*, p. 405f. Unfortunately he does not offer clues to the connection between both motives.
33. Cf. Marleigh G. Ryan, "Modern Japanese Fiction," p. 262, and Kōsaka, *Japanese Thought*, p. 292.
34. Cf. Itō Sei, "Rise of Naturalism," p. 512.
35. Cf. e.g. Hasegawa Tenkei's essay "Genmetsu jidai no geijutsu" (Art in the Age of Disillusionment, 1906) in which he describes the despair of modern man as a reaction to the "disillusionment" brought about by modern science, in particular Darwin's theories of evolution, and concludes: "What people demand in the age of disillusionment is an unadorned art which portrays the truth" (*Kindai hyōronshū I, NKiBT*, LVII, 220–229, here p. 226). In the article "Genjitsu bakuro no hiai" (The Pain at the Revelation of Reality), published in 1908, Hasegawa speaks of a lost paradise, of his generation's lack of a refuge or home and of the pain of those who have lost their stability in philosophy and religion. ". . . it is the literature of so-called naturalism (*iwayuru shizenha*) which embodies this pain best" (ibid., pp. 230–243, here p. 231).
36. Cf. e.g. Shimazaki Tōson's enthusiastic reception of Zola and his faith in science. Individual quotations on this subject in Arima, *Failure of Freedom*, p. 92.
37. William F. Sibley and Kōsaka Masaaki, amongst others, comment on the significance of *shizenshugi*. However, Sibley's appraisal of *shizenshugi* as a literary current which, for the first time, produced "works free of undigested influences" from Europe (Sibley, "Naturalism in Japanese Literature," p. 169) seems to me to be just as problematical as Kōsaka's exaggerated evaluation given in the statement: ". . . naturalism brought about a complete change in emotional life, in the Japanese ethos, and was the catalytic agent that caused the residues of the past to be swept into discard" (Kōsaka, *Japanese Thought*, p. 396) or even his condemnation of *shizenshugi*: "Its only achievement was that it liberated the emotional life of men" (ibid., p. 429).

3 · Tayama Katai— A Japanese Naturalist

The general discussion of *shizenshugi* as a literary movement in the preceding chapter will now be completed by considering Tayama Katai, a typical representative of Japanese naturalism. A closer look at his development will give us a clearer picture of the roughly sketched tendencies and problems characterized above. The second important objective is to consider the sequence of works (*literarische Reihe*) in Katai's writing that culminated in the short story "Futon." We shall initially base our discussion on the judgments of Katai's contemporaries and Japanese literary scholars up to the present day who see this story as crucial to the development of shishōsetsu, and this again requires an examination of his early works.

The second son of a former samurai, Tayama Katai grew up in the shadow of the castle of the former Tatebayashi Daimiate, in what is now Gunma prefecture. The Meiji restoration of 1868 and the reinstatement of the Daimiate to the Tenno a year later were particularly serious blows to the samurai because they robbed them of their established position within society and their security. Katai was born five years after the Restoration and witnessed the decline of his family. Many Japanese literary historians see a decisive influence on Katai's later development in his traditional education and in his longing for the paradisical[1] security of the feudal period, which explains the unusually large number of voluminous studies of Katai's early years.[2] In contrast, the number of works published on his productive literary phase is quite modest.[3]

In the years before Katai began writing, the following events are worth mentioning. After his father's death in the Seinan Battle in 1877, the uprising of former samurai from Satsuma against the central government, the 11- or 12-year-old Katai had to work for some time as an errand boy for a bookshop in Tokyo. This was a humiliating experience but, when he returned to Tatebayashi, he was inspired by the ideal of *risshin shusse* (establish oneself and rise in the world) of the early Meiji period and determined to overcome his experience through hard work and ambition. He wrote his first poems while still at school, in the Chinese style (*kanshi*), within the traditions of Sinologically educated samurai. In 1886, he moved to Tokyo. He considered embarking on a military career but then changed to a language school, where he took up English in order to study law or politics. Thus, he began by planning a career in public service, as did numerous other writers of the Meiji period, for example Futabatei, Tōkoku, Doppo, Hōgetsu, and Ishikawa Takuboku (1886–1912). A friend introduced him to European literature which aroused his interest in Hugo, Dumas, Dickens, and Wilkie Collins. He read Futabatei's *Ukigumo* and his Turgenev translation *Aibiki* (The Rendezvous, 1901)[4] and, under this influence, turned enthusiastically to contemporary fiction. Soon he was writing stories himself. The first known work, discovered by Iwanaga Yutaka,[5] is a tragic love story written in 1889 entitled "Aki no yūbe" (An Autumn Evening). Wada Kingo sees in this first work "colored with platonic sensitivity and fantasy" an early manifestation of the fundamental characteristics of Katai's literary style.[6]

In 1891, Katai gained access through Ozaki Kōyō to the "literary world" (*bundan*), then dominated by Rohan and Kōyō and their Ken'yūsha circle.[7] The Ken'yūsha writers adopted a classicist style based on Saikaku and favored predominantly sentimental love stories and mawkish tales about women. Katai enjoyed the literary atmosphere, and he soon began to produce works in a similar vein—a short story in the Saikaku style of the Meiji period entitled "Uribatake" (The Melon Field, 1891) and another, "Tera no aki" (Autumn in the Temple, 1892), in which the influence of Rohan's *Fūryūbutsu* (The Elegant Buddha, 1889) is obvious.[8] This was a romantic glorification of a sculptor's love of art and of a woman, concentrated symbolically in a statue representing both.[9] *Yamaga no mizu* then followed, an adaptation of Victor Hugo's *Les misérables* (1892). Wada Kingo sees this direct absorption of various influences and styles as a sign that Katai's desire to write arose before he had developed firm ideas or an awareness of his own.[10] An element of autobiography was characteristic of his work from the very beginning, as was the subject termed *shōjo sūhaibyō* (pathological adoration of girls) by Yoshida Seiichi.[11] Both are evident in "Shōshijin" (The Little Poet, published in 1893 in the journal *Kozakura odoshi*), the work which first won him recognition.

In the following year, Kitamura Tōkoku, the center of the romantic *Bungakukai* group, committed suicide. Katai wrote an epitaph and decided to join the group, which helped deepen his knowledge of European literature. In 1896, he met Kunikida Doppo, who was at that time, like Katai, well known as a writer of nature and love poetry in an unadorned style.

His marriage in 1899 ended this phase as a poet. The apparent relationship between the two events—curious as it may seem—should be traced back to practical material needs rather than to any psychological or artistic grounds. This is also the explanation given by Masamune Hakuchō, himself a naturalist and, as it were, eye-witness, to Tōson's change of genre from *shintaishi* poetry to prose. According to Hakuchō, the reason for his decision to publish stories was financial, not an altered view of art;[12] we may assume the same of Katai.

Katai could not, however, feed his family from prose either, and he therefore worked as an editor for various publishers. Other naturalists were also dependent on secondary incomes in this way; even at the height of their fame, they did not earn enough from their books because the numbers sold were considerably smaller than those of the great writers of Meiji literature, Natsume Sōseki (1867–1916) and Mori Ōgai, who enjoyed enormous success outside the *bundan*.[13] Financial problems and the pressure of this continuous double burden gave rise to pessimism in Katai and other naturalists, which is evident in their writing. According to Hakuchō, the desolation typical of *shizenshugi* was a reason why the average reader turned to other writers and left the *bundan* to itself.[14] This in turn merely increased the writers' penury and literary melancholy.

How, then, did *shizenshugi* develop? We see first of all a widely based reception of European literature on the part of the later naturalists, Katai in particular. We get an impression of the wide range of reading from the names of writers Katai introduced to the Japanese public in a series entitled "Seika yokō" (The Lingering Scent of Western Cultural Blossoms) in the journal *Taiyō* from May 1901 to the following year. Sasabuchi Tomoichi has counted the number of times the following names were mentioned: Hauptmann (6), Sienkiewicz (5), Maupassant, Maeterlinck, Sudermann, Bourget (4 each), Zola, D'Annunzio, Huysmans (3 each), Tolstoy, Ibsen,[15] Rod, Verhaeren (2 each), Flaubert, Hartleben, Loti, Halbe, Haeckel, Gorki, Poe, Wagner, Strindberg (1 each).[16] As we can see, the list is by no means limited to naturalist literature; indeed Katai's interest seemed to incline more towards the subsequent symbolic movement. At that time, he appears to have been impressed by Maupassant most of all[17] and wrote of him in 1901, "He is faithful only to nature; has he not completely abandoned the narrow subjectivity of the author[18] when describing nature? It is nature itself, [described] openly and courageously . . . Be natural! Be natural! How insignificant[19] are vulgarity and obscenity in art!"[20] Some explanation is needed for the importance he attributes to "nature" here. He makes use of other opportunities to draw attention to the term, for example in the foreword to *No no hana,* which appeared in the same month. Excerpts from this work were included earlier in Chapter 2 as an example of one of the first documents of *shizenshugi* theory.[21]

At the time Masamune Hakuchō criticized the divergence between the naturalist declaration of its own intention in the foreword and the product itself. As a result, Katai felt obliged to respond by explaining his ideas of naturalist objectivity. His central concept is the "subjectivity of great nature" (*daishizen no shukan*), which he contrasts with the habit in contemporary literature of making merely outward copies of reality.[22] According to Katai, the "advanced subjectivity"[23] of the writer is without doubt the same as nature's subjectivity.[24] Yoshida Seiichi explains Katai's understanding of the "subjectivity of great nature" as "the recognition of a kind of inevitability (*hitsuzensei*) which surmounts the thoughts and wishes of the individual in the course of life and society."[25]

Katai's preoccupation with what he calls "nature" (*shizen*) and "facts" (*jijitsu*), terms he used more or less identically, can be observed from 1897 onwards. In that year he spent two months with Doppo, which, according to his own statements, brought about a change of direction for him. "For Katai, who constructed his stories with sentimental fantasy, Doppo's instruction, 'You should write only factual (*jijitsu*) literature! Give up fantasy and write fact!' must have had great [significance]."[26] Should we believe Katai's version of events, he would associate the presentation of fact with self-revelation as early as this. He wrote in his memoirs, *Tōkyō no sanjūnen* (Thirty Years of Tokyo) in 1917 that it was this early impulse that explained how "[he] had come so far in completely revealing [his] inner being and in confessing [so] uninhibitedly."[27]

In considering what might have initiated the change, it is not possible to identify one single decisive element. We can safely assume that European literature served as a model in discussions with Doppo. In the subsequent phase of the intensive reception of European literature, it retained its importance as a guide in developing independent ideas, something that is evident in the frequency of references to European authors by Katai and other naturalists.[28] The change of direction was also a result of the conflict between the generations that caused younger authors to distance themselves from the established writers of Ken'yūsha in order to find their own identity. Finally, a personal process of maturing certainly also played a part in Katai's wish for unadorned realism.

THE QUESTION OF "INFLUENCE"

There is generally no doubt about the importance of European literature at the beginning of *shizenshugi*. Nevertheless, close analysis of individual works is needed in order to define such a phenomenon more precisely. Often enough, one is content to settle for the seemingly adequate description of an "influence," without much thought and in a roundabout fashion. We should, first of all, distinguish between the theoretical-programmatic and the literary-fictional statements of an author, which are often indebted to different principles even when they view each other as interrelated.[29] In Japan, works by a particular author are all too often explained through the author's own interpretation.[30] It is also necessary to find differentiated categories that enable a more precise description of these references, for example, along the lines suggested by Ulrich Weisstein, which specify borrowing, translation, adaptation, imitation, and influence (*rapports de fait*).[31] Such a differentiation would exceed the limits of our study but is nonetheless the precondition for an exact description of the function of European literature in the development of Katai's literary theory and practice, and this, in turn, could form a basis for general statements about *shizenshugi*.

These limitations notwithstanding, we shall attempt to approach the complex of questions in the case of Tayama Katai. His work includes all the forms of reference, adoption in the form of direct quotations,[32] translation,[33] adaptation, imitation and influence in the narrower sense.[34] These forms often appear next to each other in a particular work. For example, in the story "Jūemon no saigo" (Jūemon's End), published in 1902, Yoshida Seiichi identifies an idea which originated in Sudermann's *Katzensteg* and references to Turgenev's *First Love,* Flaubert's *Madame Bovary,* Zola and others: "It can at all events be called the work by Turgenbert and Zoladermann."[35]

The hero embodies the individualism represented by Takayama Chogyū, particularly popular at that time.[36] He is described as a man with pyromaniacal tendencies who is destined to be an outsider as the result of heritage and environment; eventually the villagers lynch him. His mistress, whom he incites to acts of arson, dies shortly afterward. The story is narrated in the first person by a young student who has come from the town and who observes events from a distance. Seven years later, someone who has visited the village tells the narrator that all is now peaceful and orderly again there. The story ends with these words from the narrator: "Gentlemen, thus has nature returned to nature."[37]

This obvious reference to Rousseau[38] is yet further proof of the variety of possible European allusions. (We would, however, have to identify as a next step the level in the work to which this Rousseau association refers, as it remains on the expressive plane of mere utterance.) Katai did not limit himself to naturalist literature, as we have already seen. Neither was he concerned with a logically consistent theory; he proceeded eclectically. Yet his notion of naturalism encompasses a far wider field than orthodox definitions. For example, in the series of articles "Seika yokō," "It is in any case a fact that at the beginning of the twentieth century naturalism, which united fantasy and mystic ideas, largely dominated the literary world and, equally, it is a fact that this direction had developed above all on the basis of Nietzsche's superhumanity,[39] Darwin's teachings on nature, and Wagner's theory of music."[40] For Katai, naturalism would be the generic term for various literary movements; it coincided with almost the entire spectrum of *belles lettres* in early-twentieth-century Europe.[41]

Katai himself referred to a broad Western cultural context in his literature when he described its frame of reference with the following words: "Decadence, individualism, superhuman, genius in connection with the glorification of everyday life, a sensuality bordering on satanical voracity, and the glorification of subjectivity and the ego."[42]

WEST-EAST ELECTIVE AFFINITIES

What should we think of the delight in absorbing all the educational ballast of the Occident and claiming it as his own? It seems to me that the most important function of these references to the West is in the legitimation they bestow on anyone who adorns himself with such quotations. The writer assumes what was for Japanese intellectuals at that time the immense authority of Western culture.

Yet it would be incorrect to present these references to Europe as attempts on the part of Japanese writers to deck themselves with borrowed plumes and thus to disregard their need for legitimation. We should remember that the thirst for knowledge in Japan was directed entirely towards the Western world from the beginning of the Meiji period and that great problems arose in the renewal of Japanese literature, making an even more intensive orientation towards European patterns seem desirable. Japanese writers conceived and secured their own objectives with reference to European models by patterning them accordingly.

I shall call the reference to Western antecedents, for purposes of legitimation, West-East elective affinities. In my opinion it is the most common and most typical Japanese "influence" pattern in the West-East direction and is practiced in the same way today, as I have attempted to show using examples from contemporary literature,[43] the list of which could be extended at will. The fact that the *shizenshugi* generation, of which Katai was part, was in particular need of such legitimation is easy to understand if we recall the social background and variety of literary father figures against which this generation had to struggle.

"MISUNDERSTANDINGS"

Katai and the representatives of *shizenshugi* were, however, certainly interested in the content of Western literature, which leads us to another problem, that is, distortions in reception as a result of a specific emphasis due to a different socio-cultural or individual context. Shifts in meaning due to attempted interpretation or to reading foreign elements into a discourse are, of course, not specific to any particular period or society. Yet it is obvious that greater semiotic shifts are likely when information is passed between two completely different civilizations rather than in transfer among cultures that share a common intellectual and historical context. As far as *shizenshugi* is concerned, this means that we must accept that Zola's thoughts were bound to be received differently in Japan than, for instance, in Germany, which is linked to France by a largely identical hermeneutical conception grounded in the communality of European heritage.

However obvious this statement may seem, it is certainly not superfluous, since the natural consequence from this observation, and one that is only rarely complied with, would be that the incongruity between the "original" meaning and its reception should not be dismissed as "misunderstandings" or attributed to the personal inability of the recipient, as so often happens in literary discussions.[44] If, instead, these "misunderstandings" were subject to analysis, it would open the way, in my opinion, to other more important questions concerning the specific conditions of reception and would, at the same time, help to explain the particular literary phenomena as their results.

Again, the range of questions sketched here can only find a provisional answer in the case of Katai. We begin by attempting to isolate the central issue of what Katai judged to be significant in European literature of his time, which he considered to be largely identical with naturalism, and what he intended to adopt. His theoretical writing centers on the terms "nature" and "objectivity." According to his understanding of the subject, these were the leading ideas of Western literature, ideas that he also propounded for a new Japanese literature.

However obvious it may be that Katai was referring to Europe in his use of "nature" it is also clear that his understanding differed considerably from the concept of nature that was the basis for European naturalism. There are repeated references in his writing to Darwin,[45] and there was widespread knowledge in Japan of Comte and Taine, who represented positivism and who significantly influenced the scientific attitudes of naturalism. Nevertheless, in literary practice the *shizenshugi* authors were less concerned with an analytical-scientific presentation of the effects of determining factors, such as heredity, environment, and historical situation. Nature as the "inevitability" of the event, as Katai understood it, appears in the works themselves as a mysterious automatism which rarely suggests the "naturalist" factors of race and environment.

This is also the case with "Jūemon no saigo," a work which can certainly be categorized under the rubric of naturalism as far as subject and plot are concerned: Jūemon is presented not so much as the victim of those determinants but rather as the embodiment of demoniacal powers, as the symbol of atavistic elements inherent in all people. This is conveyed by a consistent mythical narrative mode maintained right to the end, as convincingly described by Frederick Richter.[46] Thus, the rational naturalist concept of nature becomes absorbed into a traditional understanding, in mystical, irrational, fatalistic attitudes that also sift through Katai's use of the term *daishizen*—"great nature."

The concept of "objectivity" (*kyakkan[sei]*) undergoes a similar shift of meaning. The scientific-physiological foundations of naturalist aesthetics demand a precise recording of the reality to be portrayed. This scientific aspect is not featured in Katai's writing. His demand for "unadorned description," which one is initially inclined to understand as a practical consequence from naturalist theory, proves, on closer exami-

4 · "Futon"

This brings us to the crux of this first part of the discussion, the short story "Futon," published in the magazine *Shinshōsetsu* in September 1907.

The story tells of a writer named Takenaka Tokio and his secret love for a schoolgirl. The story is told in the third person, for long periods from the perspective "narrator = character" ("with" perspective).[1] In places the narrator posits himself inside a different character but the overall impression is of a singular perspective.

A period of approximately three years is described, starting with a flashback to the first half of this period, the one and a half years the girl Yoshiko spent in the writer's care in Tokyo. She has literary talent and ambition and, with her parent's permission, has come to Tokyo from the provinces in order to study literature with Takenaka Tokio, staying at his house and attending school in the capital. Tokio enjoys the cheerfulness and freshness that Yoshiko's presence brings into his life. His wife and three children have grown into something of a burden to him. Obliged to earn his living in a firm of geographical publishers, he is, at 36, dissatisfied with himself and the world and sees Yoshiko as the ideal representative of the modern independent woman. At the same time, she embodies in her beauty, grace, and youth his lost freedom. It is, therefore, no surprise that he secretly falls in love with her, always maintaining, however, his correct behavior towards her as her instructor. Since he feels sure of her admiration he is able to tolerate the inevitable inner conflict.

When he learns, however, that Yoshiko has fallen in love with a young student from Kyoto, feelings of jealousy and anger erupt in him. He drinks recklessly and becomes a tyrant at home. Towards Yoshiko he still behaves as a responsible, understanding mentor, however, and she in turn places great trust in him. The conflict becomes unbearable for Tokio when the student moves to Tokyo in order to be near Yoshiko and the two start meeting regularly. He continues to pose as the "benevolent protector" of the young, innocent love, but secretly he is tortured by feelings of jealousy and by his doubts about the purity of the relationship, despite the couple's protestations of innocence. He notes that the two young people are becoming increasingly close but remains helpless and inactive, since he fears he will lose Yoshiko completely if he interferes. Finally, however, he feels obliged to call in Yoshiko's father, who speaks to the young student and demands that the couple separate temporarily. Tokio's fears are confirmed at this point: The relationship was not platonic and he finally gives up his "protector role." Yoshiko writes him a guilty farewell letter and then travels home with her father.

Tokio again sees a dismal, joyless life before him. A short, impersonal letter from Yoshiko awakens painful memories of days gone by. He takes her bedding (*futon*) out of the cupboard in her bedroom.

> The familiar smell of her [hair] oil and her sweat caused his breast to tremble violently. He pressed his face into the quilt's velvet collar where it was evidently soiled and breathed in the perfume of the woman he loved.
>
> Desire, pain and despair pressed suddenly on his breast. He spread out the futon, put the quilt on top of it and, weeping, hid his face in the cold, dirty velvet collar.
>
> [Here] the dim room and outside the wind howled.[2]

This is a rough outline of the plot. The title was taken from the final scene, which is concluded by the above quotation.[3]

AUTOBIOGRAPHICAL ELEMENTS

The well-informed reader from the environs of the *bundan,* the world of the literati, will have been aware of similarities between the work and the author's biography. Katai made use of events from the years 1904 to 1906 when the young Okada Michiyo stayed with him to learn about literature. In a separate essay I have pointed out some of the parallels.[4]

We shall, however, consider another episode, which proves even more clearly than all the similarities in the plot that the author identifies and can be identified with his hero. At the beginning of the story, when the narrator introduces the main character as a dissatisfied writer, he says, nation, to be, above all, a battle cry in the fight against traditional "gilded" literature which required "artistry" (*gikō*).[47] Of course, Katai again invoked European literati; according to him they demanded that "everything should be unadorned, true and natural."[48]

It is obvious, however, from the example he gave that he was by no means referring solely to an exact, objectivistic method of writing such as that which characterized naturalism. He saw these very principles put into practice in *L'innocente* (1892), a work of D'Annunzio, famed for its aestheticist and subjectivist style of decadence: "The piercing quality which we feel when reading D'Annunzio is certainly not based entirely on his stylistic skill but on the fact that his description is completely audacious, completely unadorned and that he avoids nothing.... In particular, *L'innocente* is to the greatest extent unadorned, to the greatest extent fearless, and it possesses something that makes it seem inevitable for the reader to almost shudder."[49] It is illuminating to see in which connection Katai placed the term "unadorned," which was originally used in the sense of "not skillful,"[50] "objective": used together with "fearless" and "avoids nothing," it connotes frankness, directness, and thus clearly points towards an identification of objectivity and merciless self-revelation, which Katai put into practice for the first time in "Futon."

INNOVATION AS RENOVATION

This reinterpretation of naturalist principles was largely an unconscious process for Katai. He continued to refer to his European models, not in order to maintain appearances, but because he was convinced of their importance. This produced the interesting phenomenon that literary innovation was constantly explained on the basis of an adoption of foreign patterns, although these at most provided the stimulus for the largely unconscious resort to Japan's own cultural and literary tradition. The way in which the concepts of "nature" and "objectivity," which were central to *shizenshugi* or their reinterpretation, were based on particular traditional Japanese attitudes will be shown in Part Three of this book.[51] Here I only want to point out that this pattern is valid not only for Katai but for *shizenshugi* in general. In addition I consider it, next to the West-East elective affinities, to be among the most typical patterns of influence—and, for the non-Japanese student of these phenomena, the most interesting—in modern Japanese literature.

In naming these two main forms of Western influence, both characterized by the low "dyeing" effect the received literature had on the Japanese work, I do not want to suggest that interaction with the foreign in modern Japanese literature was limited to satisfying the need for legitimation and providing invisibly acting impulses which brought about a return to national tradition. Japanese authors did indeed learn from their European colleagues in many aspects, even by direct imitation, particularly where writing technique was concerned, by creating more realistic and probable plots as well as in psychological description. However, this was a process which began early in Meiji and was not limited to the period or to the authors of *shizenshugi*. It must also be said that it was the realistic novelists of the second half of the nineteenth century, rather than the naturalists, who stimulated Japanese writers to aim at more realistic and plausible description.

The most important reason why I have emphasized this "innovation as renovation" principle is that it coincides with central ideas of *shizenshugi* and that it was just these elements which brought about the breakthrough for Japanese naturalism, something that can be clearly seen in "Futon" and the reception given it.

---

1. Katai himself, in an autobiographical essay ("Shōgatsu zuihitsu"), describes how his mother and grandfather told him: "There will never again be such a paradise," cited in Wada Kingo, "Tayama Katai shū kaisetsu," pp. 11f.
2. For monographs cf., e.g., Yanagida Izumi, *Tayama Katai no bungaku,* I and II, and Kobayashi Ichirō, *Tayama Katai kenkyū.* Further titles are included in the bibliography in *Tayama Katai shū, NKiBT,* XIX, 442–456.
3. Of the monographs referring to this I consulted Iwanaga Yutaka, *Tayama Katai kenkyū.* The bibliography named mentions merely two further books.
4. "Svidaniye," a story from the collection *Zapiski okhotnika* (Notes from a Hunter), published in 1850; cf. Lewin, *Futabatei Shimei,* pp. 66f. on the translation.
5. Cf. Iwanaga, pp. 51ff.
6. Wada, "Tayama Katai shū kaisetsu," p. 19.
7. Cf., e.g., Hiraoka Toshio, "Ken'yūsha ni okeru Kōyō."
8. Yoshida Seiichi, *Shizenshugi no kenkyū,* vol. I, p. 281.
9. Cf. Ishida Tadahiko, "Rohan no naka no 'fūryū.'"
10. Cf. Wada, "Tayama Katai shū kaisetsu," p. 22.
11. Cf. Yoshida Seiichi, *Shizenshugi no kenkyū,* vol. I, p. 286.
12. Cf. Masamune Hakuchō: "Shizenshugi seisuishi" (The History of the Rise and Fall of Naturalism, 1948) in *Masamune Hakuchō zenshū,* XII, 277–381, here p. 288.
13. Cf. Masamune Hakuchō, ibid., p. 308.
14. Ibid., p. 330.
15. In the *katakana* transcription the name Furudā now follows, but in the reference books available to me it is not included.
16. Cf. Sasabuchi Tomoichi, *Meiji Taishō bungaku no bunseki,* p. 596.

45. Cf., e.g., the quotation from "Seika yōko" given above.
46. Cf. Frederick Richter, "Tayama Katai and Two Narrative Modes of Japanese Literary Naturalism," pp. 774–780.
47. "Rokotsunaru byōsha" (Unadorned Description, February 1904 in *Taiyō*), quoted from *NKiBT,* LVII, 198).
48. Ibid., p. 199.
49. Ibid., p. 200.
50. *Mugikō,* cf. the additional note 115 in *NKiBT,* LVII, 459.
51. Cf. "Theoretical Premises" (Chapter 10), and "The 'Philosophy'" (Chapter 14).

17. For details of Katai's reception of Maupassant cf. Ōnishi Tadao, "Mōpassan to sono Nihon e no eikyō," pp. 321ff. and Ikari Akira, "Tayama Katai to Mōpassan."
18. Cf. the same terminology in the foreword to his story *No no hana,* quoted in Chapter 2.
19. In the sense of "one need not fear them since they have no meaning as such."
20. On 15 July 1901 in *Taiheiyō,* quoted in Wada, "Tayama Katai shū kaisetsu," p. 30.
21. In my opinion the term *shizen* has the strong additional meaning of "natural" versus "unnatural," both in the foreword and in the quotation on Maupassant. For instance, in the foreword of *No no hana,* the truth to nature which is demanded compares with the "unnaturalness" of traditional literature, and in the Maupassant commentary, the *shizen nare* (Be nature/be natural) also points in this direction.
22. "Shukan kyakkan no ben" (On the Discussion of Subjectivity and Objectivity, 9 September 1901 in *Taiyō*) reprinted in *KBHT,* II (*Meiji-ki* II), 151–153.
23. Ibid., p. 151.
24. In contrast to "narrow subjectivity," cf. above the quotations commenting on *No no hana* and on Maupassant.
25. Yoshida Seiichi, *Shizenshugi no kenkyū,* vol. I, p. 312. Yoshida discusses Katai's ideas and terminology in detail.
26. Wada, "Tayama Katai shū kaisetsu," p. 27
27. Quoted in ibid.
28. Cf. also the quotations included in Chapter 2. On the function of the reference to European literature see below.
29. We need think only of the discrepancy between foreword and work noticed by Hakuchō in Katai's *No no hana,* see above.
30. This observation is also confirmed by modern examples, e.g., in statements about Mishima, cf. I.H.-K., *Mishima Yukios Roman,* p. 22.
31. Cf. Ulrich Weisstein, "Influences and Parallels," p. 597.
32. E.g. the exclamation "Lonely life!" in the story "Onna kyōshi" with which Katai refers to the English translation of Hauptmann's drama *Einsame Menschen,* cf. I.H.-K., "Innovation als Renovation," p. 361.
33. For example Hauptmann's *Die versunkene Glocke—Chinshō* (1903).
34. According to Weisstein, p. 597, "a more complicated pattern composed, most likely, of conscious and subconscious elements."
35. Yoshida Seiichi, *Shizenshugi no kenkyū,* vol. I, p. 317.
36. Ibid., p. 318.
37. "Jūemon no saigo," *Tayama Katai shū, NKiBT,* XIX, 121.
38. Hasegawa Tenkei, the reviewer at that time, also associated Rousseau with this work, cf. Yoshida Seiichi, *Shizenshugi no kenkyū,* vol. I, p. 318.
39. *Daikojinshugi,* literally "great individualism." Possibly *daikojin* is an earlier translation of the concept "superman," which Katai later translated *chōjin,* cf. the following quotation from *Meiji no shōsetsu.*
40. Quoted from Hisamatsu Sen'ichi, ed., *Zōho shinpan Nihon bungakushi,*, VI, 229.
41. One reason for associating "fantasy and mystic ideas" with naturalism is probably the inflexible identification of authors with particular literary currents typical for this Japanese approach. Thus, Hauptmann was "undeniably" a naturalist for Katai. A work such as the fairy tale drama *Die versunkene Glocke,* which Katai himself presented to the Japanese public in 1903, would therefore be more likely to lead to an extension of the concept of naturalism than to a revision of the scheme of literary grouping.
42. *Meiji no shōsetsu: Shizenshugi to shajitsushugi* (Novel Literature of the Meiji Period: Naturalism and Realism), p. 33.
43. For Mishima Yukio cf. I.H.-K., *Mishima Yukios Roman,* part 3, and for Abe Kōbō I.H.-K., "Abe Kōbō und der Nouveau Roman."
44. I also see this tendency in Nakamura Mitsuo, *Fūzoku shōsetsuron.*

"His literary career, which was developing only slowly, the torment of having found no real opportunity, apart from a few fragments, to put his talents into practice, the way he suffered from the bad criticism which he received in the magazines every month, all these things depressed him secretly although he was convinced that he was bound to be successful sometime."[5] The author must himself have been in this mental state since, ten years later, he described the situation in which "Futon" was written in this way:

> It was the second year after I had returned from the war and the war had already been over for a year. Although we received no reparation payments, the whole society, under the influence of victory, was full of vitality. There was also [action] on the literary front: Shimazaki had already published *Hakai* and received inordinate praise for it and Kunikida's *Dopposhū* had been given general recognition and was into its third edition. Laughing, Kunikida said, "It looks as if our time has arrived."
>
> I myself felt as if I were the only one who had been left behind. Although I had experienced the war I had not achieved anything in the literary field. It was particularly unbearable for me because I had seen how Shimazaki, who had come from Komoro, had labored in the vicinity of Ōkubo under a hot tin roof with his chest bared. This thought pursued me wherever I went, but I produced nothing. I despaired and was impatient.
>
> Then a commission came from *Shinshōsetsu*.
>
> "I'll give it a try," I said, full of enthusiasm. This time, I thought, I'll give everything I have.[6]

Frustrated ambition, pride and, as he says in "Futon," "the lonely torment of one who always stands outside"[7] motivated the author to write a work suffused with just these feelings. An important part of its success stemmed from the fact that contemporaries could obviously identify with the story.[8]

In addition to the hero, we also encounter a second character who represents the typical young intellectual of the age, this time, as it were, in more objective form, from the "outside" perspective, that is, as seen through the eyes of the writer Tokio. Tanaka Hideo, Yoshiko's lover, personifies the development of numerous young naturalists. His origins in the provinces, his self-enforced stay in Tokyo, his break with Christianity, the abandonment of his studies in order to devote himself completely to literature and the conflict with the donor of his scholarship[9]—all these situations are well known from the biographies of writers since Futabatei;[10] however, such an accumulation is typical for the writers of *shizenshugi*.[11] Nevertheless, Tokio is aware of Tanaka only as a "rival";[12]

he is never conscious of him as a reflection of himself. Instead he identifies with characters from European literature.

THE INFLUENCE OF HAUPTMANN

There is a repeated comparison with Gerhart Hauptmann's drama *Einsame Menschen* (1891) and its main character, the private tutor Johannes Vockerat, a follower of Darwin and Haeckel, who does not feel able to cope with the conflict between his conservative-pietist environment and his "advanced" ideas. He seeks reassurance in his friendship with Anna Mahr, a Russian intellectual, the complete opposite of his own bourgeois, homely wife, Käthe.

A first glance at "Futon" gives the impression of a similar triangular story of this kind—the conflict between conventional values and modern attitudes, between traditional and emancipated women and the modern intellectual's alienation and search for orientation. Right at the beginning of the work, when Tokio's inner conflict over Yoshiko's behavior is described, we find a reference to Hauptmann's drama: "Suddenly he thought of Hauptmann's [play] *Einsame Menschen*. Before things developed as they had he had intended this play to be a study subject for her. He had wanted to explain Johannes Vockerat's spiritual condition and his suffering to her. It was more than three years since he had read this drama, when he had not even known that she existed, but from then on he had been a lonely person."[13] Shortly afterwards we learn more about the reason for his loneliness: He complains about his old-fashioned, uneducated wife who shows no interest in his literary work: "Just like Johannes in *Einsame Menschen* he could not help finding the life of a housewife meaningless. This—this loneliness[14] was broken by Yoshiko."[15] To Tokio, the parallels between his own life and Hauptmann's play are so obvious that he decides not to read the work with Yoshiko after all so as to prevent any embarrassing comparisons.[16]

Katai himself saw things in exactly the same way and even went one step further. In the memoirs mentioned above he wrote: "I felt that Vockerat's loneliness was [also] my loneliness."[17]

The equation Takenaka Tokio = Johannes Vockerat = Tayama Katai illustrates the extent of the author's identification with his hero. He not only saw things with his eyes but he was himself present in the work—the name Takenaka Tokio seems to be only a half-hearted attempt at creating distance from himself.

This statement brings us into the realm of discussion about the defini-

45 · Autobiographical Elements

tive characteristics of the shishōsetsu genre, something we must put off until later. It is necessary here to clarify what function and what significance should be attributed to Katai's reference to Hauptmann's drama.

The apparent parallels between "Futon" and *Einsame Menschen* prove, on closer examination, to be mere superficial similarities. There is hardly any echo in the Japanese narrative of the specific themes of the naturalist drama, that is of conflict of *Weltanschauung* and contemporary political problems. In spite of his views about an emancipated partner with whom he would like to prove his progressive attitude, Tokio remains a conventional person in every sense. His longing for a "new woman" is nothing more than the desire for a new woman, for an erotic adventure to give him an interesting diversion and distraction. "Futon" is, therefore, not a drama about marriage and love, as is *Einsame Menschen*, but is confined to present the inner life of a man with only very limited insight into his own spiritual problems who delights in indulging himself in unrealistic, adolescent daydreams.[18]

We cannot therefore talk of "Futon" being influenced by the German play in the sense of obvious parallels exceeding the all-too-general basic pattern of an intellectual dissatisfied with his own marriage who falls in love with another woman. Nevertheless, this "influence" seems to be an accepted fact among literary historians.[19]

Nakamura Mitsuo takes a more differentiated approach to the matter. He interprets "Futon" as the result of Katai's identification with the hero Johannes but not with the author Hauptmann. According to Nakamura, the result is a version of the naturalist drama in which all the other characters are missing,[20] a "monologue from the lonely man Takenaka Tokio."[21]

Those researchers who consider "Futon" a more or less faithful copy of the German play—Yoshitake Yoshinori, for example, refers to it as a transposition (*yakuan*)[22]—base their views on the author's own interpretation when he wrote about the origins of "Futon" in his memoirs under the heading "My Anna Mahr" ("Watakushi no Anna Māru"):

> Just at that time [when he was asked for a contribution to *Shinshōsetsu*], I was involved with Hauptmann's play *Einsame Menschen*. I felt that Vockerat's loneliness was [also] my loneliness. Also, I had to destroy the form of my work up to that time and open up new paths. Fortunately, I had adopted the new current of ideas from abroad, particularly from Europe, through extensive reading. Tolstoy, Ibsen, Strindberg, and Nietzsche—the form of suffering of the fin de siècle seemed obvious in the ideas of these people. I also wanted to take this difficult course. I wanted to fight courageously not only

against society (*seken*) but also against myself. I thought of revealing what I had hidden and suppressed until then and what could destroy my spirit if I revealed it.[23]

What were Katai's reasons for his reference to Hauptmann? Katai had known the German naturalist's work since the last decade of the nineteenth century.[24] He had read an English translation of *Einsame Menschen* as early as 1901, since he later related that he had discussed it with Shimazaki Tōson and that they had both compared themselves to the "lonely person" Johannes.[25]

In this early phase, Hauptmann's influence is still conspicuous. The story he wrote in 1903, "Onna kyōshi" (The Schoolmistress), could even be called a Japanese version of the German play in many places.[26] Numerous, all-too-obvious references could be pointed out here, but this work has been largely ignored by the critics since it was not nearly as successful as "Futon." This fact alone leads us to assume that "Futon" does not owe its popularity to Hauptmann's influence. That Katai later nevertheless tried to suggest this was presumably to legitimize his great success.

If we remind ourselves that "Futon" was also a coming to terms with personal conflicts—probably to a greater degree than Katai was able to admit—then it is understandable that, ten years later, he preferred to explain the work's success by saying that it was a conscious adaptation of a naturalist play rather than ascribing it to a fortunate coincidence of private problems with contemporary taste.

Katai's statement is, however, also proof of his eclectic treatment of European literature which he quite naturally considered to be his system of reference, a typical example of West-East elective affinity. His references to Western culture do not stem from any real necessity, as we can clearly see from this quotation. It is knowledge which he has acquired and which he can call up to give his work more than a merely personal, autobiographical motivation. At the same time, by identifying himself with these European models he includes himself in the circle of "modern intellectuals" and ensures that the private problems he describes in the work will be accepted as representative of artists' and intellectuals' problems in general.[27]

THE GENEALOGY OF THE WORK

Katai had, therefore, adopted the basic pattern of *Einsame Menschen* several years earlier which he tried out and modified in "Onna kyōshi" and other stories in the subsequent series of "Yearning for Beautiful Girls."[28] The subject of "admiring girls"[29] can be traced back to the beginning of Katai's literary work, as we have already seen, and remained his favorite at least until "Futon." However, it was eventually exhausted and even a defamiliarized version, for example, adopting fairy story form in *Makoku* (Magic Land, 1906) could not conceal the fact that it was just a new variation of the old favorite. The public was gradually becoming tired of these romantic, dreamy stories, particularly because they did not differ significantly from the mawkish novels produced by the Ken'yūsha circle that had dominated the literary scene a whole decade earlier.

Katai recognized that it was necessary for him to part with this pattern, but it was obviously difficult for him, a "thoroughly emotional" person,[30] to do so. In May 1907, four months before "Futon," he published the story "Shōjobyō" (Girl Fever) about a writer dissatisfied with his marriage and fascinated by young girls—a new version of the fundamental constellation from "Onna kyōshi," based on Hauptmann—who is so enraptured at the sight of one of these perfect creatures that he falls from a streetcar and is killed.

The obvious irony and self-criticism, however, with which Katai attempted to achieve some distance from himself was no solution. His dilemma continued to be the discrepancy between the demand he stated as early as 1904 in "Rokotsunaru byōsha" for "unadorned, true, and natural" description, which damned everything artificial, constructed, and idealized—those elements he had criticized so violently in Ken'yūsha literature—and his own literary practice which would not fit in with his theories. He himself seems to have been aware of this, since he was increasingly dissatisfied with both himself and his work, as the quotations from his memoirs and from "Futon" point out. In this respect "Futon" must have been something of a last, despairing attempt.

He again adopted the constellation of characters from *Einsame Menschen*, but at this stage he had so mastered the pattern that it was possible for him to shift the narrative emphasis from the plot to the mental condition of the characters. This, on the other hand, suited his "thoroughly emotional" nature perfectly. Katai at last found his domain in "Futon." Having identified with the Hauptmann play, he was able to discover his own life as a literary subject. This was for him the solution to the problem of artificial and unreal earlier works, which he had tried to meet previously by following European literary models (since his own imagination failed him) but without producing satisfactory results. At the same time, he succeeded for the first time in putting his *shizenshugi* concept into valid literary practice. We shall go into his specific reinterpretation of the demand for "nature" and "objectivity" later which, as we had seen, he associated with "frankness" from a very early point in his theoretical considerations and which quite naturally led to the postulate for self-revelation.

"REINFORCEMENTS" IN CONTEMPORARY LITERATURE

At this point, we shall insert a short discussion of the literature produced by other authors in the period shortly before the work appeared, for it would be insufficient to explain its origins at the literary level only by, as it were, a diachronic view: in other words, a reconstruction of Katai's series of works or from the biographical facts of the author's personality. The direct references to individual new publications that Katai said, in the memoirs quoted above, stimulated him to write his own work, show us that it is also necessary to attempt a cross section through the literature of that time to identify the components in the literary process of development that specifically molded "Futon."

Shimazaki Tōson's novel *Hakai* (The Broken Commandment), published in May 1906, is of outstanding importance in this respect.[31] At the time it represented a high point and the most successful example of a series of works which had as their subject young intellectuals—in emulation of European models—a tradition established by Futabatei's *Ukigumo* and again taken up in this work. For example, Oguri Fūyō attempted to paint a picture of a spiritually homeless generation in his novel *Seishun* (Youth, March 1905–November 1906) personified by the hero Seki Kin'ya, a brilliant poseur "infected by egoistic individualism,"[32] who is clearly based on Turgenev's *Rudin* (1856). The homeless generation, disappointed at the futility of their idealistic aspirations in view of harsh reality, are left with nothing but nihilistic resignation. Readers of the time recognized themselves in Seki Kin'ya. The work deeply impressed the literati and the general public, although, as Nakamura Mitsuo points out, it suffers by trying to describe a new type of man through a traditional mode of writing. Nevertheless, it was this novel in particular that was a milestone in the development from Ken'yūsha style to "Futon's" *shizenshugi*.[33]

Yet, with hindsight, we can see that it was *Hakai* which directly paved the way for "Futon," since Tōson was the first writer to succeed in giving his generation's new feeling for life credible and profoundly motivated expression, which Fūyō had been one of the first to explore. According to Nakamura, the development from *Seishun* to *Hakai* can be seen, on the one hand, in the way author and hero begin to overlap. At the same time, the altered narrative stance, by strengthening the identification of the author with his hero, also brings about an increased seriousness in the treatment of the material. While Fūyō, talented and technically skilled, still represents the old school with his detached aloofness, Tōson's involvement reveals a more modern consciousness. Fūyō was nothing more than "an old [type of] man in new clothing," according to Nakamura,[34] whereas Tōson, three years younger, was someone looking to the future, above all because of his much more profound reception of Western literature, no longer contenting himself with outer forms but understanding that empathy, the ability to enter into the characters, was what mattered most.[35] Thus, he succeeded in amalgamating personal statement and the description of the psychic processes of his hero Ushimatsu by orienting himself around *Crime and Punishment* and Rousseau's *Confessions*. It was then only a step from this point in the development of narrative technique to the almost complete exclusion of the fictional character in "Futon."[36]

Even resorting to real events, however, had its antecedents. For example, in his *Suisai gaka* (The Painter in Water Colors, 1904) Tōson wrote a kind of *roman-à-clef* about the painter Maruyama Banka. According to Masamune Hakuchō, his real interest lay in self-portrayal, but he still lacked courage for this and so concealed himself behind a fiction taken from extraliterary reality.[37]

Tōson's "Namiki" (The Row of Trees), published in June 1907, deals with material taken from the author's immediate surroundings. The work tells of a young clerk who is unexpectedly visited by an old friend. Their conversations awaken memories of their idealistic youth. Aikawa, the hero, feels the bitter contrast between his early ideals and his present, monotonous and unfulfilled life. Thus the avenue down which he walks to work each day suddenly assumes a symbolic quality for him with its uniformly truncated trees that are not allowed to grow naturally.

If we consider "Namiki" in the light of "Futon," which dominated literary discussions three months later, we can see an astonishing number of common elements. In both works the subject matter, above all the contrast between desired and experienced reality and the dissatisfaction of the intellectual trapped in his monotonous daily life, is combined with material taken from the author's world which the public would immediately recognize. In "Namiki," Tōson introduces his former school comrade, the student of English literature and translator, Baba Kochō (1869–1940) and Togawa Shūkotsu (1870–1939) as his friend, which provoked a public discussion on the use of real persons as literary characters.[38] However, while the unskilled use in literature of real events was criticized in Tōson's work,[39] "Futons'" popularity attests to a successful handling of this aspect, too. One important reason is certainly Katai's decision to move from the use of real events and characters to confining himself solely to his personal experiences and limiting the narrative perspective to the point of view of the hero, who gradually coincides with the author.

Let us conclude by summarizing the most important lines of development which meet in "Futon." On the basis of Katai's chronology of works we can observe the linking of the "yearning-for-young-girls" theme with a subject inspired by Hauptmann's *Einsame Menschen,* which, in a process of repeated treatment on the basis of an unchanged basic pattern, is replaced by autobiographical elements. At the same time, the narrative focus moves from the outward events to the hero's inner experience. The concentration of the narrative perspective on the hero's point of view was Katai's first successful attempt at fulfilling the demand he made years earlier for "unadorned" and "flat" description, thereby relinquishing the "auctorial" narrative role—roughly corresponding to the narrator›person or perspective "from behind" pattern mentioned in note 1—which seemed unnatural and outmoded to him. His *shizenshugi* principle consisted of "depicting [something] merely flatly, as one has seen it. Therefore, one can express the feelings of the author (observer)[40] to a certain extent, but not the inner being of the characters described, since that would be unnatural in this case."[41]

As this quotation makes clear, Katai distinguishes between the point of view of the author, whom he identifies with the narrator's character, and the point of view of the fictional figures. The crucial point is that he ignores the fictional nature of the narrative function as well as of the hero, whose inner life is a central topic, and by inserting his own personal self instead, he supplies us with further evidence for the approach which was observed for the first time in "Futon." As far as his literary theory was concerned, this overlapping and merging of hero, narrative function, and the author as a real person was in evidence early on in his thought association of factual description and personal disclosure.

Katai did not write in isolation. He belonged to the *bundan,* was involved in the discussions, and played a decisive part in shaping the program of *shizenshugi*. "Futon," as an attempt to "catch up"[42] with Tōson, who had moved ahead of him in literary practice, therefore contains many of the specific elements that constituted the contemporary reader's horizon of expectation. "Futon" could be described as a kind of focusing mirror which concentrates and unites the various lines of development. These were, above all, the figure of the intellectual as a topic, and the choice of autobiographical material as subject matter,[43] which corresponded with a demand for closeness to reality, and the confessional character that began with *Hakai*. This development took place within the cultural and socio-political context outlined above which, if it were to be described using only one term, could best be characterized as a growth of individualism. This term refers to the intellectuals' search for identity, growing awareness, and longing for emancipation just as it does to their flight into the private sphere in the face of increased state control, growing nationalism in public life, and an imperialist policy towards Japan's Asian neighbors.[44]

---

1. As opposed to the constellation of narrator>person (perspective "from behind") and narrator<person (perspective "from without"), cf. Tzvetan Todorov, "Die Kategorien der literarischen Erzählung," p. 282, who adopts this classification by J. Pouillon.
2. "Futon," quoted from *NKiBT*, XIX (*Tayama Katai shū*), 194.
3. On the motivist interlacing of the final scene cf. also my observations in I.H.-K., "Innovation als Renovation," footnote 23.
4. Ibid., footnote 21. The correspondence between Katai and Okada, first published in 1939, is reprinted in Yoshida Seiichi, Ishimaru Hisashi and Iwanaga Yutaka, eds., *Tōson, Katai*, pp. 317–335.
5. "Futon," *NKiBT*, XIX, 126.
6. *Tōkyō no sanjūnen, Tayama Katai zenshū*, XV, 600.
7. "Futon," *NKiBT*, XIX, 137.
8. Cf. the reactions to "Futon" described in Chapter 5.
9. "Futon," *NKiBT*, XIX, 157f.
10. Cf. Chapter 1.
11. Cf. Chapter 2.
12. "Futon," *NKiBT*, XIX, 188.
13. Ibid., p. 126.
14. *Ronrīnesu* in the original, cf. note 33 on this.
15. "Futon," *NKiBT*, XIX, 131.
16. Cf. ibid., p. 127
17. *Tōkyō no sanjūnen, Tayama Katai zenshū*, XV, 601.
18. I.H.-K., "Probleme der modernen japanischen Literaturgeschichtsschreibung," includes a detailed comparison of *Einsame Menschen* and "Futon."

19. Cf. ibid. on the various theories of influence.
20. Cf. Nakamura Mitsuo, *Fūzoku shōsetsuron*, p. 37. However, he criticizes only the abridgement in the description of the characters in comparison with Hauptmann, while my analysis ("Innovation als Renovation") is concerned with showing that none of Hauptmann's concerns reappear in "Futon."
21. Sasabuchi, p. 611, referring to Nakamura.
22. Yoshitake Yoshinori, *Kindai bungaku no naka no Seiō: Kindai Nihon yakuanshi*, p. 281.
23. *Tōkyō no sanjūnen, Tayama Katai zenshū*, XV, 601.
24. Cf. Kobayashi Ichirō, *Tayama Katai kenkyū*, p. 153.
25. Ibid., p. 185.
26. A detailed comparison is included in I.H.-K., "Innovation als Renovation."
27. This point is considered in greater detail in I.H.-K., "Innovation als Renovation."
28. Cf. Ogata Akiko, "'Futon' zenya," p. 43.
29. As mentioned previously, Yoshida Seiichi speaks of an almost pathological tendency (*shōjo sūhaibyō*) in this connection, cf. his *Shizenshugi no kenkyū*, vol. I, p. 281.
30. Cf. Sasabuchi, p. 615.
31. Cf. Chapter 2.
32. Okazaki Yoshie, *Japanese Literature in the Meiji Era*, p. 220.
33. Nakamura Mitsuo, *Fūzoku shōsetsuron*, p. 12.
34. Ibid., p. 18.
35. Cf. ibid., p. 23ff.
36. Of course, Takenaka Tokio is also a fictional figure, but the common milieu of the literary work and the author's life, the frank, even demonstrative use of what the author had personally experienced and his consistent identification with Tokio all have the effect that the reader is not aware of him as a fictional figure but at most as the author in disguise, though more often as the author himself. Cf. Chapter 5.
37. Cf. *Masamune Hakuchō zenshū*, XII, 288f. ("Shizenshugi seisuishi").
38. Cf. e.g., "Moderu mondai no imi oyobi sono kaiketsu" (The Model Problem, Its Meaning and Its Solution), November 1907 in *Waseda bungaku*; cf. also Chapter 5.
39. Baba Kochō: "Shimazaki shi no 'Namiki,'" September 1907, reprinted in Yoshida Seiichi et al., eds., *Tōson, Katai*, pp. 75–89, here p. 89.
40. Parentheses in the original.
41. Tayama Katai: "Yodan" (Deviations), cited in Enomoto Takashi, "Tayama Katai 'Shōsetsu sahō,'" p. 142.
42. This is how Nakamura Mitsuo, *Fūzoku shōsetsuron*, p. 34, sees it.
43. Of course, works that appeared earlier also contain autobiographical elements. The most famous example is probably Ōgai's short story "Maihime" (The Dancing Girl, 1890), but the reception is decisive; it paid no special attention to the autobiographical content but understood the work on a purely literary level. Cf. "A Japanese First-Person Story" (Chapter 10).
44. Lack of space was not the only reason I decided to omit a description of Katai's development during the Russo-Japanese War, as contained in my essay ("Innovation als Renovation"), already mentioned several times. Katai was editor of news reporting from March to September 1904, and this was supposedly of great significance for the formation of the objective-realistic style of writing which characterizes "Futon" (cf., e.g., Sasabuchi, p. 614). In my opinion, there is no evidence of a direct connection between his war experiences and increased realism beyond the tendencies indicated in my essay. These were more or less limited to the field of theoretical statements in his demand for more veracity and closeness to reality. I tested this claim, also made by Ogata Akiko ("'Futon' zenya," p. 48), in scrutinizing Katai's war diary *Dainigun jūsei nikki* (1905) only to find out that, in spite of the "prosaic" subject, a romantic-aestheticistic point of view prevails.

Since this mode of observation, which always runs the danger of succumbing to reductionism, is in any case favored in Japanese analyses, I can spare myself the problem of correlating biographical facts and a (supposed) psychological development of this kind with literary "content" and stylistic innovation.

5 · The "Theoretical" Reception of "Futon"— Reviews and Essays

Why do we treat the criticisms and contemporary statements on "Futon" as so important as to warrant a whole chapter? The answer is to be found in the related question: What was so sensational and new about this work that it produced such an effect? It is unlikely that today's reader—whether Western or Japanese—will be able to answer this question. We can barely understand the originality of this work, nor would anyone today "be shocked when faced with the description of the erotic desires of a middle-aged man," to quote Ogata Akiko.[1] Therefore, in order to evaluate the importance of the story for literary development we must turn to contemporary witnesses, since they alone enable us to reconstruct the contemporary horizon of expectation and to determine those elements in the work that seemed innovative and in turn founded a tradition. This method is particularly useful in view of the marked discrepancy between the undisputedly great impact "Futon" has had on modern Japanese literature, and its much lesser literary charms, which results in the work being regarded by literary historians as more or less compulsory reading.[2] In the words of Nakamura Mitsuo:

> We can say that Tayama Katai represents Japanese naturalism in the good and in the bad sense. He made a name for himself not only as a courageous pioneer and fighter for naturalism, but his fate is also linked with the decline of naturalism. Regardless of the fact that it formed a strong current within the literary world of the time, regardless also of its enduring influence on the later period which induces us to state that it formed the basic structure of Japanese literature, and in spite of the fact that its representatives made the greatest possible efforts—the great weakness of the naturalist movement in

Japan is probably that it failed to produce any work that survived beyond that time; Katai's works are a typical example of this misfortune.[3]

As has already been noted, this is particularly true of "Futon."

The most informative document on the reception and effects of "Futon" is the special section of the magazine *Waseda bungaku* for October 1907, consisting of eight individual reviews.[4] The amount of criticism concerned with it alone illustrates the attention given to the work. Oguri Fūyō paid tribute to it right at the beginning: "'Futon' is not only a masterpiece by Tayama, but it seems to me that we are dealing with the first representative [naturalist] work since the appearance of the so-called *shizenha* literature last year."[5] His attention was drawn to this "first relatively great product of naturalism" in Japan, since, up to that time, it was possible only to "grasp at shadows," as it were, without being able to point up a single example.[6]

What was felt to be new and revolutionary in "Futon"? Let us return to Fūyō:

> What I as a writer most admire when reading "Futon" is, independent of the question as to whether the subject matter is real or not, the attitude of the author, with which he can articulate and publish his spiritual development and his emotional life unaffectedly and unadorned. This honest approach is highly enviable. But is this not an important precondition for the literary success of any naturalist writer? In any case, this attitude is present throughout, both in form and content. I would like to say that there is a completely organic relationship between the author and the work.... when first reading the work I felt the contact with a real life in a sense of excitement that persisted throughout the whole work.[7]

In this statement, we immediately encounter the central problem of "Futon" reception. The work is not treated on the basis of its literary quality, however that might be defined, but instead the evaluative criteria are the "attitude of the author," honesty, and authenticity. Shimamura Hōgetsu argued at the same level, noting: "This work is the courageous confession of an exposed man of flesh and blood."[8]

Finally, Chikamatsu (Tokuda) Shūkō wrote, "In my opinion we should disregard the question of the artistic accomplishment for once and instead pay tribute to his courage as a significant success from the point of view of literary history."[9] All these quotations document a change in critical attitude, which "Futon" was instrumental in developing. If we, for example, glance at *Hakai,* the novel which had also attracted the attention of numerous critics just one and a half years earlier, it is striking that it was evaluated solely in terms of its "artistic level,"[10] that is, in spite of its socially critical subject matter, it was judged by conventional literature-intrinsic criteria. "Futon," on the other hand—and it is this that justifies its central position in modern literary history—as a new kind of work triggered a new kind of reception, and it is here that we encounter shishōsetsu for the first time.

It would, of course, be too simple to assume that this shift of emphasis in literary reception was due solely to "Futon." Such a change does not take place overnight. The way was paved for it by the numerous articles on *shizenshugi* which steered the theoretical discussion more strongly in the direction of "reality" and which proclaimed veracity as the precondition for great literature.[11] Another important impetus for this change was the tendency to be observed in the literary productions of those years for subject matter and themes to come closer to the intellectuals' sphere of life. The involvement the reviewers felt as a result might have caused them to react in a way which in retrospect appears as a change in attitudes.

The process of such a shift of emphasis can again only be sketched out roughly through a few examples. In this connection, a contemporary commentary on Tayama Katai's previously mentioned "Onna kyōshi" is revealing. The unnamed critic of the magazine *Teikoku bungaku* made the following accusations against Katai: "He allows feeling and will to come into conflict artificially and wants to bind the reader by turning a small conflict into a small (but for the hero enormous)[12] ordeal, yet all because of such a superficial cause or with such superficial description that normally no man over 20 could shed a tear over it."[13] This is informative, not only in providing important traits of reader-response, but above all because of the clarity with which the aim and function of literature are named. If we are to infer the contemporary horizon of expectation from this and other criticism, we could do so in the following way: According to the critics and readers of the time, literature should move the reader, a fairly conventional attitude which was also the basis of Ken'yūsha literature and of traditional poetry in the pre-Meiji period.

The ability of literature to move the reader (and this is where the real development can be seen) was increasingly dependent on the credibility, the authenticity of what was described. This credibility resulted not so much from the work itself but from the relationship between the literary text and the everyday world. The following example shows how, in the ever more important correlation between literary work and non-literary fact, the latter came to be the decisive criterion in judging literature. The quality of a work changed in the eyes of the critics depending on their knowledge of the author's biography.

We refer here to the naturalist author Kunikida Doppo.[14] Masamune Hakuchō reports that Futabatei Shimei spoke of Doppo's works in terms of "Christmas publications," an ironic characterization for what he felt were overly superficial and excessively "healthy" literary products.[15] According to his own statements, Masamune then no longer took Doppo's literature seriously. He noted: "Although Doppo's 'Unmeironsha'[16] contained deep shadows, I considered them to be a product of the author's imagination."[17]

However, after reading an article in a magazine about Doppo's life and discovering similarities between the plot in "Unmeironsha" and the author's experiences, he changed his attitude toward the work: "I presumed that his [Doppo's] genuine suffering was also expressed in 'Unmeironsha,' with the result that I detected a new, genuine life (*jinseimi*) in this work."[18]

Projecting the author's biography onto the work places it in a better light, since it guarantees authenticity and reality, qualities the work alone apparently could not provide.

In their new mode of reception, which focused increased attention on the connections between art and life, Japanese critics, literati, and the general public saw "Futon" as a naturalist innovation, since they identified objectivity, factual truth, and self-revelation, as we demonstrated using the example of Tayama Katai. This specifically Japanese understanding of naturalism resulted in a literary development that first took on clear form in "Futon." The tremendous effect this development has had on Japanese literature in this century is due to the fact that it falls back, largely unconsciously, upon poetic principles and literary forms that had been vital in the cultural tradition for centuries. We shall consider this in more detail in the third and fifth parts of this book. Under the headings "claim to truthfulness," "verifiability in reality," and "experience as the source of knowledge," we can sketch out the area of traditional artistic history which was evoked by the apparently naturalist concept of "Futon."

The broad echo the story produced can, in my opinion, be explained largely by this reversion to Japan's own literary tradition, by the renovation which, when perceived as innovation, seemed to open up new ways of approaching literature for both writers and readers.

Naturally, not all the reviews were hymns of praise for Katai. Even those who judged the work positively included some criticism of detail. The unrealistic depiction of Tokio's wife was criticized,[19] for example, and the final scene was described variously as "exaggerated," "ridiculous,"[20] and "artificial."[21] However, although the critics admitted that "Futon" left something to be desired in terms of its artistic qualities,[22] this was no longer the decisive criterion: "My overall impression after reading it was first of all: this does not have the character of a work of art (*geijutsuhin-rashikunai*)."[23] The "close relationship with reality"[24] seemed to challenge contemporary readers to undertake a comparison of work and life. However much individuals may have rejected the work—Masamune Hakuchō, for example, wrote of a fellow countryman in the United States who was bent double with laughter after reading "Futon" and referred to the scornful reactions of other contemporaries[25]—the fact that no one could close his eyes to this event and that everyone of any importance in the literary world felt obliged to comment on it is proof of the impact of this work.[26]

---

1. Ogata Akiko, "'Futon' shiron," p. 43.
2. In this tenor Ogata, ibid.
3. Nakamura Mitsuo, "Tayama Katai ron," p. 342.
4. Seven of these are reprinted in *KBHT* III (*Meiji-ki* III), 417–432, as "'Futon' gappyō." The authors are Oguri Fūyō, Tokuda (Chikamatsu) Shūkō, Katagami Tengen (Noboru, 1884–1928, critic and Russian scholar), Mizuno Yōshū (1883–1947, poet and novelist), Matsubara Shibun (1884–1945), Nakamura Seiko (1884–1974, novelist, critic and translator), Sōma Gyofū (1883–1950, poet and critic) and Shimamura Hōgetsu. The contribution missing here, by Masamune Hakuchō, is reprinted in *GBRT,* II, 316 ("Shizenshugi to hanshizenshugi").
5. *KBHT,* III, 418.
6. Ibid.
7. Ibid.
8. Ibid., p. 431. Hōgetsu wrote under the pseudonym Seigetsuya.
9. Ibid., pp. 420f.
10. Ogata Akiko, "'Futon' shiron," p. 43.
11. Cf., e.g., the quotation from Tayama Katai's "Rokotsunaru byōsha," Chapter 3.
12. Parentheses in the original.
13. Cited in Yoshida Seiichi, *Shizenshugi no kenkyū,* vol. I, p. 319f.
14. Reservations concerning the categorization under the *shizenshugi* movement were indicated in Chapter 2.
15. "Shizenshugi seisuishi," *Masamune Hakuchō zenshū,* XII, 301f.
16. "The Fatalist," story, published 1902.
17. "Shizenshugi seisuishi," *Masamune Hakuchō zenshū,* XII, 302.
18. Ibid.
19. Nakamura Seiko, *KBHT,* III, 427.
20. Oguri Fūyō, ibid., p. 420.

21. Sōma Gyofū, ibid., p. 430.
22. Masamune Hakuchō, for example, considers "Futon" "wretched" (*misuborashii*) in his essay "Doppo to Katai" published in 1955, cf. *Masamune Hakuchō zenshū*, XII, 426–429, here p. 427.
23. Shimamura Hōgetsu, *KBHT,* III, 431.
24. Mizuno Yōshū, ibid., p. 423.
25. "Tayama Katai shi ni tsuite," originally 1930, in *Masamune Hakuchō zenshū*, XII, 60–63, here p. 62, and "Shizenshugi seisuishi," ibid., p. 293.
26. Ogata Akiko, "'Futon' shiron," also considers briefly the reviews in the magazine *Shinsei*. Yoshida Seiichi reports on the criticism voiced in *Teikoku bungaku* (*Shizenshugi no kenkyū*, vol. II, p. 165).

6 · The "Practical" Reception of "Futon"—Imitations and Parodies

While Shimazaki Tōson's *Hakai* was publicly discussed in statements limited to the work's artistic content,[1] "Futon" primarily aroused the feelings of the literati and therefore had a more direct effect on literature itself. That the publication of this short story could shake the literary world to this extent without any comparable public reaction is a sign of the isolation of the *bundan,* which was at that time completely dominated by *shizenshugi.*[2]

Katai's fame within the *bundan* strengthened his self-confidence and stimulated his productivity. His next work, the serialized novel *Sei* (Life, March–June 1908) was published in *Yomiuri shinbun*. He again applied his newly discovered formula using autobiographical material, and this time described his family's history in the thirties of the Meiji period. Katai subsequently remained faithful to this successful method. His next works, *Tsuma* (The Wife, October 1908–February 1909) and *En* (Bonds, March–October 1910) were also both based on his life.

According to Masamune Hakuchō, the autobiographical novels serialized in newspapers following "Futon" were not particularly interesting for the general readership, who preferred the giants of the Meiji period, Mori Ōgai and Natsume Sōseki, not least because of their incomparably greater social prestige.[3] The keenest readers of the new novels of personal revelation were probably the *bungaku seinen,* the literary adepts who formed the lowest layer, as it were, of the *bundan* and who could imagine nothing more interesting than reading gossip about the everyday lives of their idols.[4]

We return, however, to the starting point of this chapter. What was the unusual effect that "Futon" had that stimulated other members of the literati to creative confrontation with it or even to imitation of it? As we have already seen in Chapter 5, it was above all Katai's seemingly unvarnished self-portrayal and his frankness which were so impressive. Never before in the history of Meiji literature had there been such an unabashedly autobiographical work of fiction[5] and what seemed even more important, never before had anyone dared to present his "ugly nature" (*shūnaru kokoro*), his egoism and jealousy, so openly.[6]

Katai explained his attitude on the occasion of his next work, the novel *Sei,* in an essay entitled "*Sei* ni okeru kokoromi" (My Experiment in *Sei,* September 1908): "I attempted, as I have already emphasized, to employ a kind of presentation in which only objective material is written down as material without the slightest subjectivity and without construction. Not only did I dispense with the author's subjectivity, but also I did not in the least penetrate the inside of the objective subject matter, nor into the characters' psyches, but described phenomena only as I saw, heard, and felt them. So-called flat description (*heimen byōsha*) is the central concern."[7] The question as to how far Katai fulfilled this requirement,[8] which we could characterize as a consistently maintained perspective "from without,"[9] in "Futon" and the subsequent works, is of secondary importance here, since we are concerned with clarifying reasons for the "Futon" succession. One of the reasons lies in the conclusiveness and the possibility of imitating the narrative attitude Katai first expressed theoretically, an attitude he and his contemporaries felt had been put into practice in "Futon": a method of description "without explanation and analysis."[10] Such writing was much easier to copy than, for example, Sōseki's intellectualized style.[11] Thus, "Futon" presented the young Japanese literati with an important new experience which Masamune Hakuchō described as follows: "'Futon' and *Sei* not only introduced young Japanese writers to a new way of looking at life but also gave them an idea of how easy it was to write novels. They made them think: 'If this is how it is then I can [also] easily write narrative prose.'"[12] In addition, Katai readily became an idol because he was seen to be an "average person" (*heibonjin*), with whom the reader could quickly identify, in contrast to Ōgai and Sōseki, both "distanced from the average" and characterized by their foreign experience, high social position, and outstanding intellectualism.[13] The result was that, in the following years, autobiographical, confessional "stories" and "novels" flooded the literary market and "[versions of] 'Futon'"[14] written by all kinds of writers continually appeared in modern Japanese literature.[15]

The effects of the work on the young generation of writers was, understandably, visible only years later, but it persisted for a long period in that the basic pattern of shishōsetsu as developed in "Futon" has since become the most important and most widespread literary genre. "Futon" had a direct effect on established writers, as seen in literary production of the months following its publication.

When Futabatei Shimei published his novel *Heibon* (Mediocrity) in the *Tōkyō Asahi shinbun* from October to December 1907, he referred to his model in a spectacularly open way. However, he stayed within the framework of the subject he had favored since the publication of *Ukigumo*, a subject he took up again in *Sono omokage* (In His Image, also serialized in a newspaper in 1906)—family conflict, an unhappy love affair, and the figure of the intellectual, unfit for life, bearing certain autobiographical traits.[16] *Heibon*—the title gives an indication of the descriptive intention and at the same time strikes a remote ironical note[17]—tells the story of a 38-year-old writer, dissatisfied and at times resigned, who relates the individual stages of his own life in flashbacks in a humorous, ironical tone. Although Futabatei distances himself from what is described both in tone and in a final paragraph in which the writer-hero's memoirs are presented as a kind of narrative frame, the reader immediately recognizes that the work is in a sense a confession on Futabatei's part right from the beginning.

Heibon begins, like "Futon," with a description of the desolate present, lack of success, and material hardship of the hero who is forced to take up a spare-time job to make ends meet. To write down the story of his life is at once a renewed attempt to receive attention through literary articulation and to improve temporarily his financial position. This introduction, which provides a kind of secondary frame for the life story, reminds us of Katai's memoirs on "Futon" cited in Chapter 4. The parallels with "Futon" become obvious in the explanation of the choice of title: "When a mediocre person with mediocre pen writes about a mediocre life, then the title has to be 'Mediocrity.'"[18]

His explanation for his choice of presentation is satirical with obvious reference to his model: "Recently, so it is said, it has become fashionable—naturalism, I think, it is called—to write down all possible kinds of personal experiences just as they are without a trace of technique, slimily, like a drooling ox. What has become fashionable is good. I will therefore proceed in this way."[19] However, although Futabatei repeatedly distances himself from *shizenshugi* style, the work is tinged by the same sentimental, confessional tone as "Futon," with the result that one tends to ignore the element of parody which runs throughout long stretches of it.[20] Thus, in form and also intention *Heibon* is certainly a "Futon" parody, but in effect it is more like a "Futon" imitation.

Oguri Fūyō's *Koizame* (Love Grows Cold, November 1907–January 1908) is another work regarded as a successor to "Futon."[21] Yoshida Seiichi's synopsis reveals some parallels:

> The 34-year-old who appears as the first person [narrator and hero] takes his wife and children to their home town and spends some time in Nago by the sea where he meets a sick wealthy man called Shimura, becomes friendly with his younger sister, Momoeko, and gives her lessons in English. The two gradually become intimate, but the woman, having been in danger of losing her innocence one day, then stays away from him. [The hero] notes that Momoeko loves love, but that just as easily another person could have been her partner. Finally he leaves Nago; one day Momoeko's fiancé asks him about her conduct. The first person [narrator] answers: "I assure you that her behavior is steady and her nature pure" and then feels that he has been compensated for his injured pride.[22]

The plot contains powerful reminders of its antecedent as does the basic atmosphere established in the very first lines: "A friendly member of the literati once said [to me] 'Up to now, whenever love has been the subject of Japanese literature, it always used to be young love. Love in middle age, of men in their prime with family, a livelihood and a [position] in society, their bitter love, has almost never, we can say, been described. Just because we have a wife and children, it does not mean that we have already completely forgotten love,' he once said."[23] After lamenting all the missed opportunities for a love affair, he states, "I who say this am now 34, and my daughter, who is now exactly 3 years old, came into the world in the first year after my marriage. And such a man has fallen in love like a youth—I am ashamed to talk about it—as it were, a love in middle age."[24] This introduction reads like a slightly reformulated passage from the first pages of "Futon." The first-person form and the greater directness that this implies reinforce the confessional character. Thus, in following "Futon," *Koizame* undoubtedly features obvious characteristics of shishōsetsu.[25]

The prologue to the work, which Tayama Katai wrote at the author's request, is also remarkable. The two felt a kind of spiritual bond because of their experience of a "love in middle age,"[26] reason enough for Katai to include a defense of this love, which at times comes close to being a eulogy, with no lack of references to European literature, to Ibsen, Maeterlinck, Turgenev, Heyse and, above all, Hauptmann's *Ein-*

same Menschen.[27] Significantly, there is more talk of personal experience than of the literature which reflects this experience; the transitions are smooth, since one represents the other. The work and life are identified with each other as a matter of course, a further indication that the shishōsetsu manner of writing and reception had already developed.

One of the most important literary productions that was immediately influenced by "Futon" is probably Shimazaki Tōson's novel *Haru* (Spring, April–August 1908). The construction evinces parallels to Turgenev stories,[28] but its position as a successor to Katai is even more obvious and is to be seen, for example, in the autobiographical subject matter and the shishōsetsu-like presentation whereby Tōson places one character, Kishimoto, who embodies himself, at the centre.[29] Odagiri Hideo specifies the shishōsetsu quality of Tōson's works in remarking already in respect to the novel *Hakai* that experiences and occurrences flow directly into the work with the effect that the author's ego does not appear to be sufficiently "objectivized."[30]

While the fictional action in *Hakai* still functions as an important structural element in the work, the relapse into a style of writing without plot is regretted in *Haru*.[31] Consequently, *Haru* is not a further development of *Hakai*, according to Sasabuchi, since this was prevented by the intervention of "Futon."[32] Nakamura Mitsuo is even more pronounced: "A battle was fought between *Hakai* and 'Futon' and this ended, at least [if one measures it] by the influence on the literature of the time, with complete victory for 'Futon.'"[33] For Nakamura the novel *Haru* is the confirmation of this victory, a sign of the "capitulation of Tōson in the face of Katai."[34] However exaggerated this wording may seem it reaches the central truth, although the personalization of this inherent literary "conflict" of course risks misinterpretation. Therefore, Katsumoto Seiichirō is justified in attempting to make distinctions with the declared objective of allocating "Futon" a subordinate position in relation to other influences that led to *Haru*.[35] However, even in view of the evidence that the idea for *Haru* existed before "Futon" and that Tōson linked other ideas with it—for example, he intended the title *Haru* to be associated with the spring of ideals, his years in the *Bungakukai* circle described in the work, the spring of art and life[36]—the fact remains that, both in the eyes of his contemporaries and of retrospective literary studies, in this work Tōson came close to the confessional narrative tone and method that had made "Futon" famous.

We should repeat here that it is not our intention, in describing the effect of "Futon" on contemporary literature, to trace the clearly distinguishable tendency to self-revelation solely to "Futon" and so to raise Katai to the status of the exclusive creator of the new genre. Thus, the delineation of some of the strains of development that led to this work was intended as an attempt to assess its position in the context of the historical situation and the general cultural and literary changes. Not just Katai but also all his contemporaries who shared in this socio-cultural context took part in this process of change. We can therefore confidently ignore the question as to how far an individual work owes its shishōsetsu character to the direct influence of "Futon" or whether it was "only" part of the basic literary, intellectual currents of those years manifested in Katai's story.

After "Futon" there were not only several imitations—various types of reference to the work were presented here using the three examples quoted most frequently—but we also observed a general tendency following the publication of this work, which Yoshida Seiichi characterized: "It is incontestable that [after the publication of 'Futon'] the writer sees a profound sense in the placement of the ego as something absolute and the expression of truth (*jijitsu*), which is most painful for the ego without falsification and adornment."[37] There are statements of this kind in numerous shishōsetsu definitions. Until now we have used the term, beginning with "Futon," intuitively and have thus followed the historical understanding. Nevertheless in the examination undertaken here of variously focused and different-sized segments of the cultural and literary scene in the first decade of the century, we have revealed a change which, as we have said repeatedly, is most obvious in "Futon." The literary histories call this change the origin of shishōsetsu. It is therefore our next objective to produce a definition of shishōsetsu using more sophisticated analytical instruments and distinguishing the historical variables and supertemporal invariants. Essential for realizing such a goal is the evaluation of the results of previous research, to which we shall now turn.

---

1. Cf. also Yoshida Seiichi, *Shizenshugi no kenkyū,* vol. II, p. 151.
2. Cf. Masamune Hakuchō: "Shizenshugi seisuishi," *Masamune Hakuchō zenshū,* XII, 294. Hakuchō also reports on the public's criticism of *shizenshugi.*
3. Ibid., pp. 308f.
4. Ibid., p. 295.
5. With the exception of Kōyō's *Aobudō,* which I shall consider in more detail in "Shinpenmono" (Chapter 10).

6. Yoshida Seiichi, *Shizenshugi no kenkyū*, vol. II, p. 160.
7. Cited in Sasabuchi Tomoichi, *Meiji Taishō bungaku no bunseki,* p. 619.
8. Sasabuchi explains that he developed this technique following Goncourt, cf. ibid. and p. 621.
9. Whereby, however, the question remains open as to how Katai classifies the presentation of his main character. In my opinion he is concerned in this case with postulating the detachment of a cool observer, although he has access to the character's inner life. In "Shōsetsu sahō" (How to Write Narrative Prose, May 1909), he explains: "I had no particular intention with my 'Futon'; it is neither a confession nor did I intentionally select such ugly facts which I discovered in my life before the eyes of the reader." Cited in Yoshida Seiichi, *Shizenshugi no kenkyū*, vol. II, p. 163.
10. Tayama Katai: "'Sei' ni okeru kokoromi," cited in Sasabuchi, p. 619.
11. Cf. Masamune Hakuchō: "Tayama Katai shi ni tsuite," *Masamune Hakuchō zenshū*, XII, 62.
12. Ibid.
13. Masamune: "Shizenshugi seisuishi," *Masamune Hakuchō zenshū*, XII, 296.
14. Literally: "Futons."
15. Masamune: "Tayama Katai shi ni tsuite," *Masamune Hakuchō zenshū*, XII, 62.
16. On *Sono omokage,* cf. Lewin, *Futabatei Shimei,* pp. 47ff.
17. On the influence of Russian models in the selection of titles, cf. ibid., pp. 56f.
18. *Heibon, Futabatei Shimei zenshū,* VII, 99–204, here p. 102.
19. Ibid., pp. 102f.
20. Cf. also Sōma Tsuneo, *Nihon shizenshugiron,* pp. 233ff. on the satirical elements in *Heibon.*
21. Cf., e.g., Okazaki, p. 221.
22. Yoshida Seiichi, *Shizenshugi no kenkyū,* vol. II, p. 209.
23. *Koizame,* in *MBZ,* LXV, 245–282, here p. 248.
24. Ibid.
25. Cf. Yoshida Seiichi, *Shizenshugi no kenkyū,* vol. II, p. 209.
26. *Chūnen no koi.* The expression became a household word at that time. It can, however, be found as early as in Tōson's *Suisai gaka* and it was also used in relation with Hauptmann's *Einsame Menschen,* cf. Masamune Hakuchō: "Shizenshugi seisuishi," *Masamune Hakuchō zenshū,* XII, p. 322.
27. *Koizame,* in *MBZ,* LXV, p. 246f.
28. Cf. Sasabuchi, p. 322.
29. Hisamatsu, *Zōho shinpan Nihon bungakushi,* vol. VI, p. 118.
30. Odagiri Hideo, *Shishōsetsu, shinkyō shōsetsu,* p. 11.
31. Sasabuchi, p. 351; cf. also Wada, *Shimazaki Tōson,* p. 69.
32. Sasabuchi, p. 403.
33. Nakamura Mitsuo, *Fūzoku shōsetsuron,* p. 29.
34. "Tōson no Katai ni taisuru kōfukushō," cited in Katsumoto Seiichirō, "'Haru' o toku kagi," p. 242; also Wada, *Shimazaki Tōson,* p. 70. This passage is apparently missing in my edition. It is possible that Nakamura had deleted it in view of the objections of other literary historians (see above).
35. Cf. Katsumoto; also Wada, *Shimazaki Tōson,* pp. 71ff.
36. Sasabuchi, p. 418.
37. Yoshida Seiichi, *Shizenshugi no kenkyū,* vol. II, p. 11.

Part Two
Shishōsetsu Research

7 · General Observations on the State of Research

Any study with claims to scholarly seriousness includes a consideration of previous research. Why is it then not sufficient in this case to refer to the relevant studies in the course of this book, as has already been done in Part One? Because it is impossible to use the term *shishōsetsu research* in anything like the matter-of-fact way that we can refer, for example, to Katai or even *shizenshugi* research. It is daring even to use the expression *shishōsetsu research,* since doing so presumes that shishōsetsu is recognized as a firmly defined subject within modern Japanese literary studies. At present, this is true only in theory, less so in practice.

Everyone interested in examining shishōsetsu within the context of literary studies is initially confronted with the problem of entering an unusually extensive area with only a few guidelines to point the way. The secondary literature is widely dispersed and, in some cases, not easily available even though relatively recent, and there is no comprehensive bibliography. A thorough research report is similarly lacking. The most extensive bibliography on shishōsetsu[1] contains only 21 titles,[2] and the two research reports at present available devote no more than 3 pages to shishōsetsu[3] and contain even fewer titles.

In view of the meager resources for any examination of shishōsetsu it seems advisable to compile a research report which may hopefully facilitate and inspire further study. We will complement it with what is by far the most comprehensive bibliography available on the subject,[4] which should avoid the need for protracted searches for titles and the considerable work involved in supplementing the often incomplete information. For the sake of completeness, the appendix to the bibliography contains a list of studies unavailable for this study. Needless to say, this brief research report also fulfills an important function by examining the conclusions of previous research. This will show the extent to which this book is indebted to previous research and where it breaks new ground.

That alone should be sufficient motivation for this part of the book. But there is a third consideration that makes a survey of the research valuable. It is my theory that shishōsetsu research presents an exemplary reflection of central problems of Japanese literary studies. Examining it therefore heightens our awareness of questions relevant to the study of Japanese literature in general. Such matters can be of only secondary importance within this framework, but it could be a step in the right direction if our examination of the secondary literature showed that many of the phenomena referred to here are significant outside this field in characterizing Japanese *bungeigaku* or *bungaku kenkyū* as an academic discipline. It will become clear what is meant by this in the following discussion.

We turn, however, to the subject itself, the body of scholarly texts devoted to shishōsetsu. One might conclude that there has been only scant consideration of the subject in view of the meager references mentioned above; yet this would be a complete mistake, since the discussion concerning shishōsetsu has not ceased from the time when the term originated until the present. The number of book-length studies on the subject, however, is very small. If we disregard three works that appeared recently[5]—which can certainly be seen as indicating recent increased interest in the subject—only the well-known standard work by Yamamoto Kenkichi *Study of Shishōsetsu Writers* (*Watakushishōsetsu sakkaron*, 1966) is left. However, all these works are collections of essays on literary individuals; there is a complete lack of any systematic summary or historical outline.[6]

This is particularly surprising in view of the rare agreement shared by opponents and supporters, open enemies of and fanatic adherents to shishōsetsu, who all declare that the genre is of outstanding importance in modern Japanese literature. According to them, shishōsetsu is not merely one of many literary schools, but a broad basic current running throughout modern literature, or, still more, it is seen as a "way of thinking"[7] characterizing the literature of this century as "one could almost say a fatal 'Japanese reality.'"[8] This "reality" is recognized even by such committed critics of shishōsetsu as Nakamura Mitsuo. Since its birth at the beginning of the century, shishōsetsu has maintained this position, so that Howard Hibbett could state in 1977: "The narrowly personal 'I-novel' (shi-shōsetsu) . . . is still the most tenacious form of contemporary Japanese fiction."[9]

The prevalence of the genre in the literature of this century even motivated Senuma Shigeki to state in his encyclopaedia article under the heading shishōsetsu: "Among Japanese authors of the modern period there is none who did not . . . write shishōsetsu."[10]

In view of such statements, evidence of its overriding importance, it is surprising that comparatively little interest has been shown in shishōsetsu as a genre. In my view, the reason for this paradox lies in the specific epistemological interest and way of working of Japanese literary studies, which concentrate primarily on individual personalities and less on paths of development. This situation is criticized by, for example, Marleigh Ryan: "Literary historians have chosen to leap from one outstanding talent to another without adequate consideration of the whole field of literary development."[11]

Thus, systematic studies on more comprehensive topics of motifs, subject matter, or genres are relatively rare, since the favored emphasis of philology in Japan is, and always has been, individual works or individual writers.

A further problem must be mentioned here. Any systematic presentation of shishōsetsu would have to consider the term itself. Until now, however, there has been neither an operational definition, nor has any need been felt to develop one, since the "hermeneutical innocence"[12] of Japanese literary studies protects it from any doubts. The attempt to define and describe the genre thus seems unnecessary and superfluous, since a vague understanding of the subject is assumed.

The amount and kind of material available on the subject reflects this problem. In accordance with the central position of shishōsetsu, about which all are in emphatic agreement, there is a large number of scattered individual statements and innumerable references to the shishōsetsu nature of all kinds of different works, but an absence of more wide-ranging studies. As already noted, the works on the subject consist of individual biographical and analytical descriptions. However, all these works lack the secure foundation of an even remotely unified and binding concept of shishōsetsu, and it is only this which, according to Western standards of academic work, could provide the framework for comparisons of results and their further development. It is the intention of this study to contribute to such a reasoned discourse.

The specific task undertaken here is to produce a survey of the approach, the methods, and the conclusions of the texts with shishōsetsu as their subject. I refer to the following as secondary literature:

1. All those publications that clearly identify themselves as contributions to the shishōsetsu discussion. (This definition includes so-called non-academic essays, for example critical-theoretical considerations by writers. It would be impossible to exclude these contributions since many writers are critics at the same time.)[13] Excluded are all contributions to the discussion up to 1935 since, in my opinion, they are still concerned directly with the definition of shishōsetsu in a general sense; 1935 was the year when the first larger studies of shishōsetsu were published showing agreement on the term and its status as an object of scholarly consideration. (Part Three includes a discussion up to 1935.)
2. All those texts that include in their title the term shishōsetsu, one of its alternative names or subsumptions, for example *shinkyō shōsetsu* (state-of-mind fiction), or semantically related terms such as *kokuhaku shōsetsū* (confessional novel) or *jiden shōsetsu* (autobiographical novel).
3. Those sections of literary histories or systematic studies which can be said to be individual contributions either because of their length and/or because of their descriptive or analytical standard. (This prerequisite prevents the automatic inclusion in the bibliography of those literary histories that, for example, merely mention shishōsetsu, or simply list works under the label shishōsetsu or summarize their contents.)
4. Studies that deal with one or more writers or one or more works predominantly from the angle of shishōsetsu. (This excludes from the bibliography, for example, biographical studies on so-called shishōsetsu writers or analyses and essays on works which are held to be shishōsetsu which do not, however, actually consider the subject of shishōsetsu itself.)
5. Works mentioned in the publications listed above (points 1 through 4) as secondary literature on shishōsetsu.

It is obvious from the list that, however much effort is put into achieving completeness, it is an impossible aim, particularly since the criteria for selection cannot be formulated so precisely as to separate relevant texts from non-relevant texts in each and every case. A degree of arbitrariness, apparent in points 1, 3 and 4, cannot be ruled out, at least not at this stage of research. It seems reasonable always to decide in favor of inclusion whenever there is some doubt, since this prevents, as far as possible, any kind of pre-censorship.

Strict limits have been set on the length of the research report within the context of this book. Thus, there is insufficient space for either a balanced appraisal of individual research achievements, or for an extended consideration of the details of shishōsetsu research, whether of "content" or method. Some of these more specific questions are taken up in other parts of the book, and the subject index and list of persons provide easy reference to further discussion.

This research report considers the secondary literature under three headings which were decided on as the result of a rough content analysis of the most common areas of research (Chapter 9). The first four sections (Chapter 8) deal with one single study each, all of them of particular importance judged from the frequency of citation. Most of them are essays, but they are rightly counted among the most stimulating and perceptive studies on shishōsetsu. The fact that they are also the most influential fully justifies the special attention that we shall afford them. The second half of the report provides evidence of the continuing influence of these "classics" of shishōsetsu research.

1. I am talking of specialist research literature on shishōsetsu here, not, for example, of source references to the theoretical discussion from the period when the term originated which can more easily be collocated.
2. Odagiri, *Shishōsetsu*, pp. 37f. Wada, "Shishōsetsu no seiritsu to tenkai," pp. 242f., names 20 titles. Two of these are collections of source materials (see note 1).
3. Katsuyama Isao, "Shishōsetsu, shinkyō shōsetsu," Enomoto Takashi, "Shishōsetsu, shinkyō shōsetsu." Miyoshi Yukio ("Shishōsetsu ni wa donna tēma ga aru ka"—"What Subjects Are There in Shishōsetsu?") is intended as an aid when choosing subjects for examination papers.
4. The bibliography on shishōsetsu is integrated in the general bibliography to facilitate finding individual titles. The studies on shishōsetsu are indicated separately, cf. the preliminary remarks in the bibliography.
5. Matsubara Shin'ichi, *"Gusha" no bungaku*, Takahashi, and Aeba Takao, *Hihyō to hyōgen*.
6. The study by Aeba (*Hihyō to hyōgen*), which was published after this book had been completed, seems to be the most well rounded, since he places his previously published essays under the general heading of the first-person concept, analyzes the individual character and historical change of this concept and summarizes the results in a final essay (pp. 413–455).
7. *Kangaekata*, Senuma Shigeki, "Shishōsetsuron no keifu," p. 25.
8. Inagaki Tatsurō, cited in Kokubo, "Shishōsetsu no seiritsu I," p. 49.
9. Howard Hibbett, ed., *Contemporary Japanese Literature*, p. xiii.

10. *GNBD*, p. 1258.
11. Ryan, *The Development of Realism in the Fiction of Tsubouchi Shōyō*, p. 3.
12. I coined this expression in I.H.-K., "Probleme der modernen japanischen Literaturgeschichtsschreibung."
13. It is difficult to find categories for the academic character of a Japanese contribution since Japanese philology's conceptions and criteria are not identical with ours, cf. my thoughts in the Mishima research report where I distinguish between literary critics and academics using a list of critics, I.H.-K., *Mishima Yukios Roman*, pp. 25ff.

8 · The "Classics" of Shishōsetsu Research

KOBAYASHI HIDEO: "WATAKUSHISHŌSETSURON"

The essay "On Shishōsetsu" ("Watakushishōsetsuron"), which appeared in the *Keizai ōrai* from May to August 1935, is one of the best-known publications by the famous critic Kobayashi Hideo (1902–1983). He has had incalculable influence on generations of intellectuals, and his influence is undiminished today.

Kobayashi's essay appeared at a time when the occasionally passionate discussion concerning shishōsetsu, which had fascinated large parts of the literary world from the 1920s,[1] was beginning to abate. The most important questions all seemed to have been clarified, the various points of view stated, and the term shishōsetsu had been accepted as the name of the newly developed genre. Now the time had at last come to take stock and present a critical appraisal, and Kobayashi was in a position to step back and achieve some objective distance from the subject.

The "Watakushishōsetsuron" begins with the opening words from Rousseau's *Confessions*. Kobayashi explains: "What I want to say here is that the reason that something like shishōsetsu developed in modern literature is to be found just in these crazy-sounding words from Rousseau and that without this outcry at the beginning of *Confessions* the most outstanding shishōsetsu [!] *Werther, Oberman,* and *Adolphe* would not have been written."[2] This introduction contains material for a wealth of observations, but, in order to be brief, we are restricted to the following remarks.

Apart from the factual error contained in the statement—Goethe's

Werther was published in 1774, eight years before the first and fifteen years before the second part of *Confessions*[3]—it is apparent that Kobayashi sees the subject of shishōsetsu from a European angle. The problem this involves is obvious from the translation of the quotation. According to the language provisions explained in the introduction to this book, I translated "Watakushishōsetsuron" as the essay "On Shishōsetsu," since Kobayashi's subject is undoubtedly the literary genre called shishōsetsu. This is proved by the judgment contained in a statement such as that made by Ogasawara Masaru, that "Watakushishōsetsuron" is of the greatest importance in the discussion of shishōsetsu (*shishōsetsuron-shi*).[4] However, when Kobayashi uses the term to refer to European works, he forces us to decide whether we should consider a shishōsetsu to be an autobiography or a first-person novel. Both are not completely correct when referring to the novels mentioned, since only *Confessions* is a genuine autobiography, and, in the cases of *Oberman* and Goethe's *Werther* it would be more appropriate to speak of epistolary novels.[5]

If, however, we consider Kobayashi's next section, he seems to be describing the confessional novel in applying the term *shishōsetsu* to European novels, although he could have used the Japanese term *kokuhaku shōsetsu*. According to Kobayashi, shishōsetsu originated in Europe at the beginning of the Romantic period as "a direct confession written in novel form" (p. 113). In Japan, on the other hand, "there was first talk of shishōsetsu at the peak of the naturalist movement (*shizenshugi shōsetsu no undō*)" (p. 113).

The full scope of the problem becomes obvious here: Kobayashi adopts a European framework and, by applying Western terminology to the Japanese situation,[6] he succeeds in comparing what cannot be compared. Thus the two main problems when reading "Watakushishōsetsuron" are, first, the uncertainty of knowing what Kobayashi is writing about when he refers to shishōsetsu in Europe—at times his subject seems to be the psychological novel—and, second, the impossibility of following the parallels he draws between Japan and Europe.

There would be little sense in merely exposing the contradictions in Kobayashi's reasoning, since this achieves nothing. It would, on the contrary, mean inadequate reception of the text, which, like all of Kobayashi's remarks, obeys the rules of a non-Aristotelian logic.[7] Terada Tōru also points out that Kobayashi has revised the essay several times since it was first published, which has resulted in "confusion in the terminology" (*yōgo no konran*).⁸ We shall therefore restrict ourselves here to tracing the main themes of his argument.

Kobayashi developed his central argument using the term "socialized I" (*shakaika shita watakushi*), which distinguished European writers of shishōsetsu, such as Barrès, Gide, and Proust, from the Japanese. The Western writer is molded by the consciousness of a chasm between himself, nature, and society (p. 115); he can draw from a rich tradition of philosophy which favors the development of shishōsetsu. Japanese writers encountered this tradition much later. They became intoxicated by it without really understanding it (p. 117). There was no intellectual consideration of European models, and the Japanese naturalists merely adopted technical tricks (p. 118). Shishōsetsu was introduced to Japan with "Futon" (p. 118), but this work shows just as little awareness of the problem as Tōson's *Hakai* or Tokuda Shūsei's *Arakure* (Rowdy Woman, 1915). It merely demonstrates a new level of technical perfection (pp. 118f.).

In Kobayashi's view, Shiga Naoya is the author who embodies shishōsetsu theory to greatest perfection, since in him life and work achieved an indivisible unity, where the "path of shishōsetsu" was the unity of "theory of life" (*nichijō seikatsu no riron*) and "theory of creation" (*sōsakujō no riron*) (p. 120).⁹

Although there was some resistance to shishōsetsu in the literary world, Kobayashi does not detect complete rejection of this form of the novel anywhere (p. 121), since even those who were adversely disposed towards it were convinced that the concrete experiences of everyday life were the best basis for literary work (pp. 121f.). It was only with the introduction of Marxist literature that resistance grew towards the everyday life that was the subject of shishōsetsu, since it could then be opposed from the position of an ideology which conferred meaning and direction (p. 125).

Let us briefly interrupt this synopsis of Kobayashi's thoughts. They are imprinted with a curious ambivalence. On the one hand, he seems to play off the Japanese version of shishōsetsu against the European from the very beginning; on the other, he admires the perfection with which Shiga Naoya meets the shishōsetsu ideal. His attitude to Marxist literature, which he otherwise rejects decisively, is even more puzzling. In this context he seems to consider it more constructive to represent an ideology than to persist with concrete everyday life but without any kind of stable orientation, particularly since he criticized the representatives of *shizenshugi* for being capable of adopting only Western techniques but not Western philosophy. Could it be that those writers who were inspired by Marxism were perhaps even examples of the "socialized I," the positive concept for shishōsetsu he saw as a practical reality in Europe? The question remains open. There is clarity only in his attitude to *shizenshugi* narrative literature, which is, in his words, "more feudalistic than bourgeois literature" (p. 127).

Kobayashi then goes into more detail about the difference between European and Japanese shishōsetsu writers. He finds no parallel in Japan for the experimental approach of one such as Gide (p. 135), since the Japanese were, in his view, not capable of such abstraction. They could only describe and confess, but not pass from the specific to the general (pp. 140f.). Kobayashi considered the literature of *shinkankakuha* (neo-perceptionists) to be the last mutation of shishōsetsu, the attempt to adopt everything foreign and new, whether it be Proust or Joyce, as the salvation for the writer's own insecure existence (p. 141).

The Marxist, so-called proletarian literature carried its own conviction, but it had no technique. As such it would mean the end for shishōsetsu as a genre which relied on technique. "The tradition of shishōsetsu [thus] finally died" (p. 142) although proletarian literature did not replace it with any genuine individualistic literature. Furthermore no solution for the problem of the first person had been found, but, according to Kobayashi, it would merely reappear in a new form. "At least as long as Flaubert's famous formula: 'I am Madame Bovary' remains valid" (p. 142).

This final sentence highlights yet again the character and nature of "Watakushishōsetsuron." Kobayashi takes shishōsetsu, without further definition, as a global manifestation, and compares its European and Japanese variants. His brilliant and cryptic style, rich in paradox, is a barrier to anyone who expects logical, deductive argument. Kobayashi does not argue, he states; he does not analyze, but presents thoughts that take their inner coherence from the subject itself. He also refuses to be bound by evaluative criteria. He seems to have introduced a social aspect into the discussion with his concept of the "socialized ego," but even this term evades any kind of definition. Wakizaka Mitsuru comments as follows: "It is easy [to explain] what the 'socialized I' means. If we trace the matter thoroughly we find an 'I' on which remains the scent of historicity and sociality. To put it another way, an 'I' which has a deep relationship to society and nature."[10] It is probably most rewarding to understand the second half of the essay as an explanation of the "socialized I," which can then be interpreted as the consciousness of the ties between the characters and the historical and social surroundings and the possibility and necessity of generalization and abstraction from the private sphere.

Kobayashi demands sympathetic duplication of his argument, but even then much of his reasoning remains obscure. The "Watakushishōsetsuron" almost enjoys the status of a work of art,[11] since it has stimulated innumerable interpretations which have in turn been the object of analysis.[12] Even now, not all its mysteries have been solved; it continues to be "a study that contains numerous problems."[13] However, its incomparable importance is based on the fact that it became a point of orientation for all subsequent considerations of shishōsetsu and acted as a kind of catalyst. "One could also say that Kobayashi's 'Watakushishōsetsuron' was the precondition for all [later] studies on shishōsetsu."[14]

ITŌ SEI: *SHŌSETSU NO HŌHŌ*

In 1948, the novelist and critic Itō Sei (1905–1969) presented *Shōsetsu no hōhō* (Methods of the Novel), a collection of essays containing a highly original literary theory in which he attempted to analyze the relationships between art and life. He also dealt with shishōsetsu within the framework of this concept, and we shall limit our discussion to this part of his work.

Itō is much more concrete and ready with explanation in his study than Kobayashi. He develops his arguments parallel to literary lines of development since the end of the nineteenth century.

In contrast to Kobayashi, Itō considers that the influence of European literature on Japanese naturalists was not so much on their literary technique but on their desire to throw off the ties of feudalistic tradition, a desire stimulated by Western philosophy.[15] This in turn led to the formation of the *bundan,* the literary world. The group of literati, who lived largely isolated from society, were disinterested in matters of public importance, and drew their self-esteem from their consciousness of being progressive and their awareness of artistic genius (pp. 71f.). The medium of these literati was shishōsetsu, a genre that was "semi-autobiographical, containing characteristics similar to miscellanies (*zuihitsu*)" (p. 65). This literature, which limited itself solely to private and everyday matters, is not only the result of the profound alienation from society of the writers; exaggerations of its characteristics result from the interrelationship between the public and the writer. When critics pay attention only to the degree of truth of the confession and the ideological attitude (*shisō*) of the writer, "then finally the writer attempts to be precise and purist (*keppeki*) only in these two points" (p. 15). Shishōsetsu writers felt they faced stringent criticism and tried in their turn to justify themselves through their work, at which point the criticism grew still stronger (p. 16). Without any consideration whatsoever of the social or cultural contexts, the writers in the *bundan* focused only on the moral aspects of the confessions presented in shishōsetsu. This specific restriction of interest is explained by Itō on the basis of the geographical and climatic conditions of Japanese culture and the resulting social structure which prevented the development of individuality (pp. 17f.), an argument he adopts from Watsuji Tetsurō.

Itō also refers repeatedly to the European novel, although not with comparisons of Japanese and European versions of shishōsetsu (he applies the term only to Japanese literature), but in attempting to explain fundamental questions and problems by making generalizations from several individual examples. With reference to shishōsetsu, he is more interested than Kobayashi in tracing the social function of literature, although the idea of being enmeshed in the historical and social context which Kobayashi developed in his concept of the "socialized I" already pointed in this direction. However, while Kobayashi intended above all to characterize the literature itself in this way, Itō takes the writer as part of a total social context as his object of interest.

Itō's critical view of shishōsetsu writers is condensated in the formula of "runaway slaves" (*tōbō dorei*, p. 233) with their escapist mentality (*tōbō ishiki*) stylized as "renunciation" (*hōki*) on the pattern of Buddhist anchorites, who are to be identified by their sectarian seclusion. This thesis is only touched upon in *Shōsetsu no hōhō*; it was first developed in Itō's essay "Tōbō dorei to kamen shinshi" (The Runaway Slave and the Masked Gentleman), published in 1948.[16]

Itō also dispensed with detailed analysis and the presentation of evidence for his thesis, but still provided the most comprehensive model of interpretation for the shishōsetsu phenomenon, a model that has been adopted by the majority of younger critics. The high esteem in which such critical authorities as Kobayashi and Itō are held has, however, prevented any discussion of these theories beyond sympathetic paraphrase. The result is that they have acquired a function approaching the status of dogmatic doctrine without ever having been "proven" other than by purely intuitive deduction.

The chorus of critical voices raised against shishōsetsu at the beginning of the 1950s indicates the powerful influence of these theses. It seems to suggest something of a fashion, which in my opinion is paralleled by the upswing in the ideology-critical school of figures such as Maruyama Masao; it would be difficult to deny the possibility of cross connections here when, in the words of Sasaki Kiichi, young critics proceeded according to the motto: "The main thing is to squash shishōsetsu!"[17]

It has been equally impossible to produce evidence against these theses. For example, Etō Jun (b. 1933), himself an admirer of Kobayashi Hideo, was stimulated by Itō's theories to produce his own arguments against them. In his view, the explanation that made the specific conditions of Japanese society responsible for writers considering their own person the only worthy subject for their work was no longer adequate. What Etō offers as an explanation, though, falls back behind the level of insight reached by Itō, when he refers to vague "internal psychological and cultural factors, which are innate in the tradition of Japanese literature."[18] Assuming that this tortuous argument is also the explanation of his thesis, the following can be sifted out to paraphrase the "inner psychological and cultural factors."

In what is for many intellectuals—I would say, for the vast majority and certainly for Etō himself—the characteristic pattern of *Nihon kaiki,* the "return to Japan," that is the conscious idealization of traditional Japanese values following a phase of orientation towards the West, Etō sees the expression of a "vehement longing for something indispensable, that has been somehow absent, but which must be restored at any costs. They do not know exactly what this 'something' is."[19] According to Etō, this is a general feeling of crisis which is also familiar to intellectuals in other countries but which has been particularly prevalent in Japan since the beginning of the Meiji period.[20] However, presenting such a model to oppose Itō's theses means in fact relinquishing all the threads of argument, since any study which is to be taken seriously should at least systematically approach the specific Japanese longing as one of the "psychological and cultural factors."

Etō is not an insignificant figure in Japanese literary criticism. Yet this digression also provides something of a typical example of an interaction pattern within the liberal arts discourse. Characteristic here is the way available theories are touched upon and then joined to the writer's own intuitively developed thought, in order to enrich them. Resolute argumentative refutation or confirmation of theories, developed empirically or deductively, would be atypical. The style is consciously literary (this is true not only for Etō Jun's Japanese writings) in its lack of clarity and precise terminology. I again see evidence here of the powerful influence of Kobayashi Hideo, renowned for his style, although his effectiveness would be more limited if his and other philological works were not based on a common specifically Japanese understanding of scholarship and on equally specific Japanese expectations towards the functioning of language itself.[21]

Let us return to Itō Sei. The ideas expressed in his work *Shōsetsu no hōhō* and in other books, for example *Shōsetsu no ninshiki* (Novel Awareness, 1955),[22] which will not be discussed here, facilitate access to the reasoning of Nakamura Mitsuo who has adopted a more literary historical approach in his discussion of the genre.

NAKAMURA MITSUO: *FŪZOKU SHŌSETSURON*

The critic, dramatist, and novelist Nakamura Mitsuo (1911–1988) began making a name for himself in about 1935 with translations and with essays on French literature. He also developed an interest in the modern history of his own national literature at an early stage, with an eye trained through the study of European literature. His first longer contribution on shishōsetsu appeared as early as 1935, a discussion of Kobayashi's "Watakushishōsetsuron"[23] with modifications of some of his theses. This essay, entitled "On Shishōsetsu" ("Shishōsetsu ni tsuite") remains entirely within the framework set by Kobayashi of contrasting literary forms in Europe and Japan. For example, a comparison of "Futon" and *Adolphe* leads to the following conclusion:

> In "Futon" the area of contact between a character, who for reasons of principle is not analyzed, and society is described, whereas in *Adolphe* the feelings of the individual who is analyzed form a structural unit (*tan'i*) in the novel.
>
> Of course, in this case the situation described in *Adolphe* is one degree more individual than that in "Futon." And since it is individual, it has an element of sociality (*shakaisei*) that cannot be detected in "Futon."[24]

However, Nakamura clearly disassociated himself from Kobayashi in his evaluation of the role of proletarian literature. While Kobayashi had claimed Marxist attitudes as spelling the end of shishōsetsu, Nakamura considered the continued existence of the genre to be ironically ensured by the literary school which came out in opposition to it. Proletarian literature might have attacked the form of shishōsetsu, but, since it was not capable of developing a new tradition from imported ideology alone, it gave the conventional form a new lease on life.[25] Thus, Nakamura concluded, "The form of shishōsetsu may have disappeared from the mainstream of literature, but its spirit lives tenaciously on, transformed into a skeleton, in contemporary literature."[26] *Fūzoku shōsetsuron* (On the Novel of Manners),[27] published in 1950, presented a framework in which the thoughts already expressed on shishōsetsu in "Shishōsetsu ni tsuite" and elsewhere[28] could be organized. Nakamura explains his motives for writing *Fūzoku shōsetsuron* in the epilogue. He wanted to describe the "special character of the modern Japanese novel" in a larger study in order to express his "vague dissatisfaction" with this literature and open up to discussion his "continuing doubts concerning the strange 'modern' Japanese novel."[29] In contrast to Kobayashi and Itō, Nakamura restricted himself to considering the subject from the angle of literary history. However, his questioning the development of the Japanese novel was similar to that his predecessor, Kobayashi, since he also measured Japanese reality against a standard taken from Europe.

Nakamura sees, not without regret (p. 8), a fateful change of direction that casts shadows on all subsequent developments in the "clear victory [of the 'short story'] 'Futon'" (p. 29), which had won the literary world over to shishōsetsu, in the "struggle" against Tōson's *Hakai,* the work which contained possibilities of development in the direction of a social novel (p. 35). The emergence of "modern realism" (*kindai riarizumu no hassei*) culminates for him in the "birth of Japanese shishōsetsu" (p. 52), which becomes the "highest ideal for a novel" and which as a genre produced the largest number of masterworks in the following period (p. 53). Realism, as it was developed by the naturalists and the writers of shishōsetsu, consisted of describing facts from the writer's own life with the greatest possible degree of accuracy. Therefore, according to Nakamura, the "degree of truth" (*shinjitsusei*) "was determined as it were before writing," while in the case, for example, of Flaubert's *Madame Bovary,* it was revealed only in retrospect (p. 84).

The second part of his discussion is devoted to the "changes" (*henshitsu*) and the "decay" (*hōkai*) of "modern realism" in the "novel of manners" (*fūzoku shōsetsu*), which adopted the technique of presentation developed in shishōsetsu and therefore represents a kind of "extension" (*enchō*) of it.[30]

Some explanation of the term *fūzoku shōsetsu* is required, since, although it is very probably derived from *roman de moeurs,*[31] it sounds somewhat derogatory in the Japanese context. In the *Small Encyclopae-*

dia of Japanese Literature (*NBS*), Nakamura himself explains the terms as follows: "Social manners are an important subject of description for the novel, but one cannot say the most important. . . . Consequently the *fūzoku shōsetsu* is a [novel] in which the element of describing manners occupies a relatively important position. It cannot be said that this is a definite flaw in a novel, but where the [description of] manners becomes a leading [motivation] and supplants the [description] of human emotions (*ninjō*), the *fūzoku shōsetsu* begins to lose its function as a novel."[32] This extremely informative literary definition will be considered from only two points of view here. On the one hand, it reveals Nakamura's normative attitude, which took the nineteenth-century European psychological novel as its standard, and which is also fundamental to his comments in *Fūzoku shōsetsuron*. On the other hand, it also provides information about the form of the novel itself, which is really its subject.

In concrete terms he uses *fūzoku shōsetsu* to refer to the novels by Niwa Fumio (b. 1904), Yokomitsu Riichi and Takeda Rintarō (1904–1964), produced in the second decade of the Shōwa period. Representing various camps—Yokomitsu belonged to the *shinkankakuha* while Takeda stood for Marxist literature—these authors tried "to destroy traditional literature founded by naturalism with shishōsetsu at the center and . . . to revive its sociality (*shakaisei*) and fictionality" (p. 107). However, the result was a continuation of shishōsetsu in a new form, since they lacked a really new concept (pp. 94ff.) and they therefore produced nothing more than the "reversal of shishōsetsu" "as far as the technique of description was concerned" (p. 120), insofar as they replaced factual descriptions from their own lives with observations of their surroundings produced by the same means. Thus the *fūzoku shōsetsu* is the result of a "double misunderstanding" (p. 122) as it were—"the loss of sociality and fictionality" as a consequence of one-sided naturalism at the beginning of the century and the illusion that these qualities could be regained "with a method of description that presented people merely emotionally" (p. 122).

Fūzoku shōsetsuron, of which we have been able to give only a very general outline here, is representative not only of its author but of all the writing on literary history in the period following the end of the war,[33] an "epoch-making" study,[34] whose particular significance lies in having shown the persistence with which the theory and practice developed around shishōsetsu continue in recent history. Thus, Nakamura extended the interpretative model developed by Kobayashi into the future and "arranged into the horizontal what Kobayashi had, as it were, pursued in a vertical direction."[35]

HIRANO KEN: *GEIJUTSU TO JISSEIKATSU*

The collection of essays *Geijutsu to jisseikatsu* (Art and Life) by the literary critic Hirano Ken (1907–1978) was awarded the Geijutsu senshō art prize by the Monbushō, the Japanese Ministry of Education, when it was published in 1958. It is the last in the series of studies referred to as the classics and uses the ideas of its predecessors in order to develop "key terms to illuminate the problematic of modern Japanese literature."[36]

The title itself is one of these key words, naming the common subject of the various essays, which are devoted to individual writers such as Ōgai, Katai, Tōson, Kafū, and so forth, and comprehensive themes such as the "freedom of the artist" or the "antinomies of shishōsetsu." Hirano explains, "I want to examine the relationship between art and life, the distance between writer and work, the reciprocal relationship between poet and citizen and the problem of politics and literature as problems inseparably bound up with each other."[37] According to Hirano, the European artist-bourgeois problem extending from Flaubert to Thomas Mann was first discussed in Japan by Mori Ōgai (p. 69).[38] However, while Ōgai aimed at a division of art and life, this is canceled out again by shishōsetsu, which makes life itself into the subject of art (p. 70), although they appear to harmonize only since the "emergence of the notion of the artist" is purchased at the cost of the "loss" of a social role (*seikatsusha, shakaijin to shite no shikkaku*, p. 70).

In the essay on Tayama Katai, Hirano deals with "Futon," as did Kobayashi, Itō, and Nakamura before him. He sees the outstanding significance of this work in the courage, unimaginable until that time, of revealing the private self for purely literary reasons (p. 86). In addition, Hirano is also concerned with showing that "Futon" contains fictional as well as autobiographical elements. In his opinion, Katai could write a "confession" of such frankness only because of his absolute moral integrity, something doubted by nobody, which he thus exposes as fiction (pp. 93ff.). Therefore, the writer cannot be presented as a textbook author and actor in his own work, as Nakamura does in *Fūzoku shōsetsuron,* since "the shishōsetsu form—author = protagonist"—cannot be automatically applied to "Futon" (p. 97). Hirano may not agree with the commentator of the published exchange of letters between Katai and Okada Michiyo's family[39] who presents "Futon" as a hundred-percent invention, but he also rejects the idea that the work is a direct "source of shishōsetsu," since it still contains both possibilities—that of developing in the direction of shishōsetsu and towards pure fiction (p. 98). The problem of "art and life" experienced a kind of "miscarriage" with Katai's work and was then relocated in the following period to *shinkyō shōsetsu*,[40] a subgroup of the shishōsetsu of the *Shirakaba* school (p. 10).[41]

The essay "Shishōsetsu no niritsu haihan" (The Antinomies of Shishōsetsu), written as early as 1951 and included in *Geijutsu to jisseikatsu*, develops the ideas of Itō Sei. The "consciousness of guilt" (*girudo ishiki*) of the *bundan*, of which Itō had already spoken, is the precondition for the development of shishōsetsu according to Hirano (p. 19), which had consolidated its final form with Chikamatsu Shūkō's short story "Giwaku" (The Doubt, 1913) (pp. 17ff.).[42] Both Chikamatsu's style of writing, which made negative personal experiences the literary subject, and the optimistic character of the literature of the *Shirakaba* school, were based on a sense of belonging to an elite (p. 20); it was the meeting of the two tendencies that brought about the ultimate breakthrough for shishōsetsu (p. 20). The "sense of crisis" (*kikikan*, p. 24) and the desire for "salvation" (*kyūbatsu* with the *furigana erurēzunku*, for German Erlösung, p. 25) were characteristic of shishōsetsu, but these were not rooted in the metaphysical, but in problems of everyday life (p. 25).

Hirano distinguishes between two currents in shishōsetsu: the salvation literature (*sukui no bungaku*, p. 25) of the *Shirakaba* school expressed in *shinkyō shōsetsu*, which overcomes the sense of crisis and attains harmony between self and the outer world (p. 25f.); the counterpart of this is shishōsetsu proper, the literature of the "decline" literati (*hametsusha*, p. 26) escaping from the world (*gensei hōkisha*), rooted in the tradition of *shizenshugi*.

Hirano then describes the respective relationship between art and life. Whereas the authors of *shinkyō shōsetsu* sacrifice art to life, since achieving the desired harmony between self and the outer world would mean the loss of any further motivation to write (p. 35), misery in everyday life is the precondition for "decline oriented" shishōsetsu. If necessary, a miserable life must be simulated for the sake of art (p. 37). According to Hirano, this is a reversal of the relationship between art and life (p. 38).

Let us conclude this survey of the four "classics" on shishōsetsu research here and take stock. What information has come to light for us as far as shishōsetsu research itself is concerned?

One problem common to all these works is the terminology. In Kobayashi and Nakamura, *shishōsetsu* refers to a global concept with a specific Japanese variant, while in Itō and Hirano it is used for an exclusively Japanese genre. In addition, Hirano uses the term to characterize a subgroup in the genre, the counterpart of *shinkyō shōsetsu*. None of the authors is concerned with definitions,[43] but analysis of the texts reveals a surprisingly heterogeneous understanding of the term even at the point at which all the concepts of shishōsetsu meet—in its use to designate the Japanese genre. This is obvious when reading Hirano Ken's argument: He conceives of shishōsetsu solely in terms of the opposition between fiction and factual report,[44] while the other writers base their theories on a vague but more differentiated concept.

All four studies agree in the pattern of contrasting their description of Japanese literature with European. The orientation towards the Western novel is particularly obvious in the cases of Kobayashi and Nakamura, both specialists in French literature. But neither Itō, translator of Joyce's *Ulysses* and Lawrence's *Lady Chatterley's Lover,* nor Hirano, whose literary home is among proletarian literature, can manage without continual sideways glances at Europe.

Finally, all four works share a non-academic character. In the case of Hirano, Kamei Hideo refers to a "non-positivistic method."[45] This is equally true—with possible qualifications in the case of Nakamura—for the other writers. These "classics" are called *hyōron*, essays, distinguished from *kenkyū*, academic studies. Of course, the essay form does not detract from the value of the intuitive insights revealed there, but within a scholarly discourse it would be necessary to prove or disprove them. Therefore, the expression "classics of shishōsetsu research" is misleading if it is understood to mean fundamental and exemplary studies within a scholarly context. However, in view of the peculiarities of Japanese literary studies it is nevertheless correct in the sense of referring to those works that provided the discussion framework for the academic study of shishōsetsu and which have not been replaced by any other interpretative model until now.

---

1. On the translation of the term *watakushishōsetsu/shishōsetsu* in this context cf. the Introduction and below.
2. Kobayashi Hideo, *X e no tegami, Watakushishōsetsuron*, p. 113. Future page references are given in the text.

3. Even if Kobayashi's statement is interpreted to mean that the "outcry at the beginning of *Confessions*" is intended only to symbolize the spirit of the time, it is still distorted. As far as I know, this aspect has not previously been the subject of discussion in Japan.
4. Ogasawara Masaru, "Shishōsetsu no seiritsu o megutte," p. 107.
5. Goethe's work, however, contains only letters from Werther.
6. Of course, Kobayashi did not invent the term *shizenshugi*, but his use of it does not differentiate between European and Japanese naturalism and his wording suggests a parallelism of successive literary movements in Europe and Japan.
7. Cf. Edward Seidensticker, "Kobayashi Hideo," who produces impressive evidence for his arguments.
8. Terada Tōru, "Shishōsetsu oyobi shishōsetsuron," p. 106.
9. Kobayashi repeatedly emphasized these ideas in his "Shiga Naoya" (1929) and other essays; cf. Yoshida Hiroo, "Kobayashi Hideo no 'Shiga Naoya,'" on this. Individual quotations in Seidensticker, "Kobayashi Hideo," pp. 425ff.
10. Wakizaka Mitsuru, "Kobayashi Hideo no hōhō to shisōsei," p. 21. On the application of the concept to contemporary literature, i.e. writers of the "introverted generation" (*naikō no sedai*) cf. Kamiya Tadataka, "'Shakaika shita watakushi' no tassei."
11. As a matter of fact, Miyauchi Yutaka, "Kobayashi Hideo to gendai hihyō," p. 62, for example, admires the brilliance of literary work in Kobayashi's criticisms and deplores the lack of literary flair of the younger critics (p. 64).
12. Cf., for example, Yoshida Hiroo, "'Shishōsetsuron' zengo."
13. Yoshida Hiroo, "Watakushishōsetsuron," p. 117.
14. Ogasawara, "Shishōsetsu no seiritsu o megutte," p. 107. Emphasis in the original.
15. Itō Sei, *Shōsetsu no hōhō*, pp. 65f. Further page references in the text.
16. Irena Powell, "Itō Sei's Concept of Hōki and Chōwa in Modern Japanese Literature," gives a good summary of Itō's central theories.
17. Sasaki Kiichi, "Shishōsetsu, shinkyō shōsetsu," p. 220.
18. Etō Jun, "An Undercurrent in Modern Japanese Literature," p. 436.
19. Ibid., p. 444.
20. Ibid.
21. Instead of presenting my own speculations I suggest to consult: Bruno Lewin, "Denkweise und sprachlicher Ausdruck in Japan," Wilhelm Luther, *Sprachphilosophie als Grundwissenschaft*, pp. 190f., Isaiah Ben-Dasan, *Nihonjin to Yudayajin*, p. 120.
22. Cf. also Irena Powell on *Shōsetsu no ninshiki*; on Itō's "literary theory and life" see Hasegawa Izumi, *Bungaku no kyokō to jitsuzon*, pp. 180ff.
23. Cf., e.g., his discussion on the "socialized 'I,'" Nakamura Mitsuo, "Shishōsetsu ni tsuite," pp. 80f.
24. Ibid., p. 79.
25. Ibid., p. 90.
26. Ibid., p. 91.
27. On the term *novel of manners* see below.
28. The appendix of this book contains further titles of essays by Nakamura on shishōsetsu. Yoshida Hiroo, "Shishōsetsuron no keifu," supplies brief information on contents.
29. Nakamura Mitsuo, *Fūzoku shōsetsuron*, p. 129. Further page references in the text.
30. Cf. Kawakami Tetsutarō, "Kaisetsu," p. 132.
31. None of the reference books provides any information on this.
32. *NBS*, keyword "Fūzoku shōsetsu," pp. 970ff., here p. 970.
33. Hasegawa Izumi in *GNBD*, keyword "Fūzoku shōsetsuron," p. 936.
34. Kawakami, p. 131.
35. Ibid., p. 134.
36. Kamei Hideo, "Kaisetsu," p. 323.
37. Hirano Ken, *Geijutsu to jisseikatsu*, p. 69. Further page references in the text.

38. Hirano's understanding of this problem would also require analysis, but we shall exclude it here.
39. Cf. Chapter 4, note 4.
40. On *shinkyō shōsetsu* in detail cf. "The Dispute over Shishōsetsu" (Chapter 11).
41. *Shirakaba-ha,* a humanistic and idealistic group named after its journal *Shirakaba* (The Birch, published from 1910–1923), whose members, such as Arishima Takeo (1878–1923), Shiga Naoya (1883–1971) and Mushakōji Saneatsu (1885–1976) shared aristocratic origins and a rejection of *shizenshugi.*
42. On "Giwaku," cf. Chapter 16.
43. Itō comes closest to an attempt at definition: see the discussion above, and "History of Shishōsetsu and of Shishōsetsu Theory" (Chapter 9).
44. Cf. Hirano Ken, *Geijutsu to jisseikatsu,* pp. 97ff.
45. Kamei, "Kaisetsu," p. 329.

9 · A Survey of Shishōsetsu Research

HISTORY OF SHISHŌSETSU AND OF SHISHŌSETSU THEORY

The problem of "shishōsetsu" is above all the problem of "shishōsetsu theory" (*shishōsetsuron*).

Terada Tōru, in an essay on shishōsetsu, thus justifies his approach to the discussion surrounding the genre; his contribution did not separate the two subjects.[1] His introductory words could be the motto for numerous studies which appear from their titles to deal with the history of the genre. The real subject of publications on "The Emergence of Shishōsetsu" (Kokubo Minoru, "Shishōsetsu no seiritsu" 1 and 2) or its "Emergence and Development" (Isogai Hideo, "Shishōsetsu no seiritsu to henshitsu"; Wada Kingo, "Shishōsetsu no seiritsu to tenkai") is revealed as being the discussion of the genre, presented in varying detail and in different historical extracts. Texts with more general titles, such as "Shishōsetsu" (Inagaki Tatsurō) or "Shishōsetsu and the Novel Genre" (Inagaki Tatsurō, "Shishōsetsu to shōsetsu janru") are also concerned primarily with the shishōsetsu debate.

These studies usually begin with quotations from the most famous essays of the supporters and critics of the literature at the peak of the discussion around 1925. Putting Nakamura Murao and Kume Masao and their definitions at the beginning is particularly popular.[2] This simultaneously sets a process in motion that determines the further course of the work, since the writer can then draw from a rich supply of voices for and against; even quoting them partially will ensure that the study will grow to an imposing size. Such an approach is problematical in that it remains largely at the level of a descriptive report of the discussion with little analytic depth. This is also true for the still larger number of titles that deal expressly with the debate on shishōsetsu.

Yoshida Hiroo ("Shishōsetsuron no keifu") and Senuma Shigeki ("Shishōsetsuron no keifu") provide a complete survey from the Taishō period until after World War II, while Katsuyama Isao ("Shoki shishōsetsuron ni tsuite" and "Taishō-ki ni okeru shishōsetsuron o megutte"), Usui Yoshimi (*Kindai bungaku ronsō*, vol. 1)[3] and Ogasawara Masaru ("Taishō-ki ni okeru 'watakushi'-shōsetsu no ron ni tsuite") concentrate only on the Taishō period, and Terada Tōru ("Shishōsetsu oyobi shishōsetsuron") and Yoshida Hiroo ("'Shishōsetsuron' zengo" and "Sengo hihyō e no hansatei") direct their main attention to the chain of argument from Kobayashi Hideo to Nakamura Mitsuo or Etō Jun. Kobayashi's theory on shishōsetsu is the subject of frequent individual studies, and it occupies an important place in the comments of Ogasawara ("Shishōsetsu no seiritsu o megutte") and Yoshida Hiroo ("'Watakushi-shōsetsuron' zengo"). The problem of "pure literature" (*junbungaku*),[4] raised in connection with the shishōsetsu discussion is of interest to Edward Seidensticker ("The 'Pure' and the 'In-Between' in Modern Japanese Theories of the Novel"), Hirano Ken (*Junbungaku ronsō igo*),[5] Ogasawara Masaru ("'Junbungaku' no mondai") and Teruoka Yasutaka ("Junbungaku to taishū bungaku").

The debate about shishōsetsu can be said therefore to be the most frequently discussed area and most carefully documented part of shishōsetsu research. This fact points at the same time to a problem in the research. Detailed consideration of the statements made by writers and critics on literary theory seems to have absolved literary scholars from the effort involved in critical analysis of the subject. This, at least, is the impression created in view of the frequent quotations from previous discussions, behind which the writers involved seem to hide, at great pains not to have to give an account of their own views of the phenomenon. Therefore, while these studies provide us with valuable information on the literary-theoretical background and important facts on the emergence and use of the term, they are nevertheless symptomatic of the tendency of shishōsetsu research to neglect the real subject of the genre itself.

A further characteristic of these studies is that they do not differentiate between the literary-theoretical statements of the writers and comments made by critics or scholars, but deal with "primary" and "secondary information" at the same level.[6] This is characteristic of Japanese literary studies generally, as is the following problem—the unquestioning adoption of terms that were usually created ad hoc as theoretical terminology. Words such as *junsui shōsetsu* (pure novel) or *junbungaku* are introduced in, for example, *Nihon no gendai shōsetsu* by Nakamura Mitsuo, as the "invention" of the writer Yokomitsu Riichi, only to be included straightaway in his own descriptive category: "[Yet] when he [Yokomitsu] championed the *junsui shōsetsu*, he blurred the line between pure (*junbungaku*) and mass literature (*taishū bungaku*); he created the possibility for writers of pure literature to involve themselves with trivial literature for newspapers, women's magazines, and so forth, and this merely resulted in the basis for the development of the intermediate novel (*chūkan shōsetsu*) after the war."[7] Speaking generally, the problem lies in the extensive congruence between the artistic and the scholastic discussion.

There are also critical analyses of shishōsetsu that seem predestined to provide a new stimulus. Discussions of Kobayashi Hideo's work are particularly popular. Terada Tōru pointed out the ambivalence of Kobayashi's attitude as early as 1954,[8] and, in Kobayashi's "creative criticism" (*sōzōteki hihyō*) Satō Etsuko identified a "shishōsetsu-like viewpoint" (*shishōsetsuteki tachiba*) in 1976 which became apparent through Kobayashi's interest in the relationship between the writer and his work.[9] Yamagata Hiroshi also came to a similar conclusion in 1977 when considering Hirano Ken's "Shishōsetsu no niritsu haihan"[10] which he called an "essay on shishōsetsu based on the shishōsetsu method."[11]

My observations point in the same direction.[12] The most glaring examples of this type of reception are to be found in the records of discussions (*zadankai*), for example in the conversation about "Shishōsetsu's Character and Problem Areas" (Yoshida Seiichi, Nakamura Mitsuo, Takami Jun, and Hirano Ken, "Shishōsetsu no honshitsu to mondaiten"), which is made up in large parts of nothing more than an exchange of anecdotes. However, the tea-party setting is deceptive. The subject is a comparison between literary and actual reality which can then be used to measure the quality of a work. A work can be good only if it does justice to the facts in every respect.[13] However, the literary jurors seem totally oblivious to two factors: first, that their judgments are largely colored by their pride at having inside knowledge of the *bundan*, and, second, that their criticism depends on the extent of their knowledge of the relevant author's biography.

The few isolated voices heard in criticism of this kind of literary study have not had any recognizable effect on shishōsetsu research itself. The main current of this research continues to be the question of the correspondence between work and life, thus remaining within the framework of interest dictated by shishōsetsu theory itself. It is only within the very recent past that sporadic criticism of research methodology has given way to the attempt to develop an independent interpretative strategy. One example here is Yamagata Hiroshi, "Shishōsetsu ni okeru 'watakushi' no ichi," who, encouraged by Roland Barthes and Michel Foucault among others, suggested a new method of reading shishōsetsu which would not try to determine the "genuineness" (*riariti*)[14] of a work in terms of a comparison with the non-literary facts, as was previously the case, but which would instead accept the character of the first-person narrator as a literary product who constructs his own *riariti* independent of the real world.[15]

Literary studies are interested only in individual phases of the history of shishōsetsu. There is no overall description of the subject, nor is there an example of anything like a comprehensive view of the historical development of the genre. Only Odagiri Hideo, *Shishōsetsu, shinkyō shōsetsu,* can be said to have produced a rounded survey on the history and theory of the genre, but he concentrated his study on early theory and practice.

In 1962, Ogasawara Masaru gave his attention to the subject of the origins of shishōsetsu together with the accompanying literary debate ("Shishōsetsu no seiritsu to hassan"). A number of studies have searched for the roots of the genre in *shizenshugi*, for example, Ōkubo Tsuneo, "Shizenshugi to shishōsetsu" and "'Futon,' Tayama Katai," the symposium "From the Meiji to the Shōwa Period" (Ariyama Mitsuhiro et al., eds., 1966),[16] and Sōma Tsuneo, *Nihon shizenshugiron.*[17] Kōno Toshirō considered the form of shishōsetsu developed by the *Shirakaba* school ("Shishōsetsu ni okeru Shirakaba-ha no yakuwari"). Katsuyama Isao ("Taishō-ki ni okeru shishōsetsu no keifu") and Nakamura Yū ("Taishō-ki shishōsetsu ni matsuwaru oboegaki (1)") described the first climax of the genre, while Ino Kenji (*Zōho kindai Nihon bungakushi kenkyū*) and Satō Masaru ("Puroretaria bungaku ni okeru shishōsetsu") examined shishōsetsu in "democratic" or "proletarian literature." Miyoshi Yukio ("Shōwa ni okeru shishōsetsu sakka") and Hoshō Masao ("Senjika ni okeru shishōsetsu sakka") both produced studies on the Shōwa period up until the end of World War II, including the *tenkō* (conversion) phase, while the period since World War II was the subject of publications by Morikawa Tatsuya ("Shishōsetsu hōhōka no mondai"), Torii Kunio ("Sengo ni okeru shishōsetsuteki ishiki" and "Senzen shishōsetsu to no renzoku to danzetsu"), Hirano Ken (*Junbungaku ronsō igo*),[18] Miyoshi Yukio (*Nihon bungaku no kindai to hankindai*),[19] Satō Yasumasa ("Shishōsetsu no keifu"), Matsumoto Tsuruo ("Bungaku, shishōsetsu to jiko shōshitsu no jidai") and Yakushiji Noriaki ("Shishōsetsu no hitei").

Torii Kunio distinguished between three stages of development in the genre: (1) shishōsetsu literature produced towards the end of the Taishō period under the influence of *shizenshugi* and *Shirakaba-ha*; (2) the literature that flourished after the "conversion," represented by Dazai Osamu, Nakano Shigeharu (1902–1979), Takami Jun (1907–1965) and Itō Sei; and (3) the works of the "third new generation" (*dai san no shinjin*) since 1960.[20]

According to Torii, the first phase of shishōsetsu is characterized by the writer's unbroken faith in himself as an artist, by a kind of "artist supremacy" (*geijutsuka shijōshugi*),[21] as a result of which the direct personal description automatically acquires the status of a work of art as it were. The novels of the second phase lack this presumptive character since in them "the author questions his nature as a writer."[22] Finally, in the third phase shishōsetsu is formalized (*hōhōka*),[23] that is, it is transformed from a "novel [form] which has no structure in the true sense of the word,"[24] since it is created by the direct conversion of experience into literature, to a kind of writing which recognizes a second first person in addition to the first person who appears in the work. According to Torii Kunio the author becomes aware for the first time of the fictionality of his description of himself; he is aware of the division between himself and the work, a division which did not exist for the writers of the pre-war years.[25] However, with this formalization shishōsetsu loses much of its attraction which lies, according to Miyoshi Yukio, in the immediacy of self-expression of a fascinating writer.[26]

The writers are in general agreement about this view of the development of shishōsetsu from being a "formless" literature which, tailor-made to suit the author, lives only from his individuality and his belief in himself,[27] to a less impressive literature of "loss of self"[28] in the generation after the war.

The regret audible in the words of Miyoshi Yukio or Matsumoto Tsuruo when they speak of great writer personalities (which became superfluous as the result of the formalization of shishōsetsu) betrays their orientation to a concept of shishōsetsu that they themselves say is traditional—a further indication of the tenacious survival of the "shishōsetsu spirit" in modern Japanese literary studies.

SHISHŌSETSU AUTHORS AND WORKS

By far the largest part of Japanese literary studies is still concerned with individual authors and works in the form of *sakkaron* (studies on authors) or *sakuhinron* (studies on works). This emphasis not only corresponds to the method of working and the aims of Japanese philology, it also meets to a large extent the interests of the subject on the market, where the possibility of the work's publication and its sales value are important considerations.[29] Within this rule, the following tendency holds true: The more famous and popular an author, the more prepared the market is to accept a study devoted to him.[30] This largely explains the widely varying research interest as far as shishōsetsu authors and works are concerned.

One more piece of information is important here. Sometimes critics distinguish between shishōsetsu authors (*shishōsetsuka*) and authors of shishōsetsu. There does not seem to be a universally applicable distinction between the two. On the one hand, class-conscious writing, that is, for a specific purpose, a feature alien to shishōsetsu, prevents the categorization of writers concerned—in this case Miyamoto Yuriko (1899–1951) and Hayama Yoshiki (1894–1945)—among the circle of shishōsetsu authors, although their works are counted as shishōsetsu[31] while stories and novels by Akutagawa and Ōgai "are shishōsetsu and are not shishōsetsu at one and the same time," since they do not depict daily life but adopt a critical distance in order to put the concrete in abstract terms.[32] According to Terada Tōru even Shiga Naoya is not a shishōsetsu writer, although his works could be called shishōsetsu.[33] However, the distinction made here obfuscates rather than elucidates the relationship between the two supposed groups of authors. It is more informative on the matter of theoretical considerations of the genre.

Nevertheless, a differentiation seems obvious, since there is hardly any author in modern literature who has not written a shishōsetsu, as Terada Tōru concedes. The only exceptions here in his opinion are Kōda Rohan (1867–1947), Izumi Kyōka (1873–1939), and Natsume Sōseki.[34] It is therefore the general rule to distinguish between writers who take the subject of their work solely from their own life and those who also write fictitious literature—in the Japanese sense of the word.

This categorization serves to explain why the bibliography contains relatively few titles on the well-known authors and those who are, according to the remarks made above, frequently the subject of critical studies, at least to the extent that they do not belong to the smaller circle of *shishōsetsuka*. In this case, shishōsetsu is only one aspect that has usually received little consideration, although it must be admitted that, in some of the studies I have not included, shishōsetsu may be thematically treated, so that the bibliography almost certainly contains some gaps. Completeness is in any case an impossible goal.

Naturally, the proportion of studies that consider one author or one work from the point of view of shishōsetsu—and we want to count only such works among shishōsetsu research[35]—is greatest in the case of those literati who were active only within this genre. However, seen from the viewpoint of the total number of publications, many fewer studies have been devoted to these authors than to their colleagues who did not shrink from "fictitiousness" to the same degree.[36] Shiga Naoya and Dazai Osamu are remarkable exceptions here, and have been the subject of undiminished interest among researchers for a long period; but it is significant that there is disagreement on how they should be classified. On the one hand, they are held to be model shishōsetsu writers, on the other their importance is seen to lie in the fact that their literature goes beyond shishōsetsu.[37]

As in the previous chapter, it is possible here to give only an incomplete survey of the secondary literature examined. We shall therefore limit this to references to the most frequently discussed authors and works and to their characteristic or controversial features.

To begin with, a study of a special kind: In 1962, Hasegawa Izumi produced a list of 35 shishōsetsu containing information on their first publication and content, background material, and, in some cases, secondary material. The list was arranged in chronological order, beginning with "Futon" and going as far as Kawasaki Chōtarō's (b. 1901) *Katabutori no onna* (The Sturdy Woman), published in 1957. This catalogue is interesting because of the texts selected, which allows us to draw conclusions concerning the Japanese understanding of the genre.[38]

The majority of the literature on Katai's "Futon," of particular interest to the researchers as the first example of shishōsetsu, has already been discussed in Part One. Among the titles not listed there are Ogata Akiko, "'Futon' shiron," a well-rounded, careful consideration of previous research results, and Hashimoto Yoshi, "'Futon' ni kansuru memo," which analyzes the references to reality and their function in Katai's work.

In 1971, Edwin McClellan presented an essay "Shimazaki Tōson and the Autobiographical Novel," which deals with, among other things, the novel inspired by "Futon," *Haru*. This work is one of the borderline cases. While Nakamura Mitsuo and others categorize it as a shishōsetsu,[39] others like Hirano Ken and Terada Tōru deny it this status.[40]

There is no doubt as to the membership in the shishōsetsu club of later naturalist Tokuda Shūsei (1872–1943) around whose last, unfinished work *Shukuzu* (The Miniature, 1941) Matsubara Shin'ichi revolved his *sakkaron* in 1974. Kasai Zenzō (1887–1928),[41] Kamura Isota (1897–1933), Kajii Motojirō (1901–1932), and Kanbayashi Akatsuki (1902–1980), all the subject of a chapter each in Yamamoto Kenkichi, *Watakushishōsetsu sakkaron*, are considered to be typical shishōsetsu writers.

The division developed by Itō Sei into a "decline type" (*hametsugata*), which corresponds to the mentality of the "runaway slave" (*tōbō dorei*),[42] and the "harmony type" (*chōwagata*), from the author who feels at peace with his surroundings, has been consistently adopted by researchers in general. According to Hirano Ken, the *chōwagata* line, represented among others by Shiga Naoya, Takii Kōsaku, Amino Kiku (b. 1900), and Kajii Motojirō, is real shishōsetsu.[43] However, this fairly conclusive division is disturbed by a number of additional subgroups. For example, Hirano Ken groups Kanbayashi Akatsuki, Kawasaki Chōtarō and Kiyama Shōhei (1904–1968) between *hametsugata* and *chōwagata*, while Kobayashi Takiji (1903–1933) and Hōjō Tamio (1914–1937) embody a "special *hametsugata*,"[44] since their tragic life—Kobayashi, the most famous of the proletarian writers, was tortured to death by the police and Hōjō died of leprosy—gave their literature an unusual degree of reality.[45]

Yet again shishōsetsu theory—which refers quite generally to the principles of construction and the specific, corresponding mechanisms of production and reception, all of which will be described in more detail in Part Three—sets the criteria for "scholarly" categorization, in this case derived from a synopsis of work and life. This problematic— the way in which shishōsetsu analysts are entangled in the extremely fine net of shishōsetsu norms laid over the whole of modern Japanese literary theory—runs throughout the research examined here.

Tsuruta Kin'ya has also drifted into this area, although less conspicuously, with his contribution on Akutagawa and the shishōsetsu writers ("Akutagawa and I-Novelists"), thus undermining his intention of presenting Akutagawa as more serious and intellectually demanding in contrast to the shishōsetsu writers. He pursues his aim of paying tribute to Akutagawa's rejection of shishōsetsu to absurd lengths, by interpreting the writer's lack of interest in exposing his private life to the public as an aversion resulting from his biography[46] and by finally underlining the short story "Jigokuhen" (A Hellish Event, 1918) as a real personal revelation, as if it were a more profound and more genuine shishōsetsu exceeding all the works awarded that name previously.[47]

Yet again, shishōsetsu theory has caught up with scholarly research here. Even the intention of examining the opposite of shishōsetsu does not succeed in going beyond the limits set by shishōsetsu. As for the rest, in view of Tsuruta's discussion, the question arises as to what position the autobiographical, posthumously published short story "Haguruma" (Cogwheels, 1927) should fill within Akutagawa's work. Tsuruta very wisely does not mention "Haguruma," since it would take all plausibility away from his arguments, particularly since this short story was recognized by contemporary writers, for example by Kasai Zenzō[48] as an equally worthy personal confession.[49]

The problems of conventional shishōsetsu research are particularly apparent in the example of Uno Kōji (1891–1961), since, according to Yamamoto Kenkichi, truth and lies cannot be distinguished in his shishōsetsu.[50] However, if by definition shishōsetsu requires the highest possible degree of sincerity in order to be seen in its factual truth, then Uno should give rise either to an examination of the label "shishōsetsu writer" or to a new definition of the terms reality and truth. This problem, however, does not exist for Yamamoto. On the contrary, the blending of "fiction" and "reality" in Uno Kōji's literature is for him proof of the inseparability of work and life.[51] Consequently, "fiction and truth" (*shi to shinjitsu*)[52] in Uno is also an obvious subject for Katsuyama Isao, "Uno Kōji ni okeru shi to yume," and for Matsubara Shin'ichi, *"Gusha" no bungaku,* whose discussions center on the novel *Ku no sekai* (World of Suffering, 1919).

The greatest number of individual studies are devoted to the "god of fiction" (*shōsetsu no kamisama*), as Shiga Naoya has been called in Japan since Akutagawa eulogized him in such terms.[53] This writer, who has also become the subject of research outside Japan in recent times (we shall mention here only the biographies by Francis Mathy, *Shiga Naoya,* and Stephen W. Kohl, *Shiga Naoya: A Critical Biography*) is given detailed attention and appreciation as a shishōsetsu writer by Yamamoto Kenkichi, *Watakushishōsetsu sakkaron,* and Takahashi Hideo, *Gensō to shite no "watakushi."* J. B. Power provides a good introduction to the subject in "Shiga Naoya and the Shishōsetsu," in which Shiga's writing plays only a marginal part. Stephen W. Kohl's essay on "Shiga Naoya and the Literature of Experience" (1977), on the other hand, seems to be above all intended as an explanation of the translation of two short stories and supplies, in addition to a brief glance at Shiga's views on literature, an interpretation that gets bogged down again and again in paraphrases of his work.

Akiyama Shun's study "On 'I' in Shiga Naoya" ("Shiga Naoya no 'watakushi' ni tsuite") is devoted to the protagonist in Shiga's only novel *An'ya kōro* (A Dark Night's Passing), which appeared in series from 1922 until 1937. Although Akiyama emphasizes that *An'ya kōro* is by no means a simple shishōsetsu, but rather an "extremely intellectual (*chiteki*), inner (*naimenteki*), consciously artistic creation,"[54] nevertheless his method of reception does not differ from that of works he values as the most perfect form of shishōsetsu. Miyoshi Yukio, *Sakuhinron no kokoromi,* is also concerned with the shishōsetsu character[55] of *An'ya kōro* in his careful analysis and establishes cross connections to other works.

Shiga's numerous stories and short stories are discussed in many studies as exemplary representatives or for comparisons with other shishōsetsu. The short story "Kuniko" (1927), which Hirano Ken contrasts with Dazai Osamu's *Shayō* (The Setting Sun, 1974),[56] and which Sasaki Kiichi sees as the historical end of shishōsetsu,[57] is one example.

"The Shiga Hero" is the subject of William F. Sibley's 1971 dissertation; it deals with the projection of the author in his works.[58] He traces the childhood, youth, development of consciousness, and maturing of the "Shiga hero" in typical works from psychoanalytical and mythological points of view. His analysis emphasizes the "intuitive psychoanalysis"[59] Shiga carries out on himself, but some of his results are also useful for our discussion of shishōsetsu.[60] For example, Sibley's statement that at times, in his works, the author displays greater insight than the protagonist is a point of view that contradicts common shishōsetsu opinion.[61]

Dazai Osamu, identified by Hirano Ken as the last representative of the "decline type," is held to be the counterpole to Shiga.[62] Chiba Masaaki, "Dazai Osamu sakkaron jiten: shishōsetsu," provides a synopsis of the shishōsetsu subject matter for this author. Saegusa Yasutaka, *Nihon romanha no gunzō,* examines the meaning of "I" in Dazai. Usui Yoshimi, *Shōsetsu no ajiwaikata,* chooses the novel *Ningen shikkaku* (No Longer Human, 1948) as an example of shishōsetsu; Takahashi Hideo, in his *sakkaron* entitled *Gensō to shite no "watakushi,"* also deals with this work.[63]

In these discussions of shishōsetsu, we also come across names less frequently associated with the genre. For example, Takahashi Hideo devotes one chapter each to the novelist Ibuse Masuji (b. 1898) and the poet Kiyooka Takayuki (b. 1922) who was influenced by surrealism. "Inoue Yasushi and the Shishōsetsu" is the subject of a study by Isogai Hideo ("Inoue Yasushi to shishōsetsu"). Sakita Susumu, "'Kamen no kokuhaku' shiron," interprets the novel *Kamen no kokuhaku* (Confessions of a Mask, 1949), which made its author Mishima Yukio (1925–1970) famous as a "fictionalized shishōsetsu."

Studies on shishōsetsu after the war concentrate above all on the authors of the "third new generation" (*dai san no shinjin*) such as Yoshiyuki Junnosuke (b. 1924), Yasuoka Shōtarō (b. 1920) and Shōno Junzō (b. 1921), where according to the critics the shishōsetsu tradition survives.[64] Using the example of Yasuoka Shōtarō, Torii Kunio, "Senzen shishōsetsu to no renzoku to danzetsu," examined the links to the shishōsetsu of the pre-war period,[65] while Usui Yoshimi, *Shōsetsu no ajiwaikata*, Takahashi Hideo, *Genso to shite no "watakushi,"* and Aeba Takao, *Hihyō to hyōgen*, supply interpretations of individual works by these authors.[66] The shishōsetsu discussion after the war reached a temporary high point as a result of Miura Tetsuo's (b. 1931) book *Shinobugawa* (The River Shinobu), published in 1960, which motivated studies by, among others, Miyoshi Yukio, in *Nihon bungaku no kindai to hankindai*, Nakamura Shin'ichirō, "Shishōsetsu to jikken shōsetsu," and Morikawa Tatsuya, "Shishōsetsu hōhōka no mondai."[67] Miura is counted among the "introverted generation" (*naikō no sedai*); the affinity of this generation to shishōsetsu exemplified by Ogawa Kunio is the subject of a publication by Satō Yasumasa, "Jiishiki no kussetsu."

In recent times, there have been increasingly frequent signs of a renewed interest in shishōsetsu, inspired in 1977 by the publication in book form of the shishōsetsu by Shimao Toshio (b. 1917), *Shi no toge* (The Thorn of Death), which had appeared sporadically as a series over a period of seventeen years and was completed in 1976. Matsumoto Tsuruo, "Kindai bungei yōshiki nōto (1)," comes to the conclusion that this work enriches the genre due to the considerable distance in time between the author and the events described, but at the same time this work raises doubts about the whole genre, at least in places.[68] The work did nonetheless stimulate the generation of writers born after the war, called by Odagiri Hideo the "generation of emptiness" (*kūkyo no sedai*),[69] whose work is largely autobiographical, to a reconsideration of the genre. Starting with the first work by Murakami Ryū (b. 1952), *Kagirinaku tōmei ni chikai burū* (Almost Transparent Blue), published in 1975, which aroused considerable interest, Aeba Takao, "'Watakushi' no fukami ni mukatte," categorized contemporary literary production under the motto of the search for self—by now a self that could only be perceived in a very blurred form—in 1977 and placed this in the tradition of shishōsetsu. This approach also dominates the discussion group led by Aeba (Saeki Shōichi et al., "Kyōdō tōgi 'Shishōsetsu'") and in the article by Morikawa Tatsuya, "Bungaku wa hirakareru." When a champion of the "introverted generation" such as Furui Yoshikichi (b. 1937) reviewed a literary study on the naturalist and shishōsetsu writer Tokuda Shūsei and gave the review the title "Shishōsetsu o motomete" (In Search of Shishōsetsu), this points to a growing, and relatively less critical, interest in the genre, perhaps even to a need on the part of the literati to feel part of a tradition from which a positive new evaluation of shishōsetsu could develop. However, it is still too early to establish any reliable statements about such a critical reappraisal.

We now conclude this by no means exhaustive list of the titles concerned with shishōsetsu authors and works. The studies included differ significantly in form, objective, and quality. We look in vain for traces of common scholarly literary terminology and for any consideration of the approach adopted or even an explanation of the results aimed at; at least seen from the West, this is the difficulty in the entire discipline of Japanese literary studies.

More typical for shishōsetsu research—although also not atypical for Japanese philology—is the attitude of the critic or academic towards the subject under consideration. For example, in the epilogue to his study, Matsubara Shin'ichi makes the following confession:

> Love of shishōsetsu moved me to write this book. Without exaggeration, I can say that I who believe that man must have experienced the area of the negative qualities of human experience, described by shishōsetsu as "pain"[70] wrote this book in the form of an essay *as my own shishōsetsu*. In the background was the idea that it was a task that I would have to carry out at some time and that I myself would be unable to take a single step forward until it was completed. There are already many studies that reject shishōsetsu, but I believe they are nothing more than theoretical, superficial criticism, unless the attempt has been made to penetrate as far as possible into the interior of shishōsetsu.[71]

This sense of mission as a result of absolute identification with the subject of course hinders a critical examination of it. Matsubara is on the side of the shishōsetsu writers right from the beginning. He cites them only in order to follow on with further thoughts on shishōsetsu theory. As a passionate apologist for shishōsetsu, he mentions the reservations of other critics or authors only to dismiss them with a sweeping gesture. He does not do so by producing counter arguments, since he often admits that there are none, but by announcing that these very weaknesses strengthen his love of shishōsetsu.[72] This pattern of "argumentation" runs through the entire book.

Yamamoto Kenkichi's study is more informative on the whole, but his basic attitude is the same. Again, shishōsetsu has not found in him a detached analyst but an active supporter, although his emotions are not quite so exuberant as Matsubara's. His most important objective, and one shared by most Japanese writers of *sakkaron,* including Takahashi Hideo, the author of the third study, is to strengthen the reader's identification with the shishōsetsu writer so as to facilitate a reception of the works themselves. This is achieved predominantly by making repeated recourse to the difficult lives of the writers concerned, fraught with illness, poverty, and misfortune; the tendency to create legends and a kind of cult of genius using the typical *ecce homo* gesture seems inevitable.

Consequently, the concepts of self shared by the writers of these *sakkaron* imply that the reason for a study of a literary subject is primarily to create, via feelings of pity, an emotional accord between themselves, the literary author, and the reader. Thus, as Matsubara himself admits, such a study is in fact a shishōsetsu produced by different means.

This attitude seems particularly suitable to the subject when judged from the point of view of Japanese shishōsetsu research and therefore largely dominates the whole discussion. However, it is a basic attitude characteristic of the whole of Japanese literary studies, as indicated by the central methodological term *kanshō. Kanshō,* the appreciation of the work or the author in terms of congenial empathy, is the most important element in the process of literary studies for Japanese philology. The condition for this is an adequate "ability to appreciate" (*kanshōryoku*) on the part of the receiver, which could also be translated as "empathy," and which evokes quite plainly the associations with a method of interpretation, *Werkinterpretation,* popular in postwar German literary studies.[73] Yamamoto Kenkichi's approach, described above as representative of the majority of studies in shishōsetsu research, is fully in accordance with the conventions of Japanese literary studies. Evidence of this is given by Shinoda Hajime in the *Small Encyclopaedia of Japanese Litera-*

ture (*NBS*) who characterizes Yamamoto's *Watakushishōsetsu sakkaron* as a series of "beautiful literary portraits, based on a balanced, excellent ability to appreciate (*kanshōryoku*)."[74]

Finally, one more marginal comment. Characteristically all the available studies on shishōsetsu are made up of *sakkaron* published in various places over a considerable period of time, which explains repetitions within the books. The fact that a work such as Yamamoto Kenkichi's *Watakushishōsetsu sakkaron,* published for the first time in 1943 as a collection of essays that had previously appeared individually, did not require revision in 1966 but was merely enlarged by the addition of three essays written in the same style,[75] throws light again on the truly "timeless" nature of this type of research.

SPECIAL ASPECTS OF SHISHŌSETSU

This section is concerned with surveying those studies that do not concentrate primarily on aspects discussed earlier and with questions raised particularly frequently in connection with shishōsetsu.

A large part of the secondary literature on shishōsetsu consists of contributions of a general introductory nature. They will be mentioned here only in those cases where they present specific problems in a way that deviates from the customary point of view. They are categorized as "research" following Japanese custom and in order to avoid any preliminary evaluation.[76]

In my view the best introduction to the subject in the non-Japanese field is still the work by Howard Hibbett, "The Portrait of the Artist in Japanese Fiction." The Japanese reader finds the most balanced presentation of the whole subject, and the one with the most material, in Odagiri Hideo, *Shishōsetsu, shinkyō shōsetsu.*

Numerous articles attempt a general characterization of the genre, such as one by Edwin McClellan, "Some General Comments on Shishōsetsu." Among these are much cited essays such as Ara Masahito's presentation of shishōsetsu as a "Japanese reality"[77] or Sugiura Minpei's biting verdict on "The Literature of Parasites," 1953. The literati themselves often made their voices heard, for example, Kanbayashi Akatsuki ("Shishōsetsu no unmei"), Tokunaga Sunao ("Soto kara uchi e, uchi kara soto e"), Ōe Kenzaburō ("Shishōsetsu ni tsuite"), Ozaki Kazuo ("Shishōsetsu to watakushi"), Kawasaki Chōtarō ("Shishōsetsu ni tsuite"), Miura Tetsuo ("Watakushi to shishōsetsu"), and Shōno Junzō ("Hōhō to shite no shishōsetsu"). Discussions of shishōsetsu in which authors and critics face each other are particularly interesting, for example, Yoshida Seiichi, Nakamura Mitsuo, Takami Jun, and Hirano Ken ("Shishōsetsu no honshitsu to mondaiten"), Kojima Nobuo, Hirano Ken, and Yasuoka Shōtarō ("Bungaku ni okeru 'watakushi' to wa nani ka"), or Akiyama Shun, Yagi Yoshinori (b. 1911), Shimamura Toshimasa (b. 1912), and Miura Tetsuo ("Shishōsetsu no gensen"). It is evident that the point of view and argumentation of the two sides hardly differ; yet the course of the conversation and the spontaneous reactions of those taking part present an impressive picture of the shishōsetsu authors' concept of themselves and the critics' attitudes and main interests.

A number of contributions concentrate on questions of "sociality" (*shakaisei*) and the "modern I" (*kindaiteki jiga*) in shishōsetsu. They move largely within the framework of interpretation set up by Kobayashi Hideo in his "Watakushishōsetsuron." The philosophers Saegusa Hiroto ("Shishōsetsu no 'watakushi' no minamoto") and Takeuchi Yoshimi ("Shishōsetsu ni tsuite") see the problematic of the entire modern Japanese movement reflected in shishōsetsu. For example, Takeuchi points to shishōsetsu-like elements in the philosophy of Nishida Kitarō (1870–1945).[78] Further essays on this have been written by Dōke Tadamichi ("Shishōsetsu no kiso"), Kimura Yukio ("Shishōsetsu to shakaisei"). Saitō Kiyoe (*Nihon bungei shichō zenshi*), Yazaki Dan ("Kindai jiga no Nihonteki keisei (jō)"), Hiraoka Toshio ("Sengo no bungakushi-zō to Tōkoku-zō"), Kenneth Strong ("Downgrading the 'Kindai Jiga': Reflections on Tōson's 'Hakai' and Subsequent Trends in Modern Literature"), Oketani Hideaki (*Gyōshi to hōkō*, vol. I),[79] and Aeba Takao (*Hihyō to hyōgen*).[80] Some of the theories represented here will be considered in greater detail in Part Five of this book.[81]

Howard Hibbett is not concerned as these articles are with references to the philosophical, intellectual, or socio-political context but with links in the internal literary discussion. In his "Introspective Techniques in Modern Japanese Fiction," he proves also that "writers usually thought to be well outside the 'main stream' of autobiographical fiction [by which he means shishōsetsu] are not immune from the attractions of a subjectivism that they too would regard as peculiarly Japanese."[82] Thus he also discovers shishōsetsu-like techniques in Natsume Sōseki, Akutagawa Ryūnosuke, Tanizaki Jun'ichirō (1886–1965) and Kawabata Yasunari (1886–1972). His contribution is tangential to that of Edwin McClellan's "The Impressionistic Tendency in Some Modern Japanese Writers." The examples he has chosen are Sōseki, Tōson, Tanizaki and Doppo. There are points of contact with shishōsetsu research to the extent that the subjectivist impressionism described by McClellan is often emphasized as an important characteristic of shishōsetsu.

This anti-realist characteristic of shishōsetsu is usually traced from classical literary tradition. Numerous essays contain references to pre-Meiji literature, but these usually go no further than the mere verbalization of associations, since close examination is considered unnecessary. At the same time, the historical and generic range under consideration is so extensive that any serious discussion of this aspect would have to begin by defining the concept of tradition itself. In shishōsetsu research, tradition is understood to mean *nikki* (diary) and *zuihitsu* (miscellany) literature[83] as well as *haiku* and *waka* literature which began with the *Man'yōshū*,[84] medieval Buddhist confessional literature, and Saikaku's Genroku realism,[85] the *Genji monogatari* and the classical Nō.[86] However, such global statements achieve little when the nature of the references to a particular work, group of works, or genre is not characterized more closely. Vague references in many studies to an apparently gigantic monolithic block of existing "classics" by the careless use of such theoretical terms as *mono no aware* or *fūryū* also do little to help us along.[87]

More practical, on the other hand, are thematically closely defined studies such as, for example, Wada Kingo, "Tayama Katai to 'Kagerō nikki,'" and Inukai Ren, "Tayama Katai to Kagerō nikki," even though these are still in part very general studies.

An interesting example for an approach to this complex of subjects can be found in Yoshida Seiichi (*Kanshō to hihyō*) who examines *tanka*, *haiku*, and shishōsetsu together. Kubota Masabumi ("Shishōsetsu to tankateki jojō") also critically considers the "*tanka*-like lyricism" of shishōsetsu,[88] while Tadokoro Hitoshi limits his discussions on the "Relationship between Shishōsetsu and Traditional Literature" ("Shishōsetsu to dentō bungaku to no kankei") to examples from the *nikki* and *zuihitsu* genres.

Ogasawara Masaru ("Shishōsetsu no biishiki"), however, appeals only vaguely to the "classics" in his examination of the "consciousness of beauty" in shishōsetsu, when he refers to the traditional feeling for nature as a significant element of a conventional shishōsetsu, without describing this in more detail. He contrasts this type of shishōsetsu exemplified in Kasai Zenzō which remains impassive and self-estranged[89] with Kamura Isota's literature, which is concerned only with itself and is, as it were, "short-circuited," bordering almost on "auto-intoxication,"[90] which represents the absolute extreme of shishōsetsu "consciousness of beauty" for Ogasawara. This occurs paradoxically as a result of the "distance" from every kind of "consciousness of beauty," since it is revealed in Kamura above all in his "peculiar disorder."[91]

An excessive level of abstraction or incomprehensible jumps from individual observations of detail to general statements are both of questionable value. As far as the contrast that Ogawara notes between Kasai and Kamura is concerned, nearly all researchers would contradict him. Those two are generally described as having a "teacher-pupil relationship" and are both counted among the "masochistic" (*hametsugata*).[92]

Ōta Seiichi ("Zengemichi to shite no shishōsetsu no keifu") discovered in Kamura Isota's literature a pronounced affinity to the Buddhist confession, which he traced from the powerful influence of Tokutomi Roka on Kamura.[93] However, yet again no relationship to the "classics" is revealed or any literary reference proven; instead, the spiritual kinship of two writers who treated their inferiority complexes with religious therapy is described. Miyagi Otoya ("Shishōsetsu no shinrigaku: Kasai Zenzō o yonde") adopts a strict psychoanalytical approach and arrives at informative generalizations about the structure of an author's personality and public.[94] Toyama Shigehiko's essay on the shishōsetsu reader ("Shishōsetsu dokusharon") provides extensive material which, due to his naive shishōsetsu-conformist statements will have to be evaluated in Part Five.

The united front of those who place shishōsetsu in relation to Japanese literary tradition and, together with the research "classics," acknowledge at most the "oblique" and superficial influence of European literature is broken by Karatani Yukihito who attempts, using some quotations from Shiga Naoya, Foucault, and others, to identify the "origins of modern Japanese literature in Christianity" under the grandiose title "The Genealogy of Shishōsetsu" ("Shishōsetsu no keifugaku"). However, he modifies his assertion in the course of his work when he concedes that it did not "originate from Christianity itself but from the rejection of Christianity."[95] He concludes, "It is ridiculous (*kudaranai*) to criticize the fact that shishōsetsu has reduced (*kyōshōka*) the Western novel in a one-sided fashion. The power shishōsetsu possesses is not Japanese but stems from the West and its modern movement."[96] However, his peculiar dialectic cannot contribute a great deal towards a "genealogy" of shishōsetsu or a definition of its relationship to literary tradition and to European literature.

One last group rounds off our survey of trends in shishōsetsu research. These are studies that describe related genres. The first-person novel is most frequently compared with shishōsetsu, a tradition Satō Haruo established in 1925 with his broadcast essay "Ihhi-roman no koto."[97] While Satō assumed that the first-person novel (*Ich-Roman*) and shishōsetsu were identical, Kume Masao stated in "Watakushishōsetsu to shinkyō shōsetsu" (1925) that the term is not a translation of the German but rather refers to an autobiographical novel.[98] In general there is great confusion in shishōsetsu research as far as the term is concerned,[99] which, as *ihhi-roman* even found its way into the *Kōjien*, with the explanation that it is formally similar to the Japanese shishōsetsu. The dictionary of foreign words, *Kadokawa gairaigo jiten*, in turn defines the term as a "novel written in autobiographical form and in the first person" and refers to Maedakō Hiroichirō (1888–1957) who stated in his *Shijūnisai no genzai made* (Up to My Present Age of Forty-Two) that shishōsetsu was a translation of *Ich-Roman*. However, so far as I know, Mori Ōgai was the first person who used the term in Japan in connection with his short story "Maihime."[100]

We have by no means reached a final position concerning the matter of the genre. It is significant, however, that the numerous references to the first-person novel in various studies[101] are based on a widely varying understanding of this genre. For this reason, care should be taken with the translations of *shishōsetsu* found in non-Japanese studies, since behind "I-novel," *Ich-Roman*, "private novel," "autobiographical novel," and others there may either be a reference, however well-founded or otherwise, to a European genre or simply to the translation of the Japanese term.

In my view, contrasting shishōsetsu with other genres, whether with the *Ich-Roman* for which Satō Kōichi supplies examples from *Simplicissimus* to *The Tin Drum*,[102] with the *roman personnel* (Shirai Kōji, "Roman perusoneru ni tsuite"), with the Japanese (Hasegawa Izumi, "Shishōsetsu to jiden bungaku") or the English autobiography (Nishimura Kōji, "Jiden bungaku: Igirisu no baai") or even the comparison with Michel Leiris (Okaya Kōji, "Misheru Rerisu no 'watakushi'") functions as a substitute, albeit an unsatisfactory one, for an attempt at an operational definition of shishōsetsu. Remarkably, such an attempt has never been undertaken until now. In view of the ample body of secondary literature on shishōsetsu, the lack of even a single work devoted to a definition of the term is remarkable. There is no lack, on the other hand, of hasty characterizations of the genre which, together with the divergences between them, will be examined in Part Three. Certainly there could be no more pressing proof of the state and character of shishōsetsu research than the fact that a definition is still lacking.

This survey will conclude with two exemplary problems that characterize shishōsetsu research and with it Japanese literary studies. One of these deals with a use of language that differs considerably from Western scholarly discourse.

I have already spoken of an astonishing "range" of expressions for identical content in connection with Japanese literary texts.[103] The same is true for expository texts of the kind found in shishōsetsu research. Terms rich in association and "iridescent" are highly popular, while it is often not easy to make out precisely what they mean. Instead of serving to give the most precise definition possible of the subject under analysis these "creative" words attract the reader's attention to themselves—quite in the interests of their makers—that is, the criticism itself becomes a work of art characterized by self-reflection.[104]

One example of this tendency that is prevalent in Japanese literary studies as a whole is the use of the term *mu* or *mushi* in connection with shishōsetsu. *Mu* as a "negation" of the "I" (*shi*) arouses religious associations in the sense of "selflessness," which are at most vaguely discernible in the following example.

In Takahashi Hideo's essay on "The *Mushi* of Shishōsetsu"[105] the sublating (*shiyō*) of the "I" to a paradoxical exaggeration is possible on the one hand;[106] on the other he means that "the 'I' ceases being 'I' and dies by returning to nature or being absorbed by tradition."[107] What is meant by "I," "nature," "tradition," or "die" remains unclear, but the brilliance of this powerful expression suppresses the question of its meaning. The more esoteric Takahashi's style (largely untranslatable for long passages) becomes, the more suspicious one becomes that a banal content is being presented in metaphoric excess and alien form in order to deceive the reader with complex-sounding expressions.

Yamagata Hiroshi ("Shishōsetsu ni okeru 'watakushi' no ichi") works on an incomparably more scholarly level, yet he is also not prepared to do without the term *mu,* so rich in associations. According to his view the "I" is merely "a form of giving the work reality, the point of view of the writing narrator (*sakusha*),[108] the *mu* that originates in the act of writing and is born anew in the act of reading."[109]

Apart from Takahashi's two interpretations and this "non-I" in the sense of fiction, there is a further version presented to us by Kawasaki Chōtarō. In connection with a work written from the point of view of a woman, he speaks of the necessity of "making the I into a *mu.*"[110] Probably this means only getting inside another person and the various implications that raises.[111]

The knowledge gained from puzzling over vocabulary that remains estranged from the context bears no sensible relation to the degree of interpretation required. The use of one and the same lexeme to refer to different "contents"—it would also be possible to demonstrate the unusually large variety of signifiers or their combination for a single signified[112]—is only a small example of the tendency to "literary" vague language, which can be observed in terms specific to literary studies.[113]

The second problem concerns the argumentation, its criteria, and implied objectives. Attention has already been drawn to the shishōsetsu character of the research,[114] that is, the dominant interest in biographical detail and the extensive identification of the critic with his subject have been shown to be the logic inherent to shishōsetsu, which has completely penetrated Japanese literary and artistic theory. It could also be expressed the other way round, as we try to do in anticipation of the insights to be gained in Part Three: Central theoretical postulates with a long tradition live on in shishōsetsu theory in their purest, most developed form. The "innovation as renovation" pattern[115] is consequently valid for artistic theory and criticism.

The most important consideration of this mode of observation is noting the work and the life of a writer in relation to one another, in order to deduce the importance and quality of the work from the writer's attitudes—a moralizing approach that emphasizes sincerity and serious effort but not the work itself as the central criterion of "intellectual literary" evaluation. Evaluation is consequently the real concern of this discipline.

The extent to which Japanese literary studies are shaped by this attitude can be indicated by one example that is typical of many. In his essay on "The Metaphysics of Shishōsetsu," Oketani criticized the literary specialist Nakamura Mitsuo and accused him of, amongst other things, blasphemy in a matter that had nothing to do with the subject of shishōsetsu.[116] Finally he played the shishōsetsu author Kasai Zenzō off against Nakamura, since he could "no longer suppress his annoyance":[117] "However foolish and limited in his attitudes a shishōsetsu writer may be, he has the right to maintain that he has come much closer to the real roots of literature and philosophy (*shisō*) than such a study (*hihyō*) even if it is well-versed in modern European and Japanese literary history and even if a literary-historical system has grown from it as the result of detailed comparative evidence of this literary philosophy."[118] Not only are the literary discourse and the metadiscourse placed on the same level here, the agitated critic also leaves his tertiary level of argument to join them. Shishōsetsu discourse and metadiscourse are hopelessly entangled in the research. Oketani, who at the end of his essay has to admit that "without wanting to" he has deviated from the subject he set himself, the "metaphysics of shishōsetsu" to the "metaphysics of shishōsetsu research"[119]—so that the metaphysics got lost early on the way—nevertheless remains quite within the limits of what is customary for a type of literary study that insists on the artistic character of its products.[120] Seen in this way, the statement by Kobayashi Hideo in the introduction to this study (every new discussion of shishōsetsu means a further complication of the problem) proves to be accurate.[121] Under existing conditions, the constantly increasing number of works on shishōsetsu can only be considered as impedimenta, as long as they do not reflect the central problem of Japanese literary studies hidden in the consciously postulated or even implied artistic character and which can be reduced to the following formula in the words of Karl Eimermacher: "Speaking with increased understanding is possible only . . . to the extent that the language form used is not identical or not identical in character with the form of language which it is intended to discuss."[122]

RECENT TRENDS IN SHISHŌSETSU RESEARCH, 1979–1988

In literary research, one decade may or may not be a long time. Some fields develop only slowly or even stagnate, while, in others, scholarly activities are stimulated to leap forward. It seems that shishōsetsu research in and outside Japan has gained a fresh impetus recently and, interestingly enough, the beginning of this new phase coincides with the time when the present study was first completed. Thus, in retrospect it is in itself part of the whole movement. A survey of studies written simultaneously and afterwards will serve to give us a picture of the direction shishōsetsu research is now taking and will also provide a setting into which to integrate the present contribution. Questions raised but not answered, or questions not even posed in this study, may be pursued elsewhere once the field of critical activity has been delineated. Needless to say, this survey also updates and rounds off the research report in the preceding sections, which may give initial orientation to future students and researchers in the field.[123] The Appendix to the Bibliography of this study not only lists these recent materials but also gives earlier materials not known or inaccessible to the author.[124] It should be consulted for the bibliographical data of all new titles mentioned in this section.

The first title to be introduced here deals with the wider framework of our topic: Janet Walker's *The Japanese Novel of the Meiji Period and the Ideal of Individualism* (1979) places the literary development in the beginning of the twentieth century in a worldwide context by comparing the emergence of the "modern Japanese subjective novel" with analogous trends in the West and analyzing the influence of European models such as the *roman personnel*. Walker's study is also important for her observations on the development of the personality model as reflected in Japanese literature, from the "Buddhist mode of seeing the individual" emphasizing "the interpretation of karma as fate, an external force to which the individual can only submit" (p. 117) via several stages to the shishōsetsu, which she sees as "marking the entrance into Japanese culture of a modern morality based on the individual." She convincingly states her case by describing the process of defining the self in modern Japanese prose works from Futabatei's *Ukigumo* and Tōkoku's ideal of the inner life down to Katai's "Futon" and Tōson's works, to which she devotes the second part of her book. *Hakai* is characterized as "A Novel of the Inner Life"; thus, the aspect of social criticism is heavily outweighed by a search for self-definition. Tōson's *Shinsei*, treated as "A Novel of Confession" in even greater detail, reveals, among other aspects, parallels between this author and Strindberg and expounds Rousseau's influence, but Walker also observes that "the concept of feeling that dominates the I-novel is closer to the traditional *aware*, a process of experiencing the unity of events and their perceiver, than to Rousseau's *sentiment*, a self-assertive, aggressive process of psychological analysis."[125]

Hasumi Shigehiko's "Reading Shishōsetsu" (1979) is a highly idiosyncratic essay on three shishōsetsu authors—Shiga Naoya, Fujieda Shizuo, and Yasuoka Shōtarō, whose works are subjected to a close textual reading as opposed to the biographic approach so widespread in shishōsetsu research. Being a scholar of French literature, Hasumi is concerned with the "dalliance of the group of words" that form the text from which the "writer" (*sakka*) emerges as a surface phenomenon of the work (*hyōsōtekina kotai*, p. 241) to be distinguished from the author as a real person. Hasumi's approach and terminology bear testimony to his orientation along the lines of recent French criticism, which is apt to give a new stimulus to Japanese research. On the other hand, Hasumi seems in places too infatuated with his style, his "surface form," so to speak, and might therefore in the end betray the goal of demonstrating a new approach for the attractiveness of a personal diction with some magical qualities.

The next year brought another book on shishōsetsu. Katsuyama Isao's *Research on Taishō Watakushishōsetsu* (1980) assembles a number of contributions published earlier and referred to above. That Katsuyama chose to collect them in a book and found a publisher for them as late as 1980 can be interpreted as a further sign of a newly arisen public interest in the subject.

To the general reading public, an anthology of famous shishōsetsu (*Shishōsetsu meisakusen*) edited by the Japan PEN club and selected by Nakamura Mitsuo in 1980 signals a revaluation of the genre. The volume contains twenty-six works from Tayama Katai's "Shōjobyō," published only a few months before "Futon," to "Sakana-uchi" by Tanaka Komimasa, 1978. Regrettably, Nakamura does not explain his choice nor the arrangement, which is neither strictly chronological nor thematic but seems to orient itself, with some exceptions, along the birth dates of the authors. The volume features, however, a talk with the writer Minakami Tsutomu on the "Genealogy of Shishōsetsu" ("Shishōsetsu no keifu").

In a series of studies, Saeki Shōichi has drawn attention to the Japanese autobiography in the context of world literature. Saeki deals with Japanese as well as with Western works, and although the diction in and about his studies bears resemblance to a discussion of shishōsetsu, he clearly sets his subject off from shishōsetsu in the sense that it is treated here. In relation to questions raised in this study, Saeki's books can serve as a valuable guide in contrasting studies, distinguishing shishōsetsu from a neighboring, and partly overlapping, genre. His most recent monograph on the subject, dealing with the "Century of Autobiography" (*Jiden no seiki*, 1985), also discusses Kobayashi Hideo's "Watakushishōsetsuron," and, like Kobayashi, Saeki takes the liberty of applying the term to non-Japanese literature as well. Thus, he introduces Constant's *Adolphe* as a "strange sort of 'shishōsetsu'" (*kimyōna "watakushishōsetsu*," pp. 50ff.).

Ōmori Sumio, in *Watakushishōsetsu sakka kenkyū* (1982), presents a collection of articles on shishōsetsu writers from Chikamatsu Shūkō down to Kawasaki Chōtarō and Kō Haruto (b. 1906), the results of ten years of research which took as its starting point a study of Kasai Zenzō. Ōmori provides us with carefully documented investigations of the relationship between works and biographies and rounds off his study with a documentation on two pertinent journals, *Jūsannin* (November 1919–December 1921) and *Kin to gin* (April–June 1920), so-called *dōjin zasshi* edited by Makino Shin'ichi and others.

The Yūseidō series of research materials on Japanese literature (*Nihon bungaku kenkyū shiryō sōsho*) featured a volume under the title *Shishōsetsu* in 1983. Its topic, however, is not so much the genre itself but a number of writers tacitly understood to represent the genre such as Hirotsu Kazuo, Uno Kōji, Kasai Zenzō, and Kamura Isota. Containing twenty-nine contributions on these authors previously published elsewhere and representing the editors' choices of the most substantial research in the respective fields, the volume is complemented by short comments on the articles and a bibliography that lists books on shishōsetsu in general and materials concerning the four writers up to 1982.

Another indication of the new interest in the shishōsetsu is the reprinting of Yamamoto Kenkichi's by now classical study on shishōsetsu writers, first published in 1943, again in 1952, and then, in an expanded version, in 1966. The 1983 version is identical with the 1966 but also contains a commentary ("Kaisetsu") by Takahashi Hideo, who stresses Yamamoto's self-confessed humility towards the respective authors. A critic, in Yamamoto's eyes, has no voice of his own but melds his sensibilities with his object, that is the author, in such a way that the object itself determines the approach as well as the language of criticism. The seamless identification of the critic with the author, or, in Takahashi's words that borrow a metaphor from Yamamoto himself, the act of writing by "dipping one's pen into the writer's inkpot" leads to that "selfless" state of mind (*mushi*) in which "understanding" (*rikai*) becomes possible.[126]

Whereas Yamamoto Kenkichi represents the traditional and orthodox approach to shishōsetsu, Ishizaka Mikimasa, with his metacritical stance, is a totally new kind of scholar in the field. In a series of articles published between 1981 and 1985, later rewritten and expanded for book publication, he addresses himself to the *Theory of the Shishōsetsu* (1985). In much the same fashion as this study, but in a more thoroughgoing and sophisticated manner, he analyzes what have been termed "classics" of shishōsetsu research here such as the standard works by Itō Sei, Hirano Ken, or Nakamura Mitsuo. His carefully documented inquiry into the theoretical premises and concepts abounds with stimulating observations, and his discussion of the characteristics of shishōsetsu, contrasting it with autobiography, I-novel, *roman personnel* and other related genres, as well as his chapter on the origins and conditions of formation of shishōsetsu profit from his wide knowledge of European scholarship. Ishizaka appears to be an outsider in Japanese literary research which, as he himself remarks in his Postscript, is mainly occupied with positivist studies and does not value theoretical reflection. In his opinion, however, such reflection is a prerequisite for literary studies as an autonomous science.[127] In an appendix the author gives short analytical surveys of books on shishōsetsu by the following authors: Kobayashi Hideo, Yazaki Dan, Yamamoto Kenkichi, Fukuda Tsuneari, Itō Sei, Nakamura Mitsuo, Hirano Ken, Nishida Masayoshi, Matsubara Shin'ichi, Takahashi Hideo, Aeba Takao, Katsuyama Isao, and Ōmori Sumio. It is a very helpful source of information for all future researchers in the field.

Almost half of the fourteen major studies on shishōsetsu since 1935—thirteen listed by Ishizaka plus his own book—appeared since 1979. This alone is indication of a keen interest in the phenomenon in contemporary Japanese scholarship. What could be the reason for this new development? One condition was certainly the generational change in academic society, the abdication of the towering father-figures and authors of "classical" studies, a change marked most visibly by Kobayashi Hideo's death in 1983. At the same time, the interested observer of literary studies in Japan may observe a revaluation of research subjects within the discipline that lends higher prestige to studies concerned with relatively new phenomena which, together with an increased openness towards new topics and methods, might have helped to stimulate work on shishōsetsu. (This observation can be substantiated by an analysis of the themes and special issues of representative journals in the field, to suggest only one example.)

As an extraliterary factor, the age-old quest for Japan's national identify, posed with new vigor in the early 1970s, had the side effect of awaking new interest in those cultural phenomena reputed to embody "typically Japanese" features. It is no wonder, then, that a new generation of scholars, relatively unaffected by the ideological or ideological-critical damnation of the genre prevalent in the immediate postwar period, should rediscover shishōsetsu as a topic worthy of detailed inquiry.

Last but not least, the "stubborn persistence of a much-abused genre," as I have described it elsewhere, underlined by many a critic's statements that the genre experiences a new kind of boom among writers and readers (cf. Saeki Shōichi et al., "Shishōsetsu," 1980 and others) is apt to stimulate new research.

But how about the West? Two main tendencies support, as I see it, the new interest in shishōsetsu research. One is the challenge to conventional Japanology by turning to those notoriously "Japanese" authors and works reputed to be difficult to access for their very "Japaneseness," and of which shishōsetsu literature formed the core. The late 1970s and early 1980s therefore have seen the publication of many a study or translation into a Western language, from Edwin McClellan's translation of Shiga's *An'ya kōro* as *A Dark Night's Passing* (1976) or William F. Sibley's *The Shiga Hero* (1979) to studies and translations of Kajii Motojirō, Dazai Osamu, or Shimao Toshio. Not seldom do we find a combination of both—a selection of representative works in translation combined with introductions and interpretive comments, such as Kathryn Sparling's book on Shimao Toshio (1985). Christine Kodama de Larroche renders eight stories by Kajii Motojirō into French and gives an introduction into the "world" of this writer by focusing on objects, the use of scenery, animals, and human beings, without, however, referring to any other scholarship (1987).

What Phyllis I. Lyons in her study of *The Saga of Dazai Osamu* (1985) presents us with is Dazai Osamu's life journey, seen through "the literary character he made of himself" (p. 2). Her approach is somewhat similar to Sibley's reconstruction of Shiga's "surrogate self," as he calls it, in the aforementioned study of 1979, but Janet Walker in her review of Lyons's book aptly points out that, while Sibley "uses conventional, orthodox Freudian 'constructs' to 'partially reconstruct each story' in the development of what he calls the 'myth Shiga created around his Protean hero,'"[128] Lyons's approach could be termed "ethno-psychological." To Lyons, Dazai was "archetypically Japanese" (p. 2), and by analyzing Dazai's attempt at coming to terms with his personal history and his problems through a series of stories which make up the Osamu Saga and by translating seven of them into English, she not only invites Western readers "to feel what it is to be Japanese" (p. 2), but also discloses innumerable insights into the production and reception of shishōsetsu. In an earlier essay, Lyons addresses herself more exclusively to the functioning of Dazai's texts, which establish him as an "observant scapegoat."[129] The "affective results" of Dazai's "narrative program," as she sketches them here, can be studied in detail in her 1985 publication.

Stephen Wechselblatt's dissertation focuses on six stories by Kajii Motojirō, translated by him into English; while he discusses problems of translation, he also highlights characteristic features of shishōsetsu texts. For example, he describes Kajii's stories as "performances in which self-revelation and self-concealment work hand in hand," and analyzes how the author works to "maximize reader empathy."[130] The author's "lack of interest in temporal perspective," with the typical shishōsetsu's "denial of the author/narrator and the narrator/protagonist distinctions" is another focus of his concern (p. 164).

Wechselblatt's approach also suggests the other trend in the study of

Japanese literature which worked as a stimulus to shishōsetsu research. It is the recent interest in narratology associated with scholars like Tzvetan Todorov, Gérard Genette, S.-Y. Kuroda, Ann Banfield, and others. On one hand, the challenge to apply this approach to the analysis of Japanese texts was accepted in regard to Heian literature,[131] but the impetus also affected the studies of modern literature. Representative of this are two dissertations. Narae G. Mochizuki's literary and linguistic analysis of point of view in modern Japanese narratives (1986) shows, on the basis of an analysis of forty randomly selected narratives, that the point of view, because of specific linguistic features of Japanese, is predominantly the speaker's. Thus, "the subjectivity embedded in Japanese makes speakerless narratorless sentences impossible" (p. 54) and accounts for the subjective character of Japanese narratives.[132] The value of this approach for our understanding of the nature of shishōsetsu is obvious and becomes even clearer in another study, Barbara Mito Reed's dissertation "Language, Narrative Structure, and the Shōsetsu" (1985). Her systematic treatment illuminates the interplay of Japanese sentence structure and the narrative mode, which offers very helpful clues; for example, she demonstrates, via an analysis of works by Chikamatsu Shūkō, typical examples of shishōsetsu, the temporal flexibility of the Japanese, the fusion of the narrated time and time of narration, and of the psychology of the protagonist and the narrator.[133] She concludes that "the temporal focus is oriented whenever possible to the experiencing moment itself. This shows that the narrator's interest does not lie in presenting any change or development between his past and present selves.... By choosing to dwell almost wholly on the protagonist's emotional perception of the events, the author shows that the artistic objective of the stories is not to explicate any 'whys' or 'wherefores,' but to present the emotional essence of the events in the manner deemed most moving and immediate" (p. 76). Many of the observations on the character of shishōsetsu in the following parts of this study thus find their corroboration on the basis of this narrational approach.

Given the fruitfulness of this approach, one expects its application within a larger study devoted exclusively to shishōsetsu, as is the case with Edward Fowler's *The Rhetoric of Confession* (1988). The book is based on his 1981 dissertation on "Fiction and Autobiography in the Modern Japanese Novel," which treats, in part 1, "The Watakushi shōsetsu: Its Intellectual and Literary Heritage," and introduces, in part 2, "The Dilemma of Confession: Three Approaches to Experience," discussing the relationship of Chikamatsu Shūkō, Shiga Naoya, and Kasai

Zenzō to their works. The study concludes with English translations of four representative texts. The 1988 book version was rewritten and expanded considerably and claims to be a comprehensive introduction to shishōsetsu. In the first part, Fowler sketches the literary and intellectual tradition in which shishōsetsu seems to be rooted. This includes the attempt to construct a "native taxonomy," as undertaken by Masao Miyoshi (1983) in combination with the narratological approach mentioned above. Fowler thus stresses the closeness of the shishōsetsu to the *shōsetsu* form, which is marked, according to Miyoshi, "by aspect and the first person," while the Western prose narrative is characterized by the past tense and the third person.[134] In a section added to the study later, Fowler traces the discussion of shishōsetsu and the literary development which led to its formation in part 2, "The Rise of a Form." The most original part of this section is a look at the *bundan,* the close-knit, sectarian community of writers whose platform was the literary magazines. Part 3, similarly amended and extended, explores, in a combination of narrational and biographical study, the work and life of three paradigmatic shishōsetsu authors.[135]

While the 1988 version of Fowler's study approaches the scope and intent of the present book, it does have its own focus, the narrational delineation of shishōsetsu characteristics and their basic congruence with modern Japanese prose literature. This, however, poses the problem of how to set the shishōsetsu off as a distinctive genre; that necessity is lost in Fowler's eagerness to "collapse the perceived distinctions between *shōsetsu* and shishōsetsu" (p. ix). What permits us to speak of a distinct shishōsetsu pattern in spite of its closeness to the overall prose form in modern Japanese literature will, however, have to be made clear; otherwise we cannot insist on isolating shishōsetsu from *shōsetsu.* (Chapter 14 of the present study addresses these questions in depth.)

There is, however, another aspect to the problem that deserves to be considered here. Apart from the described aporia in maintaining that shishōsetsu "not be distinguished qualitatively from *shōsetsu,*" we should ask ourselves whether it would be better to speak of shishōsetsu "as a form rather than as a genre or a subgenre" (p. xxvii), a proposal also made by Richard Bowring in his review of the present book: "It could be that the shishōsetsu is not a genre at all, but rather the dominant mode of reading in modern Japan."[136] There is much to be said for this interpretation, but the task remains the same whether we speak of shishōsetsu as genre or a form or mode: We will have to show, by constructing or reconstructing, in the words of Miyoshi, a "native taxonomy," what causes the shishōsetsu to be perceived as shishōsetsu. The "mode of reading," on the other hand, could well form one important criterion or distinctive mark within the "native taxonomy" or conceptual network which certainly works along lines other than Western genre distinctions. The term *genre*, therefore, should be understood as a heuristic device in this context, for, so long as we lack operational definitions of other modern Japanese prose genres, we cannot finally decide what to call "genre," "subgenre," or "supragenre." The fact, though, that shishōsetsu is perceived throughout as a definite form conventionally identified with a genre should justify our adherence to this heuristic classification. It still seems too early for the final word on this matter.

One more observation concerning the use of the term should be added. In the course of a reawakened interest and a less critical, nonideological attitude towards shishōsetsu, one can register a tendency to apply the term in retrospect, for example, when dealing with Higuchi Ichiyō's literature.[137]

In contemporary Japanese criticism, shishōsetsu remains an important category, a category moreover that is regaining positive associations. One notes the increasing number of references to shishōsetsu when leafing through the annual editions of *Bungei nenkan,* the *Literary Yearbook*'s documentation of representative critiques, in which the discussion of the shishōsetsu quality of a certain work is a fixed inclusion. The same holds true for contemporary literary and cultural historiography, be it Shinoda Hajime who, in an admittedly critical vein, recurs again and again to shishōsetsu in his study of the contemporary novel (1980) or Isoda Kōichi (*Sengoshi no kūkan,* 1983), who regards the reappraisal of shishōsetsu as a reaction towards living conditions in a modern industrial society. While Isoda insists that it is the anachronistic appeal of shishōsetsu necessitating a traditional setting that sets natural limits to its present development, other critics, such as Kitada Reiichirō ("Hachijū nendai no bungaku o kangaeru," 1980), predict that it is precisely the closed, *sakoku* mentality that makes shishōsetsu the genre of the 1980s, a view shared by Nakajima Makoto ("Gendai bungaku no hitotsu no hōkō," 1980), who maintains that shishōsetsu forms the main current in the literary scene of that decade. The prognosis does seem to have materialized to a certain degree if we look at the present literary scene and the winners of prestigious prizes. Writers not only seem obliged to refute (or to accept) an alleged shishōsetsu character of their works such as Ōe Kenzaburō, the reception of whose works in the 1980s got under the spell of shishōsetsu reading,[138] but they even confess that writing shishōsetsu is the best way to get a literary award: "You hardly have a chance if it is not shishōsetsu style, I was admonished," says an overjoyed winner of the Naoki prize in 1983.[139]

Whatever level we look at—literary production, Japanese criticism, or literary scholarship in Japan or in the West—shishōsetsu as a literary as well as a cultural phenomenon has entered our consciousness during the 1980s more forcefully than ever before.

---

1. Terada, p. 99.
2. Cf. Chapter 11.
3. In the section "Shinkyō shōsetsu ronsō," pp. 172–184.
4. On the term *junbungaku* see below and Chapter 11.
5. In the section "Junbungaku ronsō no imi," pp. 317–330, among others.
6. One example typical of many is Senuma Shigeki, "Shishōsetsuron no keifu."
7. Nakamura Mitsuo, *Nihon no gendai shōsetsu*, p. 81. More details on the problematic of the terminology in I.H.-K., "Theoriedefizit und Wertungswut."
8. Terada, pp. 99f.
9. Satō Etsuko, "Kobayashi Hideo ni okeru 'Shiga Naoya,'" pp. 18f.
10. Cf. "Hirano Ken: *Geijutsu to jisseikatsu*" (Chapter 8).
11. *Shishōsetsuteki hōhō ni motozuku shishōsetsuron,* Yamagata Hiroshi, "Shishōsetsu ni okeru 'watakushi' no ichi," p. 70.
12. Also cf. on this I.H.-K. "Kritische Bemerkungen," p. 57.
13. While e.g. Hirano Ken praises Sata Ineko's (b. 1904) story "Kurenai" (Scarlet, 1939), Yoshida Seiichi criticizes the fact that she fails to describe how well her second husband Kubokawa Tsurujirō cared for her and that he even wiped her face for her and warmed her feet; cf. Yoshida Seiichi et al., "Shishōsetsu no honshitsu to mondaiten," p. 71.

    A second example from another discussion: Yasuoka Shōtarō relates that Kasai Zenzō claimed in one of his works that a friend had killed the turtle over the loss of which his children were very upset—but this, Yasuoka goes on to claim, did not correspond to the facts, cf. Kojima Nobuo et al., "Bungaku ni okeru 'watakushi' to wa nani ka," p. 238. Such stories could be dismissed as meaningless talk if they did not fulfill an important function in the manner of reception, molded by shishōsetsu.
14. On the term *riariti* cf. also "Inter- and Extratextual References to Heighten the *Riariti*" (Chapter 16).
15. However creditable Yamagata's attempt to develop a new explanatory model, it seems to me that his categories are ultimately meaningless, since he completely ignores the specific context of reception without which shishōsetsu cannot be considered.
16. In the section "Shizenshugi bungaku to genjitsushugi no bungaku," pp. 92–125.
17. In the section "Nihon shizenshugi to gendai," pp. 3–11.
18. In the section "Sengo no shishōsetsu," pp. 424–438.
19. In the section "Shishōstsu no dōkō," pp. 225–264.
20. Torii Kunio, "Senzen shishōsetsu to no renzoku to danzetsu," p. 85.
21. Ibid., p. 87.
22. Ibid., p. 86.

23. Morikawa Tatsuya, "Shishōsetsu hōhōka no mondai."
24. Miyoshi Yukio, *Nihon bungaku no kindai to hankindai,* p. 253. In a different context ("Dazai Osamu: Hito to bungaku," p. 7) Miyoshi sets the beginning of this formalization as early as the shishōsetsu by Itō Sei.
25. Torii, "Senzen shishōsetsu," p. 86. Satō Yasumasa "Shishōsetsu no keifu," p. 95, similarly interprets the difference between Shiga Naoya and Ogawa Kunio (b. 1927), a writer of the "introverted generation" (*naikō no sedai*).
26. In his *Nihon bungaku no kindai to hankindai,* Miyoshi Yukio makes this point in connection with Shiga Naoya and Shiga criticism. Discussing a statement by Hirano Ken on Shiga, he concedes that it is in fact the personality of the shishōsetsu writer positioned in the center of the work which imprints the work "in all directions" (p. 249). The very principle of shishōsetsu, he writes, lies in the "strong impression of the writer's individuality" which, for lack of other structural features, forms its unifying center in equating "real life" and literature (*jisseikatsu to jigen o hitoshiku shite,* p. 252f.).
27. Matsumoto Tsuruo, "Bungaku, Shishōsetsu to jiko shōshitsu no jidai," pp. 233f.
28. Ibid.
29. I shall discuss the importance of the market for Japanese literary studies in a separate essay in more detail.
30. The rule holds only for writers of the *junbungaku,* however, since in this case the buyers of novels are largely identical with those of the secondary literature. In the case of *taishū bungaku* the potential buyers diverge.
31. Terada, p. 126.
32. Ibid., p. 127.
33. Ibid., p. 126.
34. Ibid., p. 103.
35. Cf. Chapter 7.
36. Compare, for example, the number of references in Miyoshi Yukio, *Nihon kindai bungaku kenkyū hikkei* (Vademecum of Modern Japanese Literary Studies).
37. Cf. "Shiga Naoya: 'Wakai'" and "Dazai Osamu: *Ningen shikkaku*" (Chapter 16) for more details.
38. Cf. Chapter 14.
39. Cf. Chapter 6.
40. Terada, pp. 126f.
41. On Kasai cf. also "Kasai Zenzō: 'Ko o tsurete'" (Chapter 16).
42. Cf. "Itō Sei: *Shōsetsu no hōhō*" (Chapter 8).
43. Hirano Ken in *NBS,* keyword "Watakushishōsetsu," p. 1248. This article is also included in his collection of essays, *Junbungaku ronsō igo* (Since the Argument about Pure Literature).
44. Cf. ibid.
45. Cf. Hirano Ken, *Geijutsu to jisseikatsu,* p. 25.
46. Cf. Tsuruta Kin'ya, "Akutagawa Ryūnosuke and I-Novelists," p. 26.
47. Cf. ibid., pp. 26f.
48. Yamamoto Kenkichi, *Watakushishōsetsu sakkaron,* p. 27 and Yamamoto, "Shishōsetsu sakkatachi," pp. 243f.
49. Cf. also Howard Hibbett, "Introspective Techniques in Modern Japanese Fiction," pp. 6ff. on the question of Tsuruta's discussion. On Akutagawa cf. "Kikuchi Kan: 'Tomo to tomo to no aida'" (Chapter 16).
50. Cf. Yamamoto, *Watakushishōsetsu,* p. 90.
51. Cf. ibid., p. 92.
52. Ibid., p. 90.
53. For more details of Akutagawa's admiration of Shiga, see "Self-Revelation as a Moral Act" (Chapter 18).

54. Akiyama Shun, "Shiga Naoya no 'watakushi' ni tsuite," p. 67. This attribution is important since it characterizes a position opposed to shishōsetsu.
55. Miyoshi Yukio, *Sakuhinron no kokoromi,* pp. 129f.
56. Cf. Hirano, *Geijutsu to jisseikatsu,* p. 35.
57. Cf. Sasaki, pp. 215ff., 223f.
58. Cf. William Sibley, "The Shiga Hero," p. 24. The study, slightly modified, has now been published as a book (*The Shiga Hero*). My review of this publication contains a more detailed commentary.
59. Ibid., p. 158.
60. Thus it would be easy to draw parallels between the discussion on the psycho-hygienic function of shishōsetsu for the author (cf., "'Refuge for the Heart' and 'Rescue'" in Chapter 18) and Sibley's examples for "intuitive psychoanalysis" in Shiga.
61. Cf. ibid., p. 162. My interpretation of this observation is to be found in "Irrationalism and Fatalism" (Chapter 20).
62. Cf. Hirano, *Geijutsu to jisseikatsu,* p. 38.
63. Takahashi, pp. 179–195; for more detail see "Dazai Osamu: *Ningen shikkaku*" (Chapter 16).
64. Cf., e.g., Nakamura Mitsuo, *Nihon no gendai shōsetsu,* pp. 188ff. and Hirano in *NBS,* keyword "Watakushishōsetsu," p. 1248.
65. On Torii, "Senzen shishōsetsu," cf. also "History of Shishōsetsu and of Shishōsetsu Theory" in this chapter.
66. Cf. Usui, *Shōsetsu no ajiwaikata,* pp. 163ff., Takahashi, pp. 196ff. and Aeba, *Hihyō to hyōgen,* pp. 373–412.
67. For more detail, cf. "Miura Tetsuo: 'Shinobugawa'" (Chapter 16). On Morikawa cf. "History of Shishōsetsu and of Shishōsetsu Theory" in this chapter.
68. Cf. Matsumoto Tsuruo, "Kindai bungei yōshiki nōto (1)," pp. 42f. Matsumoto's original attempt to categorize the work systematically from the point of view of the development of the genre also leads to more penetrating questions, whereby he orientates himself around European concepts such as Jauß's reception aesthetic and the studies by Albert Thibaudet and Marthe Robert. Nevertheless, he fails in the convincing application of concepts such as "horizon of expectations" (pp. 34ff.) and "parodization" (p. 43)—he would need a more detailed discussion for this—and, in spite of the advanced formulation of the problem, his description of the development of the genre remains within well-known limits, since it largely exhausts itself in reporting on the research "classics."
69. Cf. Odagiri Hideo, "Japanese Literature in 1979," p. 2.
70. *Bonnō,* originally a Buddhist term.
71. Matsubara, p. 216. My italics.
72. Cf., e.g., ibid., pp. 14, 96, 163, 228, 232, 247.
73. For more detail on this cf. I.H.-K., "Theoriedefizit und Wertungswut."
74. *NBS,* keyword "Yamamoto Kenkichi," p. 1190.
75. These are the chapters on Kanbayashi Akatsuki, Tanaka Hidemitsu, and Hara Tamiki. A new edition of *Watakushishōsetsu sakkaron* has since been announced by the publishers.
76. However, cf. the reservations expressed in Chapter 7 (point 3).
77. Ara, p. 30.
78. Cf. Takeuchi Yoshimi, "Shishōsetsu ni tsuite," p. 68.
79. In the section "Kindaiteki jiga to kojinshugi," pp. 38–47.
80. Cf. in particular the title essay of his book, "Criticism and Expression—'I' in Modern Japanese Literature," pp. 413–455.
81. Cf. in particular Chapter 21. On Dōke Tadamichi cf. also "Sanctioned Voyeurism" (Chapter 18).

82. Howard Hibbett, "Introspective Techniques," p. 2.
83. Cf., e.g., Katō Shūichi, *Form, Style, Tradition,* p. 186, and Marleigh G. Ryan, "Modern Japanese Fiction," p. 264.
84. Cf., e.g., Yamamoto, *Watakushishōsetsu,* pp. 132ff. and Takahashi, pp. 17f.
85. Cf., e.g., Howard Hibbett, "The Portrait of the Artist in Japanese Fiction," p. 350, Lane, pp. 127ff. and Kikuchi Kan, *History and Trends of Modern Japanese Literature,* p. 17.
86. Cf., e.g., Stephen Kohl, "Shiga Naoya and the Literature of Experience," p. 214.
87. More on this complex of problems in "The 'Philosophy'" (Chapter 14).
88. On Yoshida and Kubota, cf. also "'Lyricism'" (Chapter 19).
89. However, cf. below and our remarks in "Kasai Zenzō: 'Ko o tsurete'" (Chapter 16).
90. Ogasawara Masaru, "Shishōsetsu no biishiki," p. 35.
91. Ibid.
92. Cf., e.g., Ōta Seiichi, "Zangemichi to shite no shishōsetsu no keifu," p. 156.
93. Cf. ibid., pp. 156ff.
94. More detail in "'Shishōsetsu's Sentimental Esoteric' and Egocentric Speech" (Chapter 16), and "The Author of Shishōsetsu" and "The Shishōsetsu Reader" (Chapter 18).
95. Karatani Yukihito, "Shishōsetsu no keifugaku," p. 121.
96. Ibid.
97. Text in *GNBR,* I, 124–128.
98. Published in 1925, text in *GNBR,* I, 108–114, here p. 109.
99. Cf., e.g., the definition in Ariyama et al., p. 107. There it is said that the *Ich-Roman* was an extremely short-lived form in the German Romantic period, a form of the novel in which the life of the author is made the subject. Simply because of the fact that it was so short-lived this genre could not be compared with shishōsetsu, which had already existed for 80 years, i.e. since the Meiji period.
100. Cf. "A Japanese First-Person Story" (Chapter 10).
101. Cf., e.g., Sasaki, pp. 212f., J. B. Power, "Shiga Naoya and the Shishōsetsu," p. 16, Tsuruta, pp. 15f. and Satō Kōichi, "Ihi romān."
102. Cf. Satō Kōichi, pp. 10, 14.
103. Cf. I.H.-K., *Mishima Yukios Roman,* p. 107.
104. Cf. Roland Posner, "Strukturalismus in der Gedichtinterpretation," p. 143.
105. Takahashi, pp. 264–286.
106. Cf. ibid., p. 273.
107. Ibid., p. 26.
108. *Sakusha* is confronted with *sakka,* the author as a real person.
109. Yamagata, p. 75.
110. Cited in Hasegawa Izumi, "Meiji Taishō Shōwa shishōsetsu sanjūgo sen," p. 90.
111. Further titles, examined after completion of this book, in which the term *mushi* appears are Aeba Takao, "'Watakushi' no fukami ni mukatte," p. 221, and *Hihyō to hyōgen,* and Saeki Shōichi et al., "Kyōdō tōgi 'Shishōsetsu,'" p. 152. Cf. also "Documents on the Human Condition" (Chapter 18) on this term.
112. Cf. I.H.-K., *Mishima Yukios Roman,* pp. 106f.
113. Examples in I.H.-K. "Innovation als Renovation."
114. Cf. "History of Shishōsetsu and of Shishōsetsu Theory" and "Shishōsetsu Authors and Works" in this chapter.
115. Cf. "Innovation as Renovation" (Chapter 3).
116. Cf. Oketani Hideaki, *Gyōshi to hōkō,* vol. I, p. 35.
117. Ibid., p. 36.
118. Ibid.
119. Ibid., p. 37.
120. Cf. I.H.-K., *Mishima Yukios Roman,* pp. 22ff., and I.H.-K., "Wissenschaft als Kunst."
121. Cf. Kobayashi Hideo, "Cartoons," p. 215.

122. Karl Eimermacher, "Zum Problem einer naturwissenschaftlichen Metasprache," p. 257.
123. Of the contributions not known or inaccessible to me until the completion of this study in early 1979, Miroslav Novák, "Watakushi shōsetsu—The Appeal of Authenticity" deserves particular mention as it had certainly been the most lengthy and thorough study of the subject in a Western language so far as well as the only definitely theoretically minded one, considering shishōsetsu "as a literary genre or style developing gradually." Novák inquires into the formative elements of the genre and presents us with sharp insights into the characteristic features and limitations of shishōsetsu. He sees the "concentration upon the experiences of the self" whereby one individual is felt to be a good representative of any other individual (p. 29) as a reflection of the changing social conditions such as the "disintegration of the old 'big' family" and speaks of a "historically (both in the literary and social sense) determined endeavour after unimpeachable frankness and faithfulness on the part of the author" (p. 40).

In spite of its relative shortness, the paper exhibits a demand for and abundance of sources, both primary and secondary, by which the author pursues issues such as affinities with other related genres or the stylistic consequences of the "presupposed and obligatory quality of authenticity" (p. 33) or the lyricism of the genre. Altogether, the study shows a sophistication in the discussion of the problem rarely found in other works of this scope. Another major contribution we have not consulted is Nishida Masayoshi, *Shishōsetsu saihakken*.
124. However, I refrain from including in this list all titles referred to in these recent studies. They naturally form another source of hitherto unidentified secondary materials.
125. Janet Walker, *The Japanese Novel of the Meiji Period*, p. 275, an observation made in accordance with Yasuoka Shōtarō.
126. Cf. Yamamoto Kenkichi, *Watakushishōsetsu sakkaron*, pp. 246, 257.
127. Cf. Ishizaka Mikimasa, *Shishōsetsu no riron*, p. 228.
128. Janet Walker, review of *The Saga of Dazai Osamu*, by Phyllis I. Lyons, p. 459.
129. Phyllis Lyons, "Art *Is* Me," p. 102.
130. Stephen Wechselblatt, "The Translator as Reader and Writer: English Versions of Japanese Short Fiction by Kajii Motojirō with a Critical Commentary" (Ph.D. dissertation, University of Iowa, 1982), p. 108.
131. Cf. Richard Hideki Okada, "Unbound Texts: Narrative Discourse in Heian Japan" (Ph.D. dissertation, University of California, Berkeley, 1985), or Amanda Mayer Stinchecum, *Narrative Voice in the Tale of Genji* (Urbana: University of Illinois, Center for East Asian and Pacific Studies, 1985).
132. A number of Mochizuki's conclusions are as bold as they are problematic, such as when she vaguely ascribes "the trend of modern Japanese literary criticism . . . to focus on the study of author rather than on the text itself" (p. 139) to the single perspective speaker's point of view in narrative.
133. Cf. her article of 1988, pp. 74ff.
134. Masao Miyoshi, "Against the Native Grain," p. 221.
135. A more detailed discussion of Fowler's book can be found in I.H.-K., "The Darkness at the Foot of the Lighthouse."
136. Richard Bowring, review of *Selbstblößungsrituale*, by Irmela Hijiya-Kirschnereit, *Bulletin of the School of Oriental and African Studies* 45, pt. 1 (1983), p. 187f., here p. 188.
137. Matsuzaka Toshio, "Ichiyō no shishōsetsusei," or Muramatsu Sadataka, "Ichiyō nikki no bungeisei."
138. Cf., e.g., Matsumoto Tōru, "Kihon no shōsetsu," p. 222, Saitō Akira, ""Ame no ki" (Rein tsurī) o kiku onnatachi' o yomu," or Edward Fowler, *The Rhetoric of Confession*, pp. 295f.
139. Kurumizawa Kōshi, see "Naoki shō e honmyō: Kurumizawa san no aku naki shūnen," *Shūkan yomiuri*, 24 July 1983, p. 28.

Part Three
Genre Theory

10 · History of the Term

The relationship between shishōsetsu theory (*shishōsetsuron*) and practice has been described by Terada Tōru in the following terms: "It must be said that until now shishōsetsu theory was not based on an observation of shishōsetsu but that there has rather been a strong tendency towards attributing all sorts of characteristics to shishōsetsu through shishōsetsu theory."[1] Strictly speaking, shishōsetsu theory can be said to have developed only after the term came into use at the beginning of the 1920s, but, as has been shown in Part One, the genre itself developed more than a decade earlier. "Futon" was a manifestation of a change in the method of production and reception of narrative literature which established a horizon of expectation of the shishōsetsu genre; the term was both coined from these expectations and at the same time influenced them. We shall, therefore, examine both the origins of the term and the ensuing literary debate around it.

To begin with, however, we shall consider the predecessors of shishōsetsu in Meiji literature. The word *predecessor* does not here refer to a line of literary precursors which led directly to shishōsetsu, but only to related terms used to categorize groups of works or individual works at the end of the nineteenth century. The terms, listed chronologically, *ichininshō shōsetsu* (first-person novel), "I novel," and *shinpenmono* (literally "self surrounding pieces"), refer to phases that remain quite discernibly distant from shishōsetsu, both in the work and its reception. However, the three steps discussed here represent a rapprochement with shishōsetsu, which, using specific examples, could be used to trace a proto-history of the genre in terms of literature and theory. At the very least, this allows shishōsetsu to be situated in a larger literary-historical framework and clarifies the relationship between different semantically related concepts.

PREDECESSORS OF SHISHŌSETSU

THE *ICHININSHŌ SHŌSETSU*

The *ichininshō shōsetsu*, the first-person novel of the middle Meiji period, is considered a type of predecessor of shishōsetsu. At first glance, it would seem that the only affinity is similar mode of narration: what else is there to connect a work such as Tōkai Sanshi's[2] *Kajin no kigū* (Strange Encounters with Beautiful Women), a so-called "political novel" (*seiji shōsetsu*), which appeared in eight parts between 1885 and 1897, with Tayama Katai's "Futon," the model of the genre?

Kajin no kigū tells the highly complicated story of various patriots and freedom fighters, in particular the Irish woman Korlen and the Spanish woman Yolanda, which is linked together by the first-person narrator who bears the same name as the author.[3] His central concern throughout is a warning against European and American imperialism, and the book is indeed thought to have become one of the most successful and influential political novels of the time.

The comparison with shishōsetsu is based upon neither the highly imaginative plot nor the author's intentions, but on the identity of the first-person narrator and author. There is, however, one further similarity apart from this purely formal aspect: Much that is reported in *Kajin no kigū* is autobiographical and is recognized as such by the reader. This makes the reaction of contemporary critics remarkable, since it introduces us to a method of reception that was to play an important part in connection with shishōsetsu.

Takada Hanpō (1860–1938), an eminent critic of the time, wrote in March 1886 in the *Chūō gakujutsu zasshi*, that the work could not be counted among normal novels (*tsūjō shōsetsu*), where "political novels" also belonged, because, "we cannot help but recognize that we are dealing here with something particularly and curiously ephemeral, a *shōsetsu* which is not one and an epos which is not one."[4] The explanation for this is, according to Takada, that primarily the author "portrays five or six characters in *Kajin no kigū*, treats them differently and allows them to speak individually, but ultimately they are nothing more than phantom [figures] of Tōkai Sanshi himself."[5]

The author, who not only addresses the reader directly through the first-person narrator, but who also apparently uses the other characters as his mouthpieces, was accused by contemporary critics of excessive subjectivism which robbed his work of the character of a *shōsetsu*. The term *shōsetsu*, introduced by Tsubouchi Shōyō in his *Shōsetsu shinzui*[6] as the translation for *novel* and *Roman* served a purpose here similar to that of the term *honkaku shōsetsu* (genuine, real novel) in the theoretical discussions of the 1920s.[7] Fiction was held to be the decisive criterion for the "genuineness" of a novel, while extensive use of autobiographical material was considered non-fictional. We shall return later to the essential question of fiction versus non-fiction in Japanese theories of the novel.[8] At this point it is important to note the following.

The autobiographical elements obvious to the reader at the time and its "subjectivity" (in the sense described above) were sufficiently significant to elicit the use of the term *watakushishōsetsu*, coined first in 1925, by the writer and essayist Kojima Masajirō (b. 1894) in connection with *Kajin no kigū*. Even though his assertion that "this novel is a rare [example] for its time of a *watakushishōsetsu*"[9] cannot be considered valid judging by current standards of scholarship, it still provides us with valuable information about the criteria used to identify shishōsetsu and about its literary proto-history, seen from the viewpoint of a contemporary witness.

A JAPANESE FIRST-PERSON STORY

In January 1890, Mori Ōgai published "Maihime" (The Dancing Girl), a short story written in the first-person narrative form.[10] The plot was based largely on the author's own experiences during a period of study in Berlin, in particular his relationship with a young woman—in "Maihime" she is called Elis[11]—who followed him to Japan when he returned home, but was persuaded to leave again by his family.[12] The framing story describes events retrospectively, from their first chance meeting until the departure of the hero, Ōta Toyotarō, who leaves the pregnant young woman behind in Berlin.

Contemporaries read this first work as a "confession" (*zange*) on the part of the hero, who records events during his return trip to Japan with repeated expressions of regret concerning his own behavior and the unhappy turn of events. In a critical analysis that appeared in February 1890 in the *Kokumin no tomo* the young critic Ishibashi Ningetsu (1866–1926) interpreted the story as portraying the conflict between love and worldly success; Ōgai criticizes the hero who decides in favor of his career because of his own weakness.[13] It is not important for us to consider here whether this interpretation is correct, just as it is unimportant for us to consider the suggestions made later concerning the individual psychological motivation of the author in writing the work—whether to relieve his own feelings of guilt or to appease his superiors who knew of his background.[14] In this respect, it is important to realize that, when it was published, "Maihime" was received not as an autobiographical document but as literary fiction, in spite of the fact it could also have been read as a roman-à-clef in places.[15] Consequently, "Maihime" is seldom considered to be a precursor of shishōsetsu in Japanese research.[16]

Ōgai's masterly treatment of the material and his stylistic skill—both of which aroused the admiration of his contemporaries—most probably account for the work's status as fiction. His archaic style and the events that take place at a distance make them suitably remote from the world of his readers to prevent them identifying with the hero. Similarly, the descriptions of life in Berlin attracts the reader's attention to the undoubtedly exotic details of a largely unknown world, so that the question typical for shishōsetsu—the truth of the autobiographical details—is of less importance.

In addition, both Ōgai and his critics emphasized the European elements in the book. For in the same edition of the magazine *Shigarami zōshi* which contained the short story, Ōgai's friend Yamaguchi Toratarō described "Maihime" as a novella and drew parallels to *Werther*, *Wilhelm Meister*, and *Clavigo*.[17] The author himself called his work a first-person novel in the style named *Tagebuch-Lyrik* (diary-poetry) by Hartmann,[18] thus acknowledging that he had drawn upon exemplary German tradition for his literary model. This meant above all that he understood the term *first-person novel* to be a descriptive category for narrative technique. Despite the risk that this understanding of the category might become confused with the term *autobiography*, as in the case of Yamaguchi mentioned above,[19] no contemporary reader seems to have gone so far as to confuse the hero with the author.

In spite of the first-person form and the autobiographical references, "Maihime" is primarily a highly stylized romantic story reminiscent in style of German short stories[20] and was therefore accepted as "fiction" rather than as the confessions of the author.

SHINPENMONO

1895 saw a step in the direction of shishōsetsu with Ozaki Kōyō's novel *Aobudō* (Black Grapes) and the reception given it. In this case, the critics noted disparagingly that the world described in the novel was too close to reality. *Aobudō* was not accepted as a *shōsetsu*, just as *Kajin no kigū* had not been.[21] The work would have to have contained "at least as much fiction as 'Maihime' in order to qualify as a *shōsetsu*."[22]

Public reaction to the work is understandable, if *Aobudō* is compared with other works of the time, since its documentary style was indeed unusual for that period. Kōyō confines himself to describing a period of nine hours, from the outbreak of acute illness in one of his pupils at 8 p.m. until the boy is taken away at 5 a.m. the next morning. The hero records, in first-person narrative,[23] the fruitless efforts of the three doctors called in succession to help, until the suspicion that the illness is cholera is confirmed; he notes the moving attempts on the part of the pupil to conceal his condition from the teacher; and he finally makes the painful discovery that his sudden awareness of fatherly feelings towards the sick boy has come too late.

Formally, the authenticity is enhanced not only by the substitution of single capital letters for personal or place names[24]—a method that became the rule in later shishōsetsu literature and continues to be used quite frequently today[25]—but also by the fact that the author appears under his own name in one place. (This, however, is not usual for shishōsetsu.) The scene in question comes towards the end of the work when one of the policemen in charge of moving the sick boy identifies the hero with the words: "But you are Master Ozaki! . . ."[26] Kōyō based his attempt to describe "facts as they are" (*jijitsu o ari no mama ni*) on European naturalism, above all on Arno Holz and his theory that art has a tendency to become nature,[27] but at that time he encountered only strong disapproval of his factuality and so turned to more fictitious subjects after *Aobudō*.

According to Yoshida Seiichi, *Aobudō* was the only work before "Futon" with such strong autobiographical elements,[28] a situation that led Ogasawara Masaru to remark that it would be considered a shishōsetsu by today's standards.[29] It is more plausible and correct to describe *Aobudō* as a typical example of a *shinpenmono*, a work of prose concerned with the author's immediate surroundings.

The trend towards producing works colored with autobiographical themes now became increasingly apparent in the writing of Tōkoku,

Doppo, and Katai. At the same time, the attitude of the critics changed, influenced by the naturalism propagated by these authors, so that the descriptions of reality that had previously been rejected as not suitable for novels now came to be considered literature's main concern.[30] The desire of the author to describe his own life, that part of reality nearest to him, grew out of this theory. Thus, in a review of Kunikida Doppo's collection of stories *Unmei* (Fate, 1906), the fact that the various first-person narrators are apparently identical with the author is no longer criticized, merely noted in a neutral tone.[31] At this point a pronounced shift to a more favorable reception of such works occurred and was evident for the first time with the appearance of "Futon."[32]

THEORETICAL PREMISES

What do we learn from all these observations about the "predecessors" of shishōsetsu?

On the basis of the examples chosen, we can see the broad outlines of a significant literary change, manifested both in the artistic product and in its reception—as evidenced in literary criticism—a change that at the same time clearly shows us the way in which art is inextricably bound up with historical and cultural movements.

Outlining those axioms in literary theory that are relevant for shishōsetsu and discernible within the reception given to its works, we are able to trace the following highly simplified line of development:

The early Meiji period was still characterized by the traditional contempt for popular narrative literature which was called *gesaku* (literally: "made in a joke") and developed in *chōnin* (town-dweller) culture. The works counted among *gesaku* usually contained elements of fantasy; they were intended to entertain and their presence could be justified by the Confucian system of thought (which was the foundation of the state) by virtue of their didactic effect in the sense of *kanzen chōaku* (promotion of virtue and chastisement of vice). This merely served to reduce further their artistic value in the eyes of the Neo-Confucians from the school of Jinsai and Sorai. *Gesaku* was categorized with *kyo*, with all its negative connotations (also *uso* or *sorago* in the sense of empty, invented, lie, fiction) while the opposite term *jitsu* (or *makoto*) as fruit, full, sincere, true, fact, and usefulness was considered in scholarly texts and poetry to be real literature.[33] This division into an elite "art" and a lower "bourgeois"[34] literature was based on the values of the samurai class and continues to exist today in the categories *junbungaku* (pure literature) and *taishū bungaku* (mass literature).

As a result of the political and cultural upheavals caused by the Meiji Restoration, new demands were made on *gesaku* literature. The general demand for "practical/useful learning" (*jitsugaku*) was met by the "political novels" (*seiji shōsetsu*) of which *Kajin no kigū*, discussed above, is an example. This work documents at the same time the ideological exploitation of literature, which can be considered as a continued pursuit of didactic objectives in the manner of the Confucian *kanzen chōaku*.

The idea that literature should be of value in itself[35] first appeared as a reaction to experiences with European culture where novels reputedly enjoyed high esteem. In *Shōsetsu shinzui* (1885–1886) the demand for the autonomy of literature was finally expressed most clearly.[36]

The revaluation of narrative literature is generally seen to result from stimuli from Europe. However, it could also be considered as a change of paradigms in Japanese literary history most clearly evident in the change of polarity of categories related to *gesaku/shōsetsu*: the "fantastic," "fictive," and "unreal" (*kyo*) no longer characterize narrative literature but rather the possibility of describing "reality" and "truth" (*jitsu*). At the same time, by taking human feelings (*ninjō*) as the central subject of this literature,[37] Tsubouchi, and others as well, continued with traditional Japanese conceptions of literature—a further example of the pattern of "innovation as renovation." In fact Tsubouchi made exactly the same demands as the Confucian philologist Motoori Norinaga (1730–1801) concerning the real purpose of literature as the description of human feelings[38] in *mono no aware*.[39] What Motoori named as an ideal of literature free from having to serve any practical purpose, using the example of *Genji monogatari* (The Tale of Genji, completed c. 1010), where spontaneous feelings are expressed as the most profound reality[40] (something he did not find in the *gesaku* literature of his own time), won acceptance in mid-Meiji literature with its demand for reality and psychological acumen in literature. Thus, "modernization" (*kindaika*) did not change the theoretical principles of art, but the validity of these principles was extended to narrative prose, an area that had previously been excluded. That the impulse for this change came from the confrontation with Europe and that non-literary factors like the development of newspaper journalism forced literature to greater realism does nothing to alter the fact that it was only this change of paradigms which made the development of modern narrative literature possible.[41] It was only because *shōsetsu* acquired the status of art and because there was basic agreement in Japanese cultural circles about the point of connection with the *jitsu* principle that it became an active field for ambitious intellectuals and ultimately a literary form representative of modern Japanese literature.

We shall now reconsider those works described as the "predecessors" of shishōsetsu. How is the criticism leveled at *Kajin no kigū* to be interpreted? It can be explained by the traditional modes of reception, which lumped the "novel" together with (conventional) *gesaku*, and which considered autobiographical elements to be foreign to the genre. *Aobudō* was rejected for the same reason.[42] "Maihime," on the other hand, contained a constellation of characters, a plot and style that bore sufficient similarity to the *gesaku*, rendering the elements of reality and the first-person form insignificant.

The decline of the plot (a major element in *gesaku*) as seen in *Aobudō*, points to a further line of development, which can be most simply described as a turn away from romances filled with action in favor of an introverted prose form limited to only a few characters and episodes. In this way, *shōsetsu* also came closer to genres that had always been accepted as belonging to higher literature and the *jitsu* principle in the traditional view, that is, diary (*nikki*) and miscellany literature (*zuihitsu*).

When *Aobudō* was published, *shōsetsu* and *nikki* were still two clearly separate fields, but they grew closer as a result of the accumulation of *shinpenmono* and as the result of the popularity of the *shizenshugi* theory, where the demands for descriptions of reality and complete sincerity—both can be derived from the *jitsu* principle—overlap.[43] This development also culminated in shishōsetsu. The resulting genre, which originated at the beginning of the twentieth century, was bound up with the national history of art and literature, not only in the way it embodied traditional poetics, but also in its subject matter, its form and descriptive repertoire, and even in the awareness of life that it expressed.[44]

THE ORIGINS OF THE TERM *WATAKUSHISHŌSETSU*

A decision had to be made right at the beginning of this book—as early as the title—about the two possible readings of the character combination of "I" and "novel." The reasons for the reading used here, *shishōsetsu*, which in my opinion characterizes the genre more accurately than *watakushishōsetsu*, were put forth in the introduction. Apart from the semantic difference, this decision was also justified by historical arguments, since, according to Inagaki Tatsurō, the term *watakushishōsetsu* was replaced by *shishōsetsu* in the Shōwa period,[45] and there seems no valid reason why this development should be ignored by returning to *watakushishōsetsu*. The modification seems rather to point to a higher level of abstraction in determining genre while refraining from reference to the first examples known as *watakushishōsetsu*.[46]

It is our intention here to begin by examining the very first form of the term. Katsuyama Isao points out that works of this kind existed before the term originated and were merely designated differently.[47] This is easily explained: An object must exist before it can be given a name.[48]

Following the success of "Futon," literary magazines and journals were full of similar self-portrayals. Some of the works inspired by "Futon" have already been discussed in Part One. Further famous examples of this tendency are Masamune Hakuchō's short story "Doko e" (Whither?, 1908), where the main character, the journalist Suganuma Kenji, embodies the feelings of weariness with life and disillusionment typical of young intellectuals, or his autobiographical, pessimistic story of a marriage, "Doro ningyō" (Clay Dolls, 1911); Chikamatsu Shūkō's lachrymose "Letter to My Wife, Who Has Left Me" ("Wakaretaru tsuma ni okuru tegami," 1910);[49] Iwano Hōmei's "Tandeki" (Self-Indulgence, 1910)[50] and "Hōrō" (Roaming About, 1910); and Tokuda Shūsei's novel *Kabi* (Mold, 1911), often cited as the model example of a shishōsetsu.[51]

It can be said that, during this period, many authors displayed a tendency to move "from a basically objective to a more subjective" style of writing, although to claim that this was a "historical necessity"[52] does nothing to explain the phenomenon. Even such declared critics of *shizenshugi* as Mori Ōgai adapted to the prevailing taste for a time. The theme and style of his novel *Vita sexualis*, written in 1909 and banned shortly after it appeared, bears witness to this.[53] Non-literary reasons were largely responsible for this development, as shown in the first two chapters of Part One of this book. "Futon"'s success was, to a certain extent, nothing more than the most successful literary expression of the specific feelings towards life of those contemporaries who were part of the *bundan* and only on this basis did the work succeed in forming a literary tradition. Also typical of this period were the regular gossip columns concerned with writers in the newspapers which were immensely popular and which supplied the reader with the necessary background information to read this literature.[54]

We can most easily recognize what was specific for the literature of these years from the names found for it, since they signal attempts to define what was characteristic in these new works and what made them different from what had gone before. The talk was of *mi-no-ue-banashi* (stories about one's own life) and *shinpen zakki shōsetsu* (pieces in note form on the immediate surroundings)⁵⁵ or also of *wagamama shōsetsu* (egocentric) and *gakuya shōsetsu* (backstage stories).⁵⁶ So-called "friendship novels" (*yūjin shōsetsu, tomodachi shōsetsu*) or "records of *bundan* friendships" (*bundan kōyūroku*) were also widespread where the authors wrote about their relationships among themselves or about individual events; these often made sense only to the people portrayed and a small circle of the initiated.⁵⁷ All these terms share an emphasis on factual content, on the autobiographical nature of the work, whereby *wagamama shōsetsu* and *gakuya shōsetsu* allude to the accentuated subjectivism and hermetic character of the literature.

Some other concepts were *jinjō chameshi shōsetsu* (average tea-rice⁵⁸ pieces), obviously mocking the mundane, trivial subject matter, *jiko* or *jibun* (I) *jijo shōsetsu* (personal report), *moderu shōsetsu* (model) and *kokuhaku shōsetsu* (confessional novel).⁵⁹

Apart from Mori Ōgai, whom we have already mentioned, many other authors applied themselves to this subject matter and manner of writing, even though it was based on *shizenshugi*, which they rejected. Some examples are the members of the *Shirakaba*⁶⁰ circle, set up in 1910, among whom were Mushakōji Saneatsu (1885–1976), Arishima Takeo (1878–1923), and Shiga Naoya (1883–1971). Even Akutagawa Ryūnosuke (1892–1927)⁶¹ and Tanizaki Jun'ichirō (1886–1965), one of the most famous exponents of aestheticism, followed the trend for a time.⁶² This type of novel was so widespread that Chikamatsu Shūkō, himself the author of works later labeled shishōsetsu, complained in February 1916 that "I have had enough of these confessional novels (*kokuhaku shōsetsu*) in which the author describes his own experiences. . . . Works where we know that the first person is the author himself are not interesting."⁶³

These developments reached a climax around 1918 when three famous writers published works representing what Honma Hisao described as "the confessional literature we have been able to observe in the literary world recently."⁶⁴ From November 1917 until March 1918, Tayama Katai's novel *Zansetsu* (Lingering Snow), a work "more like an essay," including hardly any plot, in which the "hero is undoubtedly the author himself,"⁶⁵ was published in the *Tōkyō Asahi shinbun*. In accordance with the newly awakened religious-mystic tendencies of the time and under the influence of the humanistic idealism proclaimed by the *Shirakaba* group,⁶⁶ Katai portrays the image of a disoriented decadent that one encounters in Huysmans⁶⁷ who is purified in the Buddhist sense through his relationship with a geisha and who achieves consciousness of what is real and true.

The same mysticism characterizes Shimazaki Tōson's novel *Shinsei* (A New Life),⁶⁸ published somewhat later, in which he confessed to an unhappy love affair with his niece, something many critics held against him.⁶⁹ The third work is Tokutomi Roka's (1868–1927) collection of childhood reminiscences published under the title *Shinshun* (Early Spring, April 1918) in which the son's feelings of guilt towards his mother set the tone of the work.

As a result, the critic and novelist Nakamura Seiko (1884–1974) spoke critically of what he termed a "Fashion in Confessional Literature" ("Kokuhaku bungaku no ryūkō")—the title of his article in the August edition of the magazine *Waseda bungaku*—which went no further than "superficial self-observation."⁷⁰

Only two years later the term *watakushishōsetsu* appeared for the first time. Its first known use was found by Nakamura Yū in Uno Kōji's (1891–1961) story "Amaki yo no hanashi" (Story of a Sweet World),⁷¹ which the magazine *Chūō kōron* published in September 1920. Here Uno called such works "'I'-novels" ("*watakushi*"-*shōsetsu*), in which the first person refers to the author.⁷²

Whoever may have coined the term—whether Uno himself or another member of the *bundan* (Chikamatsu Shūkō, Kume Masao and Nakamura Murao all claim to have been its originator)⁷³—it seems to have been created with ironic intent. The negative secondary meaning of the term, which appeared in the following month without *watakushi* being introduced by quotation marks as *watakushishōsetsu*, can be seen from Eguchi Kiyoshi's (1887–1975) comments, when he described the *watakushishōsetsu* and the "friendship novels" as "trivialities from daily life, rolled together into little balls and thrown out in form of novels."⁷⁴

The term appeared at the same time in other articles in an equally critical context.⁷⁵ The arguments over the new term *watakushishōsetsu* merely set forth what had been criticized previously in the *kokuhaku shōsetsu* and similarly named works. The main points of this criticism are expressed most succinctly in a sarcastic article printed in October 1920 in *Jiji shinpō*; here is a brief idea of the content of the article. The author, not named, divides the "numerous abominable novels of recent times" into three groups: first of all there are the *hedo shōsetsu* (*hedo* = vomit), in which the author narrates his most embarrassing experience and is even proud of his shamelessness. This attitude is then praised by foolish critics. The second group is that of the *Nagasaki shōsetsu*, in which the author indirectly revenges an insult by portraying members of the *bundan* in a particularly negative way in his work, in accordance with the saying "Kill an enemy of Edo in Nagasaki." The opposite attitude is true for the third group, the *taiko shōsetsu* (*taiko* = big drum). Like the drum-beating joker at parties who is supposed to keep the guests in a good mood, the author wants to ingratiate himself with his *bundan* public and therefore portrays the relevant people in an exaggeratedly good light in his work.[76] Although the term does not appear here this text provides a description of the literary tendencies subsequently called *watakushishōsetsu*. At the same time, the most important arguments that play a part in the literary debate surrounding shishōsetsu are contained here.

Let us now summarize our observations concerning the origin of the term *watakushishōsetsu*. The continuing lack of clarity on its origins[77] suggests that it was likely to have been used by chance by a member of the literati, that is, of the *bundan* and attained importance because it—rather than one of the many alternatives—was adopted by the *bundan* because of its compactness and relative abstraction. So it became the accepted term within a short time.

These developments were probably also favored by the fact that, as the text last mentioned proves, there was a strong common affinity in the types of literature which had been given so many different names. It soon became apparent that what was criticized in *kokuhaku shōsetsu* was also true of the "idealistic" "friendship novels" from the *Shirakaba* group or of the "backstage pieces" by Kume Masao or Kikuchi Kan. A common name was needed and this was supplied in the new term *watakushishōsetsu*, which therefore rapidly subordinated the alternative terms and displaced them.

It was probably this flexibility in the usage of the word, which originally "possessed an ironical meaning,"[78] that led to its being used, by adherents of the genre as well as by opponents, until it progressed to being simply a neutral designation for a literary genre.

---

1. Terada, p. 99.
2. Original name Shiba Shirō (1853–1922).
3. The hero appears throughout as Sanshi which corresponds to the first-person form,

since the name is the same as the author's. The personal pronoun *boku* is also used occasionally, cf. the text in *MBZ*, VI, 3–110, here, for example, p. 99.
4. Cited in Inagaki, "Shishōsetsu to shōsetsu janru," p. 39.
5. Ibid.
6. Cf. Chapter 1.
7. Cf. Chapter 11.
8. Cf. "Theoretical Premises" in this chapter, and "Factuality" (Chapter 14).
9. "Bungei kōza: Meiji shōsetsushi," c. 1925, cited in Inagaki, "Shishōsetsu to shōsetsu janru," p. 39.
10. The personal pronoun is *yo*, which is used only in formal written texts.
11. There is a lack of clarity about the spelling of the name, which sounds like "Erisu" in *katakana*. Hasegawa Izumi, "Mori Ōgai," p. 241, decides on "Elise"; Thomas Rimer, *Mori Ōgai*, p. 43, writes "Alice."
12. On the biographical background cf. Miyoshi Yukio, *Mori Ōgai*, pp. 321ff., and the biographical references in Richard Bowring, "The Background to 'Maihime,'" and Hasegawa, *Bungaku no kyokō to jitsuzon*.
13. Cf. Usui, *Kindai bungaku ronsō*, p. 35.
14. Cf., e.g., Miyoshi Masao's theory which I discuss briefly in my review of *Accomplices of Silence: The Modern Japanese Novel*, by Miyoshi Masao, p. 155.
15. In addition to the main characters, Count Amakata of the short story is, e.g., identifiable as Yamagata Aritomo.
16. In comparison, Ivan Morris, *Modern Japanese Stories*, p. 15, emphasizes "Maihime" as "one of the earliest examples of the shishōsetsu"; cf. also the introduction to *The World of Japanese Fiction*, p. ix.
17. Cf. the quotation in Bowring, p. 174.
18. Cf. the quotation ibid., p. 173.
19. Cf. ibid., p. 174.
20. This is attributed above all to the fact that Ōgai read the collection of novellas by Paul Heyse and Ludwig Laistner, cf. ibid., p. 175.
21. Cf. Yoshida Seiichi, *Shizenshugi no kenkyū*, vol. I, p. 299.
22. Inagaki, "Shishōsetsu to shōsetsu janru," p. 40.
23. The personal word used is *jibun*.
24. Ozaki Kōzō: *Aobudō*, in *Kōyō zenshū*, IV, 593–728, here p. 595.
25. One interpretation of such examples in the literature of Mishima Yukio is included in I.H.-K., *Mishima Yukios Roman*, p. 233, note 40.
26. *Aobudō*, *Kōyō zenshū*, IV, 719.
27. Cf. Arno Holz (1863–1929): "Die Kunst: Ihr Wesen und ihre Gesetze" (Art, Its Nature and Laws, 1891).
28. Yoshida Seiichi, *Shizenshugi no kenkyū*, vol. II, p. 160.
29. Cf. Ogasawara Masaru, "Shishōsetsu no seiritsu to hensen," p. 34. Hirano Ken (*NBS*, p. 1246) completely rejects the association with shishōsetsu, but even the fact that he mentions the work in this connection implies that a link is at least conceivable for him too. Furthermore, both fail to explain their opinions.
30. Cf. the programmatic statements of the Japanese naturalists on this, Chapter 2.
31. Cf. the text quotation in Inagaki, "Shishōsetsu to shōsetsu janru," p. 40.
32. Cf. Chapter 5.
33. Cf. greater detail in Wolfgang Schamoni, "Die Entwicklung der Romantheorie in der japanischen Aufklärungsperiode," pp. 12f.
34. "Bourgeois" refers to *chōnin* (townspeople's) culture and is therefore distinguished from the modern European term by being set off by quotation marks.
35. Here always meaning narrative prose, i.e., *gesaku* and *shōsetsu*.
36. Cf. also Chapter 1.

37. Cf. the chapter "Shōsetsu no shugan" (The Main Objective of the Novel), text in *GNBT*, I, 182–235, here p. 194.
38. I cannot go into the possibly widely varying anthropological dimensions of the *ninjō* term in Motoori and Shōyō. Nevertheless, I am not aware that the subject has been considered in a study of this problem.
39. Cf., e.g., Ueda Makoto, *Literary and Art Theory in Japan*, pp. 196ff., and Matsumoto Shigeru, *Motoori Norinaga*, pp. 43ff. Cf. also "The 'Philosophy'" (Chapter 14) on the poetological term *mono no aware*.
40. He developed these thoughts above all in the second *maki* of his nine-volume commentary, *Genji monogatari tama no ogushi* (The Small Pearl Comb—[An Examination of] *Genji Monogatari*), published in 1799.
41. In making this statement it is not my intention either artificially to isolate literary theory nor to imply a static sequence of theory and literary practice. Of course, theoretical literary development cannot be separated from artistic practice, since both relate to each other in dialectic unity.
42. Ogasawara, "Shishōsetsu no seiritsu to hensen," p. 34, points out that this attitude was generally held in the Meiji period.
43. Cf. "'Misunderstandings'" (Chapter 3).
44. More on traditional ties in Chapters 19 and 20.
45. Cf. Inagaki, "Shishōsetsu to shōsetsu janru," p. 38.
46. My decision in favor of the *shishōsetsu* reading is additionally supported by the observation that, as early as November 1920, only 2 months after its first known appearance, the terms *watakushishōsetsu* and *shishōsetsu* were differentiated by Hayama Sankichi in an interview (*taiwa*) entitled "Sukuwarezaru shishōsetsu" (Shishōsetsu Cannot Be Saved) in *Jiyū bundan*. Ōmori Sumio, "Kasai Zenzō to shishōsetsu," p. 116, who quotes from this, considers it to be the first use of the term, whereby he possibly means the *shishōsetsu* reading rather than *watakushishōsetsu*. He is the only one to include this evidence, and I assume that the advocates of the *watakushishōsetsu* reading overlooked it.
47. Cf. Katsuyama Isao, "Taishō-ki ni okeru shishōsetsuron o megutte," p. 69.
48. We are not dealing with a case, extremely rare in modern Japanese literary history, where the work is produced following a given theory, as we can observe in Abe Kōbō or Mishima Yukio—in both these cases the model was a particular type of Western novel.
49. Cf. also "Chikamatsu Shūkō: 'Giwaku'" (Chapter 16).
50. Cf. also "Iwano Hōmei: 'Tandeki'" (Chapter 16).
51. Cf. also Yamamoto Kenkichi, *Watakushishōsetsu sakkaron*, p. 15.
52. Hirano Ken in *NBS*, p. 1245.
53. Ōgai's intended ends may have differed radically from those of the shishōsetsu authors—nevertheless he used their means. My observations have since been confirmed by Nakai Yoshiyuki, "Ogai's Craft," cf. especially pp. 230, 236. The author reacted to the ban on *Vita sexualis* with, amongst other things, his next larger work *Seinen* (A Young Man, 1910–1911). Cf. Helen M. Hopper, "Mori Ogai's Response to Suppression of Intellectual Freedom," pp. 387ff., on this subject.
54. Cf. Ogasawara, "Shishōsetsu no seiritsu to hensen," p. 35.
55. Cf. Senuma, "Shishōsetsuron no keifu," p. 25.
56. Cf. Enomoto, "Shishōsetsu, shinkyō shōsetsu," p. 45. The expression *gakuyaochi shōsetsu*, in the sense of "insider novel" was probably more common (*gakuyaochi* meaning "wit which is understood only in the actors' room") as shown by Ogasawara, "Shishōsetsu no seiritsu to hensen," p. 37 and Ōmori, p. 116.
57. Cf. Nakamura Yū, "Taishō-ki shishōsetsu ni matsuwaru oboegaki (1)," p. 165. Examples of this type are presented in "Kikuchi Kan: 'Tomo to tomo to no aida'" (Chapter 16).
58. *Chameshi*: rice boiled with tea or with a mixture of soy sauce and sake.

59. Cf. Kokubo, "Shishōsetsu no seiritsu 1," p. 50, Katsuyama, "Taishō-ki ni okeru shishōsetsuron o megutte," p. 69 and Nakamura Yū, p. 171.
60. *The Birch*, the name of the magazine published by the group until 1923.
61. Cf., e.g., Nakamura Mitsuo, *Nihon no gendai shōsetsu*, pp. 13ff.
62. Power, p. 31, and Etō, "An Undercurrent in Modern Japanese Literature," p. 437 name examples for Tanizaki.
63. Cited in Katsuyama, "Taishō-ki ni okeru shishōsetsu o megutte," p. 69.
64. Honma Hisao: "Kokuhaku bungaku to jiko hihyō," in *Bunshō sekai*, August 1918, cited in Nakamura Yū, p. 165.
65. Yoshida Seiichi, *Shizenshugi no kenkyū*, vol. II, p. 623.
66. Cf. Hisamatsu Sen'ichi, ed., *Zōho shinpan Nihon bungakushi*, vol. VII, pp. 676f.
67. The hero, Sugiyama Tetsuya, is often compared with the writer Durtal, the hero of the novels *Là-bas* (1891) and *La cathédrale* (1898) by Huysmans. In *La-bàs*, he demands a *naturalisme spiritualiste*, a term that interestingly also appears in Ōgai's discussion of *shizenshugi*, e.g., in *Seinen* (1910–1911).
68. The work appeared in 2 parts, from May to October 1918 and from August to October 1919 in *Asahi shinbun*.
69. Akutagawa Ryūnosuke, e.g., in *Aru ahō no isshō* (Life of an Oaf, 1926), comments scornfully that he had never known a more skillful hypocrite.
70. Cf. Katsuyama, "Taishō-ki ni okeru shishōsetsuron o megutte," p. 69. Nakamura Yū, p. 166 includes a detailed list of the articles that appeared from July to October 1918 on the subject *kokuhaku shōsetsu* in the various newspapers and magazines.
71. Cf. Nakamura Yū, p. 171. This work was quoted earlier because of the statements it contains on shishōsetsu, although the authors concerned were not conscious of the use of the term itself, cf., e.g., Hirano Ken in *NBS*, p. 1243, or Tsuruta, p. 14. Thus, writers concerned with finding evidence of the first use of the term overlook this and the following text from 1920 cited in Nakamura Yū, and consistently give 1921 as the "year of origin" of the term, cf., e.g., Kokubo, "Shishōsetsu no seiritsu 1," p. 50, Katsuyama, "Taishō-ki ni okeru shishōsetsuron o megutte," p. 70, and Ogasawara, "Shishōsetsu no seiritsu o megutte," p. 108. An exception is Ōmori, cf. note 46.
72. "Amaki yo no hanashi," in *Uno Kōji zenshū*, II, 410–435, here p. 442.
73. Cf. Kokubo, "Shishōsetsu no seiritsu 1," p. 50 and Nakamura Yū, p. 171.
74. Eguchi Kiyoshi: "Jūgatsu bundan geppyō," in *Yomiuri shinbun*, 6 October 1920, cited in Nakamura Yū, p. 171.
75. Cf. ibid. and Ogasawara, "Taishō-ki ni okeru 'watakushi'-shōsetsu no ron ni tsuite," pp. 63ff.
76. The text is reprinted in Ogasawara, "Taishō-ki," p. 65.
77. Nakamura Yū, p. 171, does not deny the possibility that an even earlier use of the term might be found.
78. Chikamatsu Shūkō 1920, cited in Nakamura Yū, p. 171.

11 · The Literary Debate Surrounding Shishōsetsu

It would be a valuable exercise to describe the debate surrounding shishōsetsu in detail for once, to bring an important part of a neglected field of literary studies to scholarly attention—a field that equally includes the theoretical discussion within the *bundan* and among writers, critics, and literary scholars.[1] However, within the limits of the present work, we shall have to be satisfied with an incomplete account. This means, though, that we have the advantage of being able to concentrate on the most important details; we can assume that the discussion was to a large extent repetitive, and a representative selection will fully satisfy our needs. References to further sources and to the secondary literature on the subject give some idea of the true size of this field.

Here the intention is to reconstruct the literary-theoretical scope of inquiry at the time when the term *shishōsetsu* originated and then to present the literary exchange between opponents and supporters of shishōsetsu so as to determine the historical reception of the term which is a precondition for any theoretical consideration of the genre. The following section will show how the shishōsetsu debate is imbedded in literary-theoretical considerations which are in turn the subject of the succeeding section.

THE CONTEXT OF THE DISCUSSION

The literary debates carried out in newspapers and magazines in the second half of the Taishō period (1912–1926) were much more varied than those of earlier times. Old questions were formulated anew and new subjects appeared, such as the relationship between art and society.

In view of the tacit assumption among the literati who since Tsubouchi Shōyō more or less consciously accepted the supremacy of art, this question was not raised for a long time. Neither the naturalists, who retreated into their cloistered "literary world," nor the representatives of the aesthetic school (*tanbiha*) doubted the special nature of their artistic status which removed them from the "everyday world" (*nichijōsei*) and lent their works a degree of autonomy. However, as social problems grew more severe in the years of depression following World War I, the literati became more receptive towards socialist and materialist ideas, which they took up in different ways and with different results.[2]

Before the impact of "proletarian literature" (*puroretaria bungaku*) was felt near the end of the Taishō period, a co-founder of the *Shirakaba* group, Arishima Takeo, touched off an intense debate about the role of the literati in politics with his "Sengen hitotsu" (A Manifesto), which appeared in January 1922 in the magazine *Kaizō*. As a representative of the ruling class, he ruled out any possibility of joining with the workers and taking part in their fight for liberation and future victory and declared himself incapable of taking the necessary steps towards solidarity with their cause.[3] The idea which was the basis of Arishima's "Manifesto," that forms of artistic expression are rigidly bound to a class-structure, was decisively rejected by Hirotsu Kazuo. His argument was that, "literature is not something which has to be monopolized by the bourgeoisie or by the proletariat."[4] He argued for the orthodox belief in the supremacy of art by using the idea of "pure art" (*junsuina geijutsu*) which would be meaningful regardless of class barriers, nationality, and historical situation and the objective of which was to express "pure feelings" (*junsuina kimochi*).[5]

In answer to Hirotsu's criticism Arishima directed attention to the question of the relationship between art and life. He distinguished three types of artists. In the first category are those whose lives are completely devoted to art and who show no interest in anything else. The second group is characterized by attempts at a conscious relationship between life and art and the third group tries to subordinate art to life.[6] According to Arishima, the first type embodies the true "pure" artist; the second, in which group he places himself, contains the equivalent of amateurs and the third group represents, in a negative sense, the moralists. The political dimensions of the "Manifesto" were also the subject of further articles by Katagami Noboru (1884–1928), Sakai Toshihiko

(1871–1933), and Kawakami Hajime (1879–1946), but, since these bear no direct reference to the shishōsetsu debate, they will not be discussed here.[7]

The attempt described above to conceive of the relationship between art and life in the form of three different types points to a subject that greatly interested the literati of that time and that is directly related to the understanding of shishōsetsu.

On the one hand, there is the question as to what the artistic character of a work really consists of. Kikuchi Kan claimed in an article about "Art and Talent" ("Geijutsu to tenbun") in March 1920 that everyone was capable of creating works of art, and relegated the idea of artists being chosen individuals to a past dominated by aristocrats. Modern art, on the other hand, should adapt its outlook and subject matter to the needs of the normal citizen (*heibonjin*) who would then find art at all engaging.[8]

Even more noteworthy, it seems to me, than the democratic spirit of this idea, which Kikuchi himself characterized "everyman-writer theory" (*sakka bon'yōshugi*, literally "writer mediocrity"), which stamps it unmistakably as a product of his epoch, is the possible connection with the traditional art concept of *gei* as a form of dilettantism.[9] This idea reveals a further reference to shishōsetsu theory in confining the concept of literature to a report of experience.

Naturally, Kikuchi's theory was contested, but no new objections were raised. It seems to me that the debate about the "value of the subject matter of literary pieces of art" (*bungei sakuhin no naiyōteki kachi*) which Kikuchi initiated two years later was more important. He argued in his article that the quality of a work is determined not only by its artistic value, by which he apparently meant a certain degree of technical perfection, but also by a "content value" which he also refers to as "life (worldly) value" (*seikatsuteki kachi*) and which he further divided into a "moral" (*dōtokuteki*) and an "ideal" (*shisōteki*) value. He demanded accordingly close relationship between literature and the real world.[10]

Satomi Ton dismissed Kikuchi's ideas as *sozaishugi* ("content-ism") and redefined Kikuchi's "content value" as "external value" (*gaizaiteki kachi*).[11]

In his reply Kikuchi declared that he had not intended an ideological use of literature, but merely demanded that the subject matter be related to life in a useful sense.[12] However, he was thereby merely paraphrasing himself without achieving clarification of what had been said.

All these debates did not develop along "straight lines" by examining and focusing upon the problem under discussion; they often wandered off into dealing with side issues and eventually ran out of steam, although that is typical for a literary discussion in Japan. From today's point of view, these debates also seem so unsatisfying because there was hardly any awareness of the scope nor implications of the problems under discussion. However, we do not intend to carry out an analysis of these neglected issues. The intention here was merely to show the framework and scope of inquiry of the theoretical discussion within the *bundan*. One main emphasis, as we have seen, was on the legitimation of art, on the questions as to its function within society which were raised as a result of the new ideas introduced by socialist and Marxist theories. Questions such as these point to the increasing importance of proletarian literature and its theoreticians.

The second main emphasis was on the relationship between art and life, a subject doubtlessly stimulated by the existence of shishōsetsu works, which in turn determined the outline of the main shishōsetsu debate. However abstract and unreal the model of the types of artist thought of by Arishima may appear, the fact that they were revived in Hirano Ken's *Geijutsu to jisseikatsu* (1958), the last "classic" work of shishōsetsu research is proof of the continuity of concepts and modes of thought in the Japanese literary world.

THE DISPUTE OVER SHISHŌSETSU

Even before a final name had been found for it, shishōsetsu was the target of criticism from all sides. As we have already seen, accusations were made that the subject matter was insignificant and too intensely private, that it lacked skill and was banal. Interestingly, it was often the authors of shishōsetsu who were themselves its critics. For example, Kume Masao (1891–1952) declared himself against this genre as late as 1919,[13] although he published a series of *moderu shōsetsu* and ultimately became one of the most active proponents of the genre.

A further example is Akutagawa Ryūnosuke, who was often cited by his admirers as criticizing shishōsetsu, although this does nothing to alter the fact that a not insignificant part of his output was, if not shishōsetsu, at least autobiographical in character.[14] He expressed his reservations relatively early in an essay on "The World of Literature in 1920," in which he criticized the "bad habit" of autobiographical writing which he called *moderu no tame no moderu* (a model for the sake of a model). It is inevitable that members of the author's family and his friends appear in a work with autobiographical character. However, in contrast to European literature, the social environment of a Japanese writer is so limited that it consists of only a few other thinly-disguised writers, who would then populate the work. The condemnable aspect of these novels is that the characters are often included not for artistic reasons but for quite different motives. It is this "shameless tendency" which he refers to as *moderu no tame no moderu*.[15]

The third author I wish to quote here is Uno Kōji with his shishōsetsu "Amaki yo no hanashi" in which he "invented" the term himself.[16] It seems somewhat curious that he described the literary tendency to which he attributed his own work with an ironic undertone. It is interesting to note what displeased him about it: He describes shishōsetsu as a type of novel in which a mysterious person appears who calls himself "I." Although we discover nothing about this person's appearance, profession, and character, we gradually discover similarities with the author himself while we are reading. Finally a tacit understanding is reached between author and reader which says that the personal pronoun "I" should refer to the writer each time. It is deplorable (*nagekawashii*), however, that the reader concludes from this that the novel corresponds "completely with fact."[17] We must doubt the seriousness of this criticism, however, when we learn that he probably found it tiresome when the truth of his works was tested. As a result of readers' letters he felt obliged to apologize to the geisha Yumeko, who appeared in one of his stories and whose name he had changed to Yumiko.[18]

The remarkably ambivalent relationship of these authors towards shishōsetsu may be explained by personal reasons in each case. However, it is also an indication of the fascination shishōsetsu must have engendered at that time, which made it so difficult for those involved to resist, in spite of all their reservations. We can almost speak of two seemingly contradictory but related parallel levels of discourse at work here. While shishōsetsu was the most popular form for the writer's literary work, literary criticism was increasingly concerned with the shortcomings and weaknesses of this genre without, however, being able to affect the output of the literature itself. The fact that the shishōsetsu writers joined in with the choir of criticism seems to me, at least to some extent, to be explained by their need for a plausible excuse. Anyone who openly admits to his weaknesses can expect additional sympathy when he falls back into bad habits. On the other hand, even the most strident opponents of shishōsetsu never fully rejected it and granted at least its right to exist.[19]

The examples cited show that those authors who had a bad conscience about shishōsetsu and who tried to distance themselves from it were apparently most troubled by the fact that it was so closely related to reality. This argument was also raised by Ikuta Shungetsu (1892–1930), who complained that shishōsetsu was all too firmly based on and dictated by facts, yet was too imprecise to be autobiography.[20] Other criticism, apart from that listed above, dealt with the obvious lack of perspective for the future, the basic pessimism, and the apparent lack of any creativity.[21]

The discussion phase, which has become known as *shishōsetsu ronsō* (the dispute over shishōsetsu) in literary history, was opened in January 1924 by the writer and critic Nakamura Murao (1886–1949). In an article in the magazine *Shinshōsetsu*, he contrasted two forms of narrative literature, the *honkaku shōsetsu* and the *shinkyō shōsetsu*. He began by defining what he meant by *honkaku shōsetsu*, the "genuine" or "real novel": "By genuine novel I am speaking purely formally of third-person as opposed to first-person narratives. As opposed to a subjective approach, this novel has a strictly objective approach (*ikikata*). A novel in which [the author] does not describe his own moods and feelings directly but in which the author's point of view becomes apparent from descriptions of characters and their lives."[22] He described the *shinkyō shōsetsu* as the complete opposite of this (*shinkyō* is literally "condition of the soul"). This term, the origins of which are uncertain,[23] is sometimes used to describe a special kind of shishōsetsu but is also often used, for example by Nakamura, as an alternative name for the genre. When used for a subgroup of shishōsetsu, *shinkyō shōsetsu* refers to a variant that concentrates particularly on ambience and contains very little plot, corresponding to the "harmony" type so called by Itō Sei and Hirano Ken.[24] Kume Masao derives the word from the "spiritual condition" (*shinteki kyōchi*) of *haiku* poets. He makes a similar claim for this narrative literature, since, in both cases, it is not only important to describe the object precisely, but also to convey a sense of the feelings of the observer.[25]

It is also this characteristic that Nakamura emphasizes in *shinkyō shōsetsu*: "It is a [form] of the novel in which the author himself appears in the work; a novel in which the author begins to speak directly in the work; no, it is rather a work that consists of the author's speech. . . . A novel in which the emphasis lies not on what was written, but on who has written it. A novel in which such things as descriptions of a character, a life or a society play no part, but in which the sole concern is to describe the spiritual condition of the author."²⁶ Nakamura argued that this, like *tanka* and *haiku* poetry, was a typically Japanese phenomenon, as it was the *honkaku shōsetsu* that was widely known abroad. To prove this he listed a number of Russian authors. Considering the recent fashion for *shinkyō shōsetsu*, he admits to having read many of these works, but they do not represent what he holds to be the "genuine novel" (p. 22), the perfect example of which would be *Anna Karenina* (pp. 23f.). In addition, this work contains all the qualities of a *shinkyō shōsetsu* and is therefore decidedly superior (p. 23). Finally, he regrets that literary criticism has been so blinded by fashion that it no longer knows how to appreciate the "genuine novel" (p. 24). Ikuta Chōkō joined in with this unequivocal vote against shishōsetsu in a criticism of the "Bad Tendency Towards a One-Sided Emphasis on Everyday Life."²⁷ This time he used the examples of Goethe, Nietzsche, and Shakespeare to argue, as Nakamura did, that an exceptional artistic personality does not need to seek the reassurance of the public by clinging closely to descriptions of everyday life. Instead these writers can express in their works what is universally human and this is what gives them great artistic value (p. 100).

Kume Masao responded to this criticism in his famous essay "Watakushishōsetsu to shinkyō shōsetsu" (January-February 1925 in *Bungei kōza*).²⁸ Starting from a definition of shishōsetsu as an artistic "personal report" (*jijo*), which removes from it both a formal obligation to the first person as in a first-person narrative and also distinguishes it from a documentary autobiography (pp. 544f.), he nominates it as the "genuine path of the novel" (*shōsetsu no hondō*, p. 547). Works such as Balzac's *Human Comedy* appear artificial (*tsukurimono to shika omowarenai*, p. 547) and inauthentic (*shin'yō ga okenai*, p. 548). Kume writes, "Tolstoy's *War and Peace*, Dostoevski's *Crime and Punishment*, or Flaubert's *Madame Bovary* may be outstanding, but ultimately they are nothing more than excellent light fiction because they are basically artificial and nothing more than reading matter (*yomimono*). . . . The basis of all literature lies in 'I.' Therefore, works in which this 'I' . . . is expressed directly—these are shishōsetsu as far as prose is concerned—represent without doubt the genuine path of art, its basis and its core" (p. 548).

Kume counters the possible criticism that a shishōsetsu is bound to be boring if it is written by an uninteresting personality (*tsumaranai hito*) by saying that this is equally true for the *honkaku shōsetsu* (pp. 550f.). Referring to Kikuchi Kan's *sakka bon'yōshugi*, he argues that the author is fully entitled to be a boring and ordinary person, since the only thing that really matters is whether the work is genuine—this alone determines whether its existence is justified or not (pp. 551f.). However revolutionary his theories may have sounded, they are basically a repetition of the main theoretical concepts of *shizenshugi*.[29]

Uno Kōji adopts the same position as Kume when he explained his view of the shishōsetsu phenomenon in an article in the magazine *Shinchō* ("Watakushishōsetsu shiken"—My View of Shishōsetsu, October 1925). Taking up Nakamura's dichotomy of *honkaku shōsetsu* and *shinkyō shōsetsu*, he succeeded in establishing a decidedly diplomatic compromise between the supporters of both types of novel. He adds to them the attributes objective and subjective respectively and calls the former "like a novel" and the latter "unlike a novel" (*shōsetsurashikunai*),[30] which would be a confirmation of Nakamura except that his conclusions strengthen the position of the opponents again, for Uno argues that it is ridiculous to expect an objective novel from the Japanese. The *shinkyō shōsetsu* corresponds much more to the Japanese character and that is why Japanese authors produce the greatest masterpieces in this style of writing (pp. 21f.). These contributions marked the culmination of the shishōsetsu debate. Most authors apparently agreed with Kume and Uno—at least that is what can be assumed by looking at the literary products of the time.

Further attempts at definition followed, which variously inflected the relationship between shishōsetsu and *honkaku shōsetsu* or defined shishōsetsu as first-person novel, in opposition to Kume.[31] The critic Hirabayashi Hatsunosuke (1892–1931) argued "Against the Improvised Novel" ("Sokkyōteki shōsetsu o haisu," January 1927 in *Shinchō*),[32] but all these essays brought no significantly new contribution to the discussion. It is astonishing that, at this stage of shishōsetsu criticism, arguments concerning the lack of social awareness in the works played hardly any part.[33] This aspect became important with the increasing influence of Marxist literary theory[34] and reached a high point in the years following World War II with articles such as Sugiura Minpei's attack on shishōsetsu as the "Literature of Parasites" (1953).

The literary-theoretical discussion of the following years moved in any case to concentrate on the growing strength of proletarian literature, to questions of the social relevance and function of literature in the class struggle. This area of discussion is represented in literary history under the name of *mokuteki ishiki ronsō* (the dispute over the consciousness of the ends of literature), following the title of Aono Suekichi's (1890–1961) famous essay, which appeared in 1926.

The debate concerning shishōsetsu, on the other hand, continued with the discussion of questions concerning the "purity" of literature (*junsui shōsetsu ronsō*) and the artistic significance of the plot. Purity, which implied non-fiction and genuineness, was the expression of the highest artistic value attributed to shishōsetsu as early as Kume Masao's thoughts on "Shishōsetsu and *shinkyō shōsetsu*."[35]

These arguments were taken further by Akutagawa Ryūnosuke in his controversy with Tanizaki Jun'ichirō concerning the plot in the novel (*shōsetsu no suji/purotto ronsō*), a central event in the literary world of 1927. Tanizaki expressed the following thoughts on the meaning of the plot: "To put it another way, the fascination of the plot lies in the fascination of the construction and the structure, [that is] in its architectural beauty. It cannot be claimed that there is no artistic value in this . . . naturally, this is not its sole value, but I believe that in literature generally it is the novel that is most capable of manifesting structural beauty. Doing without the fascination of the plot means going without the particular strength the novel form offers. And this is what Japanese novels are lacking above all, this strength to structure, the ability to fit together geometrically the plots of various interrelated stories."[36] Akutagawa argued against this in his "Novels without Story-like 'Stories'" ("'Hanashi'-rashii hanashi no nai shōsetsu").[37] In his opinion, it is not the influence of the plot structure which decides the artistic value of a *shōsetsu* but rather the "purity" (*junsuina . . .*) which is seen in the "poetic spirit" (*shiteki seishin*) which is at the same time characterized by an absence of "trivial interest" (*tsūzokuteki kyōmi*).[38]

By judging the literary value of a work on the basis of how close it is to poetry and by warning of the dangers of "trivial interest," that is, the "interest in an event for its own sake"[39] in the case of works with a narrative character, Akutagawa was perpetuating the traditional dichotomy of higher and lower art, of *bungaku* versus *gesaku* or, to put it another way, of poetry versus narrative literature. The conflict between *jitsu* (*makoto* = truth, genuineness) and *kyo* (*uso* = lie), which is linked with this dichotomy, is also the basis for the poetic theory of shishōsetsu. As opposed to Akutagawa, the advocate of shishōsetsu principles, Tanizaki represented a more progressive approach for Japan since he—having taken to shishōsetsu in his early years—now placed greater emphasis on plot and fiction, that is, on the *gesaku*-like character, referring to models of European literature.

As Nakamura Mitsuo has pointed out, this discussion did not resolve the issues at stake. The reason was that it dealt with two representative attitudes rather than individual differences: Akutagawa represented the Taishō and Tanizaki the following Shōwa epoch (1926–1989).[40] This does not imply, however, that Akutagawa's traditional attitude was replaced by Tanizaki's ideas.

The theoretical discussion continued in fact to make use of the criterion of "purity," whose varying connotations arose from the context of its use. In contrast to proletarian literature, *junbungaku* is characterized by an "art for art's sake" view. The "neo-perceptionist" Yokomitsu Riichi (1898–1947), on the other hand, was referring to a synthesis of *junbungaku* and *tsūzoku shōsetsu* (light fiction)[41] when he spoke of *junsui shōsetsu* in his much admired "Essay on the Pure Novel" ("Junsui shōsetsuron," April 1935 in *Kaizō*). His characterization of these two extremes agreed essentially with that of Akutagawa.

It would require an examination of the terminological history in Japanese studies of the poetics of the novel to determine just how the subject has been molded since the Meiji period by the dichotomy of *jun* versus *tsūzoku* (trivial) or *taishū* (mass). The term *junbungaku* appeared for the first time in Tsubouchi Shōyō's[42] writing, was used frequently in a first phase around 1925,[43] and was completely established in the categories *jun* versus *tsūzoku* by the end of the war at the latest. As has been said repeatedly, this dichotomy can be traced back to a traditional schema and the obstinacy with which it persists up to the present day becomes clear when one considers Nakamura Mitsuo's 1977 evaluation of the Akutagawa-Tanizaki controversy. Nakamura deplores Akutagawa's capitulation in the face of the greater strength of shishōsetsu so that it might seem he is critical of shishōsetsu.[44] However, at the same time he regrets that Tanizaki's theories valourized the plot and led to a trivializing (*tsūzokuka*) of literature, losing thereby the "purity" achieved during the Taishō period, which was its real nature and value.[45] A glance at the sources shows us that not only Nakamura but practically the whole of Japanese literary studies has remained in the worn-out tracks of this traditional model of interpretation which constitutes some of the basic axioms of the Japanese view of literature and which is, at the same time, directly related to shishōsetsu theory.

The results of the shishōsetsu controversy can be summed up as follows: After the term had become established in the early 1920s in the context of an often critical discussion, attention was focused upon the theoretical consolidation of the literary concept. A far-reaching consensus was reached in the *bundan* concerning the understanding of the genre as a result of the discussion with opponents of shishōsetsu, which included the traditional artistic ideal of non-functionality[46] and the truth manifested in "non-fictionality," "non-construction," and unsparing personal statement. The affinity to poetry in the Japanese view which resulted from this confirmed shishōsetsu's membership in the higher sphere of *bungaku* or *junbungaku*. Even repeated attempts to overturn the opposition or, more often, to shift the emphasis within this dichotomy does not dispense with such a structure and even if—the question remains an open one—the border between both areas should have changed, there is no doubt that shishōsetsu is still today held to be part of "higher art." Looked at another way, it seems to me that it is this very dichotomy, an unspoken precondition for the Japanese concept of art, that is one reason for the continuing existence of shishōsetsu today.

1. Among the few European-language examples of this kind are, in addition to the previously mentioned studies by Schamoni and Powell, also Ekkehard May/Karl Maurer, "Eine japanische 'Theorie der Prosa'?" and Ueda Makoto, *Modern Japanese Writers and the Nature of Literature*, as well as one on a special field which also touches on the shishōsetsu debate, the *junsui shōsetsuron* (see below, "The Dispute over Shishōsetsu" in this chapter), Seidensticker, "The 'Pure' and the 'In-Between.'" Ueda's study, as is the case with the majority of Japanese works on this subject, has the character of a documentation compiled with regard to a particular complex of questions. There is a predominant lack of the analytical insight one would expect from a study of this subject. Nevertheless, as a collection of important and previously largely unknown material, his book is extremely valuable.
2. The beginnings of social criticism are evident early in the literature of the Meiji period (cf. Chapter 1), but this tendency could not assert itself within *shizenshugi*, nor was working-class literature heard outside a relatively small circle of followers. Left-wing literature succeeded in achieving national significance only after important magazines such as *Tanemaku hito* (The Sower, published February 1921–April 1921, October 1921–August 1923) were established, until it came to form an important phase of modern Japanese literary history as "proletarian literature." Cf. amongst others *Linke Literatur in Japan: 1912–1923* (Left-Wing Literature in Japan 1912–1923) on this, particularly the section "Von der Sozialistischen Literatur zur Proletarierliteratur" (From Socialist Literature to Proletarian Literature), pp. 140–164, and G. T. Shea, *Leftwing Literature in Japan*.
3. Cf. the text in Hirano Ken et al., eds., *Gendai Nihon bungaku ronsōshi*, pp. 11–14.
4. "Arishima Takeo shi no kyūkutsuna kangaekata" (Mr Arishima's Narrow Way of Thinking), published 1922 in *Jiji shinpō*, reprint ibid., pp. 14–18, here p. 16.

5. Cf. ibid.
6. Cf. "Hirotsu shi ni kotau" (An Answer for Mr. Hirotsu), published from 18 to 21 January 1922 in *Asahi shinbun*, reprint ibid., pp. 17–21, here p. 18.
7. Cf. the reprints ibid., pp. 21–45 and the discussion in Arima, pp. 147–151.
8. Cf. Kokubo, "Shishōsetsu no seiritsu 2," p. 37.
9. Cf. "The *Makoto* Principle" (Chapter 20) on the term *gei*.
10. Cf. the reprint of "Bungei sakuhin no naiyōteki kachi" (published July 1922 in *Shinchō*) in Hirano et al., pp. 49–52.
11. Cf. his answer: "Kikuchi Kan shi no 'Bungei sakuhin no naiyōteki kachi' o bakusu" (I Contradict Kikuchi Kan's . . . , August 1922 in *Kaizō*). Reprint ibid., pp. 52–58, here p. 55.
12. Cf. "Sairon 'Bungei sakuhin no naiyōteki kachi'" (And again: . . . , September 1922 in *Shinchō*), reprint ibid., pp. 59–66.
13. Cf. Katsuyama, "Taishō-ki ni okeru shishōsetsuron o megutte," p. 68.
14. Cf. further details in "Kikuchi Kan: 'Tomo to tomo to no aida'" (Chapter 16).
15. Cf. "Taishō kunen no bungeikai," in *Akutagawa Ryūnosuke zenshū*, V, 244–248, here pp. 246f.
16. Cf. "The Origins of the Term *Watakushishōsetsu*" (Chapter 10).
17. *Kotogotoku jissai no dekigoto no yō*, cf. "Amaki yo no hanashi," in *Uno Kōji zenshū*, II, pp. 442f.
18. Cf. ibid., p. 443.
19. Cf. Katsuyama, "Taishō-ki ni okeru shishōsetsuron o megutte," p. 72.
20. Cf. "Jiden to jidenteki sakuhin" (Autobiography and Autobiographical Works, *Jiji shinpō*, 1920), cited in ibid., p. 69.
21. Cf. for detail Katsuyama, "Taishō-ki ni okeru shishōsetsuron o megutte," pp. 70ff.
22. Nakamura Murao, "Honkaku shōsetsu to shinkyō shōsetsu to," p. 19.
23. Kume Masao considers himself to be the inventor at a time when the word had already become part of common language use, cf. Kume Masao, "Watakushishōsetsu to shinkyō shōsetsu," p. 543; Yoshida Seiichi opposes this by arguing that Tayama Katai used *shinkyō* as early as 1909, cf. Yoshida Seiichi et al., p. 63.
24. Cf. "Itō Sei: *Shōsetsu no hōhō*" and "Hirano Ken: *Geijutsu to jisseikatsu*" (Chapter 8).
25. Cf. Kume, p. 543.
26. Nakamura Murao, p. 19. Further page references in the text.
27. This is the title of his article "Nichijō seikatsu o henjū suru akukeikō," published in July 1924 in *Shinchō*, reprint in Hirano et al., pp. 97–108.
28. Cf. Kume, page references in the text.
29. Cf. Chapter 2.
30. Uno Kōji, "Shishōsetsu shiken," p. 21. Further page references in the text.
31. Cf. Satō Haruo: "Ihi-roman no koto" (The First-Person Novel, 1926) and "'Shinkyō shōsetsu' to 'honkaku shōsetsu'" (1927), reprinted in Hirano et al., pp. 119–128.
32. Reprint ibid., pp. 128–132.
33. Cf. Katsuyama, "Taishō-ki ni okeru shishōsetsuron o megutte," p. 69.
34. Cf. Chapter 8.
35. Cf. above and Kume.
36. "Jōzetsuroku" (Garrulous Jottings, published in March 1927 in *Kaizō*), cited from *Tanizaki Jun'ichirō zenshū*, XX, 76f.
37. In "Bungeitekina, amari ni bungeitekina" (Literary, All Too Literary," published in March 1927 in *Kaizō*), cited from *Akutagawa Ryūnosuke zenshū*, V, 130.
38. Ibid.
39. Ibid., p. 131.
40. Nakamura Mitsuo, *Nihon no gendai shōsetsu*, pp. 14f.
41. Cf. the text in *KBHT*, VII, 143–154.

42. Cf. Seidensticker, "The 'Pure' and the 'In-Between,'" p. 175.
43. Cf. Ogasawara, "'Junbungaku' no mondai," p. 27.
44. Nakamura Mitsuo, "Shishōsetsu e no kuppuku" and "Hanashi no nai shōsetsu' o megutte," p. 42.
45. Nakamura Mitsuo, "'Hanashi,'" pp. 43f.
46. Non-functionality, however, only in the sense of the dilettantism in art idealised in the pre-Meiji period, which rejected an ideological function for literature and corresponds to the repudiation of "purposiveness" (*mokuteki ishiki*, Aono Suekichi, see above) in the 20th century.

12 · Conventional Definitions of Shishōsetsu

We have noted earlier that, although numerous vague characteristics of shishōsetsu exist, there has been no scholarly attempt at definition, since one takes for granted a broad agreement among all those who were involved with the genre. Therefore, in order to describe the concept of shishōsetsu in Japanese literary studies it is necessary to study the secondary literature where the basic assumptions concerning shishōsetsu—only partly named but largely implicit—become obvious.

We begin with a fundamental consideration. The Japanese concept of shishōsetsu is attributed with certain characteristics without any consideration of the fact that these might be interdependent. The simple sum of these criteria produces the definition which secures the genre a place within prose literature and which automatically distinguishes it from other genres. Problems arise when there is no order of importance among these criteria; it is unclear when one or more characteristics are lacking if the work can still be classified as shishōsetsu. One attempts to avoid this aporia by distinguishing between shishōsetsu writers and shishōsetsu authors[1] or between shishōsetsu and shishōsetsu-like works.

Which characteristics are essential to the Japanese understanding of shishōsetsu? It will be seen that conceptions of the genre have remained the same for decades. Shishōsetsu poetics of the 1920s continues to provide the main points of reference. Thus, the most important criterion is the contrast of "fiction" versus "reality." However obviously shishōsetsu is categorized under "reality," the individual interpretations that correspond to the theoretical term *jitsu* (*makoto*) are many and various.[2] The "reality" that characterizes shishōsetsu refers to the restric-

161

tion of the subject matter to "the life experienced by the author" as "fact."³ Any fabrication (fiction) is immediately excluded as lacking in complete sincerity.⁴

The conceptual framework behind our understanding of *jitsu* is comprised of three main parts and is already evident here. On the one hand, a one-to-one relationship between literary and real-life events is assumed,⁵ wherein some slight deviations from fact are acceptable. The second main group understands "reality" to mean the spiritual condition of the hero, the "inner reality." If this is the subject of the work, then factual accuracy is of secondary importance, since events have a largely symbolic function. Nakamura Mitsuo sees something of the kind in his interpretation of "Futon."⁶

A third group concentrates not on the relationship between the work and the author but on the impression the work creates on the reader. A *shōsetsu* has a claim to "reality" if it seems to be "natural" and "unaffected." This point of view is represented by, for example, that master of shishōsetsu Shiga Naoya when he praises one work because it does not seem planned (*shikumi to iu yō na mono naku*), while he rejects another on the grounds that it seems "constructed" (*koshiraemono*).⁷

In view of this breadth of interpretation, even the attempt to define the criterion "reality" in terms of its opposite, "fiction," fails. We turn therefore to the second criterion often cited to distinguish shishōsetsu from other genres. It is concerned with a formal aspect: first-person form versus third-person form. The first-person form as a specific characteristic is suggested by the name of the genre, and a number of shishōsetsu descriptions make use of this criterion. It was used, for example, by Yoshida Seiichi⁸ and by Fukuda Rikutarō.⁹ On the other hand, even the very first users of the term *shishōsetsu* pointed out that it should not be understood in the sense of a work in the first-person form. Kume Masao may well have presented the most well-known example: He demonstrates this in his essay "Watakushishōsetsu to shinkyō shōsetsu," with reference to Natsume Sōseki's novel *Wagahai wa neko de aru* (1905–1906, *I am a Cat*) which is written in first-person narrative form but which is nevertheless not a shishōsetsu, while a group of works by Kikuchi Kan, written in third-person form and named after the protagonist the "Keikichi Pieces" ("Keikichi-mono") can definitely be said to be shishōsetsu.¹⁰ What then remains as a distinguishing characteristic if even the category of first-person form is not valid? Japanese secondary literature supplies numerous further attributes, all derived from the first criterion. The one most often mentioned is the autobiographical character of shishōsetsu, which stems from their claim to "reality." However, even this characteristic is not universally valid, since, in the case of those works included by Shiga, whose claim to "reality" depends on their effect, the question as to whether they are autobiographical or not is irrelevant.

Some reference to emotionality and subjectivity as defining elements is also seldom missing from prospective definitions of shishōsetsu. Kikuchi Kan, for example, has posited the following demarcation between shishōsetsu and autobiography: "[The Shishōsetsu] is *much more 'personal'* and has perhaps a greater depth of feeling and thinking instead of being a mere account of [the author's] life story."[11] What could the classification of shishōsetsu among biographical literature (*denki bungaku*) then mean if the condition for this is an "objectification of the first person" (*jiko no kyakkanka*)?[12]

The "lyrical capacity" often used to characterize shishōsetsu is also a result of its classification under *junbungaku*. For example, Inagaki Tatsurō wrote that shishōsetsu "possesses in its depth the character of prosified poetry (*sanbunka sareta jojōshi*),"[13] but this kind of labeling can hardly be of much value as long as "lyrical capacity" is not defined more precisely.

We have now exhausted the reservoir of characteristics used by conventional definitions of shishōsetsu.[14] As we have seen, they do not even come close to defining the genre, since, even where there is some terminological agreement, the breadth of interpretation is so wide that no real clarity is attained.

This statement is, however, somewhat irritating, and it raises a fundamental question about Japanese literary studies. If our observations were of equal importance in Japan as they are in the context of Western literary studies, then we would either be forced to assume that shishōsetsu research has not yet been established or that it was still involved above all in the primary task of defining its subject, which seems of prime importance to us. However, both assumptions are incorrect. The latter, because there are still no scholarly attempts at definition and the former, because it would be absurd to deny the existence of shishōsetsu research in view of the voluminous secondary literature discussed in Part Two. It is more the case that the research interest in literature is different in Japan and that the function of *kokubungaku* as a discipline of literary study is not the same as in the West. Consequently, the importance of a definition of genre is viewed differently. The following brief digression on genre theory in Japanese literary studies attempts to illustrate this difference.

1. Cf., e.g., Terada, p. 126.
2. Cf. "Theoretical Premises" (Chapter 10).
3. Nakamura Mitsuo, "Hanashi," p. 42.
4. Cf. "'Misunderstandings'" (Chapter 3).
5. Cf., e.g., Sasaki, p. 215.
6. Cf. "Jiko to shizen—'Futon' no kyojitsu" (The Ego and Nature—Fact and Invention in "Futon") in *Bungakukai*, March 1969, cited from *NKiBT*, XIX, 434, note 23.
7. Cited in Kōno, "Shishōsetsu ni okeru Shirakaba-ha no yakuwari," pp. 27f.
8. In the second part of his *Hyōshaku: Gendai hyōron, zuisō* on the endpaper at the back of the book, keyword "Shishōsetsu."
9. Cf. his "Japanese Writers: No Longer Insular?" p. 1367.
10. Cf. Kume, p. 546.
11. Kikuchi, p. 16; my emphasis.
12. Cf. *NBS*, heading "Denki bungaku," p. 799. On the other hand it is astonishing to observe that, in his monograph on *Methods of Biography and Autobiography* (1971), Yahagi Katsumi does not consider it necessary to make a dividing line to shishōsetsu, nor does he mention this genre in connection with questions that raise obvious points of contact to Japanese shishōsetsu research. There are, however, interesting observations in Saeki Shōichi, "Kindai Nihon no jiden (1)," on the relationship between shishōsetsu and autobiography in modern Japanese literature.
13. Inagaki, "Shishōsetsu," p. 93.
14. Not just for the sake of completeness but also because it is a remarkable exception, I refer to the most recent contribution of which I am aware to this subject. Morikawa, "Bungaku wa hirakareru," recognizes the need for a definition more clearly than his predecessors and he attributes the failure of the most recent *zadankai* on this subject (Saeki et al.) to the lack of a clear understanding of shishōsetsu (p. 191). His definition is new in that it contains a kind of politico-sociological criterion. According to Morikawa, the writer as the main character of shishōsetsu differs from the well-behaved average citizen in his hostile rejection of the existing social order, and only as a result of this can the "I" in the work take on its particular version of the "truth" (*shinjitsusei*) (p. 193). This argument does not really present us with a characteristic trait of the genre since its literary and non-literary premises are extremely hard to verify, for example, determining social conformity and aberrance both at the level of the literary work and of non-literary reality. On the (supposed) outsider nature of shishōsetsu authors, cf. "The Institutionalized Outsider" (Chapter 18).

13 · Genre Theory in Japan

This short summary cannot attempt to provide a representative view of this subject within Japanese literary studies. It is, instead, intended to show that the apparently ill-considered definitions underlying the understanding of genre, which seems so problematical from the standpoint of Western literary studies, is not a shortcoming of the shishōsetsu research itself. Instead, such a theoretical foundation arises from the nature of Japanese literary studies and thus it acquires an exemplary character within this field of research.

The relative unimportance of genre in Japanese literary research is evident from a glance at the relevant reference works; in most there is no entry under the heading *genre* nor any of its compounds. It is missing, for example, in the *Great Encyclopaedia of Modern Japanese Literature* (*NKBD*), in the *Terminological Dictionary of Modern Literary History* (*KBYJ*), and in the *Dictionary of Japanese Linguistics* (*KGJ*) which includes a considerable number of literary terms in the twelfth section entitled "Bungaku."

General reference books, on the other hand, inform us that the term for genre in the Japanese form *janru* or *yōshiki* is of European origin— *yōshiki* was originally the Japanese equivalent for *style*. (The interchangeability of *genre* and *style* in Japanese sheds an illuminating light on the problem discussed here.) The first use of the term *janru* cited by the dictionary of foreign words *Gairaigo jiten* (Arakawa Sōbei, 1970) was in 1912. Those encyclopaedias that include the heading are based on the European triad, poetry-narrative literature-drama, and proceed to list a series of historically disparate European and Japanese styles of writing.[1]

It is only on the level of the individual subtypes—that is, the texts grouped together under particular characteristics—that we begin to understand the Japanese use of *genre*, which is based on the existence of various "kinds" (*shurui*) or "types" (*ruikei*) of works. This is reflected in labels such as *shōsetsu*, *setsuwa bungaku* (folk-tales), *gunki monogatari* (war tales) and also *katei shōsetsu* (family novels), *fūfu shōsetsu* (novels about marriage) and *sararīman shōsetsu* (novels about employees).

The criteria according to which these groupings are made are as various as the history of their origins. However, these groups all are alike in that they were neither originally nor subsequently influenced by much theoretical consideration. It is characteristic of the extremely pragmatic attitude of Japanese literary studies that these categories, often formed ad hoc, are taken up enthusiastically and then acquire the status of scholarly terminology.[2] As soon as one of these terms is used in practice and works well enough within the context of established conventions of literature, it renders prior theoretical delineation superfluous, since that can now be deduced from practice. That this opens up the danger of a methodological short circuit is an observation Japanese literary researchers would not understand; they would point to their own work which leaves no room for doubt—and this appears perfectly correct as long as they remain within their own pattern of circular thought.

An impressive example of this method is Ōba Shunsuke's *System of Japanese Literature* (*Nihon bungaku no keitō*, 1965). Dividing the book into three sections of poetry (*shika* or *jojō bungaku*), prose (*shōsetsu* or *joji bungaku*), and drama (*gikyoku* or *kahaku/serifu bungaku*), Ōba has presented a chronology of the history of Japanese literature from its beginning until the present by breaking it down into a series of individual genres. The result for the subgroup *kindai no shōsetsu* (the modern *shōsetsu*) within the section *shōsetsu*—here it becomes clear that Ōba is making use of two different meanings of *shōsetsu*, without being aware of it—is a confusing number of subgroups and further divisions, which at times seem to be involved with labeling individual works. The "Novel of the Transitional Phase of the Early Meiji Period" ("Meiji shoki no kadoki shōsetsu"), for example, is divided into five types. One of these is the *jitsuroku shōsetsu* (documentary novel), which is divided into "historical" and "contemporary pieces" (*jidaimono* and *jitsuwamono*[3]). The latter forms three subgroups; that of "love pieces" (*ninjōmono*) is again divided into "love madness" and "love story pieces" (*jōchimono* and *jōwamono*).[4] The text does not give any reason for this categorization or say anything about correlations between the specific criteria for parallel genres. Instead, it simply formulates the list of divisions in the opposite order by attributing to those works for which the categories were created the characteristics which were used to create the division originally—a perfect tautological definition!

Ōba's book, however, is typical not only because of its circular structure, but also in the way it is oriented towards traditional European theories of genre. In the same way, many other Japanese literary scholars base their theories on outmoded concepts. Very occasionally, when an attempt is made to discuss this subject—largely superfluous as a result of the pragmatic attitudes of the Japanese—an extremely vague concept of world literature is described which is generally identical with that of European literature. The Japanese genres are then merely fitted into the given structure which is itself not subjected to analysis.[5]

This suggests that literary genre theory is not an independent, productive field of research in Japan. Added to this is the fact that the acceptance of Western theories—in particular, the ideas of Brunetière, Bovet, Staiger, Kayser, and Ingarden[6]—itself produces problems in the context of specifically Japanese understanding. One clear point of departure from European concepts arises, for example, because the question of how the genres are formed is largely ignored in Japan. These are all problems that can only be touched on here.[7] However, we can clearly see that this area of Japanese literary studies—if it can be said to be a separate area—is a strange amalgam of traditional objectives and methods and assimilated newer theories and techniques.

Returning to shishōsetsu research, we see now quite clearly why a definition of the term has not yet been developed and why it has not been missed. Just as in the case of Ōba's "system of literature" mentioned above, the genre is explained in terms of individual works and the works in the term of the genre. Genre history, that is, the chronological listing of works labeled shishōsetsu, replaces genre definition, and even makes it superfluous in the Japanese view. The lack of a Japanese tradition in genre theory however, exposed by the orientation towards European works, may help us understand the shortcomings of those attempts at definition that we do find.

---

1. Cf., e.g., the heading "Janru" in *Nihon kokugo daijiten* (Large Dictionary of the Japanese Language), vol. X, or in *Heibonsha sekai daihyakka jiten* (Heibonsha's Large World Encyclopedia, 1965), vol. X. *The Annotated Encyclopedia of Literary Terminology* (Fukuda Rikutarō/Muramatsu Sadataka, eds.) additionally includes the different arts under *janru*.

2. Examples for this in I.H.-K., "Die nicht existenten Probleme."
3. Literally, "true story pieces based on facts."
4. Cf. Ōba Shunsuke, *Nihon bungaku no keitō*, p. 180.
5. Cf., e.g., Saitō Kiyoe, "Kokubungaku no janru."
6. In the short article under the heading "Janru" in the supplement to the *Large Encyclopedia of Japanese Literature* (*NBD*), the names Brunetière, Hartl, Petersen, and van Tieghem are listed.
7. Cf., e.g., Hasegawa Izumi, *Kindai bungaku kenkyūhō*, pp. 125f. on Japanese concepts of the genre which refer to European theories.

14 · Shishōsetsu—an Attempt to Define the Genre

PRELIMINARY THOUGHTS

It seems fitting to begin this chapter with a pause for critical thought so as to avoid the danger of a false interpretation of the previous chapters. The reader may well have gained the impression that the previous discussion has served merely to introduce this chapter. This impression arises when one views the intent to create a new definition against the background of a seemingly growing trend to criticism of conventional shishōsetsu concepts and regards the connection between the two as an implicit justification of the present author's attempts. For this reason, it is necessary to demonstrate the importance of the previous chapters for our subsequent considerations of genre theory. That in turn raises the question as to the value of a renewed attempt at defining shishōsetsu.

First let us consider the structure of this part of our investigation. It contains various threads of argument, as does the whole work. In the first chapter, concerned with the "predecessors" of shishōsetsu, the threads were woven together. On the one hand, the examples listed chronologically provided evidence of an increasing convergence towards shishōsetsu with respect to particular characteristics in the text and their reception—this could be called the literary-historical dimension of the discussion. At the same time, however, we considered the change in concepts of the theory of the novel, which provides the background to literary practice, and the use of particular terminology in contemporary Japanese literary studies with respect to shishōsetsu. Next, we considered the way theories of the novel since the Meiji period were rooted in older concepts by examining certain constants within traditional art theory. This study of the literary-historical premises proved to be particularly useful in clarifying shishōsetsu theory. The origins of the term *watakushishōsetsu* provide much information as far as the understanding of the genre at the time is concerned, as does the discussion of the subsequent literary debate, concerned with showing the argument carried on largely by the authors themselves. The following chapters concentrated increasingly on metacritical comments to do with the theoretical content of and background to the conventional understanding of shishōsetsu. This could be misunderstood as intended only to lead up to the author's own definition of the term. However, it resulted from the "higher" level of discussion, since the subject had shifted from the idea of shishōsetsu held by writers or contemporary critics to the term as used within shishōsetsu research.[1]

As shown above, the conventional definitions of shishōsetsu, which also form the basis for present-day secondary literature, are not satisfactory: They consist of a list of supposed characteristics of the genre, but include no criteria by which to judge which are really specific to shishōsetsu; nor are the individual characteristics placed in any kind of defining relationship to each other. Nevertheless, it would be foolish to decide hastily about the necessity of forming a new definition; such an undertaking should be more carefully motivated since identifying the lack of an operational definition of shishōsetsu does not automatically justify the search for one. One should at least make it clear why such a definition seems indispensable.

It is important to remember that there is hardly any publication on Japanese literature in this century, however brief or general, that does not mention shishōsetsu. It is even considered to be *the* typical genre which, more than any other, represents Japanese literature. Also, it is assumed that—as Terada Tōru puts it—there would be not a great deal left if the shishōsetsu writers were removed from modern literary history,[2] or, in the words of Morikawa Tatsuya, "There is a *shōsetsu* type which makes up the main current or the core of Japanese literature. And this is the so-called shishōsetsu [literary] series (*keifu*)."[3]

What is remarkable about all such statements is that it is still considered worthwhile to point out the shishōsetsu character of a work, in spite of the genre being so widespread. It would have been quite understandable if the success of this method of writing had also led to an engrained recognition of its specific characteristics, but there continues to be a feeling that there is a definite difference between shishōsetsu and non-shishōsetsu. Thus, it is held to be a typical, representative genre but not the equivalent of the modern Japanese "novel" per se. Were this the case, there would be no need to speak of shishōsetsu, since the term would be coextensive with *shōsetsu* and therefore become redundant.

Since, however, a distinction is made between shishōsetsu and non-shishōsetsu, this distinction should be explained if it is to be used within a scholarly study. After all, this entire book is based on the assumption, widely held in Japan, that shishōsetsu exists, that it stands apart from other literary prose forms.

This brings us to an important matter as far as the definition to follow is concerned: It will have to be framed according to the Japanese understanding of the term. This statement has significant methodological implications. The author must not develop her own catalogue of determining criteria using selected texts, since this would mean that these criteria would then impose their own theoretical premises on the analysis. It is irrelevant here whether these criteria be personal or based on the norms of the European novel; it is important only to point out that they would be inadequate for a definition of shishōsetsu. Shishōsetsu can only be defined in relation to other Japanese genres. The author's own attitudes are unimportant, regardless of how well they might be expressed. The most crucial points of reference are Japanese statements from which a theoretical system of rules can be built up to form the basis for the definition.

We can identify the elements of shishōsetsu that are relevant for the definition only on the basis of Japanese observations and evaluations. This is an important condition in view of the fact that, basically, every conceivable literary characteristic of shishōsetsu could be used as a distinguishing feature of this literary form. However, only those elements that are perceived, within the context of Japanese literature, to possess characteristics contrasting with immediate predecessors and also with contemporary literary products are of any significance. Consequently some criteria that are of great importance in genre definitions for Western literature never appear in Japan, while others that seem completely irrelevant in the West acquire central importance.

The reason for all that precedes in Part Three now becomes clear, since it is immediately obvious that it was more than mere preparatory work towards a definition. Rather, it is the indispensable prerequisite for what follows. Although the Japanese descriptions cannot be used directly to define the term, since they have no real basis in scholarly reasoning, they, together with the arguments supplied in the literary debate, do supply the points of reference from which the Japanese understanding of the essential characteristics can be determined.

Since it is necessary to derive the elements relevant for the definition of the genre from Japanese reception, an unbiased attitude towards all opinions and observations on the specifics of shishōsetsu—and not merely those that appear particularly interesting—is a precondition here. We began to classify the definition criteria by attributing them to two basic assumptions and three groups of derived characteristics. This hierarchy of criteria requires further content definition and is an important step in the direction of the definition of shishōsetsu itself, since it points to connections or even more, a structure of relationships, between characteristics that are customarily listed cumulatively and considered virtually equivalent and interchangeable. Our attempt at definition here will consist of setting up a unified hypothetical model in which each of the specific characteristics we earlier arranged in five individual groups is fixed in its relation to the others.

In order to do this it will be necessary to rearrange and interpret the selected collection of characteristics despite the possible disruption of a subjectivity which enters at this point and which we could not completely exclude anyway—otherwise the author would be accused of "hermeneutic innocence"! It is almost impossible to avoid an "intuitive leap" when attempting to define a genre.[4] However, it is decisive that the "divinatory apprehension of what is typical of the genre" (Karl Viëtor)[5] is strictly controlled, since it must submit to a threefold examination. On the one hand, it must be orientated towards the Japanese understanding of genre; it must also be able to provide a precise, clear, and conclusive description of the texts said to be shishōsetsu; finally it must enable us to distinguish between supertemporal invariants and historical variables,[6] that is, those characteristics of shishōsetsu that are critically regarded to be constant throughout the history of the tradition and their varying manifestations that, subject to the effect of extraliterary, historical influences, alter noticeably over the period of the genre's existence.

The third of these conditions seems to be the most difficult to fulfill, since it leads to a morass of as yet unresolved theoretical-methodological complications which we do not wish to add to our attempt to summarize them.[7] Since the possibility of collision cannot be excluded were we to attempt to report on this subject—these questions are by no means settled in literary studies—we intend to avoid the area by referring to the secondary literature available, which the author used to increase her own awareness of the problem. Included here, apart from the previously mentioned works by Hempfer and Lockemann and "classics" such as Lämmert, Jolles, Stanzel and others, are publications by Jauß, Anderegg and Hinck.[8] It is more important here to apply in practice the knowledge gained from these authors than to devote a great deal of effort to discussing their theoretical premises.

In order to determine the importance of the third condition (the difference between genre invariants and historical variables) for our inquiry, we need only indicate how one should not set about defining a genre. One could base a definition of genre on criteria derived from the subject matter of the text, that is, from those themes that seem to be treated specifically by shishōsetsu. Howard Hibbett, for example, does just this and lists what he considers to be the characteristic themes of the genre—sickness, poverty, adultery, loneliness, alcoholism, and the society of prostitutes as well as a craven desire for literary success.[9] Such an approach, however, if it attempts to present certain themes as being canonical definitions of the genre rather than simply descriptive in nature, misjudges the extent to which they are historically overdetermined: the thematic content of shishōsetsu is intimately bound to the author's personality which in turn is largely determined by his social and historical milieu. The themes poverty and friendship with geishas, for example, are of a completely different and usually lesser significance to an author of the postwar years than to one living in the 1920s. A definition of the shishōsetsu genre based on such thematic criteria would be bound to fail since it would be too dependent on fluctuating historical factors.

We now move on after these preparatory remarks to formulate a hypothetical model of the genre for shishōsetsu. It consists of two basic, dialectically related elements which I will call factuality and focus figure.

An explanation of the terms will follow. However, the separate consideration of both elements, undertaken for practical reasons, should not give rise to the conclusion that they exist independently of each other. They are meaningful only in combination. The following sections are intended to clarify what this means.

We could even go one step farther and speak of the "factuality of the focus figure," but then the interdependence of both elements would appear to have been replaced by a one-sided dependency. In order to avoid this, we shall continue to keep both components separate.

OUTLINE OF A STRUCTURAL MODEL

FACTUALITY

Factuality describes the relationship presumed in the view of the Japanese reader between the literary work and reality. It represents a rule which states that the work reproduces the reality experienced by the author.

As a result, factuality does not depend on the actual relationship between literature and the reality portrayed, which would involve the consideration of many other factors,[10] but on an agreement in the process of literary communication—the trust which the reader places in the textual version of reality created by the author's use of certain textual "signals."

It seems remarkable that this basic condition was grasped intuitively as early as what we today assume to be the "invention" of the name of the genre by Uno Kōji, since he indeed described it as being a type of tacit agreement between author and reader.

He also did something else no less remarkable and equally important for us—he described how this agreement was established by the use of the reading process from the reader's point of view. In this context, I take the liberty of returning to a text from Uno's 1920 shishōsetsu "Amaki yo no hanashi"[11] already used in another connection: Uno introduces a "strange phenomenon of recent times from part of the Japanese literary world" "which the intelligent reader certainly knows already." According to Uno, this consists of the fact that, in the said works, "a mysterious person simply appears who calls himself 'I.'" We search in vain for information about his appearance, his profession, and his character; instead there are descriptions of "strange feelings." "However, if we are very observant then [it becomes clear] that the writer of the novel is similar to this 'I.' This is usually the case. That is why the narrator is a writer by profession. And so neither the readers nor the authors are in the least skeptical about the strange phenomenon that, when there is talk of 'I,' the reference is to the writer of the novel."[12] The description of the reading process shows precisely how this agreement functions. The reader depends to begin with on particular signals. Uno describes them as the abrupt appearance of the first-person character which is not preceded by any discursive description, who then proceeds to expound on his own feelings. Since the text keeps this information from the reader, he undertakes the search himself and discovers that the first-person narrator and the author are identical. At this point, agreement is reached between the reader and the work or the author: The reader concludes, on the basis of the signals found in the text, on the basis of a certain similarity between the hero and the author, and on the basis of his experience of other similar works ("this is usually the case") that this text also "corresponds to the truth." From then on he concludes conversely: If the hero and first-person narrator are identical with the author, then his profession must be that of writer, then he looks like this, has a . . . character and so forth.

Uno Kōji set out an ensemble of various signals to which the reader reacts before he assumes factuality. We will consider these in more detail.

He began by describing text-immanent signals such as the lack of particular pieces of information, which seem absolutely essential to the reader in view of the nature of the text. For example, a first-person narrator appears and demands undivided attention while seeming to pay no consideration at all to the reader. In my opinion, it is just this experience that Yoshida Seiichi was referring to when he made the strange sounding observation that the writer of shishōsetsu is "not nice to his reader" (*dokusha ni shinsetsu de nai*).[13] We can see here a principle of organization of the text specific to the genre which relates to our second basic element, the focus figure. The author allows his first-person narrator and hero no oblique glance at the audience. In order to give the impression of a reality directly experienced and reproduced during the experience, the writer lets the narrator describe everything as if he were doing so only for himself or for a friend who knows about all the details of his life. Many things that are only hinted at acquire a highly allusive nature. If the reader wishes to understand what is being discussed, he must acquire knowledge about the book's background and its particular correspondence to reality. To achieve this he can use other books by the same writer or the numerous reviews and articles, which are concerned more with the character of the author than with his books.

In fact, we can assume that the average Japanese reader knows a great deal about the characters and lives of the authors whose works he reads so that he appreciates the significance of the allusions to these.

Of course, this raises the question as to whether the average Japanese reader's greater background knowledge concerning the author, when compared with the equally hypothetical "average German reader" of belles-lettres, is a result of or a condition for the shishōsetsu style of writing. Probably both are true. It would be pointless to attempt to measure how much of each is present, since this would be much the same as trying to solve the insoluble chicken-or-egg problem, and just as useful. We shall have to consider the historical conditions for the reader's background knowledge later in this chapter. We return for the moment to the facts in the text which establish relationships with non-literary reality.

Some of the allusions mentioned previously are to particular localities with which the reader is familiar at least in name, as well as to real people, particularly the author's writer colleagues, whose names are so obviously coded that the reader feels obliged to decode them, which is easy enough in the case of the author's contemporaries. The author frequently used the first letters of the person's surname; sometimes imaginary names were invented which bore an obvious relation to the person concerned, for example a name made up of parts of the names of two writers Tōan and Kason, which referred to Tōson and Katai, or the formation of Uchiyama by altering the second and third characters of the name Osanai (Kaoru, 1881–1928) so that the reading of the individual parts changes at the same time.[14]

In this way, the text is interspersed both with direct references—including mention of recent events—and allusions to reality that the reader can check at any time. Examples of this will be given in Part Four where several individual works will be discussed.

Factuality means that the reader assumes a direct correspondence between what is portrayed and actual reality—he reads the novel as an autobiographical document. In this way, the method of reading shishōsetsu is similar to that for memoirs and autobiographies.[15] However, there is a difference in that memoirs and autobiographies are openly presented as such—usually in the title or a preface—so that the testing process as described by Uno, which is typical for shishōsetsu, is superfluous. Of course, the Japanese reader usually knows in advance if he is dealing with a shishōsetsu, either because he has read the reviews or the dust jacket or because he knows other works by the same author. It is not, however, a convention, as in the case of autobiographies and memoirs, to declare the work a shishōsetsu in advance.

There is a further difference that is more important. The claim to factuality in a European autobiography is in itself of no aesthetic value: quite the contrary, the more documentary a work of this kind purports to be, the less space for "fictionalizing" and the fewer the levels of signification it possesses, therefore, at least according to Western ideas, the smaller its claim to be artistic. The Japanese understanding of art, on the other hand, is never bound solely to particular text or decoding strategies but always expects a certain relationship between the piece of art and reality—we have frequently discussed this *jitsu* or *makoto* (truth/genuineness) principle which includes a strong ethical and moral component. A work that implies that it portrays reality or can claim to do so on the basis of an agreement reached through literary communication possesses, according to Japanese ideas, a high artistic value on these grounds alone.[16]

A specific difference to European literature however, allows our assessment of factuality in shishōsetsu. In Japan the effect of factuality is achieved largely by non-representational means. (The references to reality described above represent only one, almost secondary, form of securing authenticity.) We must assume a completely different relationship between *riariti* (genuineness), *kyakkansei* (objectivity), and factuality than in Europe, because we would otherwise have to believe that even the most prosaic press report was counted as great art in Japan. We shall deal with this question in more depth later.[17] In this connection, it is important to note that factuality is linked to a different kind of writing than in European literature and that it is the foundation of the artistic value of a work of literature.

Before we characterize this method of writing as a manifestation of the second structural element of shishōsetsu, the focus figure, we must explain how the mutual pact between author and reader of the text's factuality is reached—shishōsetsu does not have its origins in autobiography, from which it could have adopted the claim to truth, but, as was shown in the first part of this book, from the literature of *shizenshugi*, that is from "fictional" narrative literature.

THE HISTORICAL CONDITIONS FOR THE ORIGINS OF THE FACTUALITY PACT. One condition for the development of shishōsetsu was the *bundan*, the close secluded world of the literati, consisting of separate, often competing groups of poets, writers, and critics. Within this group, concentrated in Tokyo, everyone knew everyone else. Artists met regularly in cafés—a custom copied from the European Bohemians—and found in each other support and recognition at a time when the social position of the literati still needed to be confirmed.

In addition, the specific interpretation of the naturalist demand for truth in the sense of unsparing personal revelation and its adoption in literary practice by Katai, Tōson, Hōmei, and others gave the *bundan* the character of a controlling body, which could attest to whether the work involved corresponded to the facts and could so certify or deny the degree of sincerity, that is, the artistic value of a work. Reviews were essentially an examination of the relationship between fact in the work and in reality, which the general reader could follow upon their publication.

The readership of shishōsetsu, however, was very small to begin with, since the average self-respecting Japanese reader preferred the "fictional," stylistically elaborate literature of authors like Natsume Sōseki and Mori Ōgai, who were held in high esteem in society. It was only after *shizenshugi*, and with it shishōsetsu, had become popular in the literary world that they increased in importance beyond the *bundan*.

In the early phases, the authors, literary characters, and readers were largely identical. It is therefore not surprising that when a new work appeared, the public was most interested in who had been chosen as the protagonists this time, apart from the author, and whether they had been suitably portrayed. Because the work could be checked so easily, the authors could not risk any deviations from fact if they did not wish to be accused of insincerity. Even the slightest attempt to give individual events a different emphasis or to give them a new interpretation met with criticism. Of course, controversy raged permanently concerning supposed exaggerations or biased descriptions, in which those concerned—usually writer colleagues—replied with essays putting the matter right or with books of their own.[18]

An episode from Uno Kōji's "Amaki yo no hanashi,"[19] already cited in a different context, shows how great was the pressure to be true to the facts. The author complains about the difficulties of his profession, which requires an exaggerated consideration of the facts, since shishōsetsu has now become popular and is read by an alert readership which protests all too quickly when it feels truth is neglected. He is not even allowed to change the name of a geisha from Yumeko to Yumiko—a (cautious) attempt at "fictionalizing" (*kyakushoku suru*)—and felt obliged to apologize.[20]

This episode makes it quite clear that reality was the final standard by which both reader and author judged a work. The agreement is based on a relationship to literature and life that permits no doubts in principle as to the possibility of describing reality. The degree of agreement as to how an acceptable description of reality should look is astonishing, and, since the real object itself is always present as confirmation, the reader gradually comes to trust shishōsetsu more and more. The plausibility of shishōsetsu as a direct objectivization of the author's experience increased as the number of works grew which had withstood the careful scrutiny of the work's strict factuality by the *bundan*.

This willingness to trust, however, became a practical necessity as readers increased beyond the narrow circle of the *bundan* itself, since the general reader could no longer make a direct comparison between reality and the work, due to a lack of background knowledge, and depended on the author's keeping his promise to be true to reality.

There is therefore a point—though not one that can be pinned down in time—not only when reading an individual work, but also in the development of shishōsetsu as a genre, when an unspoken agreement between author and reader concerning factuality is made. To put it more precisely, factuality as a structural element of shishōsetsu is the form of discourse specific to the shishōsetsu genre and established within the text, but ultimately put into practice by the reader who accepts shishōsetsu qua factuality and focus figure as such.[21]

FOCUS FIGURE

In order to describe the structural element of factuality it has continuously been necessary to do so in terms of the second element, the focus figure, because the two are dialectically interrelated. Factuality does not exist without the focus figure and the focus figure presupposes factuality. In order to go into this in more detail it is necessary to describe the focus figure element.

The focus figure element is more than a combination of the characters of first-person narrator, hero, and author—the last for reasons of factuality. It is in evidence in all the relevant levels and aspects of the work.[22]

We begin with the relatively formal aspects—"relatively" because every element of a work, even the formal ones, contributes to its meaning, although this may sound like a platitude in literary studies, a fact that needs to be emphasized in the context of Japanese studies.[23]

THE NARRATIVE PERSPECTIVE. In terms of narrative technique the structural element focus figure is manifested in the perspective "with" (narrator = character) which is largely maintained throughout, that is, the author exposes the interior view of his hero while describing all the characters "from the outside." This would be the ideal form of a consistent "with" perspective, which is however frequently interrupted when the narrator moves behind another character, so that there is then the perspective as seen "from behind." If these examples are studied in more detail, it can be seen that they are usually concerned with describing the thoughts and feelings of characters with whom the hero is close so that the reader is given a feeling that he is intimately involved in the state of affairs. However, it is very unlikely that the Japanese reader is at all aware of this interruption in the perspective, since we must assume that even the author uses this method as a matter of course. If this is the case, then the statistical frequency of the "with" perspective proves that it is a structural necessity, that is, a manifestation of the focus figure. Some further observations using an example will underline this.

Shiga Naoya's novel *An'ya kōro* (1927–1937, *A Dark Night's Passing*), generally categorized as a shishōsetsu,[24] is narrated consistently from the point of view of the hero, Tokitō Kensaku. However, there are a number of passages where the author interrupts that point of view, apparently because he does not feel able to present the material without doing so. One such passage is in the last scene of the four-part work, published in two volumes. Kensaku, who suddenly becomes seriously ill after a visit to Daisen, the sacred mountain, at the climax of the novel, is lying exhausted in bed. His wife, who has been summoned by telegram, reaches the remote house in which he is being cared for. Her condition, her thoughts when she is told that she cannot disturb him now, the conversations with the doctor—all this cannot be presented from the viewpoint of the hero. This is a case of an author-narrator speaking from a different point of view. The very last sentences of the novel show Kensaku from "outside," from the point of view of his wife Naoko: "Kensaku seemed to be exhausted, and, his hand in hers, he closed his eyes. His face was peaceful. It seemed to Naoko as if she were seeing such a face for the first time. And then she thought, maybe he will not survive. But, strangely, this thought did not trouble her greatly. Naoko spent a long time watching this face from which she seemed, as it were, to be sucked in. And all the time she thought: 'Whatever happens I shall not leave him and will always stay with him.'"[25] The change of perspective is in this case an extremely effective method of allowing the picture the hero has painted of himself[26] to be confirmed "objectively." It verifies the catharsis the hero had hoped to achieve by climbing the mountain and proves, through Naoko's reaction, that he has really, definitely changed into a person one *must* love. However, the change of perspective does not mean a change of the "order system"[27] in the work, that is, of the ethical-moral evaluation; instead, it confirms it even more effectively.

In addition to this final scene, the further implications of which we must ignore here, there is one more outstanding example of the interruption of the point of view. In chapter 5 of the fourth part, the authorial narrator describes Naoko's extramarital adventure and what led up to it—an event that took place while the hero was absent but which could just as well have been described from Kensaku's point of view when Naoko tells him about it.

Yasuoka Shōtarō describes this as a particularly successful narrative trick when discussing this chapter, because by means of the perspective "from behind"—in Yasuoka's words, the "objective description" (*kyakkan byōsha*), which presents events from a neutral point of view—Shiga succeeds in doing justice to this delicate subject. According to Yasuoka, he found the optimal solution among all possible methods of description—the emotionally charged inner view of the hero or Naoko's equally subjective rendering.[28]

In this respect it is not so much Yasuoka's interpretation that is interesting but rather the fact that such a feature is considered at all, since Japanese literary criticism usually excludes "technical" questions of the kind. The change of perspective was so obvious in this case that it could not be ignored. By recognizing the anomalous imposition of the authorial point of view and admitting that it gives the impression of a technical fault to begin with which could have led to the "destruction of the harmony of the whole,"[29] Yasuoka confirms that the hero's point of view should be counted as a constitutive element of the shishōsetsu genre even when it is not strictly maintained throughout. If the Japanese reader is aware of such deviations from normal practice, his critical reaction confirms the validity of the rule.

The novel *An'ya kōro*, cited previously several times and written in the third person, also shows that the difference between first and third person has no specific meaning for the genre; it is not the personal pronoun that is important but the narrative perspective. This was understood intuitively right from the beginning, for example, by Kume Masao in his essay "Watakushishōsetsu to shinkyō shōsetsu."[30] Yasuoka Shōtarō also confirmed this when he wrote: "[The novel] does not differ from a shishōsetsu, in which the first-person narrator and the author are identical."[31]

The opposition between the first- and the third-person narrative form is also of less importance in Japanese because the number, gender, and the grammatical person of the subject of a sentence, which is in any case often unnamed, have no influence on the syntax. Instead, the manner of the interpersonal relationship determines the lexical and grammatical forms—but this is in turn decided by the narrative perspective. In the case of shishōsetsu, the first-person narrative form is used in the majority of cases, which is to be expected in view of its autobiographical nature. In order to simplify matters, we shall therefore refer to the "first-person narrator" or the "first person," since we can assume that the use of the third person does not lead to any alterations in the structure of the work.

THE TEMPORAL STRUCTURE. The subject of shishōsetsu is at the center of the events described. His life or the part of it described forms the temporal axis, a significant point of articulation for the work as a whole. Considering the standpoint of the narrator both as narrator and protagonist of the events described, it follows that the temporality of the narrator must accompany and be distinct from the temporality of the narrated events in which the narrator plays a part. This two-fold narrative standpoint is characteristic of shishōsetsu but leads, however, to problems of narrative technique.

Strictly speaking, the active first person and the narrator can never be identical—an extreme case would be using the moment of writing as the subject for the work, but we can exclude this in the case of shishōsetsu. We have, therefore, to assume a "dichronous nature of the double ego,"[32] which is, however, concealed as much as possible in shishōsetsu.

Usually, a shishōsetsu does not begin at the real end of the narrative, as many autobiographies do. This would mean a loss of immediacy, since the reader would then know that the narrative was merely a reenactment of events already passed. Japanese readers and writers enjoy the illusion that the work has been created parallel to the events described, that the active and narrative first person are identical—something that is not possible in practical terms.

This ideal conception of the work has consequences for the temporal structure of the genre. Shishōsetsu is confined to relatively short episodes from the author's life, the first of which should not be too far in the past and the last of which should take place in the narrative present, close to the time of publication.

Events are related chronologically, corresponding to the order in which they actually happened. Incidents from the more remote past, such as childhood experiences, only may be alluded to in association with the present described in the work—they cannot be treated as the main theme because they are too far removed from the author's present.

Long works are few and far between. They are written, as in the case of *An'ya kōro*, over a correspondingly long period of time and are basically nothing more than individual stories subsequently joined together, written successively and held together by the main character's chronology of experience.

Shishōsetsu are concerned with spontaneous reactions to experience; there should be no perceptible distance from that which is related. A large time interval means an increasing risk that a gap will develop between the experience and its description which the author then attempts to conceal by casting back his mind to the experiential moment.[33]

There is some substance to the argument that the temporal separation from the occurrence of the events is really a relevant aspect in Japanese literary theory in statements such as the following in an encyclopaedia article on Kawabata Yasunari's short story "Izu no odoriko" ("The Izu Dancer," 1926): "[The work] is not a true-to-life account but rather reminiscence." (*Shasei de naku kaisō de aru.*)[34] It is of great importance for Japanese literary criticism that the encounter with the dancing girl, which is the subject of the short story, really took place eight years earlier. The ultimately unattainable ideal of a shishōsetsu remains "a true-to-life account" (*shasei*) as the momentary image of the "spiritual condition" (*shinkyō*). These two terms taken from traditional *haiku* theory reveal the way shishōsetsu is rooted in traditional attitudes and literary concepts. Before we go into the description of the focus figure on the "higher" level of the work, we should examine the problematic nature of shishōsetsu narrative method and its evaluation in Japanese literary studies.

The dichotomy between reminiscence and instant perception postulated in the encyclopaedia article can lie only in a relative difference in distance to real events. It does not correspond with, for example, the opposition between distance and immediacy, since the latter, as has been previously stated, cannot be achieved.

We do not suggest that Japanese authors, readers, and critics know nothing of these facts; but they seem to suppress this knowledge by assuming that immediacy can be achieved. (Why they do this can be seen from the following and from the observations in Part Five.) They are probably thinking of the figure of the *haiku* poet who spontaneously translates his impressions of scenery and mood into poetry. This ignores the fact that, at the moment of writing the poem, the poet is no longer concentrating on the object but on the process of composing, so that even in this ideal Japanese case there is a distance between experience and narration. Given this situation, it is untenable to distinguish between reminiscence and instant perception. The distinction is, however, instructive in another connection.

Any decision as to which of the two possibilities entailed in this distinction are involved must be based on knowledge of the biographical background. Kawabata's work itself supplies no concrete clues. His is a timeless story which could have taken place ten or twenty years later without any significant changes to events or even to their presentation.

The type of literary criticism which sees its most important task in relating the work to its factual background makes use of the customary way of approaching shishōsetsu as discussed in Part Two. However, this insight is of no use for making a generalization about the genre—although the encyclopaedia article seems to be aiming at exactly that—because it means that the recognition of the opposition between reminiscence and "true-to-life account" would be dependent on previous knowledge about the actual reality which is assumed to be referred to in the work.

On the other hand, the distinction between an "accompanying" and an "overseeing" narrative perspective is useful and significant for the definition of genre. The ideal first-person narrator in a shishōsetsu is completely inside that which is being presented and knows no more than the reader. It would be just as impossible for the narrator to have a fixed position outside events, for example in the form of a retrospective frame story, as it would be for the first-person narrator to plan to surprise the reader and make it necessary for him to reinterpret that which has previously been related. Shiga Naoya has clarified this by contrasting his literary ideal and the "fictional" works of Akutagawa: "I prefer to see the reader observing events from the same place as the writer.... However, in the case of Akutagawa the reader is occasionally tricked at the end."[35]

Let us now return to the example of "Izu no odoriko." We can at last put the Japanese categories "reminiscence" and "instant perception" to the test. They made no sense as a description of the time interval between literary and non-literary reality, as Japanese literary studies use them. However, they are valuable for describing intra-textual characteristics, as synonyms for the "overseeing" and the "accompanying" narrative perspective.

"Izu no odoriko" is a typical example of "accompanying" narrative as it characterizes shishōsetsu. No implications about the future let the reader know that the narrator already knows how the story will end. The open ending is also characteristic, so that a reader without knowledge of the biographical background could assume that the story ends in the year of the publication. This also makes it quite clear that it is not the relationship to non-literary reality which is decisive for the definition of the genre, but rather conventions in literary communication which can be identified in the work itself. Otherwise, literary studies would be concerned not with the work but with the character of the author, and it could best observe this subject by surrounding every writer with a horde of detectives—a logical consequence of shishōsetsu research up to now.

THE LEVEL OF PLOT. The factuality of the focus figure means that the first-person narrator of a shishōsetsu is the author himself. In addition, the focus figure signifies that nothing outside the experience of the first-person narrator is the subject of the work. Thus, shishōsetsu has an autobiographical quality.

Here we can clearly see the interdependence of factuality and focus figure. If they were independent of each other and were both merely separate characteristics ascribed to shishōsetsu, then factuality could be identified by references to historical events or real places, things that can be just as easily found in literature which is not shishōsetsu. On the other hand, the focus figure is also dependent on factuality, since it can be justified within the framework of the shishōsetsu doctrine only by its claim to truth.

The dialectical unity of factuality and focus figure results in a rigorous restriction of the breadth of authorial vision. Only what is of immediate concern in a certain period of the first-person narrator's life is described; everything else is left out. Thus, factuality as a structural element of shishōsetsu can never mean that the reader can expect information of general interest from the time period concerned, since it is not objective reality that is being described but rather the first person who is experiencing and narrating it and his relationship to it.

It is much too imprecise, however, to describe the limits of the subject as what is of immediate concern for the first-person narrator, since, depending on his personality, he might be concerned with fundamental philosophical matters, contemporary political events, or the problems of writing itself. We find nothing of this sort in shishōsetsu. Instead, there are descriptions of day-to-day monotony, financial problems, arguments with the family, marital problems, and brief moments of contented harmony with oneself and nature. It would be wrong to conclude that this monotony, which approaches banality at times, is a result of the lack of imagination and dullness of the authors; such an insinuation—apart from its being insulting—could not claim the right of being an explanation of a typical characteristic of shishōsetsu. The structural model we have been using must be applied here.

The structural element denoted by focus figure corresponds to a specific mode of experience, a particular relationship to the world, which is primarily emotional. The subject matter of shishōsetsu is not self-observation, self-criticism, the search for meaning, or the rational attempt to come to terms with oneself and the world but rather an emotional conception of the relationship between subject and empirical reality. Using a distinction between various functions of language in literature based on Bühler's Organon model, shishōsetsu could be classified as a mixture of subjective and descriptive literature[36] in which the subjective function of expression dominates.

Seen in this way, events at the level of plot in a shishōsetsu are relatively "excentric." The experience of reality in a narrative event is certainly an absolutely essential condition for securing factuality—but the descriptive intention is directed towards valorizing neither the subject nor the reality described within the limits of its experience. The meaning of shishōsetsu is not to be found in the description of periods of the author's life so as to raise them to an exemplary status; nor is it to be found in the general representative significance of the writer's personality itself. Thus, it does not intend either to instruct the reader or to satisfy his curiosity. It is furthermore not intended as means of self-interpretation or self-justification, which both imply that the subject can maintain a certain distance from itself and is open to rational thought processes.

Shishōsetsu is concerned above all with the expression of subjective experience. In this way it is close to both egocentric speech and, at the same time, traditional poetry.[37]

Let us now return to consider the level of plot. As we have seen, the events portrayed are not valued for themselves as an aid to entertaining—for example, in creating tension or simply creating an interesting story. They have no representative, symbolic character either.

The relative unimportance of the plot can be seen in many shishōsetsu which include only inadequate descriptions of real events, so that the reader has problems following what is happening. A typical example of this is Tokuda Shūsei's novel *Kabi* (Mold, 1911) which presents even the professional commentators with insoluble problems.[38] Yoshida Seiichi is right when he claims that the shishōsetsu writer is "not nice to his reader."[39] However, we know from the previous discussion that he cannot be "nice," because it is just his unconcerned egocentricity that guarantees his sincerity and spontaneity, qualities that would be destroyed by any consideration of the effects of what he writes.

According to Kobayashi Hideo, "The logic of everyday life itself becomes the logic of literary creation" in shishōsetsu.[40] We can now express this more concisely: To the extent that factuality as a structural element in shishōsetsu signifies an analogy between the work and reality, it is a precondition for the work. However, "everyday life" as such does not enter the field of vision and does not determine "the logic of literary creation," but it is the experiencing and narrating subject who selects and filters from the manifold of everyday life to comprise the reality of the work. He is the axis for the plot narrated from the "with" perspective and in "accompanying" form. It is, however, not the events themselves that are important but the way in which the subject perceives them.

THE "PHILOSOPHY." In the last section we attempted to characterize the plot in shishōsetsu. It became clear that this is determined not only by the reality involved, but also to a large degree by the person, the subject, who experiences and portrays this reality. The two aspects of speech—as statements about reality and as statements that provide information about the speaker—are particularly difficult to separate in shishōsetsu. That is why we were forced when discussing plot to anticipate matters that should have been the subject of this section.

All the factors that characterize the statements that provide information about the speaker in shishōsetsu can be summarized under the heading "philosophy": the system of values inherent to the work, the specific relationship to the world, and the resulting basic outlook with its corresponding manner of presentation. The "philosophy" is thus part of all the levels of text and can be "traced back" to the lexical-semantic level.

As we have already said, the structural element of focus figure corresponds to a subject who is at the center of the work from the point of view of both action and narrative technique. However, the values of the first-person character become part of the work, because the perspective is his, and since they are not confronted with values of equal rank held by other characters or institutions, they become absolute. A further factor reinforces this effect.

Shishōsetsu contains no discursive explanations of the first-person narrator's character, his appearance, or the motives for his actions, since this would betray to the reader that the author and first-person narrator was aware of him, that the narrator was not spontaneously putting down his experiences on paper but processing them so that they were "fictionalized" and therefore falsified. The work would be disqualified as a shishōsetsu. Just as the narrator cannot see himself from the outside, so the reader expects no information about things that are either inaccessible to him or obvious.

Shishōsetsu aims at the reader's complete identification with the first-person narrator. The reader becomes part of this character, so to speak. He is aware of the world through the narrator's eyes. However, since this takes place in an emotional way, largely excluding rational elements, it produces a mutual bond of understanding that precludes all intellectual thought processes. This manipulation of the reader's response results in his identifying so completely with the narrator that, in spite of the proximity between events described and his own reality and in spite of his familiarity with the situations described, he never attempts to judge the narrator's attitude or behavior. The hero does not reflect on his behavior, nor is the sympathetic reader perturbed by this in any way.

The narrator in shishōsetsu is characterized by his irrationality. He presents himself as the victim even when he himself has created the situation that makes him suffer. Poverty is portrayed as a destructive natural force; he is controlled by his own dissatisfaction with himself and frustrated ambition. He is at the mercy of his environment, is sacrificed to it, and reacts in a way that characterizes the basic mood of shishōsetsu—with sentimentality.

At last it is possible for us to locate the connection between shishōsetsu and classical literature so often mentioned by Japanese critics but never described in detail. We can cautiously apply two central concepts from traditional theories of art—*mujōkan* and *mono no aware*. To refer to sentimentality in shishōsetsu as an intensified emotion, as "escapism from a reality full of suffering to a world of aesthetic illusion,"[41] would blind us to the fact that this idealization has a long tradition in Japan and that shishōsetsu is not a new use of the concept but the continuation of a major trend.

Even a brief definition of the concepts named above leads to difficulties, caused on the one hand by the range of meaning which changes throughout their long history and, on the other, by the broad use of the concepts. The Buddhist concept *mujō* (ephemeral, unstable)[42] and its combination with *kan* (which means, depending on how it is written, "sentiment" or "view," "perspective")[43] is found in literature not only in medieval diaries and miscellanies. One of the most famous examples is the *Genji monogatari*, written ca. 1000 and generally called a tale of courtly love, in which all events are accompanied by melancholy reminders of the earthly ephemerality. The fact that *mujōkan* has continued to exist as an aesthetic ideal is due in no small degree to the canonical status of this work in Japanese literary history, reinforced by Motoori Norinaga's important commentary *Genji monogatari tama no ogushi* (1799).[44]

Closely connected with this concept is *aware* or *mono no aware*, the "beautiful pathos,"[45] "the sighing acknowledgement of the 'Ahness of it all,'"[46] which Brower and Miner describe: "Touching, pathetic, beautiful, moving the sensibilities, evoking the proper emotional response. Applied to those aspects of life and nature or their embodiment in art which stir the sympathies of the sensitive person of cultivation and breeding, impressing him with a deep awareness of the ephemeral beauty of a world in which only change is constant. Also applied to the person's response itself, which is usually one of bittersweet melancholy, although often combined with joy, delight or awe."[47] A constant and obvious reminder of the ephemerality of everything is the change of the seasons. The individual is exposed to the most perfect experience of *mujō* and *mono no aware* in nature. It now becomes clear why the world of nature and detailed observations of insects and other living creatures play such an important part in shishōsetsu. They correspond to the theme of *waka* and *haiku* poetry which perpetuated in modern times the *mono no aware* tradition.[48]

The last step follows automatically: The "subjectivism" of the focus figure, the emotional approach to reality and the specifically Japanese sentimentality are suitably expressed in affective language. The basic attitude and the intention of the expression are closest to the poetic first person; this explains why shishōsetsu is so often said to be poetic.

The great affinity among *mujōkan* and *mono no aware* and poetry becomes obvious in the following words by Emil Staiger, an attempt to characterize the nature of poetry: "In the flow of poetry we hear the river of the ephemeral which flows on incessantly so that nobody, since Heraclitus, has entered the same river twice. Man lowers himself into the river reminiscently, from the present, and swims along on the waves."[49] This quotation can be contrasted with the beginning of the *Hōjōki* (An Account of My Hut) written ca. 1212 by the monk Kamo no Chōmei (1153–1216), often cited as one of the most famous examples of *mujōkan* in Japan: "The river's flow never ceases, but it is not the same water. In still water the foam disappears and forms again, but it never remains for long."[50] It may seem idiosyncratic to place two texts from such different historical and cultural traditions next to each other, but the Staiger quotation should be considered of use as a commentary for the *mujō* text. We are hereby consciously excluding all the specific elements in the field of signification implied by the Japanese term, which it would be difficult to include here but which are also subject to varying interpretations in Japanese research.[51] At least we restrict the term more closely than, for example, Isobe Tadamasa, who, in his book *"Mujō" no kōzō* (The Structure of "Mujō") understands *aware* to mean, quite simply, human consciousness: "For the Japanese living means living with nature. Mountains and rivers, grass and flowers, birds and four-legged creatures, they are all the fellows of man. If there is anything in which he differs from them by nature, then it is that man is conscious that he is alive, that is, he feels *aware*."[52] Let us define the terms for our purposes: *mono no aware* is expressed in an increased emotional receptivity which results in *mujōkan*, a secularized melancholy of Buddhist origins.[53] We can recognize in it an affective schema[54] which is widely spread and has such a long history in Japanese culture that it has come to be regarded as the "most natural" relationship between man and the world, as the last quotation shows. Isobe's restriction of the world to nature which he moreover describes in terms of the traditional stereotypes—"mountains and rivers"—shows us how this pattern is tied to particular objects that have hardly changed at all in the course of Japanese history.[55]

We seem to have moved unnecessarily far away from our subject, the structural model for shishōsetsu. However, this attempt to find a working definition of the terms *mono no aware* and *mujōkan* is essential in establishing a link with literary tradition. We have not yet succeeded in breaking through this monolithic block. It is of no use to speak of a continuation of the classical heritage and refer to such varying epochs as we find in shishōsetsu research, where *nikki* and *haiku* literature, No and Saikaku, to name but a few, are all said to be predecessors of shishōsetsu,[56] since such an approach has not yet established which aspect of shishōsetsu correlates with which characteristic of the relevant classical genre.

We shall attempt to do just that with our definition of *mujōkan* and *mono no aware* as an affective schema. Shishōsetsu is related to those genres in Japanese literary history that also display this pattern. Since it is very widely spread, as we have already said, the relationship is correspondingly broad. This also explains the diversity of the classical genres with which shishōsetsu is linked, since this schema is not bound to only one particular structural element of the work but is equally relevant to its plot and other formal aspects. The affective schema is also not bound to particular forms of presentation, that is, it is not limited to one particular genre.

In tracing the connection with this affective schema we have avoided the paradox that would have arisen had we attempted to prove a relationship between such disparate genres as shishōsetsu and *haiku* on the basis of structural similarities or identical use of language. It is also unimportant whether the points in common depend on conscious or unconscious references being made. Finally, we can avoid having to list all shishōsetsu's classical relations, since this would depend on identifying the pattern in classical literature and that is not our objective.

Let us now conclude this discussion of the hypothetical shishōsetsu structural model with a summary: Shishōsetsu can be characterized by two elements which we named factuality and focus figure. Factuality refers to the supposed relationship between the work and reality and focus figure characterizes the way the text is organized. Important characteristics of the focus figure are the "with" and the "accompanying" narrative perspective and the central position the first-person narrator and hero assumes in the world of the "novel." He is not only the axis along which the plot develops, but he also carries out the implicit evaluation. He experiences emotionally; cognitive conception is considered to be an intrusive factor because it destroys the impression of immediacy essential for "genuineness" and therefore of decisive importance for the quality of a shishōsetsu. This emotional relationship with the world corresponds to a basic sentimental mood expressed in a poetic-impressionistic form of presentation. In this sentimental experience of the world we recognized the concepts *mujō* and *mono no aware* from classical tradition, which we interpreted as an affective schema. Shishōsetsu is related to various genres of pre-modern times by the transformation of this scheme in literature as a cultural pattern of action.

The outline presented here is bound to be approximate and abstract. Much has been stated only in theoretical terms, since further references would have made the definition intolerably long. However, the following two parts of the book will be concerned with the necessary detailed examination. Part Four will show whether the model is capable of producing satisfactory descriptions of various texts. It will then be necessary to find examples for those points that are at present merely unproven statements supporting the definition. Finally, Part Five will illustrate and expand the hypothesis put forward here.

In concluding, we ask how this structural model for shishōsetsu differs from previous definitions of the genre. Does it not contain the same statements as most earlier shishōsetsu descriptions? Was then the whole attempt unnecessary? The intention was not to produce a "completely new" definition of the term, but to replace all the characteristics attributed to shishōsetsu, the catalogue of criteria which can be shortened or lengthened at will, with a model that situates these characteristics in relation to each other. Only then can decisions be made as to whether a particular criterion is of constitutive importance for the genre or not. (It has been possible to deny this in the case of the first-person form.) And this means nothing more and nothing less than that we can now decide, for the first time, what is shishōsetsu and what is not.

---

1. Even if this is oriented towards shishōsetsu poetology; but this observation is itself a result of the analysis.
2. Terada, pp. 100f.
3. Morikawa, "Bungaku wa hirakareru," p. 191.
4. Cf. Hempfer, *Tendenz und Ästhetik*, p. 25.
5. Cited in ibid., p. 24.
6. Cf. ibid., p. 21, and Hempfer, *Gattungstheorie*, p. 224.
7. On this condition cf., e.g., the critical note by Wolfgang Lockemann, "Textsorten versus Gattungssorten oder ist das Ende der Kunstwissenschaft unvermeidlich?" p. 298.
8. Further titles are included in the bibliography.
9. Hibbett, "The Portrait of the Artist in Japanese Fiction," p. 35.
10. Cf., e.g., Siegfried J. Schmidt, "Ist Fiktionalität eine linguistische oder eine texttheoretische Kategorie?"
11. Cf. "The Dispute over Shishōsetsu" (Chapter 11).
12. *Uno Kōji zenshū*, II, 442.
13. Cf. Yoshida Seiichi et al., "Shishōsetsu no honshitsu to mondaiten," p. 65.
14. These examples come from Iwano Hōmei's story "Dokuyaku o nomu onna" (The Woman Who Took Poison, 1914), cf. "Shizenshugi seisuishi," *Masamune Hakuchō zenshū*, XII, 303.
15. This refers initially to the European genres. Bernd Neumann, *Identität und Rollenzwang*, has developed a terminological distinction. He sees autobiography characterized by a contemplative recollective attitude which studies the process of the formation of identity; he considers memoirs, on the other hand, to be the self-presentation of a subject who is in harmony with the social role which he is documenting (pp. 60ff.). It is not possible here to examine possible points of comparison with the traditional Japanese genres *zuihitsu* (miscellany) and *nikki bungaku* (diary literature), however, cf. "Diaries and Miscellany Literature" (Chapter 19).
16. This is considered in more detail in "The *Makoto* Principle" and "Empiricism" (Chapter 20).
17. Cf. "Inter- and Extratextual References to Heighten the *Riariti*" (Chapter 16), and "Shishōsetsu as an 'Automatic Text'" (Chapter 18).
18. Cf. examples in "Kikuchi Kan: 'Tomo to tomo to no aida'" (Chapter 16).
19. Cf. "The Origins of the Term *Watakushishōsetsu*" (Chapter 10).
20. Cf. "Amaki yo no hanashi," *Uno Kōji zenshū*, II, 442f.
21. Having completed this chapter I became aware, through two more recent monographs

on autobiography (Klaus-Detlef Müller, *Autobiographie und Roman*, and Peter Sloterdijk, *Literatur und Organisation von Lebenserfahrung*) of a study by Philippe Lejeune ("Le pacte autobiographique") in which he examines the specific reader reference of autobiography. His theory of a *pacte autobiographique* seems to equate with the claim to factuality postulated here even to the extent of the same mode of expression. However, it differs from our outline not only as far as the subject is concerned, which contains no equivalents of the distinctions worked out by Lejeune between autobiography, autobiographical novel, autobiography and biography, etc., but also above all in the meaning which factuality possesses as the realization of the *jitsu/makoto* principle in Japanese theory of art. Cf. critical notes on Lejeune in Müller, pp. 18ff.
22. The use of the word *relevant* is intended to draw attention to the fact that the possibility of isolating text levels has been carried out only to the extent to which it seemed useful in the context of modern Japanese literature, i.e. considering aspects which are significant in European literature is superfluous in this context when they are not significant in Japan and vice-versa.
23. The necessity for this repetition is explained in I.H.-K., "Kritische Bemerkungen."
24. Cf. below and our observations in "Shiga Naoya: 'Wakai'" (Chapter 16), and "The Myth of Immediacy" (Chapter 20) for the justification of this categorization.
25. *An'ya kōro, kōhan*, in *Shiga Naoya zenshū*, VIII, 264.
26. See below on the use of the third-person form and on the shared identity of character and author.
27. Cf. Todorov, "Die Kategorien der literarischen Erzählung," p. 289.
28. Cf. Yasuoka, *Shiga Naoya shiron*, pp. 247–263.
29. Ibid., p. 249.
30. Cf. "The Dispute over Shishōsetsu" (Chapter 11).
31. Yasuoka, *Shiga Naoya shiron*, p. 248.
32. Müller, pp. 68f.
33. "The Myth of Immediacy" (Chapter 20) contains impressive examples of this.
34. Yamamoto Kenkichi in *NBS*, p. 284.
35. "Kutsukake nite: Akutagawa kun no koto" (In Kutsukake: About Akutagawa, 1927), *Shiga Naoya zenshū*, V, 29–40, here p. 37.
36. Cf. Hans Dieter Zimmermann, *Vom Nutzen der Literatur*, pp. 105ff.
37. Ibid., p. 112. Cf. also "'Shishōsetsu's Sentimental Esoteric' and Egocentric Speech" (Chapter 16).
38. Cf. the annotated edition in *NKiBT*, XXI, 53–231.
39. Cf. "Factuality" in this chapter.
40. Cf. Sibley, "The Shiga Hero," p. 1.
41. Ilka Büschen, *Sentimentalität*, p. 127. The sentimentality concept, which here refers to European (Middle High German) literature, can also be used to advantage for the Japanese literature we are considering, cf. the discussion ibid., pp. 43ff., 64.
42. Abe Akio, *Kokubungaku gaisetsu*, pp. 157f., argues that *mujō* awareness corresponded to the feelings of the Japanese at a time when Buddhism did not have a dominating influence on spiritual life as it did in the Middle Ages. He sees a change of consciousness running parallel to Buddhist thought (*bukkyōteki shikō to onaji kōsu o tadorihajimete-ita*, p. 158) for the literati of antiquity, e.g. for the famous poets Kakinomoto no Hitomaro and Ōtomo no Yakamochi, who are represented in the poetry anthology *Man'yōshū* (Collection of Ten Thousand Leaves/Generations, late 8th century). Their poems breathe *mujōkan*, although they could hardly have been influenced by Buddhism (p. 158).
43. Cf. the semantic distinction of these different ways of writing in Karaki Junzō, *Mujō*, p. 10.
44. Cf. Kōnoshi Takamitsu, "Genji monogatari no isō," pp. 114ff., also Matsumoto Shigeru, pp. 54ff. on Buddhist thought in *Genji monogatari* and on Motoori's belittling of Bud-

dhism in *Genji monogatari tama no ogushi*, since he considered that it rather ran counter to *mono no aware*.
45. William LaFleur, "Death and Japanese Thought," p. 233.
46. Jay Gluck, *Ukiyo*, p. xxiv.
47. Robert H. Brower/Earl Miner, *Japanese Court Poetry*, p. 503. Cf. also O. Kressler, "Mono no aware," on the *mono no aware* concept in Motoori.
48. Cf. Mathy, "Mono no aware," pp. 150ff.
49. Staiger expresses this in connection with tense equivalents in the main kinds of poetry, *Grundbegriffe der Poetik*, p. 215.
50. *Hōjōki*, text in *NKBT*, XXX, 23–52, here p. 23. Karaki, pp. 220ff., includes similar passages from three further works of this time.
51. There are numerous studies on *mujōkan* in individual medieval works. An example of historical terminological differentiation is the section in Kobayashi Chishō's "Atmosphere of Mujō in the Heike Monogatari" (from *Zoku chūsei bungaku no shisō*, 1974), which is included as text no. 8 in Bruno Lewin, ed., *Japanische Literaturwissenschaft*.
52. Isobe Tadamasa, *"Mujō" no kōzō*, p. 102.
53. Cf. also Karaki, p. 209, on the relationship between *mono no aware* and *mujōkan*.
54. Cf. Hans Dieter Zimmermann, p. 126.
55. More detailed explanations in Part Five.
56. Cf. "Special Aspects of Shishōsetsu" (Chapter 9).

Part Four
Transformations in Shishōsetsu

15 · Literary Evolution— an Outline

The hypothetical, structural model of shishōsetsu set up in the previous part of this book was based on the assumption that a genre is not merely an arbitrary grouping of texts but a reality of literary communication. We described this aspect of the communication process at a significant point within the history of the genre—its first important appearance and reception—before attempting to construct the model of the genre formally.

Thus our model is neither a substratum abstracted from a cross-section of representative examples of the genre (choosing a body of texts would immediately disqualify this method as arbitrary) nor does it imply the aprioristic existence of "universals" in the Platonic sense.[1] Instead, for us the genre consists of a collection of certain norms of communication which we have attempted to incorporate into our model.

The individual works are related to the model in the same way that concrete "historically determined and historically explicable" surface phenomena are related to "deeper structures of relative or absolute constancy."[2] There is a specific relationship of dependency between these two levels which determines the limits of historical change. Our intention in concentrating here on a historical body of texts is to characterize them as the transformation of the deep structure that determines the specificity of any genre.

We must expect, however, that the examples used may also be subsumed under other conceivable genre structures. It is therefore possible that, in addition to a specific superstructure that coincides with one transformational possibility of the shishōsetsu structural model, a work also contains further elements that could refer to one or more other genres. We shall not follow up such information if it should arise in course of our examination of the works, since we would then run the risk of digressing from our real subject, shishōsetsu: this would be inexcusably negligent in view of the present state of research on the subject.

There is one more important point in which we must dampen some hopes that may have been raised by the title of this part of the book. It is not possible within the framework of our inquiry to present a diachronic cross-section of the genre in the sense of a developmental process that could be interpreted using intra- and extratextual facts. There are several reasons for this, one of which is that the necessary philological groundwork has not yet been carried out in this field.[3] In any case, such an undertaking would exceed the limits of this book.

The most important argument against such a project, however, arises from the problematic nature of assuming the validity of a historical process of development. It would be pointless to assume deterministic principles from which to conclude the inevitability of historically manifested change. Such an attempt would be no more than a "pseudo-explanation . . . on the basis of historical-philosophical speculation."[4] If, instead, evolution is understood in terms of a system change, then we can concur with Hempfer in assuming the following kind of process: "In view of the empirical conditions it seems possible at the present to give only the dialectic of genesis and structure as a general principle of development, which constitutes a non-deterministic, non-teleologic process of destructuring existing structures and of restructuring new entities. The process can, in each case, be derived in concrete terms not from general principles but from specific antecedents in the relevant system and/or from such conditions in higher systems."[5] These statements are useful in two ways. First, they make it clear how much analysis is necessary before we can adequately describe shishōsetsu genre history as a historical process of change. However, since literary evolution cannot be concluded from immanent literary factors alone, it will be necessary to include the relevant influential factors from other "higher systems," and for this we shall have to formulate the "explicit conditions necessary for different systems to be able to correlate."[6]

Even the task of testing conscientiously to what extent any possibly relevant "higher systems"—whether political, philosophical, religious, or whatever—may have affected the development of shishōsetsu would require the cooperation of several scholars, if possible on an interdisciplinary basis. However, such a joint undertaking within the field of shishōsetsu research is unlikely to occur in the foreseeable future and makes it painfully clear just how modest our contribution is in view of the problems that remain to be solved.

This book has taken, however, an important step in the right direction by discussing both a method and its premises with which genre history can be meaningfully tackled in the future. This is one important step beyond all the historical attempts at description which, buoyed up by naive positivism, try their luck with questionable teleological theories.

If this book can, despite all limitations, claim to make a contribution to the history of genre, then it lies—alongside the description of a decisive period of development outlined previously in the first part—in the concept we have presented of a process of evolution originating both within and outside the field of the literature in question. What we can hope to achieve through our inquiry must be accordingly redefined. Paradoxically, our contribution to genre history lies precisely in the recognition that it is not capable of producing a definitive theoretical construction of genre-history.

Such self-satisfaction should not lead us to be complacent; there are enough questions left open that we can see a partial solution to the question of genre through practical examples. In the following chapter we concentrate on eight selected shishōsetsu which cover the period from the origins of the genre until the present. The criteria for selection were, on the one hand, a relatively even distribution as far as possible within this time frame, although the concentration of examples from the early phase is intended to point out the frequency of shishōsetsu in that period. Just as important is the selection of representative examples. Works which were considered by contemporary readers or by the critics to be typical shishōsetsu or characteristic for an author were chosen wherever possible, as well as works that have a secure position within literary history.

The number of possible examples was, of course, much greater than could possibly have been discussed here. There had to be a further limitation: Preference was given to those texts capable, in "formal" or other respects, of illuminating the range of possibilities and variations in the model for the genre.

In the interpretations we can concentrate only on certain aspects, which automatically introduces some bias; but it would be impossible to provide a full analysis of the relevant works here. Similarly, we can dispense with the "synopsis" which is customary in many studies of Japanese literature and which would mean an over-emphasis on the level of plot, something that is not at all justified in shishōsetsu. It is easy to find an outline of the plots in reference books and literary histories[7] so that I can restrict myself to describing important scenes and sketching out the general context, as may be necessary. Should this lead to protests that this method is too subjective, one might reply that a "synopsis" is also interpretive to an extent. Certainly, there is nothing to replace reading the original.

Despite all these restrictions, we can still hope that our observations made of the examples will as a whole give an impression of the essence of the genre and that they will provide a preliminary descriptive and interpretative framework, if not a systematic historiography, for a history of the genre which would clarify the context of historical transformation.

---

1. Cf. Hempfer, *Gattungstheorie*, pp. 30ff.
2. Ibid., p. 141.
3. Only a few essays are concerned with giving a coherent description of different examples of the genre, and then in a very general way, often using completely inadequate means, cf. the research report in Part Two of this study.
4. Hempfer, *Gattungstheorie*, p. 227.
5. Ibid. In addition, the following studies were consulted on the evolution problematic: Jurij Tynjanov, "Über die literarische Evolution," Alexander von Bormann, "Ansatz und Reichweite," Hans Günther, "Die Konzeption der literarischen Evolution," and Ingrid Strohschneider-Kohrs, *Literarische Struktur und geschichtlicher Wandel*.
6. Hempfer, *Gattungstheorie*, p. 227.
7. Cf., e.g., Hisamatsu, *Zōho shinpan Nihon bungakushi*, vols. VI and VII, or Yoshida Seiichi, *Shizenshugi no kenkyū*. To my knowledge, of the texts discussed here in detail, there is an English translation only of Dazai Osamu's *Ningen shikkaku: No longer human*, tr. by Donald Keene.

16 · Shishōsetsu—Examples and Analyses

IWANO HŌMEI: "TANDEKI" (1909)

The story "Tandeki" (Self-Indulgence) was published in February 1909 in the magazine *Shinshōsetsu* and overnight transformed its author Iwano Hōmei (1873–1920) into a typical representative of *shizenshugi*. At the same time it is "in many ways a model [example] of his literature."[1] According to Wada Kingo, the work is obviously influenced by "Futon," published in 1907.[2] The story tells, in first-person voice (*boku*), of the experiences of the writer Tamura, identified in the reference books as Hōmei himself.[3] The events related in the book are supposed to have occurred in Nikkō in 1906.

"Tandeki" contains the first example of the narrative concept of "one-dimensional description" (*ichigen byōsha*),[4] a technique developed by Hōmei himself, which we have called the "'with' perspective" (narrator = character) and which proved to be a typical characteristic of shishōsetsu derived from the structural element of focus figure.[5] One essential characteristic of the work is at this "formal" level—the assumption of absolute subjectivity.

"I AM PROUD TO BE DECADENT!"—A WEST-EAST AFFINITY

The first-person narrator in "Tandeki" is in many ways similar to the hero of "Futon." He is a member of the literati in his mid-thirties, though not very successful, unhappy in his marriage, who supports himself by teaching English. We learn little of his writing career. We know only that at the beginning of "Tandeki" he has withdrawn to the seaside

201

resort of Kōzu to write a play there during the summer. The majority of the events described in the story take place during his stay. The subject of the work is the relationship between the first-person narrator and the geisha Kichiya, from the time they meet each other until their final separation some months later.

Although literature and art seems to play at the most only a subordinate role in the life of the first-person narrator, he still feels that his is a great artistic existence. He repeatedly compares himself to the character of Leonardo da Vinci from Merezhkovskiy's novel of the same name (published in 1901). It is remarkable that he is not satisfied with justifying his existence by the similarities brought out by the comparison with Da Vinci. We met this method—which is one of the standard devices in West-East affinities—in Katai.[6] Instead, he accentuates the points of contrast with Da Vinci: "When I think of my family problems, of my relationships with women, and the pain and weariness which they cause, then I somehow long for [a life like] Leonardo's—I would have been happier as a bachelor, noble and ascetic. But when I think about it again, I realize that I experienced this noble, ascetic, half monk-like life both as an ideal and in practice more than ten years ago. I know by now that my present ego could not be satisfied with such a naive (*uiuishii*) [attitude]. I think my nerves are five or ten times more sensitive than Leonardo's."[7] For Tamura, Leonardo embodies the disciplined, "noble," "classic" type of artist. He sees himself, on the other hand, as an impulsive person of excessive sensibilities—in his own words, a decadent. "Decline, decay, lassitude and weariness—I was overwhelmed before I was proud to wander around in the field (*bun'ya*) of decadence" (p. 84).

"Decline," "decay," "lassitude," and "weariness" seem strange in view of the world depicted in the book, which is concerned throughout with love affairs and the financial problems they lead to. Such vocabulary would be applicable here in a very superficial, banal sense and its use can be explained only in terms of the relationship with "decadence."

Tamura confesses to being a decadent. He sets out in detail what he understands by the term in the way he leads his life: It is the overbearing, inconsiderate, egoistic life of a man whose conduct is entirely determined by his own needs and moods. The price he has to pay for such a life is, in his view, that of financial difficulties and permanent "over-sensitivity," but he decides towards the end of the book to bear such burdens, since his way of life is the fulfillment of an artistic ideal which he places higher than that of Leonardo:

I greatly envy his [Leonardo's] great energy and absolute patience, but it makes me dissatisfied that he maintained classical attitudes quite contentedly until the time of his death. A decadent, on the other hand, takes on incertainty as such.

When such smart-aleck thoughts went through my head while I was writing it seemed as if a voice from somewhere above me said:

"Yes, but you're being self-indulgent!"

And from somewhere out of the depths came a groan:

"Indulgence is life!"

However that may be, it can only have been my inner being which is free of self-indulgence which invented such arguments. But it became painfully clear to me that my present misery and my over-sensitivity would remain with me for my entire life. (p. 96)

However difficult it is on the basis of the evidence of the life described in the book to distinguish decadence and self-indulgence from exaggerated egoism, or to recognize in what way the repeatedly invoked hypersensitivity of the first-person narrator expresses itself, it is easy to see the way in which these concepts refer to European literature. Leaving aside questions concerning the adequacy and the specific "misunderstandings" in Hōmei's assumptions,[8] we shall describe the circle of authors and ideas to which he refers.

It is possible to see from the way these European concepts appear in the work just how poorly they are incorporated: they are included merely as a list of authors' names whose works are to be found on the writer Tamura's bookshelves. (Significantly, only non-Japanese books are mentioned.) However, the fact that the list begins with names such as Tolstoy, Maeterlinck, and Browning (p. 91), who have little or nothing in common, and is then extended shortly afterwards by completely gratuitous references to Bismarck and Gladstone (p. 92) makes it likely that Hōmei was more interested in the references as such than in the explanation of clearly defined concepts. He adorns himself with this West-East affinity; it serves as self-apology and self-stylization.

The first-person narrator in "Tandeki" mentions several times a "Treatise on Decadence" ("Dekadanron," p. 89) published shortly before his stay in Kōzu, but rather than use the opportunity to explain his ideas he merely connects his treatise with worries that he might lose his job as an English teacher (p. 92). By the "Treatise" he probably alludes to his essay "Shinpiteki hanjūshugi" (Mystic Semi-Animalism, 1906), where he refers to Emerson, Swedenborg, Maeterlinck, Schopenhauer, and Nietzsche, among others.[9] The essence of the essay is expressed in the formula *bungaku soku jikkō*—"literature = action." "Tandeki" is intended to glorify life and document the affirmation of suffering. The result is the reverse of the formula: "action = literature."

WOMAN AS AN OBJECT OF DESIRE

In view of what has been said up to now we can assume that Hōmei was aiming at a demonstration of his decadence theories in the story "Tandeki." However, the unprepared reader encounters a story that reappears in a similar guise in many other shishōsetsu and verges on banality and bad taste. This opinion is based not so much on the events as such—the relationship of a writer to women engaged in the business of entertaining (*mizushōbai no onna*) appears so frequently as a theme of modern Japanese literature that it contains nothing of the profligate character a European reader might read into it. Dissatisfaction with the work arises, rather, from the fact that the events and feelings are unmotivated.

The story is a familiar one. The writer Tamura falls in love with the geisha Kichiya, or, to put it more precisely, he decides to "pamper" (*kawaigatte yarō*, p. 66) her during his stay in Kōzu and perhaps take her back to Tokyo. Kichiya is neither beautiful nor attractive in any other way. She has the nickname "crow geisha" (*okarasu geisha*, p. 72) because of her dark skin. It displeases him that she gave herself up to him on the very first evening, but one can become fond of a creature who behaves so freely, whether a pet or a person, for that very reason (p. 66).

The relationship, which begins on such an odd note, is overshadowed by two further affairs Kichiya is having with local men. Nevertheless, Tamura continues to make use of her services. At the beginning of their friendship, he decides to make an actress of her, because, although she can neither sing well nor play the samisen, she does have large eyes and a long nose and in any case he is writing a play in which a woman appears (p. 67). It then seems as if he feels himself bound to her more because of his promise to bring her into the theater than of erotic passion, even though he repeatedly has reason to doubt whether Kichiya is at all interested in an acting career (p. 75). His attempts to persuade writer colleagues to help Kichiya into acting fail (pp. 68, 88). Ultimately, it is purely out of pride and fear of losing face—rather than heartfelt ties to the geisha or even the conviction that her talent must be supported—that the writer continues stubbornly with his plan: "After all, I am a man, and I do not intend to lose my honor by not keeping a promise I have made. I will not ask anyone else but will take full responsibility myself in every situation" (p. 89). His sense of honor rather than sexual desire binds him to Kichiya, to whom he does not even feel attracted. The fact that he still continues to call himself one of her helpless slaves (p. 74) arouses suspicions that Hōmei is attempting to enact his theoretical understanding of passion;[10] it is however in no way convincing.

WOMAN AS A BURDEN

If we are to believe the narrator, the jealousy and doubts Kichiya causes are nothing compared to the suffering his wife inflicts upon him. She and the three children with whom he can develop no real relationship (p. 90) are nothing but millstones around his neck, the dismal background to his daily existence, the embodiment of all the suffering inflicted on men.

It is astonishing how similar the heroes of "Futon" and "Tandeki" are. They hold European women up as an ideal and long for similarly "free" and "modern" Japanese women. In reality they just have love affairs: "When I feel dissatisfied, have spiritual pain, or feel lonely, then my wife and the children are no consolation. Once Japanese, as opposed to foreign, women have children, they generally direct all their energy towards them and mostly believe that it is adequate to be dutifully faithful to their husbands. How can they win the heart of a man who wants to be something in society and encourage him in this way (that is what I call true living love)?[11] For me my wife is merely a lame animal (*hanshin fuzui no dōbutsu*). I wondered if I should make Kichiya my mistress and forget the whole acting affair" (p. 74). He tells his wife in a letter that his relationship with Kichiya is much more intense than his feelings for her (p. 75) and asks her for money to support his pleasures. When her letter of reply does not come with a cheque, he throws it aside unread and later complains how little understanding she shows for the new life that his love has infused him with (p. 86). Repeated demands for money and Tamura's announcement that he will bring Kichiya to Tokyo as his mistress bring his wife to leave for Kōzu with their youngest child, a baby. We learn nothing of any discussion between the two. She remains in Kōzu as security for the rent of the room and to maintain supervision of Kichiya secretly, while Tamura pawns her clothes in Tokyo in order to get money to pay his debts and to buy Kichiya's freedom, who then returns to her family in Asakusa, Tokyo.

While Tamura is sorting out his wife's clothes for the pawnshop, his feelings upon glimpsing a red undergarment reveal that, at the beginning of their marriage, he was as much in love with his wife as he now (supposedly) is with Kichiya. He imagines he can scent his wife's young skin in the material (p. 93). This is not the only scene that arouses associations with "Futon."[12] We are led to ask why the heroes of these works are subject to such violent changes of feeling.

INNER VOICES AND HIGHER POWERS, OR
THE IMPOTENCE OF THE INDIVIDUAL

Fourteen or fifteen years ago, when the narrator married, it seemed to him that his wife appeared inexpressibly lovely when she blushed charmingly after only a few sips of sake (p. 81). Nothing remains now of his affection—a development he feels to be an obvious consequence of the process of aging.

The heroes in "Tandeki" and "Futon" are in their more lucid moments aware that their present love affairs will end with them growing tired of their partners, just as in their marriages, since their relationships with women are restricted to a purely sensual level. However convinced Tamura may be of having been bewitched by Kichiya, he simply turns his back on her at the end.

He visits her one day in Asakusa and notes, with some satisfaction, that she is suffering from an eye complaint, obviously the result of venereal disease (p. 97). His wife's secret pleasure in the news of Kichiya's suffering may seem understandable to the reader, but Tamura's similar reaction is not and can only be understood in terms of the vindictive feelings that arose after he had bought Kichiya freedom from bondage without receiving anything in exchange.

The narrator visits Kichiya once more, this time after a night spent in Yoshiwara, the red-light district. Malicious curiosity seems to motivate him, and he takes a friend with him to witness his triumph. Kichiya's condition has declined rapidly. Tamura suggests that she ask her former lover for the money she needs for treatment (p. 100). After a while he wants to leave:

> "Cold-blooded! Cruel!"—a voice that could not be ignored was raised, but I contradicted it secretly. If the odor of my family is firmly in my breast in spite of the fact that it is so abominable, then Kikuko's [the geisha Kichiya's common name] evil smell will cling to my heart eternally. I am sure I will encounter other women in the future and taste the bitterness that this will bring, but that will be no reason to dig myself a narrow stereotyped (*kata ni hamatta*) grave. I do not know if it is cold-blooded or cruel, but strong injections are needed for weak nerves. What I need is an injection that takes effect quickly. It is most potent, like sake or absinth, while the smell is strongest.

And when all this slowly and naturally comes to plague me, then it is nothing but love and longing.
While I was thinking this, I was surprised to find myself in the entrance to the house.
"Best wishes to your wife." [Kikuko's] mother said. Kikuko seemed to feel weak and showed us a sad, painful smile: "If my eyes were healthy I would love to go with you . . ."
I did not answer this; however, I felt that my goodbye wishes were like a song of victory, and my friend pulled me away. (p. 101)

This last scene has been quoted in full because it throws light on the story as a whole. The narrator never thinks about his own behavior. He describes himself as a creature driven by inner voices, by inexplicable commands coming from above or below, who is incapable of assuming responsibility for his actions (even when he plans to do so). Feelings—or rather compulsive behavior—take hold of him suddenly and disappear again just as quickly. Usually they are external stimuli to which the subject can only react. In their strongest form, these reactions increase to the level of "love" and "longing" (cf. the quotation) all of which he accepts as though it were his fate. Nothing leads him to thought or reflection. He feels himself like someone who suffers and acts; there is no place for reflection in a life in which ominous voices are assigned to the task of removing the hero's last scruples.

How little the hero is prepared to consider the consequences of his actions is exemplified in a scene such as that at the end of the story, when Tamura and his friend realize, after their night in the red-light district, that they do not have enough money to pay their debts. Their attitude, that this predictable calamity is "really funny" (*jitsu ni kokkei*, p. 100), seems peculiarly superficial and fatalistic. However, it is just this "Drifting"—this was also the title of a work ("Hōrō") which appeared two months after "Tandeki"—which Hōmei idealizes as the type of behavior that characterizes a decadent and that turns his life itself into a work of literature.

Contemporary reception of "Tandeki" maintained none of the critical distance from which we have considered the work. On the contrary, it was the hero's impulsiveness in particular which was admired. It seemed to the public to be more genuine and convincing than any story in which the motives for actions were easy to recognize. *Tandeki* became a catch-phrase, as did *chūnen no koi*—"the love of a man in his middle years," and the subject of many shishōsetsu at that time.[13] Nobody was greatly disturbed by a fact that may seem curious to us—that Hōmei was well known for wanting to turn every woman he met into an actress.[14] Even if Masamune Hakuchō declared as early as 1928 that neither "Tandeki" nor "Futon" were great works of art,[15] it seems that the intellectuals in 1909 saw themselves reflected in the writer Tamura. The following examples will show that many of the characteristics of "Tandeki" can also be found in works where there is no such elevated "theory of decadence."

CHIKAMATSU SHŪKŌ: "GIWAKU" (1913)

The "short story" "Giwaku" (Doubt), published in September 1913 in the magazine *Shinshōsetsu*, is more than twice as long as, for example, the "story" "Kurokami" (Black Hair, 1924) by the same author, showing us that Japanese generic concepts like *tanpen*, *chūhen*, and *chōhen shōsetsu*, based solely on length, are somewhat self-contradictory. According to the critic and shishōsetsu scholar Hirano Ken, it is not only the high point (*pīku*) in the literary career of its author Chikamatsu Shūkō (1876–1944), but also an unsurpassed masterpiece (*zeppin*) in the shishōsetsu genre.[16] Ōkubo Tsuneo claims that "Giwaku" is the provisional end of a process of purification (*junka*), during which the author achieves ever greater openness and sincerity. While he wrote in "Yuki no hi" (Snowy Day, 1910), an earlier work, "How could anyone bare his own private life in front of the eyes of the masses to earn his living!"[17] this is just what he himself does in "Giwaku," according to Ōkubo. Thus, not only would this be an important development for Shūkō's literature but it would also represent a higher degree of refinement in shishōsetsu as a whole.[18] Given that it is possible to trace a division between "public" and "private" life (*kōteki* and *shiteki seikatsu*) in Katai, only private life would then exist for Shūkō.[19]

We intend to place such an attitude, with no further comment, at the beginning of our discussion of "Giwaku," as a typical example of the methods and assumptions of conventional shishōsetsu research. However, it is important to identify those points over which we take a decidedly different approach from Ōkubo: We do not share his opinion that, when the thematic range of shishōsetsu is limited to the relations between the sexes—Ōkubo himself talks of "stories of obsessive love" (*jōchi shōsetsu*)[20]—which in turn means for him the exclusion of public life, that this automatically leads to a "refinement" in the sense of a qualitative improvement of shishōsetsu. Nor can we accept his method of taking fictional statements—since they appear within the context of a literary work—as comments on the work, or of making no fundamental distinction between "objective" and "literary" reality.

INTER- AND EXTRATEXTUAL REFERENCES TO HEIGHTEN THE *RIARITI*

According to the Japanese view, a shishōsetsu can be deemed truly good only when it creates *riariti*. This concept is so central to Japanese literary standards that it no longer needs definition. But what does it really mean?[21]

Riariti presupposes factuality, but factuality in the sense of the structural element as we defined it in the framework of the shishōsetsu definition, that is, as the reader's establishment of a correspondence between literary and "objective" reality. While factuality in the sense used above refers to the reader's expectations, the term *riariti* expresses the effect on the reader. Thus, while factuality is by definition an indispensable condition for all shishōsetsu, *riariti* is, on the other hand, a quality largely effected by the specific configuration of an individual work.[22]

Inter- and extratextual references, such as those in "Giwaku," are important means of securing the effect of *riariti* in shishōsetsu. The work is a shishōsetsu in its own right, but it is generally considered to be the "continuation" (*zokuhen*) of "Letter to My Wife Who Left Me" ("Wakaretaru tsuma ni okuru tegami"), published in 1910.[23] There was also a sequel to "Giwaku,"[24] so that one can definitely claim that the works form a series. However, the connection is less dependent on intertextual references than on the thematic content of these works, that is, the author's own biography. It is thus the chronological development of nonliterary events that welds these texts into a larger unit. To the extent that all shishōsetsu have an autobiographical character, all the books by a particular shishōsetsu writer could be regarded as one long "serialized novel."

Why is it, then, that this feature is so especially emphasized by the critics in the case of "Giwaku"? It seems that one important reason is that Shūkō assumes, more than other authors, the unity of the whole work and therefore merely refers to matters he has dealt with in detail in earlier works. The first-person narrator (*watakushi*) is not the least bit concerned with informing a reader who knows no other of the author's works. Thus, we are never told throughout the entire book why the hero sets out to search for the woman who left him two years ago, although this search becomes more important to him than anything else, even more important than reading and writing novels; it becomes his "only reason for living."[25]

But this is a question the ideal shishōsetsu reader would not raise, since he knows that women play a particularly important part in Shūkō's life. For this reason, Ōkubo concludes according to a shishōsetsu logic: "For Shūkō, *woman* was indeed *literature* itself (onna *to wa* bungaku *sono mono de ari*) [emphasis in the original]), and it was his life's work to search for her."[26] To question this trinity of woman, life, and art would imply inadequate response to the text.

Shūkō introduces the reader to the story very abruptly. The first sentence delivers information about the time of year and establishes the general tenor, while the second sentence surprises by elucidating, in a characteristic manner, the subject of the entire book, which is the broken relationship between the hero and a woman. "At the time, it was spring, which put one in a sensual mood. I imagined the moment when I would kill you using various different means" (p. 284). A little later precise indications of the time of narration ensure that the reader recognizes the topical nature of the material and no longer questions the factuality of the book: The narrative present is April 1911 when the hero places a missing-person report concerning the woman who left him in autumn 1909 (p. 284).

Here the informed contemporary reader should now be able to see the connection with "Letter to My Wife Who Left Me." That the woman is called O-Yuki, while her name in "Giwaku" is O-Suma, raises no doubts as to the real identity of both characters; since as far as names are concerned shishōsetsu are awarded a small measure of "poetic license."[27] Ōkubo Tsuneo would probably call the change from a purely fictional name such as O-Yuki to the name O-Suma, derived from the name of the real model, O-Masu, a "process of refinement."

The following sentence must puzzle the reader somewhat: "As I already said in the previous letter, I particularly wanted to see the fan or the sake dish from this Shin in Nikkō, but this is impossible" (p. 285). The previous letter to which the narrator refers can only mean the earlier published work "Wakaretaru tsuma ni okuru tegami." However, it is interesting to note that this contains no reference to the person named here nor the objects and their history; Shūkō obviously believed he had explained everything necessary. The objects themselves are unimportant; their sole significance is to raise the name Nikkō and so orientate the narrator on a path through the rest of the "short story."

"This Shin" (*sono Shin san*) appears to the reader a complete stranger until this moment. It is only gradually possible to identify him as O-Suma's brother-in-law. It is just this type of narrative organization in which the author, to use Yoshida Seiichi's words, "is not nice to the reader"[28] which proves that it is "genuine" and is one method of achieving *riariti*.

THE "HOLY FOOL"

The first-person narrator in "Giwaku" is a typical shishōsetsu hero of the type already encountered in "Futon," "Tandeki," and other books. The hero of "Giwaku" feels he has been betrayed by a woman who was no longer prepared to act the part of his wife unless he legally marry her. It is not clear why he is not ready to marry her, since he considers marriage—and this is his argument against official bonds—as nothing more than a piece of paper (p. 306). The lack of real love between them cannot be the reason, since he feels drawn to her by a "long-lasting, secure relationship, tied by profound bonds and unfathomable secrets which could only be mutual—just the thought of it makes me happy" (p. 309). Of course, none of this means that the hero does not sometimes have another woman live with him (p. 313).

We learn about this in a flashback while the narrator is in Nikkō. He went there in order to have his suspicions confirmed that his mistress spent several days there with Kojima Kinjirō a year and a half earlier. Kojima is a student and his former tenant. When he finds their names in an old guest list he cries tears of joy (p. 290) and is so delighted at his success that he "wants to thank God, if there is one" (p. 291).

The rest of the short story consists of the flashback mentioned previously which describes the life of the three characters in Tokyo. It soon becomes clear to the reader, from the long sequence of short episodes, what "doubt" means for the narrator until his journey to Nikkō—that O-Suma is having an affair with Kojima. She presents the hero with the choice of marrying her or doing without her, but he is merely evasive: she is free to leave him, he says, but not during his current period of difficulties (p. 306). O-Suma wants to clear the matter and presents him with an ultimatum. He has fifteen days to decide to marry her or she will leave (p. 306). The narrator sums the whole affair up with the words: "There was nothing for me to think about. I could do nothing but wait until you had calmed down again. But without success" (p. 306). O-Suma then moves to her family's house, taking the tenant with her. There are scenes of jealousy, which are not without a degree of comedy. For example, one night the hero wants to break into the house, armed with a knife, but turns back when he is sure that O-Suma is not sleeping next to Kojima (p. 310). The narrator also lives with O-Suma's family for two months, until she eventually vanishes with her lover, but we learn nothing of this presumably dramatic phase of the triangular relationship because, at this point, the narrator switches back to the narrative present, that is, his journey back from Tokyo by night. The story ends abruptly with the conjecture that the pair are staying with Kojima's family in Okayama.

It is not very difficult to find the story and its hero ridiculous, with his continuous wild swings of emotion, his boundless egoism, his unreasonableness and utter disregard for reality, his vanity,[29] and his surges of emotion which all end in tears (cf. pp. 286, 288, 290, 292, 310, 314). However, according to Matsubara Shin'ichi, it is just this which makes this work so appealing. For him, "Giwaku" is the prime example of a "literature of fools" (*gusha no bungaku*)—also the title of his book on the subject.[30] The general conduct and types of behavior described in such literature which would be normally completely unacceptable are the "nourishment" (*jiyōbun*) for an art form that wishes to emphasize what is considered truly human.[31] Therefore, no one has the right to ridicule Shūkō and his literature.[32] According to Matsubara it would be more fitting to bow down before the "halo" (*gokō*) of someone so thoroughly foolish.[33]

SHIGA NAOYA: "WAKAI" (1917)

The story "Wakai" (The Reconciliation), which was published in October 1917 in the magazine *Kokuchō*, is one of the best-known works by Shiga Naoya (1883–1971), the "god of fiction" as he is known in Japan's literary world, following the coinage from his admirer Akutagawa. The subject of the story is a period of the author's life dominated by a dispute with his father, which ends with their reconciliation in August 1917. The literary histories emphasize the documentary character of the story.[34]

Even his contemporary critics, in spite of their open admiration for Shiga's literary masterpiece, criticized the fact that the reader never finds out the reason behind the conflict with the author's father.[35] Shiga defended himself in his own inimitable way: "I should like to say to that: why does no one give me credit for the fact that I was able to portray the reconciliation without writing anything about the reason for the quarrel."[36]

We are not interested here in the biographical background, about which a large number of works have been published,[37] but shall instead emphasize some important aspects of the work which illuminate Shiga's particular style of writing and at the same time show what is typical of shishōsetsu in his work.

SHISHŌSETSU NARRATIVE STRATEGIES— THE ILLUSION OF IMMEDIACY

"Wakai" consists of sixteen sections. The story starts on 31 July and continues until the second half of September. It could almost be said that the narrative present ends at the time of publication, since the reader who ignores the fictional character of literature and the reader with knowledge of the biographical background both place the events in this period of 1917 and know that the work to be published in October, mentioned repeatedly in "Wakai,"[38] is identical with the story itself. However, the narrative structure is by no means as simple as it may appear. As far as I know, this feature of the work has not yet been analyzed, so we shall now consider it briefly.

Let us start at the end of the story, which provides the most important information about the time during which the events took place. The reconciliation between father and son has already been recounted in section 13; from section 14 to 16 the first-person narrator (*jibun*) revels in his newly found inner balance and describes endless scenes of blissful domestic happiness which take place only a few days after the "peace settlement" of 30 August. The last paragraph in this last section begins as follows: "I felt uneasy [when thinking of the] deadline for my work, because one day passed after another. Finally I decided to write about the reconciliation with my father which occupied me most of all at the time" (p. 145). At this point, immediately before the end of "Wakai," we first discover when the work was started and the motivation for writing the story. Thus, the circle outlined in the title is closed: The reconciliation is the final point of the action; the story is told with this given end in mind, which is confirmed in the course of the work as being the desired aim. Astonishing though it may seem, this is not the end of "Wakai"; the next sentence is: "Almost half a month went by" (p. 145). This "half a month" is a reference to the time during which "Wakai" was written while the impression of what the author had experienced was still fresh in his mind. Thus, the last two sentences pin down the time frame; the whole story can be inserted chronologically within the period which they mark out.

This time information apparently corresponded with reality since Shiga remarked in "Zoku sōsaku yodan" (Conversations about My Literary Work, Further Installments, 1938): "As I have already said in the work, I wrote 'Wakai' out of joy and excitement over the reconciliation with my father which proceeded so smoothly during the time that I wrote about it that I worked without a break. I wrote ten pages[39] a day on average and was finished within half a month. There was only one evening when I couldn't write, because we had a guest, but there was also one day when I wrote twenty pages, so that on average it was ten [per day]. An average of ten pages a day for fifteen days, that is a record that I have never equaled either before or since."[40] By bringing the "narrated time" so close to the date of publication, Shiga heightened the sense of up-to-dateness in "Wakai." The quotation from "Zoku sōsaku yodan" also proves that the first-person narrator and the author are identical. Thus far, everything corresponds with the simple pattern of narration in shishōsetsu.

But the work is complicated by the various time levels which can be fully distinguished only after often difficult calculations. The following are some of the results of an analysis of the time structure.

Altogether, "Wakai" contains three different time levels. The "middle" one and the one the reader is most aware is the period between 31 July 1917 and the beginning of September, that is, shortly after the "reconciliation." To begin with, the story is told chronologically until 18 August. From this point there is a flashback in section 10, which begins in the spring of 1915 and continues until shortly before the time at which the story starts.

However, between sections 10 and 11 there is a leap into a new time level of which the reader cannot be aware. Section 11 begins: "And the following took place about four weeks ago, [seen from] now" (p. 118). For the reader the narrative present is the time at which the narrator inserts the flashback, and therefore the second half of August. He cannot know that, when Shiga speaks of "now," he no longer means this time level but a third, that is, that point in real, non-literary time where he finds himself after completing the 10th section. By using "now" or, to put it more precisely, by using the new temporal narrative perspective to which it refers, the author projects the process of writing "Wakai" as an additional level onto the work. Thus "now" refers to the second half of September. The author has nearly finished his book which is due to be published in the October issue of the magazine. The time the reader believes to be the narrative present in section 11—it is by now 23

August—is a continuation of the flashback. In this way, Shiga skillfully divides the story into two parts—by shifting the temporal point of reference in the narrative.

Why should we be interested in the kind of confusing temporal structure that is so complicated that it eludes the reader? The answer lies in the reasons given for the lack of awareness of the complicated temporality, which in turn is explained by the structure of the work: Shiga marks out the changes of time level neither explicitly—apart from the not very helpful "now"—nor implicitly.[41] That is to say, the different time levels do not correspond to different levels of consciousness or awareness on the part of the narrator, who is always entirely enclosed within the time level he is describing and who gives away none of the knowledge he possesses with hindsight. We even find the narrator taking up a separate temporal "accompanying" narrative standpoint during the flashback, which the reader can now easily identify as being "fiction." For example the narrator writes of the sudden illness of his first daughter in July 1916 as if he did not know in section 5 that she would soon die. Towards the end of this part, the reader and the narrator are still hoping for her recovery. Section 6 releases the tension that has been built up with the laconic comment: "But finally there was nothing more that could be done for the baby" (p. 98). Nor does the change from the "middle" to the "third" time level imply a change in the narrator's consciousness. He is again completely involved in what he is describing without even hinting that he is dealing retrospectively with memories. This unity in the narrator's point of view, despite the different time levels that take the form of the "accompanying" narrator typical for shishōsetsu is, in my opinion, the reason one can easily overlook the complicated construction of the work.

We are now, however, ignoring the fictionality of this method of writing, which this study set out to investigate. The shishōsetsu public and even the writers depend on the illusion of "immediate" writing which seems to be confirmed by the technique of the "accompanying" narration. Indeed, some shishōsetsu succeed in creating the impression that the narrated present and the narrative present are identical. Kasai Zenzō's "Ko o tsurete," which is discussed below, is a typical example. Even if we ignore the "dichronous nature of the double ego"[42] fundamental to all shishōsetsu, since it is neither explicitly thematized by the works themselves nor considered worthy of mention by Japanese writers and readers, nearly all shishōsetsu still contain retrospective passages that would seem to weaken the fictionality of "accompanying" narrative. However, the process of reception in Japan functions exactly the opposite way and such a narrative technique merely serves to reinforce the impression of authenticity without which *riariti* would become impossible to achieve.

FANTASIZED REALITY AND REALISTIC FANTASIES

In section 7 we discover a flashback within the flashback in the form of associative memories of a stay in Matsue in 1914. The memories are reawakened by the worsening of the narrator's relationship with his father following the death and the circumstances surrounding the funeral of his first child. He tries, on the one hand, to avoid any contact with his father, but, on the other, the presence of his grandmother, who seems to be the most important person in his life, attracts and keeps him almost magnetically bound to his family's house in Azabu, part of Tokyo. The hero fears nothing more than the death of his grandmother before he is once more free to visit her, and it is largely because of this fear that he is gradually prepared to consider a reconciliation with the master of the house. This forms the background to the following passage from section 7, which contains the flashback mentioned earlier. The particular relevance of this quotation is that it highlights the peculiar interpenetration of fantasy and reality, of the hero's wishes and reality, and how he attempts to solve his problems by means of such reversals. Literature becomes a substitute for life, fiction is intended to suspend reality. It seems to me that here the relationship of the writer Shiga to his art is reflected on a literary level:

> I do not know how often I have planned during the last five, six years, [to use] this argument with my father as the subject for a novel. But it ended in failure every time. One reason may have been an inner resistance towards voicing my anger at my father [in this way]; but more than that I found it depressing to imagine what kind of tragedy would be created by the publication of the work. In particular, I could not bear to think how it would mar my relationship with my grandmother. When I was in Matsue three years ago, I drafted the following plan for the novel in order to avoid such a tragedy at all costs: A young man with a sad face comes to me. He is someone who at that time wrote serialized novels for the newspapers in Matsue. I read what he lays in front of me. He has written about an argument with his father. Suddenly, this serialized novel no longer appears in the newspaper. The man comes to me in an agitated state. He tells me that his father has learned of it, in spite of the fact that he writes under a pseudonym, and that he has sent someone from Tokyo with a sum of money [to demand] that the newspaper discontinue publication of the story. There are then some unpleasant incidents between the father and the young man. And I write this all down as the third party. Nearing desperation, the furious young man

leaves for an unpleasant discussion with his father. The father orders that his son may under no circumstances enter the house. By describing some more unpleasant things which could in fact take place between me and my father, by openly writing them down, I wanted to prevent them from actually taking place. I thought we could prevent it all coming so far by putting it down on paper. The high point was to be at the end when I would describe the tragedy which would take place on the occasion of the grandmother's death. The fight between the father and the young man who, beside himself with rage, would not be stopped from entering [the house], a fight which is probably more than just a simple brawl—when I imagined this plan I thought I would write either that the father killed the son or the son the father. But suddenly I imagined a scene where, at the climax of the fight, the two suddenly embrace each other and cry. This scene which suddenly appeared [in front of my eyes] completely surprised me. Tears came to my eyes.

But I decided against writing down the catastrophe (*katasutorōfu*) in this novel. I thought I would not be able to write it up in this way. I thought, one does not know how things will develop before I reach [the scene]. But I did think how good it would be if things really did turn out like that as a result of the novel.

I started the novel but did not finish it. After I had prepared the draft, my relationship with my father deteriorated as a result of my marriage. Nevertheless, I still felt that this scene of the catastrophe in the novel, which occurred to me quite unintentionally and naturally, could at some point happen to us. I had the feeling that it was not impossible that it would happen when relations between us had reached their lowest point. Of course, one only knows it when it actually happens, but I felt that both I and my father possessed something which could make such a sudden change possible.

(pp. 103–105)

It is essential to quote at length here so that the reader can observe the fascinating process of reality-fiction osmosis on a literary level, which I would not be able to convey by paraphrase. A detailed discussion will be contained in a separate essay on "Wakai."

Shiga translated his own personal conflict into literature—the result is the story "Wakai." A further translation takes place when the narrator turns his own problems into the story of the young man who does exactly the same as Shiga—he turns a conflict with his father into the subject of a novel. The course of events provided by this is in turn the draft for the narrator's novel. Shiga here describes the interweaving of a novel within a novel within a novel. The result is an infinite series of reflections, a mise-en-abîme, which make it possible to move unnoticed from one level to another. If we read Shiga's novel simply as an auto-therapeutic attempt to overcome a situation of conflict, which of course it also is to a large degree, then we lose sight of the aesthetic qualities of shishōsetsu which may arise independently of the author's intentions. What I find so exciting about this example from "Wakai" is the observation that such an aesthetically intriguing pattern of textual organization can even result from an authorial motive so "external" to literature, that is, from a personal attempt to overcome conflict.

GOOD AND BAD MOODS, OR
THE UNPREDICTABILITY OF FEELINGS

"Wakai" is notable for the frequency of "characterizing adjectives" (J. Erben) and compounds of words naming the moods and feelings of the narrator. In this way, those characteristics that are typical for the focus figure are already evident at the level of language—the dependence of the focus figure on his own emotional condition and on the emotional significance of the given situation. The thought of holding back his feelings seems to be as alien to the hero as the idea that he could dictate the emotional pitch of a given situation. Instead, he is convinced that he is the helpless victim of his own moods. The consequence is his total inability to steer the course of events in the direction he wishes, since he is hardly in control of himself. Thus, in "Wakai" the father's first attempt to bring about a reconciliation with his son is doomed because the protagonist feels himself unprepared: "At that time I could not have dreamed that a real conciliation could have taken place" (p. 79). For this reason, the father, who has come to Kyoto (where the hero has been living) solely to achieve a reconciliation, is forced to return after a few days without even having met his son. It does little to appease the father that he receives a letter in which his son makes it quite clear that he does not wish to see him. The narrator describes the scene as follows: "I imagined how my father would read my letter, ill-humoured and alone in his hotel room. I also became displeased. But I thought, it cannot be changed" (p. 80). His other experiences follow the same pattern. The narrator's egocentrism, his fatalistic attitude towards his own moods to which he reacts each time with the statement *shikata ga nai*—"it cannot be changed"—is boundless even when he plays the active role in his relationships with other people. He vents his bad temper on his wife but considers this—as we can conclude from other similar situations—to be more honest and "moral" than suppressing his mood. It is only the thought that his wife might not be able to continue nursing the baby if she is placed under too much mental pressure that prevents his working himself up into a complete rage (p. 78).

Even when he becomes more balanced and conciliatory as a result of contact with his colleague Mushakōji he still continues to make any attempt at reconciliation dependent on external factors. When his mother[43] suggests reconciliation, he tells her: "But I cannot just close my eyes and apologize [to father] if my feelings are not in accord . . . But I will try to talk to him. It is mainly a matter of feelings and I cannot guide events as I thought I could; I do not know if my mood will be more conciliatory than I now think it is when I am standing opposite him" (p. 132). The fact that the reconciliation takes place at all is therefore due not only to the hero's initiative but also to the fortunate coincidence that he does not find the situation unsympathetic towards him, as is so often the case. He sees his father's "gentle face" through the open door. His "manner of speaking" makes a "good impression" on him (p. 133), and they make peace after both have expressed their desire for reconciliation. There is absolutely no need for any discussion in this emotional situation as father and son, both in tears, reach an understanding.

If the first half of the story is dominated by an almost monotonous selection of expressions of negative feelings—there is repeated mention of *fukai* (displeasure), *fuyukai* (unpleasant), *hara ga tatsu* (to be annoyed) and *katto suru* (to be enraged)—the phase after the climax is completely dominated by peaceful, pleasant, loving emotions. "I now felt deep love towards my father. And I felt how all the bad feelings of the past melted away" (p. 141). "Wakai" portrays a world of emotions. The hero's life is dominated by spontaneous actions that reflect his own psychic condition, and he allows no time or space for thoughtful consideration. His psyche also characterizes the form of the work. The story does not proceed according to a logical, comprehensible inner development that would make the reconciliation a conceivable result of a gradual process, but it consists of a loose string of recollected events that are highly emotionally charged. The reader often fails to understand the actions and reactions of the characters, since he is not given the necessary background information. However, if we recall Shiga's defense, quoted previously, it is clear that he did not intend to describe a process of inner development. In addition, shishōsetsu does not demand that the writer be "nice to the reader." In this sense, Shiga is an exemplary shishōsetsu writer.

The subjectivism which is expressed through his literature, his excessive self-righteousness, and his boundless egoism have been emphasized by many critics. Kobayashi Hideo's verdict of "ultra-egoist" from his first essay on Shiga in 1929 has become famous.[44] There is also frequent mention of his "willfulness" (*wagamama*).[45] However, Usui Yoshimi maintains that it is just these characteristics that produce the "purity" and therefore the attraction of the work.[46]

KASAI ZENZŌ: "KO O TSURETE" (1918)

According to Odagiri Hideo, Kasai Zenzō (1887–1928) is the author of the "most shishōsetsu-like shishōsetsu" (*mottomo shishōsetsurashii shishōsetsu*).[47] Such a distinction was awarded to Kasai's first work "Kanashiki chichi" (The Sad Father, 1912). The sequel to this story was the short story "Ko o tsurete" (With the Children), whose publication in March 1918 in *Waseda bungaku* magazine first brought him widespread recognition and facilitated his breakthrough as a writer. Even in early discussions on shishōsetsu, Kasai's works were held to be model examples as the following quotation from Uno Kōji's "Views on Shishōsetsu" ("'Shishōsetsu' shiken," 1925) shows: "If one wishes to characterize shishōsetsu briefly various [works] could be named, but the best examples are probably those by *Kasai Zenzō* [emphasis in the original] which I believe to mark the high point in this novel literature. By this I mean that no single real novel (*honkaku shōsetsu*) written by a Japanese writer reaches the standard Kasai Zenzō [achieves] with his novels on the condition of the mind (*shinkyō shōsetsu*)."[48] Kasai invented the name *jiko shōsetsu*—"novel of the self"[49]—and also called them ironically *jisseikatsu no kamikuzu bungaku*—"the scraps-of-paper literature of life"[50]—since his subject matter was the same as other shishōsetsu writers, his own biography.

"SHISHŌSETSU'S SENTIMENTAL ESOTERIC" AND EGOCENTRIC SPEECH

In "Ko o tsurete"[51] Kasai portrays an almost hopeless situation: The writer Oda is pressured by his landlord to leave his flat by the 10th of the month because he cannot pay the rent. His wife has gone to her parents in the country with their second daughter in order to procure some money, but he has heard nothing from her. Thus, Oda is left with his other two children in Tokyo, completely on his own. His friends have broken off relations with him because he has asked them for money too often. Only his writer colleague Kei still stands by him and gives him one yen (p. 9). Oda cannot answer his friend's question as to how he plans to support himself in the future, but in his "weak way of thinking" he hopes that things will somehow work out alright (p. 10). His fatalism worsens when he thinks of his numerous creditors who seem to him to be cruel bloodhounds:

In order to resist their exploitation he takes flight. He decides to eat and drink nothing and tries to hide under a stone or something similar, but again he is pulled out.

To think that he already has children. Such is fate! But he can no longer bear it. And again he flees.

This time, full of desperation, he tried to stay hidden under a stone for three or four months. But the only result was that he was imprisoned by walls and stones. (p. 12)

Just as Oda's attempts to run away from his problems are ridiculous and ineffective, so is he incapable of communicating with other people. Although he has hardly any remaining human contact to the world, he cannot even talk sensibly to the one friend who is concerned about his problems. The characters in "Ko o tsurete" are frequently at cross purposes with each other, for example, when Oda is looking for a flat and meets a policeman he had known ten years earlier when both were being tutored (pp. 22f.). While the hero repeatedly asks him for help, the policeman advises him to improve his powers of mental concentration through training (p. 26).

The reduced capacity for communication is a reflection at the level of plot of a shishōsetsu characteristic that the psychologist Miyagi Otoya has described as a kind of autism. He also considers Kasai and his works to be typical of the genre and, using these works, has made a study which is important to a psychoanalytical understanding of this literary phenomenon. In contrast to the biographical studies, which are so popular in Japan and which aim only at comparing the work with the life of the author, making free use of psychoanalytical language in the process, Miyagi is interested in what is exemplary in the case of Kasai and is as much concerned with the work as with the person. He notes that his literature emphasizes an emotional sphere to the exclusion of the intellectual sphere (which for him also means "fantasy" [*sōzō*] and "interpretation" [*kaishaku*]).[52] Utopian thinking, the possibility of alternatives, does not arise, and, when fantasy does appear, then it is restricted to the past, as Miyagi proves from a textual example. Just as in Shūkō or Shiga, there are parts of Kasai's works that can be understood only from the context or which demand biographical knowledge. We should mention at this point that Kasai neglects to check whether the times given in the work, which deals with only a few days, are consistent. For example, we are told that Oda must leave his flat by the 10th at the very latest and can expect no extension of this limit at all (pp. 2, 19); we are therefore more than a little surprised to read that he also spends the night of the

10th there (p. 26). I consider the author's lack of interest in the formal structure proof of the lack of a communicative process in Kasai's literature, a point Miyagi emphasizes: "Kasai Zenzō's texts are very similar to those written by children. Children talk a language that is not intent upon communication. Even conversations are close to monologues. Piaget called this state of absolute introversion (*naiheisei*), which is typical of children, egocentric and to the extent that things which are totally unrelated are written down in Kasai's texts just as they occur to him, they are also egocentric."[53] The studies of shishōsetsu texts we have undertaken in this book may have concentrated on other aspects, but I hope they were of sufficient breadth to point towards the conclusions of Miyagi's statement.[54] An underlying self-pity and sentimentality, as the natural result of the dominating subjectivism and fatalism, is typical of all the examples, as it is of "Ko o tsurete." Kasai's short story also illustrates this feature, which Hiraoka Tokuyoshi names as one of the basic characteristics of the genre when referring to the "sentimental hermetic . . . which shishōsetsu as such implies."[55]

LIFE IS SUFFERING

The hero in "Ko o tsurete" invites us to take part in his suffering. One piece of bad luck follows another in the manner of a series of natural disasters. He believes he can only wander around aimlessly in this situation—the idea that his misfortunes were foreseeable and could have been overcome through his own initiative would not suit the atmosphere of misery the author creates through the blind and enraged masochism portrayed. According to Ōmori Sumio, the author is motivated by his feelings of guilt towards his family who have suffered because of his profession. However, he needs art and the feeling of being an artist in order to compensate for his permanent inferiority complex.[56] His suffering is, both for him and his public, part of his art. Yamamoto Kenkichi sums it up with the words: "The only thing he can do is bare his wounds publicly."[57]

Oda suffers in a number of ways. He suffers not only because of his hopeless financial situation, but also because of the subtle insults from *bundan* colleagues (pp. 13–18); he suffers at the sight of villas (pp. 20f.); he suffers from a lack of helpfulness shown by those around him (p. 26); and he suffers from the feeling of being no longer capable of any emotion (p. 33). However, if we maintain a certain critical distance when reading "Ko o tsurete," it seems obvious that Kasai has subjected his hero to more suffering than is really necessary. In order to heighten the dramatic effect in the final scene he portrays an almost inexplicable change that rounds off the completeness of the misery: On the 11th, Oda sold his last belongings to a furniture trader and now wanders aimlessly through the town with his 8-year-old son and 7-year-old daughter and a basket full of books—that is all he still possesses. Tired and hungry they enter a bar, where he lets the children choose a meal while he is satisfied with only a sake (pp. 30–32). Then a desperate search for somewhere to spend the night begins. An old couple in the house of an absent friend are moved by the daughter's tears and offer them a place to stay, but, because the girl goes on crying, the hero decides to continue his search with the two completely exhausted children. It is 11 o'clock at night when he finally sits in the train with them again, completely incapable of thought, "since"—such is the last sentence—"his head and his body demanded sleep just as his children did" (p. 36). It is quite normal for a child to want nothing more than to sleep in such a situation, and it really seems completely unreasonable that Oda rejects the couple's offer even though he has no hope of an alternative. However, this provides an ending that accords with the desolate atmosphere of the book as a whole, and Kasai proves to be a worthy representative of what Hirano Ken named "the literature of ruin." According to his statements, Kasai is one of the shishōsetsu writers who destroyed his own life for the sake of art.[58] This much at least is certain: Kasai believed he was sacrificing his life for art.

KIKUCHI KAN: "TOMO TO TOMO TO NO AIDA" (1918)

Between 1918 and 1920, there were a large number of literary productions which were generally called "friendship novels" (*yūjin shōsetsu, tomodachi shōsetsu,* or *bundan kōyūroku*) and which are a subgroup of shishōsetsu.[59] Kikuchi Kan's (1888–1948) story "Tomo to tomo to no aida" (Between Two Friends) will serve as our example of these works. It was published as a serial in the *Ōsaka Mainichi shinbun* from 18 August to 8 October 1919. The work not only includes numerous cross-references to other shishōsetsu, which enable us to illustrate the way these works are closely interrelated, but also supplies us with valuable insights into the way the *bundan* functions, into the way it produced and received literature and its significance for the genre as such.

THE "FRIENDSHIP NOVELS" AS DOCUMENTS OF THE *BUNDAN*

According to Hirano Ken the "records of *bundan* friendships" (*bundan kōyūroku shōsetsu*) are a cross between *moderu shōsetsu* and *shōsetsu*;[60] the term *moderu shōsetsu* (model novel), which has been given various meanings in Japanese literary studies, is to be understood here as roman-à-clef. The subject matter consists of events concerning the literary circle around Natsume Sōseki in 1916 and 1917. At the center of the story are the attempts of two friends of the author Kikuchi, the writers Kume Masao (1891–1952) and Matsuoka Yuzuru (1891–1969), to win the favor of Sōseki's daughter. Matsuoka—in the book he is called Sugimura—finally succeeds in marrying Sōseki's daughter Fudeko, while Kume—the story character is Hisano—suffers greatly as a result of his defeat. The writer Kikuchi, who introduces himself in the third person as Yūkichi, relates the story from his point of view, as an observer who is a close friend to both rivals. He is not an immediate witness to events since he learns what is going on only from those involved. Thus, the story deviates from what has previously been shown to be the shishōsetsu pattern; the narrating subject places events which do not directly affect him at the center of the story, though the events described do originate from within his milieu and never move beyond it. For this reason and because the subject matter, the side of life portrayed, and the narrative techniques deployed comply with shishōsetsu, it is certainly reasonable to include this "friendship novel" within the genre.

"Tomo to tomo to no aida" is a shishōsetsu that manifests factuality and focus figure; however, the role of narrator, usually traceable to the focus figure and assigned exclusively to the subject, is extended here to secondary characters who as a result become essential to the plot and compete with the focus figure for the role of the hero. However, Yūkichi ultimately remains the most important character, since Hisano's and Sugimura's romantic pursuits are only one, albeit central, part of the story, and the various elements that determine the chronology and the descriptive perspective of the novel coalesce around Yūkichi's character.

The events described in "Tomo to tomo to no aida" actually took place, and it was no problem for contemporary readers to distinguish the facts through their thin veil of fictionality. Certain literary conventions were helpful in this respect. For example, the author appears in this work, as in others, under the name Yūkichi, so that he is immediately recognizable. The number of literary pseudonyms an author invents for himself is usually not very large. The well-read public know when they see, for example, "Keikichi-mono" that they are dealing with a different group of works in which Kikuchi has become Keikichi. In the case of Shiga, the name of one focus figure also appears in several works.[61]

Natsume Sōseki appears thinly disguised in the book as Matsumoto Sōseki[62] and the title of his work *Meian* (Light and Darkness) is changed to *Hikari to kage* (Light and Shadow) (p. 121). There can be no doubt that these references were made deliberately. Sōseki's death at the end of 1916, described in detail in the story (pp. 121–125), is a historical event, which underlines the factual basis of the work.

The other characters are easily recognizable by their relationship to one another given that the reader knows a little of Kikuchi's biography or knows any works written by the authors hidden behind the fictional names. For example, in his short story "Ano koro no jibun no koto" (Myself at That Time, 1919), Akutagawa Ryūnosuke cites a letter he wrote to Kikuchi Kan suggesting that he himself should get to know the impressive Sōseki who so fascinated both himself and Kume: "When you come to Tokyo, you must see him; it would even be worthwhile coming to Tokyo just to meet him."[63]

Kikuchi Kan spent three years studying at Kyoto University under Ueda Bin (1878–1916), who appears in the book as Doctor Nakata (p. 117). "Tomo to tomo to no aida" starts at the point where Akutagawa's short story ends: on returning to Tokyo, Yūkichi discovers that all his friends have become admirers of Sōseki, and he finally meets the great man himself. As a result, he overcomes his feeling of isolation, since, by conforming in this way, he again feels himself to be a full and worthy member of the circle of friends and no longer needs to complain incessantly of being lonely—something he does no less than six times in the first three pages of the story.

Namikawa alias Akutagawa is not the only friend in the book who can be identified through literary clues. It is even easier to spot the identity of the two rivals. Thus, one notes that not only did the happy victor Matsuoka turn events into a story he called "Yūutsuna aijin" (The Melancholy Lover), but also that nothing would stop Kume, considered the loser, from writing about the affair from his point of view. He did not hold back from describing the story in a total of eight literary works: for example, in "Hotarugusa" (Firefly Grass [the botanical name of an annual plant], 1918), "Haisha" (The Loser, 1918), "Warei" (Harmonious Spirit, 1921), "Hasen" (The Wreck, 1922) and "Bosan" (Visiting the Grave, 1925).[64] At the beginning of a further "friendship novel," "Ryōyū akuyū" (Good Friends, Bad Friends, 1919), he also refers to the affair, claiming that the spiritual wound was slowly healing and, with the help of his friends, he would also succeed in overcoming the dreadful inner emptiness this unhappy love had caused. He threw himself into pleasures and defended his debauchery against the criticism of friends on the grounds of the pain he had suffered. He soon came to expect that the others would condone anything just because of that, as he himself did. The following sentences could be taken as a commentary on the numerous works in which he uses his own defeat as subject matter:

> At first, I was afraid of being the object of scorn; I was unobtrusive and tried to hide my misfortune in love. But, when I realized, completely unexpectedly, that everyone's sympathy was fully concentrated on me, I suddenly felt whole again, displayed my unfortunate love [to the public], exaggerated and enjoyed it and even cashed in [on the affair] to an almost shameless, brazen degree. And, since everyone silently allowed it, I concentrated on it more and more and imagined that the people would always accept me as affected by the affair. Of course, on the one hand I felt pretty miserable about it, but on the other hand I also thought that my present life of excess would be accepted.[65]

Repeated and unequivocal references to the same events in different works by various authors tend to make the reader ignore the literary character and concentrate solely on the reality he describes. Thus, "Tomo to tomo to no aida" contains a large amount of factual detail as do other "friendship novels." It provides biographical information, in particular about the relationship between the writers. The way in which any one of the colleagues are described alternates between extremes, a method one critic in 1920 named *Nagasaki* and *taiko shōsetsu*, referring to literary continuation of a personal enmity on the one hand and flattering exaggeration on the other. The latter took place in the hope that the person so favored would in turn show his appreciation.[66]

One much quoted example of a feud carried out in the literary field is Satomi Ton's (1888–1983) short story "Kimi to watakushi to" (You and I, 1913) in which Shiga Naoya felt himself to be unjustly treated and, as a result, not only wrote an essay of protest, the "Model's Protest" ("Moderu no fufuku," 1913), but also gave free rein to his hostile feelings towards Satomi in his novel *An'ya kōro*.[67]

"Tomo to tomo to no aida" also provides us with information about the relationship of shishōsetsu writers to their literature. We are given a clear picture of how smooth the transition between life and literature is. Each affects the other, and for the writer any demarcation line between the two is of little value. The need to record in literary terms everything the writer experiences acquires an almost compulsive character. Even when he will suffer personally as a result, nothing can stop Kume from revealing all.[68]

It originally seems to everybody in "Tomo to tomo to no aida" that Hisano, that is Kume Masao, will win the competition for Fudeko, and Natsume's widow hints that Fudeko is intended for him. However, many of the master's pupils and admirers are against a marriage between Fudeko and Kume, and one day Mrs. Natsume receives a letter accusing Kume of having all sorts of love affairs, with the intention of disqualifying him as a suitor. The letter does not have the intended effect, since Mrs. Natsume chooses to ignore it. The candidate himself however raises suspicions by publishing some stories that seem to confirm the contents of the letter (p. 133).

It is only after a further indiscretion, however, that Kume is finally eliminated from the competition. His need to record everything on paper leads him to reveal to the public the secret promise Sōseki's wife made him. She is so annoyed at this that she decides to go back on her word (p. 135). It is not only Kume's behavior that is revealing: the reaction of those involved illustrates how they read ostensibly fictional literature as though it were reality.

The second reason for Kume's defeat throws light on the narrow world of the *bundan* with its rivalries and cliquish behavior. He fails as a suitor because no one believes he will succeed in his career. Among Sōseki's pupils, he is considered to be merely a "good light-fiction writer" (*kōkyūna tsūzoku sakka*, p. 133) and Fudeko's mother lets it be known that she has a pessimistic view of his future prospects. Dismayed, Kume seeks out his friend Kikuchi and together they try to decide why Mrs. Natsume has chosen to voice her opinion at precisely this moment. She has led Kume to believe that his works are no longer discussed in public. Kikuchi makes the following conjecture: "When she says no one talks about your works she must mean September's criticism. Mr. Kusata has taken over September's criticism, hasn't he? Isn't it true that this man has a strange antipathy towards you and that he therefore tries to suppress your work?" (p. 136). To Kume it seems useless to set about changing the poor opinion people have of him. He is resigned to making way for his friend Matsuoka. At the start, Sōseki's pupils are also opposed to him (p. 144). After marrying Fudeko he became a famous Sōseki specialist—a further indication of the extent to which art and life are bound together in Japan.

CROSSING LITERARY BOUNDARIES

In the discussion heretofore, we have treated "Tomo to tomo to no aida" and other "friendship novels" not as works of literature but as documents from which to extract particular information, as we would from letters or diaries, concerning the real-life background to the work. What justification do we have for this and of what value is it?

The "friendship novels" are characterized, as are other shishōsetsu, by the way they emphasize their connection with reality, repeatedly referring to non-literary facts or making such a show of disguising these so that the reader automatically notes the disguise. This is an effective method of authenticating the factuality that is a precondition for shishōsetsu. It is a matter of decisive importance for our interpretation that there is no categorical division between the focus figure in shishōsetsu and the author. The work is thus a direct expression of the life of the author; he knows no more than that which he expresses through the first-person narrator. The hero's outlook on the world is thus identical with that of the author. It is this observation that allows our approach to the works.

Such an "identity test" between a section of the work and its corresponding basis in reality is one of the most common methods employed in Japanese literary studies. This excessively biographical approach can largely be explained by the practice of shishōsetsu. Terada Tōru seems to have reached this same conclusion intuitively when he claims that "the fact that Japanese literary criticism is particularly meticulous when compared to every other country seems to be largely thanks to shishōsetsu."[69] The implicit assumption made here, however, that a one-to-one correspondence between life and literature is the only possible relationship that can exist between the two has had fatal consequences for Japanese philology, since the same method has been applied to other types of writing where such a principle is not valid.

Even if we can accept the suitability of this method in the case of shishōsetsu, it is of little value as far as the work itself is concerned, since the origins, motivation, and factual background of a piece of literature are of only limited use in interpreting it as a work of art. Such an approach is valuable only when it supplies us with information of the kind required here. We attempted to reveal the facts and their relationship to the literary product and discovered that the author's aim was to duplicate the facts in his literature. "Tomo to tomo to no aida" proved to be particularly instructive as far as this aspect was concerned.

By using shishōsetsu in the sense of biographical or autobiographical documents and by stating that shishōsetsu are to be considered as direct representations of the author's life, we have touched on a problem that cannot be solved here. It is the question as to whether and in what way shishōsetsu are distinguished from "functional texts" such as private diaries. It is quite customary for a writer to take material from the notes he has made in his diary, particularly if he is writing a work of autobiographical character. However, how are we to interpret a relationship of identity between the "raw material" (diary notes) and the "end product" (the literary piece)?

We refer for example to some notes from the diary of Akutagawa Ryūnosuke from 26 May 1919. He records that Tanizaki Jun'ichirō visited him in the afternoon. He was wearing a red tie. After the two had rummaged through the secondhand bookshops in Kanda they went to a cafe where the waitress admired Tanizaki's red tie.[70] He describes the same episode, omitting the visit to the cafe, under the same date in a second version (*bekkō*) of the diary.[71] The existence of two parallel diaries leads to the assumption that at least one was intended for publication, but neither the commentary to the complete edition nor the literary form of the documents themselves provides any information about this; both versions exhibit an equally unpolished and sketchy style.

The incident appears again a third time, in the form of a 1924 sketch about Tanizaki. It is outlined in greater detail this time, but the somewhat terse style of the narrator, who refrains from making any comment whatsoever, remains the same.[72] In my opinion, there is practically no criterion that would enable us to make a categorical distinction between "artistic literature" and "functional literature" in this case. With regard to shishōsetsu, where this would also seem to be the case, it is however possible to differentiate between the two.

Shishōsetsu is "artistic literature" as far as its intention and place in the literary field are concerned, since it belongs to *junbungaku* (pure literature) even if it is at times no different in formal terms from "functional literature." However, in Japan a private diary or other document often acquires the character of "art" simply by virtue of being published, so that we can conclude that there is no strict segregation of "artistic literature"; the great respect for the *zuihitsu* (miscellany) and *nikki* (diary) genres, both of which enjoy a long tradition in Japan, explains such fluid lines of demarcation.

Finally, the fact that shishōsetsu authors are themselves aware of these flexible literary boundaries can be seen from a remark made by Shiga Naoya: "'Yuki no hi' [A Snowy Day, 1920] is a journal from Abiko;[73] if I continued sketching the following day, it would have become a story, but because I was under pressure to give the newspaper [the manuscript] I concluded it there."[74] The difference of one single additional day is enough to decide whether a piece of literature may be called a "journal" or a "story." In view of this seemingly trivial formal dividing line, one can at least assume that a change in the designation implies no real change in the generic status of the work as "functional" or "artistic" literature.

HAYASHI FUMIKO: *HŌRŌKI* (1928–1930)

In the previous chapter we considered an example that seemed to point in one particular direction within the variety of shishōsetsu that we set up in the structural model. The work in question here, the *Vagabond's Diary*—*Hōrōki*—by Hayashi Fumiko (1903–1951) presents, in the form of a diary, a formal variant of shishōsetsu. *Hōrōki* consists of three parts, the first published in several episodes beginning March 1928 in the magazine *Nyonin geijutsu*. In 1930, the publishers Kaizō brought out parts 1 and 2 in book form with the unexpected result that the book became a bestseller. Hayashi published the third part from 1947 to 1948 in *Nihon shōsetsu*. According to her own account, this contains those sections from the first two parts which, it was feared, would not have passed the censor.[75]

It is difficult to state exactly which period of time is covered by this novel. The only certainty is that she started the diary on which *Hōrōki* is based in 1923. The great earthquake, which occurred in that year, is one of the few historical facts referred to in the novel and which allows it to be dated accurately.

SHISHŌSETSU AND DIARIES

Is it possible that in *Hōrōki* the genre shishōsetsu is superimposed by the diary, "overwhelmed" as it were, or can we justifiably assume that this case represents merely a formal variant of our structural model?

The affinity between shishōsetsu and the diary was recognized early on in the theoretical discussion. In April 1918, the genre, which was given the name shishōsetsu shortly afterwards, was criticized in the magazine *Shinchō* as consisting of "cheap, vulgar confessional novels or useless records of someone's life, the kind of diary where the date has been left out and in which dialogue is inserted,"[76] and the writer Sasaki Mitsuzō (1896–1934) mocked "the present day, where diaries are considered to be novels."[77]

If we start with the abstract structural model for shishōsetsu, it is easiest to recognize similarities and points of comparison. A diary presupposes factuality, as does shishōsetsu, and it can contain the focus figure.

However, the latter is not an essential element, since it is quite conceivable for a diary to include philosophical thought or observations of the surrounding world that do not refer to the subject. However, Japanese diaries in general tend to conform to the focus-figure pattern, so that they also bear a strong affinity to shishōsetsu in this respect. There is therefore only a superficial difference between the two which is summed up by the formula given above of a "diary where the date has been left out and in which dialogues are inserted." Seen in this way, the diary is merely a variant of shishōsetsu.

It is now necessary to ask why Hayashi uses this form. In the epilogue, she herself characterizes her style of writing as follows: "At that time I was still innocent and did not think about my writing, let alone about technique or style. It was a matter of spontaneously expressing my feelings when I felt like crying, when life was difficult, or when I wanted to fly away somewhere—this was my literature [written] with great energy."[78] In order to satisfy her need for spontaneous expression of emotion only this method presented itself: "At that time I changed my job extremely frequently and, because I was completely occupied with work, I had no time to sit peacefully at my desk and write. When I did have time, I wrote in the form of a diary so that it gradually grew and so [the publishers] Kaizō published parts one and two of the vagabond's diary in 1929."[79] Thus the literary form of the book was determined by the circumstances surrounding its composition, which became its subject matter.

Even though the book is written in the form of a diary, Hayashi reworks the narrative material into an identifiably fictional form. She favors dialogue and elaborates on some scenes in a way that can have been possible only after an interval of time had elapsed since their actual occurrence. *Hōrōki* is undoubtedly a diary made literature and various references in the book confirm the observation that it is based on another, the "real" diary.[80]

The advantages of this form of presentation are obvious as far as Hayashi's intention of expressing her feelings spontaneously in literary form is concerned—the diary provides her with the greatest possible freedom. She is bound by no narrative rules. She describes experiences within a time frame the reader cannot accurately reconstruct, since she names only the month but not the day or year, and provides no information as to the background to these events. There are no discursive transitions and when, for example, there is a sudden unexplained jump from December to April (pp. 16–18) or from May to November (pp. 22–24), it is left to the reader's imagination to complete the work and understand how the situation in the subsequent entry has evolved. The inconsistencies and unevenness of description imply that even the chronological order of events is unclear to the reader. In addition, it seems strange that the third part covers the same period of time as the first two, the division of which is not internally motivated. Seen as a whole, the entries in the third part are longer and seem to have been thought out more carefully, so that the reader concludes that the writer must have worked on the text again at some point during the long interval—seventeen years, in fact—between the two publication dates. The attitudes and narrative perspective remain, despite the possible re-working of the text, the same in both publications.

Since neither entries in literary dictionaries nor Itagaki Naoko's explanatory essay (1977) mention the difference between the first two parts and the third part, we shall include a short explanation here. It must have been clear to the writer from the very start that much of the material first published in 1947 could not possibly have been printed in 1930. In particular, the numerous references to the Tenno and the Imperial Family would have fallen victim to the censor. In some places, Hayashi's conscious violations of taboos rise to blasphemy, as, for example, when she imagines the Empress defecating (p. 280). Her repeated expressions of sympathy for the mentally disturbed Tenno (pp. 194, 275) represent an audacity inconceivable at that time.

In addition to these qualities, Hayashi's directness in sexual matters and her "political" comments would have also led to the book's being banned. She would have been considered politically oriented, however, only by the type of hypersensitive censor who would take seriously her declaration of loyalty to anarchism (p. 190) or her desire to go to Russia (p. 203). In actual fact, out of longing to escape from cold reality she also imagined herself just as readily in France (p. 195) or in Sicily (p. 207), and her anarchism is more obviously attributable to her life as a vagabond than to political conviction. She did not think politically but sentimentally.

It seems remarkable to me that the paperback edition of the book, now in its 77th edition,[81] contains only the first two parts of *Hōrōki* without even mentioning the existence of a third part. We shall, however, include it in the following discussion of the work.

MONEY, MEALS, AND TEARS

The fragmentary outline of the plot of *Hōrōki* consists of the experiences of the heroine, who continually changes her job and who struggles through life alone and on the verge of starvation. A short introduction, written in the first person and entitled "Hōrōki izen" (Before the *Vagabond's Diary*) prepares the reader for what follows and provides some information about the main character. We learn that she was constantly on the move in her childhood with her mother and stepfather, that she left school after only four years, and that she was never able to establish permanent relationships with children of her own age (pp. 5–11). At the very beginning she is said to be destined to lead a life of wandering (p. 5). These details only foreshadow what is to come; the diary begins abruptly and seemingly without any reason.

The book consists of a continuous succession of experiences, always based on the same pattern and characterized by the elements money, meals, and tears. In each diary entry, at least two of these items are important. No matter what kind of situation the heroine finds herself in—whether as a maid in the house of the writer Chikamatsu Shūkō (pp. 12ff.), as a worker in a celluloid factory (pp. 24ff.), or as a waitress in a cheap cafe (p. 55)—her thoughts center on the money she lacks, on food she longs for; the scene invariably ends in tears. The following examples represent many similar extracts:

> In the evening I grill a small cheap fish and at last I eat rice again. Tears come to my eyes. (p. 195)

> I have eaten nothing since morning. If I had sold three or four fairy-tales or poems it would not even have meant that I would have been able to eat white rice for a month. When I am hungry my head works sluggishly and even my thoughts become stale. Then there is neither proletariat nor bourgeoisie in my head. All I want is a cake of white rice to eat.
> "Please give me some rice!"
> When I think how they would react to that by frowning it seems it might be better to throw myself into the rough sea. (p. 60)

> "Miss Hayashi, a registered letter!"
> My landlady's voice sounds unusually good-tempered and, when I pick up the envelope lying on the stairs, [I see] that it is a registered letter from Mr. Shiragi. [It contains] 23 yen! The payment for a fairy-tale. Now I need not starve for a while. Elated, I exclaim: Oh, how happy I am! Oh God, I'm so happy that I feel terribly lonely . . . I open the window wide and hear the bell from Ueno. This evening I will eat delicious sushi. (p. 96)

The last two examples remind us that the first-person narrator is a writer, a fact the reader could easily overlook, since her writing is itself never thematized.[82] We learn from such references only that she produces literary work in her spare time, and it is apparently worth mentioning only in connection with the money she receives for it. We can conclude from other references that she has contacts with various members of the literati, but, again, there is never any mention of her discussions with her colleagues, only descriptions of their common attempts to procure food: When the poet and anarchist Hagiwara Kyōjirō (1899–1938) visits her she sells her blanket in order to buy some spirits. Since there is not enough money left over to buy rice they eat noodles (p. 47). The author visits her colleague Hirabayashi Taiko (1905–1972) with the poet Tsuboi Shigeji (1898–1975) and his wife, the writer Sakae (1900–1967), because they have learned that she has acquired some rice (p. 45). Only once is there an allusion to a literary theme, when the writer friends discover in a common experience a parallel to Knut Hamsun's novel *Hunger* (*Sult*, 1890). The comparison is, however, not developed any further and the conversation ends in the usual way with the decision to steal some bamboo shoots for the next meal (p. 43).

The mention of Hamsun's novel raises one issue to which repeated reference is made in *Hōrōki* and which is intended to justify a West-East affinity. Just as the hero of "Tandeki" continually draws parallels between himself and the literary figure of Da Vinci, so Hayashi compares herself to Hamsun's hero and decides that she is much worse off than he is: "In the evening I read Hamsun's *Hunger*. This hunger is paradisical [compared with mine]. It is the novel of a man from a country where one can think and move around freely. He speaks of evolution and revolution. I no longer have such patience. I live in the murky cauldron of longing, without thinking at all" (p. 283f., cf. also p. 261). In the epilogue, the author writes that it was Hamsun's novel that motivated her to write her *Vagabond's Diary*, so emphasizing the significance of the allusion.[83] In addition, she refers to other European writers in *Hōrōki*, as one might expect, such as Goethe, whose *Werther* serves as a model for her (p. 286) and Chekhov and Tolstoy, whom she also emulates (p. 240). She calls Chekhov, Artsybashev, and Schnitzler the "home of her heart" (*watakushi no kokoro no furusato*, p. 49). However, just as in other shishōsetsu, she never goes any further than invoking their names. Any decision as to whether the book is really influenced by one or more of these writers, beyond mere citation of their works or mention of general thematic parallels, would require detailed structural analysis.

THE WILL TO LIVE AND THE WISH TO DIE

The book maintains an essential sentimentality. With a sigh the author bemoans her lot: "I am lonely. [Everything] is futile. I need money" (p.

41). Then again she exclaims: "How difficult everything is in this transient world!" (*Nan to suminikui ukiyo de gozaimashō*, p. 43). We encountered earlier this wistful melancholia, so typical of much of classical Japanese literature, under the name of *mujōkan*, as a characteristic of shishōsetsu which links the genre to the literature of earlier epochs. A second example will illustrate this. Upon seeing a sunflower in the neighboring garden Hayashi muses: "I should like to be born again as a flower in my next life. The thought makes me feel sad. The yellow of the sunflower—a generous color. In this disc of colors there is a joy which only nature [possesses]. I think how strange it is that only people must suffer" (p. 262). Yet, in *Hōroki* there are sudden changes from dismal thoughts and the frequently expressed wish to die to an energetic will to live. It is often the thought of something to eat that lifts her out of depression. Such a change can be found at the beginning of the book: "Whether I am asleep or awake it is inevitable that I will die, but so what! Sometimes I shall still buy five measures of rice [I think], laughing" (p. 21). It never takes long for cold reality to wake the heroine from her maudlin, tear-filled daydreams:

> A gentle wind blows, but I lie on the tatami [mats]. I become weary and sad. I don't want to die at all, but I start wanting to write to him[84] that maybe I shall die.
> Although I don't really want to die at all, sometimes I do want to. My imagination swells [and becomes big] as an elephant. The elephant becomes full of air and totters towards me. There is a smell of grilled salmon coming from somewhere. (p. 199)

Thus the wish to die and the will to live tend to balance each other. Pessimistic phases are brightened by glimpses of light, and the basic impression is of a woman who, sad but courageous, fights her way through life's adversities, in the words of Nakamura Mitsuo a woman with "great vitality, coupled with nihilistic feelings."[85]

THE BOOK AS THE READER'S "FRIEND"

When *Hōroki* was published as a book it achieved enormous success—within a short period 600,000 copies were sold.[86] How can such success, also obvious from the many editions through which the book has run, be explained?

Itagaki Naoko wrote a commentary on the book in which she remarks on a letter from a young man in a remote mountain district. He wrote: "Hayashi Fumiko's *Vagabond's Diary* is my friend."[87] Itagaki continues:

"As is common today, he cannot move to the town for reasons to do with his family and he therefore [has to] continue with his studies, in addition to his job, in the country. The intrepid, yearning attitude of the heroine of the *Vagabond's Diary* must surely have a powerful influence on the young man."[88] The young man's statement and the way it is interpreted by Itagaki illustrate that the *Diary* was felt to be helpful to people. *Hōrōki* is the place where Hayashi Fumiko voices the feelings of the readers and consoles them with the thought that at least she is no better off than they are.

The process of identifying with literature is staged within the *Diary* itself when, for example, the heroine has to pawn all her books and keeps only the shishōsetsu "Ko o tsurete" by Kasai Zenzō and "Wakai" by Shiga Naoya (p. 60). She probably finds moral support in "Wakai" and feels drawn to it by the harmonious family life described, something she values highly. The similarly desperate situation of the hero in "Ko o tsurete" probably serves as a consolation for the heroine in *Hōrōki*. As a result, she begins to compare her own situation with the misfortunes described in the books: "Yesterday, having decided to sell my bedclothes, I then slept peacefully: it is impossible to sell them when it is so cold. It seems to me that everything is becoming hopeless as in Kasai Zenzō's novels" (p. 208). We turn from the intratextual level back to the relationship between the work and the reader having ascertained the overall symmetry between both levels. In the epilogue, the author remarks on another reader's reaction, which confirms our previous observations: "Recently a formerly prosperous woman, who had returned from Manchuria, told me that she had previously not wanted to read the *Vagabond's Diary* at all, but now that she was completely destitute and living in misery she understood the spirit (*kokoro*) of the *Vagabond's Diary* for the first time. I felt the tears coming to my eyes at hearing this."[89] Hayashi's conclusion, which follows immediately after the above quotation, concentrates on the essential bond in the relationship between book and reader: "It can be assumed that the *Vagabond's Diary* means little to those who lead a comfortable life."[90] This not only implies that the book can be read appreciatively only by those who are able to closely identify with the heroine; it also assumes that such an ability can only be found in those who find themselves in a similar situation, which seems to be confirmed by the woman refugee's statement.

This underlines the book's power to console the reader, it bestows a feeling of personal well-being upon a reader who can identify with a literary figure in a situation which seems similar to his own, another sense in which *Hōrōki* is an exemplary representative of the shishōsetsu genre.

DAZAI OSAMU: *NINGEN SHIKKAKU* (1948)

"And when Dazai's other works are forgotten, this will be remembered forever as a work that describes the nature of human existence." These words introduce an article written by the famous Dazai scholar Okuno Takeo on the work which we discuss in this section.[91] Japanese literary criticism as a whole agrees with the statement, if in somewhat less expansive terms. *Ningen shikkaku* (No Longer Human) is considered to be the "epitome of Dazai literature"[92] and its author an intellectual representative of the postwar period.

The enormous impact of this book, published from June to August 1948 in the magazine *Tenbō*, was undoubtedly due to an extent to Dazai's death in June of the same year, which was claimed to be a double suicide.[93] *Ningen shikkaku* is a particularly interesting example for us because many Japanese critics assume as a matter of course that the novel is not a shishōsetsu. As usual, little is said about the reasons for such an assumption. Okuno Takeo, for example, writes: "*Ningen shikkaku* is the inner, spiritual autobiography of the author Dazai Osamu. Of course, it is not a shishōsetsu dealing with just the facts (*jijitsu sono mama*), but it expresses a profound and fundamental experience through fictional methods."[94] However, since he has just traced all the events in the book to experiences the author had around 1936,[95] he immediately undermines his own argument; *Ningen shikkaku* contains no less factual validity than a typical representative of the shishōsetsu genre.

Since the verifiable facts in the novel were obviously correct, it was then insinuated that Dazai was "insincere" when dealing with such matters as the beginning of his sexual relationship and so forth.[96] These events are, however, impossible to verify and can thus play no part in explaining why the work should not be called a shishōsetsu,

In the attempt to distinguish the work in question from the genre, shishōsetsu is presented in a completely new light, one that largely contradicts conventional concepts. For example, Takahashi Hideo succeeds in defining Dazai's work as a non-shishōsetsu only by asserting that the author melts into the background in an orthodox shishōsetsu and is perceived only in relation to his environment; *Ningen shikkaku* builds an obvious contrast to such an assertion, as it is composed entirely from the self-portrait of the author, his relationship with others playing no part at all.[97] Until now we have considered the situation to be quite the opposite. According to such a picture, *Ningen shikkaku* would represent a typical example of the genre.

Other arguments contradict themselves, for example the following statement from the Dazai biographer O'Brien: "Dazai is not a shishōsetsu writer, primarily because he does not attempt a minute and sustained recollection and reconstruction of the past."[98] Here shishōsetsu is considered to be something that it is not.

The fact that none of these arguments is sound is, however, no reason to dismiss the doubts about whether or not the book belongs to the genre. Instead we should pursue the matter in a less direct manner than we have done up to now, in order to find out the reason for such doubts and reach our own conclusion. For this purpose, we shall begin by studying the critical reception of the work; this will show that *Ningen shikkaku* was and is read as a "normal" shishōsetsu in every respect. We shall then turn to Dazai's motivation in writing the book and its effects on the text itself. Our analyses will also confirm the shishōsetsu nature of the work. Finally, we shall turn to the question of how the work differs from the genre and argue that it ought to be considered a shishōsetsu.

"SUBLIMATING WOUNDS TO THE HEART"

Okuno Takeo presents an impressive picture of the effects the book had upon publication. He begins by describing the author's large readership, to which he himself belonged. He claims that Dazai was the only writer who spoke directly to the heart: "We saw in him the only writer who expressed our feelings for us. It may sound exaggerated, but I can say that we entrusted the literature of Dazai with the entire basis for our existence, our reason for living. At least for me, the whole world seemed at that time to revolve around Dazai Osamu. Not only I and the young literary afficionados around me had this feeling, but it symbolized what were more or less the feelings of many young people of that epoch. It is difficult to explain today, but there really was a time when many young people identified spiritually with Dazai Osamu and dedicated their life or death to him."[99] The publication of *Ningen shikkaku* was therefore awaited with great excitement. When the first of three installments appeared in *Tenbō*, the editor's epilogue proclaimed that Dazai considered the novel to be the peak of his achievements and added that no other work of his presented such a frank confession.[100]

Everything in our account up to now points to typical shishōsetsu attitudes in the way the book was received. The reader's obvious disposition corresponds with the reading process. Okuno recollects that the public was already concerned about the author's well-being as a result of the works published previously: "And when one read the 'prologue,' which evoked such a strange mood that one could only define it as his yellowed nihilism, [the 'prologue'] which begins [with the words]: 'I have seen three pictures of the man,' then one felt, alongside our expectations of the book, an ominous sense of foreboding concerning the author. Reading the book with the suspicion that the author wrote *Ningen shikkaku* as an advance warning for his suicide even gave the reader a secret feeling of complicity. Unfortunately, this presentiment proved to be true."[101] A public that concentrates so intently on the person "behind" the work will to an even greater extent consider it to be a personal document after his death and will begin searching for clues and motives for the anticipated outcome of events. Thus, the most widespread literary approach to Dazai's works is the comparison with the biographical facts and the reduction of the "meaning" of these works to their therapeutic value for the author. Okuno even goes as far as to say that *Ningen shikkaku* was not written for the reader but for the author.[102] Here, according to Okuno, Dazai tried again to digest the shock he received in 1936 when he was committed to a psychiatric clinic where he acquired a feeling which he was subsequently unable to cast off, that of being shut out of human society.[103] "He lived in order to sublimate the wounds in his heart through literature, through art; we can even say, he lived only to write *Ningen shikkaku*."[104] A literary scholar who makes such statements and who admits that he is unable to read the book critically and that he cannot help but be moved every time he reads it,[105] reveals that he is reading it as shishōsetsu. He thereby refutes his own assertions that the work does not belong to the genre. The implicit inclusion of the work within the shishōsetsu genre is seen most clearly in the following quotation, where he mentions the principle of intertextuality typical of shishōsetsu[106] and calls upon the reader to find the missing information in the author's other works: "The character of the hero is developed rather hastily, and the reader does not necessarily fully accept him. I think the author was mentally and physically quite weak and exhausted at that time, and it is possible that he could not translate his motives into literature convincingly enough. However, a Dazai fan can of course complete the author's idea of the life and fate of the hero from his numerous other works."[107]

WRITING AS A "WAY OUT"

Having established that both the immediate reaction of the reader and the literary analysis comply with what one expects of shishōsetsu, we are faced with the question of Dazai's attitude towards the affinity of the work with the genre, both as a person and as it is expressed in the work.

We cannot, in this short section, provide a balanced picture of the writer's personality. We can still put forward some soundly based observations on aspects of Dazai that enable us to see how far the parallels between his biography and the reality portrayed in *Ningen shikkaku* extend. These observations will then be related to our inquiries into this writer's poetics as far as shishōsetsu is concerned.

Dazai Osamu, born in 1909 under the name Tsushima Shūji, was the tenth child in one of the most influential landowning families in Aomori prefecture. His weak physical constitution and his parents' lack of affection for him forced him early on into the role of outsider in his own family. This feeling of deprivation in early childhood prevented his developing self-esteem and led to his asociality. The only chance he had of attracting attention was to assume the role of family clown which encouraged his own narcissistic tendencies. From then on, his entire life was determined by "histrionic self-display,"[108] "buffoonery" (*dōke*) as he himself called it. Only when acting out the role of the notorious outsider could he find fulfillment and overcome isolation. He was never sure of his own feelings. His uncertainties concerning the genuineness of both his and others' emotions meant that the question of sincerity or hypocrisy was central for him throughout his life. His role-playing also enabled him to act out his feelings of hatred towards his father and the society that he felt had rejected him, feelings that were, however, accompanied by a strong sense of guilt for which he tried to compensate through Christianity.[109]

Marxism, which became increasingly influential in Japan in the late 1920s, was initially attractive for Dazai because it was a movement against the establishment; he felt an affinity with it in his status as an outsider. However, although he joined the movement, he was not able to identify with it. Consequently, Tsurumi Kazuko describes him as a "perennial deviant" in her study on the personality development of Japanese intellectuals, that is, he was fundamentally incapable of committing himself to a group or an ideology.[110] Tsurumi locates the reason for his deviance in his strong feelings of guilt and shame.[111]

Dazai became aware of his problems early on. In his first work,

"Memories" ("Omoide," 1930), he states that he decided to become a writer as early as 1925, while he was still at school: "My inner unrest began around that time. Nothing fully satisfied me, and all my efforts were in vain. Because I wore ten or twenty masks I could not decide which was the sorrowful [mask, let alone decide on] the extent of [this sorrow]. However, I finally found a sorrowful and lonely way out—writing. Here there were numerous like-minded people, or so I believed, who, like me, gazed on this inconceivable trembling. I secretly wished, I shall be a writer, a writer."[112] It is customary to interpret this statement as a direct personal declaration on Dazai's part, and indeed it fits easily into the picture of the writer's personality. Nevertheless, it seems necessary to point out that, as early as this first work, we perceive a kind of literary crossing of the borders, whereby artistic creation is judged to be simultaneously self-evaluation. If this method is used in early works, then there is no doubt that it applies to *Ningen shikkaku* as well, which means that we are inevitably interpreting it as a shishōsetsu.

Let us now turn to the content of Dazai's statement. He sees in literature a "way out" of his problems, which makes it possible for him to identify them objectively. In addition, art enables him to act out his narcissism, his histrionic, exhibitionist tendencies and his aggressions. In "The Flowers of Buffoonery" ("Dōke no hana," 1935)—the title is, in my opinion, an obvious reference to Baudelaire, whom he admired—he wrote: "Why do I write novels? I should not have said that! Now it is too late. It sounds unpleasantly like coquetry, but I will try answering with one word: 'revenge.'"[113] What conclusions can we draw from the foregoing observations? We should exclude one methodological approach right from the start so as to distance ourselves from Japanese literary studies: We are not concerned with tracing the entire contents of the book to biographically verifiable facts or with identifying the decisive circumstances under which the literature was produced in its final form. And it is not our objective to characterize Dazai's literary works as the product of a psychopathic personality—he is said, among other things, to have exhibited schizoid tendencies.[114] Such statements are of little value, since not every psychopath becomes a writer nor would this help in judging the literary value of Dazai's work.

For us it is important only to recognize that Dazai produced his literary work largely in order to overcome his own problems and that he therefore used it as a medium for portraying himself, providing personal testimony, and self-justification. Thus, his relationship to literature is similar to that of the shishōsetsu writers, for example, Shiga Naoya. The strong mutual dislike felt by both writers is not, as O'Brien argues, proof of their spiritual differences;[115] on the contrary, it seems to point to their unconscious awareness of an inner kinship. (The same is true of that other great Dazai opponent, Mishima Yukio.)

"BUFFOONERY" AS AN ACT OF DESPAIR

We now turn to the novel itself. It consists of a short prologue and epilogue from a first-person narrator (these provide the narrative framework) and the central part which is presented in the form of three notebooks by another first-person narrator. The use of the framing story was undoubtedly one of the reasons why the shishōsetsu label was rejected for this book. We shall, therefore, have to consider this feature later in more detail. The foreword begins abruptly with the sentence: "I have seen three pictures of the man."[116] There then follows a description of "the man" of the photographs, which show him in three different stages of his life. The first-person narrator finds him to be increasingly disagreeable, first as a child, then as a student, and finally as an older man. Without telling us anything about the character of the narrator, who merely conveys his impressions of the photos, the first notebook then commences with the words: "Mine has been a life of much shame" (p. 366/p. 21).

This narrator, who calls himself *jibun* in contrast to the *watakushi* character of the frame, is the figure in the photographs. The three phases in his life correspond to the three notebooks. The first describes his childhood; the second his time at school and as a student, a period which extends to about 1930 in Dazai's biography; and the third notebook, divided into two parts, concentrates on the time until he left the psychiatric clinic, which is according to the biography at the end of 1936. A final passage in the last notebook indicates an elapse of over three years which has, however, as far as I know, been generally ignored by the critics. If the work is read in parallel with the author's life, then the lapse should indeed be ignored, since the notebook ends with the statements: "This year I am twenty-seven. My hair has become much greyer. Most people would take me for over forty" (p. 467/p. 170).

The name of the hero, Ōba Yōzō, known to the Dazai reader from "Flowers of Buffoonery" ("Dōke no hana," 1935), is also reminiscent of shishōsetsu practice; the underlying mood of the book, from the first sentence, is familiar. The title of the novel seems to be the Japanese version of the English words *Human Lost*, the name he gave to a work in the form of a diary written in 1937, partly based on the same experiences as *Ningen shikkaku*.

The narrative present of the first person remains a mystery. It does not seem to change much from one notebook to the next, so that it can be assumed that all three have been linked retrospectively until one arrives at the present moment at the end of the third notebook. The periods of childhood and adolescence are described in loose chronological order, and the author emphasizes only those events that seem to the hero to have an exemplary character in the light of his subsequent development. The episodes are linked together by self-critical, sometimes ironic commentary which informs the reader about the narrator's insight into his own problems. He recognizes even in his early childhood that he is different from others and incapable of making social contact, concluding, "This was how I happened to invent my clowning. It was the last quest for love I was to direct at human beings" (p. 370/p. 26). His lifelong clowning is stylistically expressed through the abundance of verbal inventiveness which at times extends to sarcasm, but which cannot disguise the fact that the hero cultivates a feeling of pity and resignation towards his own weaknesses, something expressed more directly in other shishōsetsu. The hero of *Ningen shikkaku* is, however, different in that he possesses an unusually clear awareness of his problems though this brings him no nearer to solving them. For example, he admits:

> I am congenitally unable to take much interest in other people.
> (p. 416/p. 99f.)

> Though I have always made it my practice to be pleasant to everybody, I have not once actually experienced friendship. (p. 421/p. 107)

> I know that I am liked by other people, but I seem to be deficient in the faculty to love others. (I should add that I have very strong doubts as to whether even human beings really possess this faculty.)[117] It was hardly to be expected that someone like myself could ever develop any close friendships—besides, I lacked even the ability to pay visits. (p. 422/p. 107f.)

His self-hatred is expressed in thoughts like the following: "The toad. (That is what I was—a toad. It was not a question of whether or not society tolerated me, whether or not it ostracized me. I was an animal lower than a dog, lower than a cat. A toad. I sluggishly moved—that's all.)" (p. 433/p. 122). He expects affection and attention from society but feels at the same time contempt for it because of its falseness and wickedness, and presents himself as its victim (for example, p. 421/p. 106f.). Thus he feels simultaneously an outcast and the chosen one, inferior and superior, despairing and proud. Such ambiguity is reflected in the title where shame at not belonging to human society is coupled with a feeling of moral superiority. In this, *Ningen shikkaku* is a typical shishōsetsu, since such a self-image on the part of the narrator is one of the genre's most important characteristics. Dazai evinces as little development as other shishōsetsu writers, as Tanizawa Eiichi rightly points out.[118] The situation of the poor misled hero who seeks refuge in buffoonery against the corrupt, false world remains constant from beginning to end. Thus, the narrator's experiences do not differ at all from those in other shishōsetsu, where there is a similar opposition at work.

"THE MOST MODERN VERSION OF SHISHŌSETSU"

Having shown that there are significant arguments in favor of classifying this novel under the genre shishōsetsu, we should now examine the previously mentioned arguments against this. Probably the most important argument against labeling *Ningen shikkaku* a shishōsetsu is the framing story format. This does indeed imply a break in perspective, which seems to conflict fundamentally with the principle of "one-dimensional" and "immediate" narrative. However, a detailed analysis is essential in order to establish the function of the particular narrative framework in question. We begin therefore with the short prologue.

As already implied, the first-person narrator remains a depersonalized figure who simply conveys his impressions of the photographs of Ōba Yōzō. The very first sentence, "I have seen three pictures of the man," creates tension through the cataphoric function of the demonstrative; this is then heightened at the level of "content" by the descriptions of the photographs, illustrating three different stages of the man's life and anticipating in condensed form the story within the frame. The description of the individual photographs prepares the reader for the mood of the three notebooks because the first-person narrator of the framing story views Ōba Yōzō from the same perspective as the notebook narrator. The childhood photograph shows the hero as the family clown; the narrator recognizes this in the prologue, but leaves the detailed interpretation to the notebook. The impression of artificiality, of play-acting, is irrefutably present in the second photograph. The third photograph completes the negative image that we gain of the hero and directs the reader's attention to the proceeding notebooks much more effectively than a pale description could have done. We can recognize the careful construction of the prologue by three sentences of parallel construction with which the narrator summarizes his impressions of the photographs:

> I have never seen a child with such an unaccountable expression.
> (p. 365/p. 14)
>
> I have never seen a young man whose good looks were so baffling.
> (p. 365/p. 15)
>
> I have never seen such an inscrutable face on a man. (p. 366/p. 17)

The way this prologue is connected with the main story can be seen from the following sentence: "It is quite impossible in this one even to guess the age, though the hair seems to be streaked somewhat with grey" (p. 365/p. 15). As mentioned above, the third notebook ends with the words: "This year I am twenty-seven. My hair has become much greyer. Most people would take me for over forty" (p. 467/p. 170). This illustrates the function of the prologue as a whole: the fact that a detached and, in terms of time, remote observer, having seen the photographs, makes the same statements and reaches the same conclusions as the narrator in the main story, convincingly authenticates and reinforces the latter's opinions. The narrator's views are thus not merely the subjective truth of a shishōsetsu focus figure, but are objective insofar as they are intersubjective and independent of time. In addition to the prologue's aesthetically pleasing nature and its skillful means of increasing tension, it also serves to underline Dazai's theme.

The same is true for the epilogue where the narrator, who turns out to be a writer, describes the way in which the three notebooks came into his hands. One of Yōzō's mistresses, a barmaid, gave them to him with the suggestion that he use them as the basis for a novel, but he decides to publish them as they are. The woman says that the books were sent to her ten years earlier, but that she has only recently read them. She felt the events described are now so remote that she did not even cry while reading (p. 470/p. 176). In the short conversation about Yōzō, the writer plays the part of the uncomprehending public who can only shake their heads in exasperation: "If everything written in these notebooks is true, I probably would have wanted to put him in an insane asylum myself if

I were his friend" (p. 470/p. 177). This is the prompt for the barmaid's statement: "It's his father's fault" (*Ano hito no otōsan ga warui no desu yo*, p. 470/p. 177). This judgment is a complete explanation of Yōzō's development and behavior, which the narrator can assess only from the point of view of "others." She places the responsibility on Yōzō's father and the bourgeois society he embodies.[119] Her opinion is made all the more convincing because she expresses it "unemotionally" (*nanige nasaō ni*, p. 470/p. 177) as if it were quite obvious and not because she is forced to find some defense for Yōzō because of an emotional identification with him. The author emphasizes the objectivity that arises out of an emotional and temporal detachment from the events and invests her last statement, the last sentence of the work with the highest possible degree of objective validity: "The Yozo we knew was so easy-going and amusing, and if only he hadn't drunk—no, even though he did drink—he was a good boy, an angel" (p. 470/p. 177). The book ends by presenting the assenting reader with a positive picture of the hero based on a reliably objective judgment. Such an authenticated impression removes any doubts left among the more naive readers who may have interpreted the hero's self-hatred too literally. Dazai puts words into the barmaid's mouth that he could not himself express directly as a notorious clown or, on the literary level, as an intellectual overly prone to sarcasm. In the epilogue, he ensures that the image he has of himself is conveyed plausibly to even the most naive reader. At the same time, by describing in the framing story how the notebook manuscripts came to be published, he heightens the documentary character and the impression of "genuineness." Thus, the framing story format for *Ningen shikkaku* proves to be an effective means of "objectifying" a shishōsetsu. The effect of the additional perspective is enhanced further as it is identical with that of the focus figure.

We can thus reject O'Brien's assertion that the epilogue "creates an entirely new perspective"[120] and necessarily destroys the reader's interpretation of the events described, or, at the very least, makes him feel unsure of it.[121] We can similarly repudiate Alyce Morishige's attempt, based on Wayne Booth's theories, to label both narrators "unreliable,"[122] an approach that raises many doubts, since it is based on a fundamental misunderstanding of what the book intended.

One last observation further supports the theory expressed here. In the context of the narrative framework, the barmaid's statement that Yōzō's father is to blame for everything is really quite unrealistic, since she can hardly be expected to possess such insight. This proves that the author is using her as Yōzō's mouthpiece. Kazamaki Keijirō's remark that we perceive Dazai's self-love in the words of this woman appears to be valid.[123]

Our evaluation of the function of the narrative framework is also confirmed by the results of detailed analyses of style undertaken by Ōkubo Tadatoshi and Tachibana Yutaka, which show that the language of the first person in the frame and of the hero hardly differ.[124] This indicates that the author was not aiming to distinguish the perspective through language. Everything points towards a text that complies with our generic model of shishōsetsu.

In addition to these formal criteria, it is possible that the style of *Ningen shikkaku*, which is more "philosophical" than other examples of shishōsetsu, could have led to the conclusion that the book does not belong to the genre. There is no doubt that the narrator differs from other shishōsetsu narrators in being less concerned with describing banal trivialities. In attempting to give a characteristic picture of his own personality, he reaches back into childhood and so distances himself from the pattern of "immediate" description. However, we have seen that his rational insight does not radically alter the plot, and his view of the world corresponds with that of the "naive" shishōsetsu writers. His critical, ironical tone and rationalization are the literary stylistic manifestation of his buffoonery.

In using new formal methods and by including a stronger "philosophical" component, *Ningen shikkaku* proves to be a further, more modern development of the shishōsetsu pattern, and we must agree with Usui Yoshimi's statement that in this novel, "The tradition of Japanese shishōsetsu was developed to its most modern form."[125]

MIURA TETSUO: "SHINOBUGAWA" (1960)

None of the doubts raised concerning Dazai's *Ningen shikkaku* and the shishōsetsu genre were voiced when "Shinobugawa" was published in October 1960 in the magazine *Shinchō*, a short story for which the author, Miura Tetsuo (b. 1931), was awarded the 44th Akutagawa Prize, Japan's most respected literary honor. All the critics and literary scholars agree that "Shinobugawa" is a shishōsetsu.[126] For example, Hirano Ken writes that the work evinces "the basic weakness of the shishōsetsu style of writing."[127] Uno Kōji remarks that it makes an "old fashioned" (*furumekashii*) impression,[128] and Kawabata Yasunari, who was also a member of the jury selecting the prizewinner at the time, agreed with the decision but added that the work gives the impression of being "inexperienced and old-[fashioned], but genuine and deeply moving."[129] The shishōsetsu writer Takii Kōsaku, one of the book's supporters, explains that it is just this old-fashioned style of writing, reminiscent of the *haiku* form, that makes it so attractive. Finally, Funabashi Seiichi proclaims, "Among the many new-fashioned works which [give the impression] of being dirty because they are so difficult to understand, what is new is to be found in its very old-fashionedness, unpretentious and yet not novel."[130] At least all were in agreement that this old-fashioned and new work, a shishōsetsu, should be awarded Japan's most prestigious literary prize.

"PURITY" AND "LYRICISM"

There is widespread agreement in all the statements characterizing Miura's literature, whether they are made in encyclopaedia articles, essays, or the jury judgments. All arguments center on the keywords *purity* and *lyricism* as illustrated in the commentaries quoted above. Kawauchi Mitsuharu emphasizes that the author succeeded in "sublimating" his work to "pure lyricism" and should therefore be highly valued.[131] Akatsuka Yukio, in turn, waxes poetically when he compares the "lyrical work" "Shinobugawa" with seaweed that floats back and forth deep in the water and has nothing to do with the rough currents of time.[132] The material on the book's jacket contains similar metaphors.[133]

The combination of the words *purity* and *lyricism* can easily be explained, since each implies the other in the Japanese context.[134] This observation makes quite clear just how deeply the literary-theoretical association of poetry with "pure literature" (*junbungaku*) is rooted in the general consciousness, something we emphasized earlier as an unchanging premise of Japanese artistic theory.

In consequence, in order to characterize the work it is sufficient to concentrate on its "lyricism," since this would at the same time provide evidence of its "purity." Since there is, as usual, no more detailed explanation of these characteristics, we are dependent on the short story itself. Which of its features could create the impression of lyricism in the Japanese sense of the word?

In "Shinobugawa," a student living in Tokyo relates, in first-person narrative (*watakushi*), the story covering the time of his first meeting with his future wife, Shino, until their wedding night and the beginning of their honeymoon. The story starts at a time when the two already know each other and have just begun going out together. They visit a red-light district in Fukagawa, where Shino grew up. Here the narrator learns about her childhood in these unpleasant surroundings.

The next scene describes how their friendship developed. Shino works in a Japanese restaurant (*ryōtei*) called Shinobugawa. On the occasion of a farewell party, the narrator and some fellow students visit this restaurant, which, as a penniless student, he had always found overly exclusive. He meets Shino and is immediately captivated by her (pp. 22–24). He visits the restaurant again during the next few days and realizes that Shino also finds him attractive. So, on her first, eagerly awaited day off, the two undertake the pilgrimage to Fukagawa (pp. 25f.).

After she has revealed her past to him there, he decides to be just as honest and describe his family history to her. Since he lacks the courage to tell her immediately, he reveals in a letter to her that two of his five siblings have committed suicide and two have vanished without a trace. Only one extremely poorly sighted sister and he are left (pp. 26f.). Shino stands by him, and the attempt made by another person to separate them is unsuccessful. The narrator proposes to her on the spot (p. 32).

One day Shino is called to her dying father. Her family lives in poverty in the country. She asks the narrator to join her later, and thus her father dies with the comforting knowledge that his daughter will marry out of love just as he had always wished (pp. 38–40). At the time of the New Year's celebrations, the couple travel to northern Japan to the groom's home, where the wedding is celebrated among close family and friends and with touching simplicity. Neither the family nor the bridal couple could be happier. On the morning after the wedding night, they travel for their honeymoon to a nearby seaside resort for the day. Only the beginning of the honeymoon is described. The work ends with a scene in the train where Shino, whose family has always lived in temporary accommodation, sees her husband's house and, filled with enthusiasm and childlike innocence, keeps exclaiming, "Look! My house!" (pp. 51f.).

The plot which we have outlined is presented in approximately eleven scenes,[135] each one carefully constructed to emphasize a single point. Shino's touching innocence is emphasized in the first and last scenes. At their first meeting, it is the way she grants the hero's request for a glass of water with such womanly charm (p. 22) that is emphasized for the reader and in the farewell scene, before she travels to visit her sick father, it is her seriousness that receives similar attention (p. 35). Okuno Takeo admits that he is somewhat jealous of the hero, because he feels so attracted to Shino: "This is the ideal woman as Japanese men have always longed for her to be from the depths of their hearts—the image of a wife."[136]

However, the author also includes impressive descriptions of other characters and events. One typical example is the arrival of the narrator in the station of the small town where Shino awaits him while visiting her dying father. Her sister does not take him straight home. When she is asked for the reason behind the detour she replies: "I have heard that father will not die until you come, but when you are there he's bound to die immediately, isn't he?" (p. 37).

The powerful effect of all these scenes is based on a consciously developed contrast. In the last example, it is the contrast between humorous naiveté and a particularly serious situation; in other cases, that between childish innocence and the corrupt environment, an opposition that epitomizes Shino, since her naiveté and honesty are a strange contrast to her reputation as the "figurehead" (*kanban musume*) of a Japanese restaurant.

The effect of these scenes is complemented still further by highly evocative descriptions of nature. An example is the scene of the couple's arrival at the hero's home village: "At home the snow fell gently. As we got out of the train and walked along the platform under the open sky it lay like silver dust on Shino's . . . shining hair. When my mother saw us she said only, 'Oh, oh!' Her face became furrowed with lines as she smiled and opened her arms as if she wanted to embrace us, and she said [again], 'Oh, oh!' Shino went straight to her without hesitating and greeted her and my mother bowed lower than she and answered her greeting in the lilting dialect [of my home country]" (p. 41). Nature provides the background that intensifies the impression of a friendly, open and affectionate country family. The work culminates in the description of the wedding night. In the distance, the bells of a horse-drawn sleigh can be heard. Shino wants to see it:

> We wrapped ourselves, naked as we were, in a padded winter kimono and crept out of the room. As I opened the sliding door in the hallway just a fraction, a beam of light of almost cruel brightness fell on Shino's naked skin.
> The sleigh, a black shadow behind it and its bells ringing, passed by on the lane, while the snow covered countryside was as bright as day. (p. 50)

We can assume that scenes of such idyllic intensity as these largely contribute to the "lyricism" of the work. "Shinobugawa" does not include metric structures, which would most clearly identify it as being lyrical.

We can, however, still identify a specific use of language that, in addition to the previously mentioned elements, creates the lyrical effect—it is namely an aphoristic succinctness of content inside a simply formulated sentence that marks the high point or end of a scene.

The death of Shino's father and the account of his advice to Shino, "If you have fallen in love, then get married soon," is followed by the sentence: "On New Year's Eve of that year I set off with Shino on the night train from Ueno" (p. 41). The next scene begins with their arrival in the hero's home village, which we have previously cited.

At times, such language sounds archaic. As the narrator prepares to write about his first meeting with Shino and has finished describing the restaurant which he never previously dared enter, we encounter the phrase, "Shino was a woman from the Shinobugawa" (*Shino wa Shinobugawa no onna de atta*, p. 20). The peculiar *Shinobugawa no onna* heightens the poetic effect of this sentence, which stands out from those before and after it in a paragraph of its own.

All these methods of enhancing the poetic effect of the text, which is interpreted as lyricism, could be subsumed under the concept of aestheticism. This concept, which is in my opinion more comprehensive, will be considered in the following section.

"BEAUTIFUL POVERTY," OR SUSPECTED FICTIONALITY

That which one critic praises as the special quality of "Shinobugawa" leads another to suspect fictionalization, which would mean a considerable lessening of the book's artistic value. One representative of the first group is Ibuse Masuji: "It is difficult to be poor beautifully, but he described poverty in a beautiful way."[137] Okuno Takeo represents the second group. In his interpretation of the short story, we can trace the process by which the identification of the work's aestheticism leads to a negative evaluation of the work.

Okuno admits that his eyes were filled with tears when he read "Shinobugawa," but he continues with the question, "Is this really a work where [the author] has described his own experiences, his wedding, honestly, as it really was? I'm not really convinced. The facts and details written down here are probably based on reality as he experienced it. But the pervasive atmosphere of the book as a whole corresponds to 'fiction' rather than to 'realism,'[138] and I cannot help feeling that it is a fictional work which the author has created according to his aesthetic tastes (*biishiki*). It seems to me that it is like a fairy tale treated aesthetically, one which was sublimated onto a different level from [that of] reality. Has not the author written a dreamy fairy tale by using the actual facts?"[139] He then goes on to explain why the work no longer seems to him to be a shishōsetsu, but only "a fairy tale drawing upon the [ideal] way of being, which makes uses of the shishōsetsu form": "Reality cannot have been so beautiful and manageable for these two people. There must also have been the dirt of reality, which inevitably clings to us during our lives, groundless doubts, envy, suffering, and ugliness. . . . There is no difficult fight here where the characters are stuck deep in the dirt, as we have seen it in earlier shishōsetsu, where we did not see how life could go on."[140] Okuno, and other Japanese literary scholars see the aestheticism purely in terms of an exclusion of negative experiences from the description of reality. However, if we wish to argue more precisely, we should add that such aestheticism is in evidence at other levels of the work which are of less interest to Japanese literary studies. We referred to some of the aspects in the previous section. One further peculiarity of the text will suffice to substantiate our theory.

The title of the short story not only emphasizes the importance of the place where the two first met. It is also intimately related to the "content" of the work. *Shinobu* means "suffer," "endure" and thus refers to the lovers' unfortunate states. The wedding night scene proves that this is not merely an arbitrary interpretation of the text: After they have made love they lie and think about their future. This is clearly meant to be a turning point when the dismal past both have led will be wiped away by their common, bright future. Shino says:

> "But I am ashamed; I can't do anything. From now on I want to learn a lot. It is only now that I think about it that I realize how wastefully I have spent the first twenty years of my life. I have never put myself first and I have always endured, endured (*shinonde shinonde*) only for others, for those around me, regardless of whether I wanted to or not . . ."[141]
> "Shino from Shinobugawa."
> "No, I have already completely forgotten that Shinobugawa; starting from tomorrow I shall be another Shino and from now on I shall think only of me and you. Let us lead a good life!" (p. 49)

There can be no doubt that the author consciously emphasizes this turning point by using the lexeme *shinobu*, so making the meaning of the name "Shinobugawa" even clearer, and he then goes on to demonstrate this even more emphatically by naming it again towards the end of the citation. The phrase *Shino from Shinobugawa* also makes it clear that the consonance of both names was intended, as does the sentence *Shino wa Shinobugawa no onna de atta* (p. 20).

"Aestheticism" in the sense of conscious, "aesthetic" selection of the particular reality to be portrayed and a heightened poeticity arising from the many different functions carried out by a text-element produces the result that the work is no longer considered a shishōsetsu. Nakamura Shin'ichirō comes to the same conclusion as Okuno. The hero's life seems to have gone too smoothly. Real life must have contained more setbacks and he concludes therefore that "Shinobugawa" is a "non-shishōsetsu" (*hi-shishōsetsu*).[142]

If we look at the reasons behind such arguments, we can see that these critics are not speaking about shishōsetsu as such but rather a particular historical exemplar of the genre. This is most obvious in the case of Okuno. His understanding of the genre, like that of the majority of his colleagues, is based on the "decline" type written by Kasai Zenzō or Dazai Osamu. For him this type of writing embodies shishōsetsu-like "realism," a hint that he obviously fails to see that Kasai "fictionalizes" just as much as Miura. The difference is merely a matter of emphasis. The "decline" literature concentrates on a description of negative aspects, adversities, and pathetic, tragic situations and uses "fictionalization" as a means of heightening the effect of despondency, as we could see from the example of Kasai.[143] This literature also includes poetic images and symbols that create *mono no aware* and *mujōkan* moods, features we referred to only in the context of Hayashi Fumiko's *Hōrōki*,[144] but which is no less typical for "Ko o tsurete."

The profound effect of this frequent variant of shishōsetsu is revealed in the way the style of writing is considered to be "natural" and true to reality to the extent that the particular reality described in it is held to be *the* reality (*jijitsu sono mama*). Anything which deviates from this kind of engrained recognition is felt to belong to the realms of the "artificial."

Using our structural model of shishōsetsu and not a historical variant as our criterion, nothing can be said against the inclusion of the short story "Shinobugawa" in the genre. At most, it would mean casting doubts on its factuality, since, if a critic asserts that he did not read the book as a shishōsetsu,[145] one basic condition would not be met—the public's expectation that there is a direct correspondence between the reality described and non-literary reality. It is easy to find a practical reason for this argument: Since the author first became well known as a result of this work and there was no previous biographical knowledge about him, it was not possible to apply the typical method of reading a shishōsetsu. However, there can be no doubt that, in spite of all these protests, the work was accepted as shishōsetsu. The most convincing proof of this is found under the heading "Miura Tetsuo" in the *Concise Encyclopaedia of Japanese Literature* (*NBS*) where we find not a list of the author's works but rather a description of his family background as we know it from "Shinobugawa." What could be better proof of the shishōsetsu method of inquiry in Japanese literary studies than the removal of statements from a fictional text and their subsequent misuse in a critical reconstruction of the author's personality, as happens here? That is namely the case when the assertion is made that the author's tragic family history brought him to literature and that this in turn was an attempt "to purify his blood" (*chi no jōka*). The metaphor of "sick blood" originated in Miura's short story "Shoya" (The First Night, 1961), a sequel to "Shinobugawa," in which the first-person narrator decides that his wife's first pregnancy should be aborted for fear the child will inherit a pathological disposition—he considers his family's fate to be genetically determined. However, after his father's death, he decides to create "new blood" with Shino's help which will overcome the "sick blood" of his dead brothers and sisters.[146] There is also mention in this work—in the same language—that he wants to free himself from the shadow of the past through his work.[147]

This reference to "Shoya" introduces us to a practice we have already met in other shishōsetsu authors, such as Chikamatsu Shūkō, Shiga Naoya, and Dazai Osamu. Miura uses the same and later material from his life in a number of further works which would produce a Japanese "novel" (*chōhen shōsetsu*) if they were all joined together. Shiga Naoya's approach in the case of his famous novel *An'ya kōro* is evidence that a writer can consciously adopt this method. He himself wrote: "I once considered writing some short stories (*tanpen*) and then joining them up to make a novel (*chōhen*)."[148] According to his own statement, he then actually proceeded in this manner.[149]

In "Shoya" Miura picks up the thread of the story again at the beginning of the honeymoon and describes events until Shino's—this time eagerly awaited—second pregnancy.[150] "Kikyō" (Returning Home, 1962) describes the couple's life of extreme poverty in Tokyo. In spite of taking in work and regular visits to both the pawnshop and the secondhand bookshop to sell their own books, they eventually give up and return to the country.[151] In "Haji no fu" (The Inheritance of Shame, 1961), Miura again uses the material from "Shinobugawa," this time going into his father's death in greater detail than in "Shoya."[152] Finally, "Gentōgashū" (Magic Lantern Collection, 1961)[153] provides a postscript to the deaths of Miura's brothers and sisters, a theme present as a tragic background in all the stories.

These close connections between the individual works and the intertextual references are evidence of the shishōsetsu character of "Shinobugawa," which can be said to be at the center of the referential web. The subject matter of a short story such as "Kikyō" should also be sufficient to satisfy even a reader such as Okuno, since the act of having to pawn a kimono belongs among other similar events to the basic repertoire of "decline" literature.[154]

We return to Okuno's interpretation. Having determined that the effect of "Shinobugawa" was created consciously, he is ashamed of his tears since a "wrought" and therefore "artificial" work (*tsukurimono*) should not be able, according to his view, to elicit profound human emotions.[155] There can then be no doubt that the literary value of the short story has fallen, while a comparison with Dazai's writing merely serves to confirm Okuno's opinion that Miura's "optimism" contains a "redeeming" element but is ultimately a flaw. He maintains that "the color of suffering," as in Dazai, is always of higher artistic value.[156]

Japanese literary scholars referred to a "formalization" (*hōhōka*, literally "methodization") of shishōsetsu when discussing "Shinobugawa" in order to overcome the problem that arose from the recognition that the short story was "definitely a shishōsetsu" but, on the other hand, not like a "real" shishōsetsu.[157] This dilemma is not solved by asserting that "Shinobugawa" is a shishōsetsu only in respect to form.[158]

It is reasonable to speak of "formalization" if the term is interpreted to mean creating a tradition. The process of canonizing the generic form, which began with the first example of the genre, was carried out by the readers and critics themselves who formed their own increasingly clear idea of the genre. The example of Okuno showed that this idea was based above all on the "decline" type of story and that this became the model for the genre as such. Only deviations from their rule would make the public aware of the otherwise constant and unnoticed "formalization" of shishōsetsu.

A desire to reject "Shinobugawa" as part of the shishōsetsu genre would mean clinging to a variant of shishōsetsu that has obviously become obsolete. Miyoshi Yukio's contribution to the discussion is certainly more telling. According to him shishōsetsu's naive, spontaneous style was replaced after the war by a more thoughtful style of writing, by an "awareness of method" (*hōhōteki jikaku*) which corresponds to the "formalization" carried out by the reader. The "awareness of method" would also entail a recognition that the genre is a series of literary works structured according to an inherent system of rules.[159]

1. Masamune Hakuchō, "Iwano Hōmei," p. 383.
2. Cf. *GNBD*, p. 114, heading "Tandeki."
3. Cf., e.g., Hisamatsu Sen'ichi, *Zōho shinpan Nihon bungakushi*, VI, 318.
4. Cf. Yoshida Seiichi, *Shizenshugi no kenkyū*, vol. II, pp. 449ff.
5. Cf. "The Narrative Perspective" (Chapter 14).
6. Cf. I.H.-K., "Innovation als Renovation."
7. "Tandeki," text in *GNBT*, vol. XXI: *Iwano Hōmei, Kamitsukasa Shōken, Mayama Seika, Chikamatsu Shūkō shū*, pp. 63–101, here p. 84. Further page references in the text.
8. Cf. the discussion in "'Misunderstandings'" (Chapter 3).
9. Cf. for details the sections "'Shinpiteki hanjūshughi' nōto" (Notes on '...') and "Hōmei to Nīche" (Homei and Nietzsche) in Ōkubo Tsuneo, *Iwano Hōmei no jidai*.
10. Masamune, p. 384, expresses similar thoughts.
11. Parentheses in the original.
12. Cf. I.H.-K., "Innovation als Renovation," pp. 353ff.
13. Cf. Masamune Hakuchō: "Shizenshugi seisuishi," *Masamune Hakuchō zenshū*, XII, 301.
14. Cf. Masamune, p. 385.
15. Ibid., p. 384.
16. Cf. *NBS*, p. 764, headings "Chikamatsu Shūkō" and "Giwaku."
17. Cited in Ōkubo Tsuneo, *Iwano Hōmei no jidai*, p. 206.
18. Cf. ibid., p. 208.
19. Cf. ibid.
20. Ibid., p. 206.
21. In I.H.-K., "Kritische Bemerkungen," p. 57, I have already referred to some aspects of this concept and its origins in shishōsetsu tradition.
22. I do not here wish to examine the other aspects on which it could also depend.
23. Cf. Uno Kōji, "Chikamatsu Shūkō," p. 398.
24. Cf. Hirano Ken, *NBS*, p. 764, heading "Giwaku"; also Miyagi Tatsurō, *GNBD*, p. 717, heading "Wakaretaru tsuma ni okuru tegami."
25. "Giwaku," text in *GNBZ*, vol. XIII: *Iwano Hōmei, Chikamatsu Shūkō shū*, pp. 284–314, here p. 285. Further page references in the text.
26. Ōkubo Tsuneo, *Iwano Hōmei no jidai*, p. 208.
27. One example of the public's stricter standards was given in "The Dispute over Shishōsetsu" (Chapter 11).
28. Yoshida Seiichi et al., "Shishōsetsu no honshitsu to mondaiten," p. 65.
29. While looking for O-Suma, he says that she is 30 years old. She is really 35, but he is ashamed of running after such an "old" woman (p. 286).
30. Cf. Matsubara, p. 98.
31. Cf. ibid., p. 108.
32. Cf. ibid.
33. Cf. ibid., p. 98.

34. Cf., e.g., Kōno Toshirō et al., eds., *Taishō no bungaku*, p. 20ff., also Usui, *Shōsetsu no ajiwaikata*, p. 155.
35. Cf., e.g., Nanbu Shūtarō's review "Shiga Naoya shi no 'Wakai'" of 22 October, 1917 in *Mita bungaku*, reprint in *KBHT*, IV, 454–456, here pp. 454f.
36. Cited in Usui, *Shōsetsu no ajiwaikata*, p. 154.
37. I consulted Agawa Hiroyuki, *Shiga Naoya*, Kohl, "Shiga Naoya," Sibley, "The Shiga Hero," Usui, "Shiga and Akutagawa," Yasuoka Shōtarō, *Shiga Naoya shiron* and "Kaisetsu" on this.
38. "Wakai," text in *Shiga Naoya zenshū*, VI, 69–146, cf., e.g., pp. 78, 141. Following page references in text.
39. To be precise, he was counting in sheets of standardized manuscript paper.
40. *Shiga Naoya zenshū*, X, 181–198, here p. 193.
41. A Western reader is struck by the parallels to European literature in this discussion, to Victor Hugo's *Dernier jour d'un condamné* (1829) as far as the time structure is concerned, but in the case of Hugo's novel the reader can manage with the aid of French tense rules (such as the change between *passé défini* and *passé composé*, depending on whether 24 hours have passed or not).

The associations with Marcel Proust's *A la recherche du temps perdu* (1913–1927) which might become apparent in "Wakai" as a result of my description of the way the story becomes coextensive with the act of writing, are more likely to increase the awareness of the differences between the two works, since the concept of time, so central to *Recherche*, is not a subject of Shiga's shishōsetsu. The complexity of the time structure in "Wakai" is largely a result of the author's unconscious use of it (which, of course, does not alter its aesthetic effect), and the fact that Japanese studies are hardly even aware of the question of the complex temporality confirms my theory.
42. Müller, p. 68.
43. It is his father's second wife. His mother died in 1895, an experience he also made use of in his writing and to which he also refers in "Wakai," cf. p. 101.
44. "Shiga Naoya," text in *Kobayashi Hideo zenshū*, IV, 13–27, here p. 16.
45. Cf., e.g., Tanikawa Tetsuzō, *Shiga Naoya no sakuhin*, p. 115.
46. Usui, *Shōsetsu no ajiwaikata*, p. 154.
47. Odagiri, *Shishōsetsu, shinkyō shōsetsu*, p. 24.
48. Uno, "Shishōsetsu shiken," p. 21.
49. Ōmori, p. 119.
50. Cf. ibid., p. 118f. and Yamamoto, *Watakushishōsetsu*, p. 14.
51. The text used was the first edition of the work, published in 1919 by Shinchōsha. It contains a total of 12 works. "Ko o tsurete," from which the book takes its title, is the beginning (pp. 1–36). The page numbers given in the text refer to this edition.
52. Cf. Miyagi Otoya, "Shishōsetsu no shinrigaku," p. 44.
53. Ibid., p. 45.
54. Kindaichi Haruhiko, *Nihonjin no gengo hyōgen*, p. 91 also confirms this, on the basis of an examination of Shiga Naoya's short story "Kinosaki nite" (1917). Statements by the hero about the kinds of animals he likes, dislikes, or about which he is indifferent have no function according to Kindaichi—only children speak in this way. However, he also claims that this work is a model example of shishōsetsu.
55. Hiraoka Tokuyoshi, "Shishōsetsu no suitai to tensei," p. 154.
56. Cf. Ōmori, pp. 110f.
57. Yamamoto, *Watakushishōsetsu sakkaron*, p. 20.
58. Cf. Hirano, *Geijutsu to jisseikatsu*, pp. 25ff., 43.
59. Cf., e.g., Nakamura Yū, p. 165.
60. Cf. *NBS*, p. 1244.
61. E.g. the name Junkichi in "Wakai" and "Ōtsu Junkichi" (1912).

62. "Sōseki" is, however, written differently, cf. "Tomo to tomo to no aida," text in *Kikuchi Kan zenshū*, III, 117–145, here p. 117. Further page references within the text.
63. "Ano koro no jibun no koto," text in *Akutagawa Ryūnosuke zenshū*, VI, 309–313, here p. 313.
64. Cf. the table of dates (*nenpu*) and the bibliography in *GNBT*, vol. XXXXV: *Minakami Takutarō, Toyoshima Yoshio, Kume Masao, Kojima Masajirō, Sasaki Mosaku shū*, pp. 441ff.
65. "Ryōyū akuyū," text ibid., pp. 213–220, here p. 214.
66. Cf. the quotation in "The Origins of the Term *Watakushishōsetsu*" (Chapter 10) for details.
67. Cf. Yasuoka, *Shiga Naoya shiron*, pp. 56ff., 292f., Furuki Akira, "Kaisetsu," p. 303, and Kōno Toshirō, "Satomi Ton 'Kimi to watakushi to,'" on this.
68. If one really wants to, it is possible to see a parallel to André Gide here who wrote his voluminous diary (*Journal*, published 1939–1950, in 3 parts covering the years 1889–1949) from an early stage with the intention of publishing it as a work of art, and who also, while writing, enjoys his set-backs with a similar need to confess.
69. Terada, p. 135.
70. "Gakikutsu nichiroku" (Daily Sketches from the Cave of the Hunger Devil, 1919), Gaki (from Sanskrit *preta*) is a pseudonym of the author. Text in *Akutagawa Ryūnosuke zenshū*, VI, 132–146, here p. 132.
71. Cf. "Gakikutsu nichiroku (bekkō)," ibid. pp. 138–146, here p. 138.
72. "Tanizaki Jun'ichirō shi," ibid., p. 177.
73. Shiga lived in Abiko in Chiba prefecture from 1915 to 1923.
74. "Sōsaku yodan" (Conversations about My Literary Work), *Shiga Naoya zenshū*, X, 170–180, here p. 179.
75. Cf. Hayashi Fumiko: "Chosha no kotoba" ([After]word by the Author), in *Hayashi Fumiko zenshū*, II, 289–293, here p. 291.
76. Cited in Nakamura Yū, p. 171.
77. Cited in Ogasawara, "Taishō-ki," p. 64.
78. Hayashi Fumiko, "Chosha no kotoba," *Hayashi Fumiko zenshū*, II, 292.
79. Ibid., p. 291. The reference works *NBS* and *GNBD* both agree on 1930 as the year of publication.
80. Cf., e.g., the reference to the diary in *Hōrōki*, *Hayashi Fumiko zenshū*, II, 91. Further page references in the text.
81. This is true for my edition from 1977. By now further impressions must have been published.
82. The third part also differs from the first two in this respect, since at least here she repeatedly expresses her desire to write a novel.
83. Cf. "Chosha no kotoba," *Hayashi Fumiko zenshū*, II, 292.
84. It is unclear who is meant. He is probably one of her earlier male friends.
85. Nakamura Mitsuo, *Nihon no gendai shōsetsu*, p. 172.
86. Cf. *GNBD*, heading "Hayashi Fumiko," here p. 918.
87. Itagaki Naoko, "Kaisetsu," p. 320.
88. Ibid.
89. "Chosha no kotoba," *Hayashi Fumiko zenshū*, II, 291.
90. Ibid.
91. Cf. *GNBD*, heading "Ningen shikkaku," p. 679.
92. Thus, for example, on the cover of the paperback edition (71st edition, 1977) or Usui Yoshimi in *NBS*, heading "Ningen shikkaku," p. 737.
93. It is no coincidence that the belief in the double suicide legend is maintained, even though Saegusa Yasutaka revealed as early as 1958 that Dazai was murdered by his mis-

tress. Wagatsuma Hiroshi and George A. De Vos, "Alienation and the Author," p. 547, give an interpretation of the death.
94. Okuno Takeo, "Kaisetsu," in *Ningen shikkaku*, by Dazai Osamu, p. 146.
95. Cf. ibid., p. 141.
96. Thus Sugimori Hisahide, cf. James O'Brien, *Dazai Osamu*, p. 154.
97. Cf. Takahashi, pp. 179ff.
98. O'Brien, p. 152.
99. Okuno, "Kaisetsu," in *Ningen shikkaku*, by Dazai Osamu, p. 138.
100. Cf. ibid.
101. Ibid., p. 139.
102. Cf. ibid., p. 143 and *GNBD*, heading "Ningen shikkaku," p. 679.
103. Cf. Okuno, "Kaisetsu," in *Ningen shikkaku*, by Dazai Osamu, p. 142.
104. Ibid., p. 143.
105. Cf. ibid., p. 140.
106. See "Inter- and Extratextual References to Heighten the *Riariti*" in this chapter on intertextuality.
107. Cf. Okuno, "Kaisetsu," in *Ningen shikkaku*, by Dazai Osamu, p. 144.
108. Wagatsuma Hiroshi and George A. De Vos, "Alienation and the Author," p. 524.
109. Cf. ibid., pp. 542ff. and Okuno Takeo, *Dazai Osamu ron*, pp. 47ff.
110. Kazuko Tsurumi, *Social Change and the Individual*, pp. 52ff.
111. Cf. ibid., p. 58.
112. "Omoide," *Dazai Osamu zenshū*, I, 22–60, here p. 45. Cf. also the translations by Wagatsuma Hiroshi/George A. De Vos, p. 527, and O'Brien, p. 45.
113. Cited in Okuno Takeo, *Dazai Osamu ron*, p. 53.
114. Cf. Kakeda Katsumi, "Hametsugata sakka no seishin byōri," Kawai Hiroshi, "Dazai Osamu no byōshi," and Shimazaki Toshiki and Fukumizu Yasuo, "Seishin igaku kara mita Dazai Osamu," on this.
115. Cf. O'Brien, p. 152.
116. *Ningen Shikkaku, Dazai Osamu zenshū*, IX, 364–470, here p. 364. Quoted from Donald Keene's translation (*No Longer Human*), p. 13. In the page references in the text below the first number refers to the Japanese edition, the second to Keene's English version.
117. Parentheses here and in the next quotation in the original.
118. Cf. Tanizawa Eiichi, "Dazai Osamu," p. 187.
119. On the identification of the father with the "authority structure" of society cf. Wagatsuma Hiroshi and George A. De Vos, p. 527.
120. O'Brien, p. 145.
121. Cf. ibid., p. 154.
122. Cf. Alyce Morishige, "The Theme of the Self in Modern Japanese Fiction," pp. 50ff.
123. Cf. Kazamaki Keijirō, *Sakuhin o chūshin to shita Nihon bungakushi*, p. 295.
124. Cf. Ōkubo Tadatoshi, "Dazai Osamu," p. 212, and Tachibana Yutaka, "Dazai Osamu," p. 155.
125. *NBS*, heading "Dazai Osamu," pp. 734–736, here p. 736.
126. See below on the reservations made subsequently.
127. Cited in Akatsuka Yukio, "Senpyō to jushō sakka no unmei," p. 128.
128. Cited in ibid.
129. Cited in ibid.
130. Cited in ibid.
131. Kawauchi Mitsuharu, "Akutagawa shō sakuhin jiten," p. 231.
132. Akatsuka Yukio, "Senpyō to jushō sakka no unmei," p. 128. E.g. Nakamura Shin'ichirō, "Shishōsetsu to jikken shōsetsu," p. 6, also speaks of a "lyrical work."

133. Cf. Miura Tetsuo, *Shinobugawa*; the paperback edition I used contains 6 further works by the author in addition to "Shinobugawa." The page references in the following text refer to this edition.
134. The fact that this really is an established combination is confirmed by a comparison with works of prose characterized as lyrical which are also regularly said to be "pure," e.g. "Izu no odoriko" by Kawabata Yasunari, cf., e.g., *NBS*, heading "Izu no odoriko," p. 284.
135. The information is deliberately not made any more specific, since various ways of counting are possible.
136. Okuno Takeo, "Kaisetsu," in *Shinobugawa*, by Miura Tetsuo, p. 323.
137. Cited in Akatsuka, p. 128.
138. *Fikushon* and *riarizumu* in the original.
139. Okuno Takeo, "Kaisetsu," in *Shinobugawa*, by Miura Tetsuo, p. 323.
140. Ibid., pp. 323f.
141. Omission dots in the original.
142. Nakamura Shin'ichirō, p. 6.
143. Cf. "Life Is Suffering" in this chapter.
144. Cf. "The Will to Live and the Wish to Die" in this chapter.
145. Cf., e.g., Nakamura Shin'ichirō, p. 6.
146. Cf. "Shoya," in Miura, *Shinobugawa*, pp. 54–78, here p. 72.
147. Cf. ibid., p. 69.
148. "Zoku sōsaku yodan," *Shiga Naoya zenshū*, X, 185.
149. Cf. ibid. Other authors such as, e.g., Kawabata Yasunari also made use of this method.
150. Cf. Miura, *Shinobugawa*, pp. 54–78.
151. Cf. ibid., pp. 79–121.
152. Cf. ibid., pp. 177–204.
153. Cf. ibid., pp. 205–236.
154. Cf. ibid., pp. 96f.; see also "Woman as a Burden" in this chapter.
155. Okuno Takeo, "Kaisetsu," in *Shinobugawa*, by Miura Tetsuo, p. 324.
156. Cf. ibid.
157. Cf. Morikawa Tatsuya, "Shishōsetsu hōhōka no mondai," pp. 1ff.
158. Cf. ibid., pp. 3ff.
159. Cf. Miyoshi Yukio, *Nihon bungaku no kindai to hankindai*, p. 263.

Part Five
*Shishōsetsu Within
the System of
Literary Communication*

17 · Introductory Remarks

The preceding section of this book was concerned with analyzing individual works and using them to point out various features typical of the genre. There, and in the discussion of the relevant research, it was possible to demonstrate the usefulness of the structural model of shishōsetsu set up in Part Three. This section will now concentrate on underlining the exemplary character of the results produced up till now and on showing the way they are linked to the observations made in Part One through Part Three. Our inquiry will thereby turn to the function of shishōsetsu in the literary communication system, an aspect that has until now received only marginal attention. However, a presentation based on literary history, theoretical, or metacritical considerations cannot adequately grasp the phenomenon of shishōsetsu if these are not complemented by at least some information on the various communicative functions of the genre. In view of the foregoing discussion, it would be all too easy to give the impression that shishōsetsu can be adequately "explained" if it is considered in its relation to the immediate literary tradition and theoretical postulates. Therefore, it must be made doubly clear that one cannot neglect the diverse non-literary contexts, since a genre is also an "answer . . . to the concrete cultural and social demands of [its] time,"[1] and, strictly speaking, judgments as to the "meaning," the "sense," or the aesthetic value of a genre can only be made when all elements in the literary communication have been included.[2]

The extratextual references in shishōsetsu provide researchers with a wide field of interest not only because of the structural element of factuality, but also in view of the genre's specific function as a "life support" of which both writer and reader are consciously aware and which we have already identified in an example. However, until now research has tended to concentrate on the author-work relationship which corresponds to the tendency we have repeatedly pointed out to concentrate on an obsessively biographical approach. Important questions that have been excluded from Japanese philology (and from Western studies of Japanese literature) include those on the relationship between literary and empirical reality, that is, the model of reality presented in the literary text, and also the possible and the actual response of the reader to literary reality. There has also been no consideration of the elements of the cultural code, that is, specific value judgments, and patterns of thought and behavior that influence the texts. In the case of shishōsetsu, the patterns concerned all have a long tradition. If these references are overlooked, there is a danger that the phenomena will be interpreted as unrelated individual cases, which would not do them justice. A glance at the contents of Chapter 20 makes it clear which types of theme are meant here. The list is by no means complete. Thus, we could include the concepts of *mujōkan* and *mono no aware* as well, but refrain from doing so, particularly since they have been discussed briefly in the context of the theoretical discussion of the genre and their role will be repeatedly implied in connection with "Aspects of Traditionalism" (Chapter 19).

It is not a matter of chance that some of these sections overlap. The *makoto* principle, empiricism, and the myth of immediacy are connected in the same way that nature mysticism, the diary, and lyricism are, and both groups refer directly to each other, as is proved by the relatedness of the concepts and, as it were, the homogeneous conceptual framework of the genre structured by these diverse elements. We are dealing with a thematic continuum in which it would be justifiable to select any of several key concepts, that is, to consider the same phenomena under key concepts that occupy a different place on the continuum, for example under the headings *sentimentalism, amae, mujōkan, mono no aware,* and others.

It is necessary to examine the references to literary tradition in more detail in view of the large amount and great variety of information in the secondary literature, which generally restricts itself to a process of free association or attempts to uncover "parallels" in a questionable and unsatisfactory way. Although the short sections on the diary, miscellany, lyric tradition and nature mysticism in Japanese literature cannot provide a well-defined analysis, they nevertheless suggest possible starting points for future studies.

What is true for the chapters "Aspects of Traditionalism" and "The Cultural Code" is also valid for the chapter called "Shishōsetsu's Communicative Function." It has been my main intention here "to discover homologous structures between author, text, and recipient,"[3] for example, identical interests, intentions, and expectations which we hope to correlate to one another at various levels of communication. More preliminary study is required before a model of literary communication on several levels such as that introduced by Günter Waldmann can be of use in shishōsetsu research. Waldmann assumes two levels of communication external to the text, the "pragmatic level of social relationships" and a level of "specific literary relationships" as well as a textually internal and a fictional level of communication, which would be identical in the case of shishōsetsu.[4]

In view of the present state of shishōsetsu research, where such an approach is completely neglected, a detailed analysis of the subject is yet impossible at present and in the foreseeable future. It is the intention of my comments on the author, hero, and reader to emphasize the relevance of this approach and to gather observations and results from Japanese shishōsetsu literature and secondary literature and from my own work in order to establish the basis for a solidly founded classification of the genre within the literary communication system. The individual points are attributed to any one of the three nodes of the triadic structure author, hero, and reader somewhat arbitrarily, since the particularly strong author-reader homology in shishōsetsu produces innumerable cross references—according to my theory—which cannot possibly be all mentioned. For example, if the subject is the "writing disease," the excessive need on the part of the author to confess, it then corresponds to the public's interest in the writer's character. However, the latter could just as well have been considered as a "model" character trait in the section on the heroes of shishōsetsu. The fact that shishōsetsu's psychological function affects the writer and reader analogously is easily understood, as are other cross references within Chapter 18.

These observations also serve to disclose elements and mechanisms of the rituals of self-revelation performed in shishōsetsu. We gain insight into the rules of confession and recognize the way in which both reader and author contribute to the process, something which is equally discernible in the patterns of expression and behavior in the work itself. The concept of the ritual of self-revelation thus refers to the specific nature of this genre within the literary communication system.

The following chapters each serve several purposes. In addition to the thematic summary and further development of the arguments in Parts One to Four, this time considered from the point of view of the communications aesthetic, we sketch possibilities and directions for future shishōsetsu research. Therefore, the following section is more evaluative and interpretive, but, since the observations and hypotheses expressed here are based on what has gone before, they will, I hope, be conclusive. Although somewhat fragmentary, they may be of value in view of the lack of a general survey of the phenomena. One reason for the incompleteness of our inquiry is limited space, a continual problem considering the wide-ranging subject of this book. The following part—and each of the other four—could easily have taken up the entire book. This would have done more justice to the subject, but not to my aim of providing a clear picture of the complex and intertwined themes. Let us now mention some of the themes and questions that we had to leave aside.

An important topic in Chapter 18 would have been to distinguish between the real author and the role of the author and between the actual reader and the role of the reader or also between the "implicit" and the real reader, as suggested by Iser.[5]

The repercussions of shishōsetsu literature on the private life of the author is a subject I should like to consider at another time.

One extremely broad area of study is indicated by the term *kindai jiga* (modern ego), which plays an important role in the secondary literature on shishōsetsu but is defined only vaguely.[6] I am not at all certain that this subject is really as important for the genre as it is generally held to be, since the majority of shishōsetsu authors certainly do not consider their literary activity to be a search for the "modern ego." The problems of modernization and individualism are at most subjects only for *shizenshugi* and the very first examples of the genre and are of no real consequence for its subsequent development, since its anti-intellectual, intuitive, and "lyric" character prevents the conscious discussion of such a subject. The question of *kindai jiga* is therefore neither more nor less relevant to shishōsetsu than it is in the case of other cultural products of the twentieth century which also do not explicitly thematize the subject.[7]

It seems to me that Kenneth Strong manages to avoid most adeptly the inherent difficulty in defining the problem of "modern ego," which results from a complicated mixture in the relationship of European and Japanese concepts of personality and modernity. This relationship varies in turn according to the situation, the individual, and whether the term is used consciously or unconsciously. Strong considers that a work as early as Tōson's *Hakai* can be said to be "prophetic of the *non*-expression of the *kindai jiga* in most of modern fiction."[8] We agree insofar as shishōsetsu is concerned.

As in other parts of our inquiry, the numerous source quotations fulfill two functions. They not only provide information about a particular subject but also about the way in which it is seen and understood. One desirable side-effect of this book would be if the quotations and their interpretation could stimulate non-Japanese literary studies to form closer contacts with its Japanese counterpart, since I am also interested in showing how valuable the study of Japanese texts can be to the field of literary studies in general. My ideal view of "Japanology" is—at the risk of sounding pompous, naive, or even too obvious—of mutual give and take and not of two parallel sets of research, one Japanese and one foreign, which have no points of contact. The subjects in this part of the book concerning the interdependence of communicative elements, the much-discussed traditionalism and the cultural subsystem that highlights the general sociological character of certain values and expectations, all underscore the necessity for international and interdisciplinary cooperation.

---

1. Eberhard Lämmert in Walter Hinck, ed., *Textsortenlehre—Gattungsgeschichte,* p.v.
2. On Frege's terms "meaning" (*Bedeutung*) and "sense" (*Sinn*) cf., e.g., Wolfgang Iser, *Der Akt des Lesens,* pp. 244f.
3. Günter Waldmann, *Kommunikationsästhetik 1: Die Ideologie der Erzählform,* p. 50.
4. Cf. ibid., pp. 50ff., 70; emphasis by Waldmann.
5. Cf., e.g., Iser, pp. 50ff.
6. Cf., e.g., Yazaki Dan, "Kindai jiga no Nihonteki keisei (jō)," or Saegusa Hiroto, "Shishōsetsu no 'watakushi' no minamoto."
7. In the most recent contributions that have appeared since I finished this book, the term at times again plays a more important role, cf., e.g., Saeki Shōichi et al., "Shishōsetsu," p. 167, Morikawa, "Bungaku wa hirakareru," p. 194 and, in particular, Aeba, *Hihyō to hyōgen.* There is general agreement that the Western model of a "modern ego" could not be put into practice, but the argumentation differs from mine.
8. Kenneth Strong, "Downgrading the 'Kindai Jiga,'" p. 407; emphasis in Strong.

18 · Shishōsetsu's Communicative Function

THE AUTHOR OF SHISHŌSETSU

KAKITAGARU BYŌ—THE "WRITING DISEASE"

What motivates a shishōsetsu author to write? Many writers have themselves responded to the question and Miura Tetsuo's answer is representative among these: "When I was preparing to write my first *shōsetsu*, the first subject I thought of was what had secretly plagued me for years and what I had always carried with me, and I was impatient to get it done as quickly as possible. I wrote it all down without hesitating."[1] Later Miura expanded on what he had written about himself to make a general statement on literary creativity: "Everyone who starts writing a *shōsetsu* must be full of things he wants to write down. Listen to my story!—this feeling is strong. And then you write as if you were gradually vomiting everything up; the most accessible style for what one wants to express is, after all, the letter or the diary style . . . I started by writing a *shōsetsu* in letter style. And only when I heard from a critic that that was a *shōsetsu*, I thought, aha, so it is."[2] According to Miura, writing is based on an overwhelming need to communicate, the need "to spew everything out." Significantly, private "functional texts," such as diaries and letters, seem to him to be the most suitable form both for the writer and the reader of such literature. The aesthetic function is of secondary importance when compared with the need to make a personal statement.

Akutagawa Ryūnosuke spoke even more openly about the need to speak out which was obviously the basis for his writing. He stated that he was overcome by an incurable compulsion to write, which he identified using the Latin name *cacaothes scribendi*, translating this into Japanese as *kakitagaru byō* (the disease of wanting to write).[3] Here he answers critics who accused him of a lack of literary quality, saying that he was interested only in the writing itself. The question as to whether the writing was successful or not would thus be of only secondary importance.[4] His exaggeration suggests an element of ironic detachment for which there could be several reasons. Even if Akutagawa did not ultimately mean the statement to refer to himself, it points to the crux of what the genre meant for the authors as individuals.

The importance of shishōsetsu's function as an outlet can be illustrated by an observation from Yagi Yoshinori (b. 1911): "Not only young literary enthusiasts but also old men and women who lead ordinary lives proclaim: Listen to my life [story], it is a novel! That is what nearly everyone says."[5] On the basis of this need to communicate through literature, which is apparently so extreme in Japanese society, Yagi assumes that shishōsetsu will always continue to exist, an opinion numerous critics and writers share.[6]

"REFUGE FOR THE HEART" AND "RESCUE"

What effect do the personal statements made in shishōsetsu have on the character of the author? There have been numerous responses to this question. For example, in the epilogue to *Hōrōki*, Hayashi Fumiko writes: "I started writing the *Vagabond's Diary* with the feeling that writing was a kind of refuge for the heart and I was comforted by writing."[7]

Writing helps the author maintain psychological balance. It is an extremely successful means of coming to terms with life, as we can see from the following episode from Ozaki Kazuo's (b. 1899) shishōsetsu *Atami yuki*, the report of a visit to Shiga Naoya. Ozaki, who has only just recovered from an illness, learns from the great master, Shiga, that a writer's strength lies in his ability to translate his problems into literature. "One can also say that this rescues us from our sufferings or that we thereby overcome them."[8]

Any kind of written personal statement is felt to have this comforting and healing effect in Japan. The fact that every Japanese schoolchild must keep a diary over a long period of time indicates the importance attributed to it. It is also no coincidence that diaries are used in Japanese psychotherapy.[9] The social anthropologist W. Caudill and the psychologist Doi Takeo have, in addition, noted that the Japanese find it difficult to express themselves orally and are much more capable of frankness in writing.[10] Should this observation be used in conjunction with shishōsetsu? In view of the therapeutic effect openly admitted by the writers and sanctioned by literary communication it seems quite possible to me, and Caudill and Doi do in fact draw parallels: "Adult Japanese find it easier to communicate in writing, and the use of diaries in Japanese psychiatry is not unrelated to the exuberant development in Japan of the *shishōsetsu,* or 'I' novel."[11] The existence of this genre thus points to specific psychological problems both of the individual and of society in Japan.

SHISHŌSETSU AS AN "AUTOMATIC TEXT"

It is part of the Japanese understanding of shishōsetsu that it is a spontaneous expression of life which precludes not only everything "invented" but also any kind of planning or construction. It is not the author who decides that shishōsetsu is the right style of writing for him, but rather the genre that reduces the writer to being merely its instrument. One interpretation that constantly reappears in statements made by the writers of shishōsetsu is that they did not intend to write a shishōsetsu but that it was the result of a "natural" and spontaneous creative process. For example, Ozaki Kazuo,[12] Takami Jun,[13] and Miura Tetsuo[14] all make statements to this effect. According to Kanbayashi Akatsuki, the shishōsetsu form takes hold of the writer "like a magician." It would be impossible to free oneself.[15]

Takami traces this back to a kind of "calling of the blood," a Japanese tradition that flows in the veins of all generations (*nagai chi no nagare*),[16] and no doubt the same idea is behind Inagaki Tatsurō's pronouncement that shishōsetsu is "Japanese reality" and "Japanese destiny."[17]

These explanations, which form their own literary critical topos in Japan, are illuminated somewhat by Kanbayashi in the following statement: "Shishōsetsu is not a form of literature which is based on theories or ideas (*shisō*) but on the person and life of the author."[18]

This brings us back to the question of shishōsetsu as an "automatic text" by means of a dichotomy, typical in my opinion for Japanese thought of this century, between intellect (including *shisō*) and feeling, whereby cognitive thought is in its widest sense considered "nonessential" while feeling constitutes our actual existence. According to the Japanese view, authenticity as an evaluative criterion for shishōsetsu demands a quasi-unconscious creative process uninfluenced by any kind of intellectual interference in order to register the "facts as they are" (*jijitsu o ari no mama*). Thus, the writers' protestation that they did not intend to produce shishōsetsu as such is the best proof of the "genuineness" of their literature.

In this way, the artist is merely a seismograph who registers fluctuations without being able to exert the slightest influence on the development of the product. Shiga Naoya repeatedly made statements to this effect.[19] Here is another quotation from Kanbayashi Akatsuki: "It is my opinion that one cannot plan to write a shishōsetsu, and any shishōsetsu written with this intention is not a genuine shishōsetsu. I believe that a genuine shishōsetsu is created when one has written what could no longer be held back, when it is impossible to do anything but write it down."[20] Hayashi Fumiko supports the idea of the "automatic text" which "grows" organically and, as it were, without any effort on the part of the author: "I have never planned out the plot of a novel before I started writing it. Even if I were to plan to write something in particular, my pen often skims off unexpectedly in another direction. I usually write by giving myself up to the natural flow just as one never knows where ice will float."[21] If authors themselves have so little influence on their "creation," then it is obvious that the circumstances that produced this literature are worthy of just as much attention, if not more, than the author's conscious effort, since he is, to put it rather strongly, nothing more than a vessel life itself uses in giving birth to a shishōsetsu. Okuno Takeo shares this belief when he praises Miura Tetsuo for making use of the rare opportunity of writing a work such as "Shinobugawa": "It is very rare for such a work to be produced. If one were to imitate it, it would inevitably turn into a horribly sentimental piece of light entertainment. When an author believes he can write such a work, then he must spontaneously give way, without hesitating, to the outflowing of his inner being (*tamashii*). The writer Miura Tetsuo seized a rare opportunity which will be presented to him only once or twice in his lifetime, and invested everything in it."[22]

SHISHŌSETSU AS A PSYCHOGRAPH

Shishōsetsu's "outlet function," its recognized therapeutic effects, and the opinion shared by both writers and readers that they are dealing with a kind of *écriture automatique* all suggest that shishōsetsu should also be considered as a kind of psychograph. However, since the psychoanalytic approach takes up a significant part of the broad range of biographical studies in Japan, there is no need to go into this question in detail here. There are large numbers of individual psychological studies available on all important authors.[23]

In his informative article on the "Psychology of Shishōsetsu" (1953), Miyagi Otoya is interested, on the other hand, in discovering homologous structures in the psyche of shishōsetsu writers as a whole. He uses the case of Kasai Zenzō to develop his theories. According to his article, Japanese artists, shishōsetsu writers in particular, have a tendency towards schizophrenia, expressed in an "incoherence of thought, action and emotion . . . a detachment from reality and withdrawal into oneself and the predominance of an inner life which has been abandoned to the products of the imagination (autism)" and in "a more or less intensive, always badly systematized manic activity."[24] This is exemplified not only by Kasai's "Ko o tsurete," as suggested in Part Four,[25] but also equally well by most of the other representatives of the genre.

We should emphasize in particular Miyagi's observation that the homologous structures on the author's side correspond to similar structures on the side of the public,[26] which he explains are the result of the effect of feudal elements in society. Rather than developing these thoughts we shall point to some psychopathic traits of personality that are obvious to the general reader when reading shishōsetsu. There is, for example, the exaggerated narcissism both of the heroes and the writers themselves. The shamelessness and exhibitionist ambition, the masochistic delight in relating private disasters that confront the reader would all be unthinkable without the high degree of eccentricity that is a result of the isolation of the subject. To become aware of this narcissism one need merely open any shishōsetsu; the structural element focus figure is in itself sufficient evidence of the egocentricity of the genre itself. It is typical of the narcissist to be incapable of relating to any other object and to be proud of his behavior. I believe that both these characteristics are embodied most purely in Shiga Naoya, the "god of fiction."

We can infer that shishōsetsu writers evinced psychopathic behavior solely from the evidence of their books, but, as expected, innumerable anecdotes have also circulated. For example, Oketani Hideaki reports that when Kamura Isota learned that his work was to be published in the respected magazine *Chūō kōron* for the first time, he shouted, "I am number one in Japan!" (*Nihon ichi ni natta!*) and fainted. (Interestingly enough, Kamura also used this episode in his literature!)[27]

It would no doubt be entertaining to continue with a series of strange and amusing stories, but in context it is more important to formulate a hypothesis about the origins of such narcissism. In my opinion, it can be traced to the *amae* structure characteristic of Japanese socio-culture, to which Doi Takeo has drawn particular attention.[28]

Amae corresponds roughly to "passive object love" as described by Balint in the oral phase of development of small children.[29] As opposed to the Western pattern, where the phase is succeeded by a "normal" development of personality, the need for *amae* does not weaken in the development of the Japanese individual but retains its extreme importance. The powerful narcissistic component is directly related to the *amae* structure. We can therefore assume that shishōsetsu writers merely possess an exaggerated form of this characteristic. Thus, they exhibit characteristic cultural traits that could lead to valuable insights into socio-cultural interrelations were they to be systematically researched.[30]

SELF-REVELATION AS A MORAL ACT

The need to confess brings the shishōsetsu writer more than merely "personal" catharsis. Confession in literary form is admired by the public. Complete frankness is awarded a high ethical-moral status. To place the knife in one's own wound and cry out with pain because of a passionate love of truth—according to Yamamoto Kenkichi it is this attitude which characterizes a genuine shishōsetsu.[31] Hirano Ken writes: "Literary genuineness (*riariti*) is guaranteed by revealing unhesitatingly the most painful part of one's own body, the most private part which one does not want to show anybody."[32] The moral value lies in the act of confession, not in the way the author-hero behaves towards his fellow humans. Reactions to Shiga Naoya's works make this particularly clear. For example, approximately one year after the publication of "Wakai" he was admired for his "inborn honesty (*makoto*) of the heart" and his "deep sincerity" (*fukai shinseriti*).[33] The immature, anti-social acts of Shiga's hero are left out of consideration for they are not to be judged. Although Shiga is "a kind of ultra-egoist" according to Kobayashi Hideo,[34] this does not imply criticism as one would usually assume in view of the Japanese ideals of community and harmony, since it is the "precise combination of reason (*richi*) and sensual desire (*yokujō*)"[35] which is of prime importance for Kobayashi, or again, ". . . for him thought is action and action is thought."[36] The "content" of the deeds and ideas are insignificant, whereas their unity is of decisive importance. It is only from this point of view that we can understand Akutagawa's admiration for Shiga, since he called him, amongst other things, the "purest writer" (*mottomo junsuina sakka*).[37]

The first (and probably most important) reason Akutagawa gives for his respect is that Shiga led an admirable life (*rippa ni ikiteiru*), that is, a "morally pure" one (*dōtokuteki ni seiketsu ni*).[38] Akutagawa does not mean by this any particularly ascetic or altruistic behavior but directs his admiration towards Shiga's posture in life, the attitude of serious sincerity towards himself, which he maintained throughout his life. This last statement indicates something that the Japanese critical tradition cannot and will not accept: Personal revelation can degenerate very easily into a mere formality. Admitting weakness thus becomes nothing more than an alibi. The act of confession removes all responsibility for personal actions. This is proved by a quotation from Shiga's novel *An'ya kōro*, a short section from the answer of the hero Tokitō Kensaku to his wife's (justified) reproaches: "As you say, if my tolerant thoughts could become one with my intolerant feelings, then there would be no problems. It is an egoistic way of thinking and at the same time maybe a utilitarian one. That's just the way I am, there's nothing we can do. I do not acknowledge you, but, regardless of this, I can do nothing but sort it out in my own way. I have always been like that . . . "[39] To praise the honesty of this attitude, as William Sibley does along with Japanese scholars of literature,[40] corresponds with the customary Japanese respect for such confessions and is certainly an elegant solution for all involved. The problem that remains with such confessions is that they become ends in themselves and not the means of personal development; public posturing as one's own prosecutor guarantees pardon. Changes of behavior, on the other hand, would not only be superfluous but would also possibly deprive the author of his confessional "material."

THE INSTITUTIONALIZED OUTSIDER

However impossible it is within the context of shishōsetsu communication to admit that much of what the reader admires in the hero is based on the author's self-stylization and conscious staging—which would inevitably destroy the core, the principle of "genuineness"—it would be equally sacrilegious or, in more scholarly terms, inadequate for shishōsetsu criticism if we were to question the topos of the artist's self-sacrifice for his art. Authors and readers—including the critics—imagine the writer of a shishōsetsu to be one of the "chosen" (*erabareta*)[41] who has dedicated his life to art and sacrificed himself to it. This idea also lies behind the commonly recognized term of *decline literature*.[42] For example, Ara Masahito writes, "There is certainly a general principle according to which the artist expresses the pain he has experienced in real life in the form of a book and so sublimates or spews out[43] his pain. But there is also a so-called opposite principle, since there are writers who are destroyed by writing. To name some obvious examples, Hara Tamiki,

Tanaka Hidemitsu and Dazai Osamu are all writers who perished through writing."[44] It is, however, certainly not the case that those named here committed suicide for primarily literary or artistic reasons. Dazai Osamu's death had more to do with his masochistic tendencies, depression, and narcissism than with artistic endeavor. In the case of Hara Tamiki (1905–1951), it would certainly not be wrong to assume that the traumatic experience of the dropping of the atomic bomb on his hometown, Hiroshima, drove such a depressive person to his death. It is just as unlikely that Tanaka Hidemitsu's (1913–1949) suicide at the grave of his friend Dazai had "literary" causes.

One might object that my interpretation is much too superficial. We therefore cite the next sentence from Ara's essay which opens up new interpretive possibilities: "In their writing they looked for difficult circumstances [in life]."[45] Assuming that Ara was not merely adding to the artistic myth with this statement, we must reformulate it in order to make quite clear what is meant: not "*in their writing* they looked for" (*kaku koto ni yotte*) but "*for the sake of their writing* they needed difficult circumstances [in life]" (*kaku tame ni*). It is not unreasonable to assume that Ara Masahito (perhaps unconsciously) shrank from making such a clear statement and therefore chose to remain somewhat vague, since it would otherwise have meant admitting that shishōsetsu could not exist without a certain contrivance. This would have rocked the very foundations of all assumptions concerning the genre.

The logical dilemma behind Ara Masahito's cautious and abstruse statement is inherent in the many critical discourses which maintain the "life for art" myth on the one hand but which also persist in upholding the principle of "genuineness." At one point there does seem to be an awareness of this paradox, although the subject—the generally held opinion that shishōsetsu can only arise out of crisis situations—was not pursued to its logical conclusion. Referring to Ozaki Kazuo, Yagi Yoshinori names four possible crises: "Whoever cannot present one of the four following crises—the health crisis, the financial crisis, the family crisis, or the crisis of ideas (*shisō*)—is not qualified to write a shishōsetsu."[46] The report written by Kanbayashi Akatsuki thirty years earlier on how he began writing reads like a parallel commentary: "About ten years ago, when I was completely down spiritually, physically, financially (*seikatsuteki*), and in my literature, I wrote about myself thinking it could be my will."[47] However, Yagi is forced to admit that some writers have to create crises artificially, otherwise they would not be able to write. He includes Dazai among the "non-genuine" artists, but concedes in his case that suicide added the otherwise lacking authenticity to his life.[48]

In answer to the question as to why crises are necessary in order to write, the following proposal may sound banal, but careful observation proves that it holds true for the majority of writers: Without a "crisis"—and even incurring debts counts as such—there would be no material to write about and the subject matter would be restricted entirely to daily monotony. Kanbayashi sensed a fear that the material would prove inadequate both in himself and in all his colleagues.[49] The obvious solution would then be to create crises in order to ensure a ready supply of new material.

The categorization of crisis situations makes clear that the typical shishōsetsu writer never leaves the realms of his own private life in his literature.[50] Questions of general social relevance have no part to play in shishōsetsu, since the author conceives of himself as an apolitical being who stands outside society. However, one topos in shishōsetsu interpretation, in spite of this, is the conviction that the writer is engaged in a battle with society, a view that is, of course, widely held by the writers themselves. Ishikawa Tatsuzō (b. 1905), for example, describes his role thus: "Writing is the fight of a lonely spirit (*tamashii*). All writers envision themselves alone in their studies, search gropingly for their spirit, and love this loneliness. It is such loneliness that fulfills us most richly. While we are sitting at our desks the battle takes place. There are no allies in this fight; one is completely alone. And the enemy is the endlessly expanding society."[51] However, it is more correct to refer to the social position of the shishōsetsu writer as that of an institutionalized outsider who is mistakenly identified with a "battle *against* society." To a certain degree the artist enjoys the privilege of a fool, and he is fully aware of the limits of his privilege. Since he behaves apolitically—and can, if necessary, be linked to an ideological cause as in the case of "conversion literature"—the freedom he is granted generates no danger to society's traditional values.

Writers had fought for their position since the beginning of the Meiji period, and it must surely have demanded considerable courage for the first shishōsetsu writer to present a "confession" to the public. The ritual of confession, however, soon developed a fixed pattern and, since their content was restricted to a few common themes such as extramarital sex, mistreatment of the family, and pecuniary problems, they were able to anticipate public reaction. Thus, the following quotation from Dōke Tadamichi is relevant only for the first shishōsetsu, since he ignores the fact that the ideal of sincerity rapidly degenerated into mere posturing, particularly under the pressure of subsequent developments in literary convention which legitimized what had begun as a crime: "To undertake a particularly 'immoral' self-revelation in view of existing, vulgar morality (*dōtoku*) was an act that demanded the writer's courage. The sincerity of total self-revelation is the highest ethos of shishōsetsu. Pleasure with geishas or prostitutes, deserting wife and children in search of free love, and stories of borrowing money and nocturnal flight [from creditors]—it becomes a matter of proof of a writer's sincerity whether he publicly confesses these things which one would normally not tell anybody."[52] Nothing could characterize the outsider element more clearly than the narrow private area of life in which, according to Dōke, it can be identified. The critical force which shishōsetsu research considers to be directed against society is revealed to be an act of defiance on the part of maladjusted egoists and lachrymose narcissists and is directed largely at themselves. The phrase coined by Matsubara terming shishōsetsu authors as "holy fools"[53] is thus useless to the extent that it allows for no distinction between genuine maladjustment and mere childish egoism and immaturity. However, such a statement is interesting as evidence of the widespread myth of the artist's "fight against society." The shishōsetsu writer would be more than content to accept the role of outsider attributed to him. He certainly never took part in a struggle against society.[54]

THE HERO IN SHISHŌSETSU

THE "OBJECTIVE" EFFECT OF SUBJECTIVITY

The structural element focus figure, the character combination of first- or third-person narrator, hero, and author, the "with" narrative perspective, the temporal "accompanying" (present time) narrative standpoint, and the concentration of the subject matter on the character of the hero who is judged by his own values all characterize the genre as "subjective" literature par excellence. The world of the individual work is identical with the narrator's world, isolated and cut off from all outside influences. "Society" does extend into the life of the shishōsetsu hero in an elementary form, since he cannot live in a complete vacuum, and even he requires contact with other people in order to satisfy his basic needs. However, it is crucial that his point of view is not influenced by any other person or any experience. Thus, even the structure of a shishōsetsu suggests autism. It is therefore hardly surprising that it proved to be particularly suitable means of expression for personalities who verge on autism.

It must now sound like a paradox to say that the Japanese public is unaware of the extent of the "subjectivity" in shishōsetsu, since how else could readers actually believe that they are faced with "facts as they are"? The Japanese reader does not perceive of the world, which is wholly instrumentalized by the first-person narrator, as a slice of life, but is convinced that he is confronting life itself, a panorama of reality where nothing is concealed. How is this effect achieved?[55]

One explanation of this phenomenon is given by Jurij Lotman, who provides an illuminating explanation of this and other aspects in comparison with techniques used in film: "Numerous experiments have proved that photographing a longer section of a film from the point of view of one of the heroes does not heighten the feeling of subjectivity but, on the contrary, leads to a reduction: The viewer begins to accept the pictures as objective. In order to present a particular film text as being the point of view of a hero, the film taken from his perspective must alternate with film that pinpoints him from outside, either from the viewer's angle ('zero' perspective) or from that of one of the other characters."[56] As we have already seen, in shishōsetsu the focus figure dominates the text in such a way that the feeling of being confronted with a subjective perspective vanishes. However, Lotman's comparison makes it clear that it is very unlikely that the subjective narrative standpoint is maintained throughout from a "with" perspective, that is, identified with the hero. Even in shishōsetsu texts, there are short sections where the perspective is changed. We can also show, however, through several examples that the change of perspective—it is of secondary importance here whether this is undertaken consciously or unconsciously—does not bring about a relativization of the subjective point of view but instead effectively emphasizes it. This can be explained by the fact that when—and it is only relatively seldom—the "with" perspective is interrupted, it is often done in order to support the point of view and the value judgments of the focus figure "objectively." Let us return to an example from Part Three: the change of perspective at the end of Shiga's novel *An'ya kōro,* from the point of view of the hero Kensaku to that of his wife. This brings about no displacement of the "system of order," since she sees him with his own eyes and judges him exclusively by his own set of values. In this way, the subjective point of view, including the "philosophy" of the focus figure, is verified "objectively" and reinforced. Thus, the "objective" effects of subjectivism can be demonstrated.

Here the reader should keep in mind the author's reaction to what Nakamura Shin'ichirō, who first noticed the change of perspective in *An'ya kōro,* pointed out. Shiga replied in an article ("Nakamura Shin'ichirō kun no gimon ni tsuite," "About the Questions from N.S.," 1948) that it was not true that he had made a mistake but that he had chosen this method consciously. (The thought that it could have been a mistake is, of course, explained by the idea of the "unconscious," automatic text.) In reference to the chapter where an authorial narrator is suddenly introduced in order to describe Naoko's extramarital escapade and what led up to it[57] Shiga wrote, "Only those people who read [the text] analytically (*kenkyūteki*) and particularly carefully may find it strange that the hero is suddenly no longer there, but such people are exceptions, and the average reader (*ippan no hito*) will hardly take any notice when he reads it through at one sitting."[58] If this statement is applicable for Japanese readers— and we have no reason to doubt that it is—then it would merely be further confirmation of what we have tried to show as the effect of shishōsetsu narrative technique: A readership only unconsciously aware of obvious changes in the narrative perspective is not likely to try to account for the subjectivity of the point of view presented.

PARADIGMATIC EXPERIENCE OF REALITY

The "objective" impression of the world of the shishōsetsu hero is also produced by the reader's familiarity with many of the details in the work. He recognizes the characters and places and the usually only slight time difference between the reader's present and that of the book ensures a feeling that he is dealing with a topical, truthful portrayal of reality. The up-to-dateness hardly diminishes with the passing of time, since the subject matter is truly timeless. Marital problems, love affairs, financial worries, and illness—the typical central shishōsetsu subjects—are largely independent of social development as a whole (which is in any case never consciously portrayed), and it does not impair the immediate effect of a book when readers of an older shishōsetsu notice that a particular cafe now has a different name.

The Japanese reader finds shishōsetsu particularly convincing when he can, to a large extent, recognize his own world in them. The first-person narrator's problems are so general that nearly everybody can find some point of comparison with his own life. Thus, shishōsetsu's thematic range is quite narrow. There are no profound reflections about the author's artistic being or his writing,[59] which might disconcert the reader and make him realize that there is a difference between the narrator's world and his own. There is a difference in degree and not kind when we consider that the hero of a shishōsetsu enjoys somewhat more freedom than the average citizen; he is however also allowed to despair more and to get himself into more hopeless situations. In addition, he is allowed to be more sensitive, more helpless, and to have a greater need of *amae* (more narcissism!). All this belongs to the image of the artist. However, the discrepancy between "normal citizen" and artist is not the basis of any fundamental difference, since the kinds of problems they share and the way in which they are experienced and overcome remain the same.

The Japanese shishōsetsu reader gains the impression of reality because the side of life described is limited to the immediate environment of the narrator, and is largely identical with that reality of which he himself is aware. Also, for both writer and reader, the primarily private, apolitical, institutional, and anti-intellectual point of view and experience of life are identical. Shishōsetsu does not, therefore, introduce the Japanese reader to a new modality within this narrow, private area—for example with self-analysis, new strategies for solving problems, different modes of perception, and so forth—but presents what is conventional in a compressed form.[60] The experience of reality portrayed in shishōsetsu acquires its paradigmatic value in that the Japanese reader recognizes in it the structure of his own experiences.

THE INTERCHANGEABILITY OF LITERATURE AND LIFE

In nearly all the works we discussed in Part Four, the heroes compared themselves with literary characters—for example, the hero of Hōmei's "Tandeki" who constantly refers to Merezhkovskiy's Da Vinci[61] or Hayashi Fumiko's first-person narrator who models herself on Hamsun's hero.[62]

It is remarkable in each case that there is no categorical distinction between literature and reality. In the case of Shiga's "Wakai" the melding transparencies of imagination and reality on the literary level were raised to a point of principle, as we have shown. The reality-fiction osmosis can also be seen in other works. Let us return to a familiar text, Chikamatsu Shūkō's "Giwaku."

The hero's wife has left him. In this situation, he suddenly identifies with Hazama Kan'ichi, the hero in *Konjiki yasha* (The Golden Demon, by Ozaki Kōyō, 1897–1902), one of the most popular novels of the Meiji period, where a wife leaves the hero for a rich man. Although he knows that it is not true, Shūkō's first-person narrator complains that his wife has also spurned him because he is poor.[63] In this case, the emphasis on the parallels to the well-known melodrama draw attention away from the fact that there is no basis for them in the story itself and prepare the reader for a similarly sentimental story.

A second example from this text is also relevant here. After the hero has satisfied himself that his wife really did spend a night with her young lover in Nikkō a year earlier, he fantasizes on his way back to the station: "I had wondered whether she had maybe married an old man around 50 in Numazu or the region of Shizuoka, and therefore I tried until recently to imagine this man's face and, with this thought in mind, examined the hotel lists. I invented a fantasy figure and was jealous of it. Fortunately, it was only a person whom I had constructed myself; nevertheless, I still have a bad conscience towards him."[64] It is astonishing that the narrator should apologize to a figment of his own imagination!

One last example from Hayashi Fumiko's *Hōrōki* will corroborate previous observations: "When we read books, they tell us everything. One never knows what to make of the words of people, but that which is written down in books seizes our hearts firmly and does not let go."[65] There is no significant difference between literary and interpersonal communication in the case of Hayashi. They seem to be interchangeable, just as in shishōsetsu the dividing line between fantasy and reality, between literature and life is blurred. From this we can assume that perhaps the shishōsetsu author experiences his life as a kind of novel, and that he is in turn convinced that his life "just as it is" can be turned into a novel. The trust of both writers and readers in a reality that can be portrayed, that is perceptible, and that can be understood, and that moreover shishōsetsu is a faithful copy of, persists in Japan.

LACK OF DEVELOPMENT

A learning process—which always demands a certain degree of consciousness—is incompatible with the intuitive and anti-intellectual nature of shishōsetsu. Shishōsetsu do not treat an individual's process of maturing, since this would require the hero to consider himself from a distance, a condition that conflicts with the principles of the genre. In addition, temporal "accompanying" narrative also suspends awareness for the difference between the narrated and narrative present. The author writes, as far as possible, by imagining himself in the situation (which he himself has experienced).

The result of this process is a chronological series of relived scenes and spiritual conditions whose meaning is self-evident or lies in the chronological order, without the necessity for the overriding perspective of an interpreting commentary. There is also no trace of a process of development in the plot. The shishōsetsu hero reacts predictably to similar situations, he seems to "learn" nothing at all from his story—how could he, since he does not have a sufficiently clear picture of himself to recognize his mistakes?

These observations are not intended to be judgments, since lack of development is in itself no more a negative concept than development is always positive. In theoretical terms, the hero's unchanging nature means, according to Lotman, that the individual moments of the hero's life that the text depicts are coextensive with the total impression on the most abstract level of representation.[66] However, it cannot be denied that speaking of development or its lack and its connotations in connection with particular epochs and cultures is nevertheless subject to definite evaluative categories, yet it would be wrong to declare that the values of our own culture or epoch are generally binding. This would be the case when shishōsetsu is criticized for its lack of development without considering that such a judgment forces it into alien categories. Again, shishōsetsu is bound to Japanese reality where there are different concepts of individuality, development, and maturity from those in the West.

In my opinion, Mishima Yukio identified the connection between text organization, lack of development of the hero, and the cultural code most precisely, and there are several extremely perceptive contributions from him on this aspect.[67] I shall quote here a section from a discussion with Itō Sei and others on "Japanese Reality and the Possibilities of a New Literature" ("Nihon no genjitsu to atarashii bungaku no kanōsei," 1956). I have emphasized Mishima's central arguments, which will also interest us in another context:

> It is difficult to paint an active picture of people using so-called Japanese realism (*riarizumu*) . . . This is because of the [Japanese] persecution complex, which I mentioned previously, which considers everything *constructed* to be *untrue* (*uso*). If a person is placed in a chronology and acts under a given particular logic, then time gradually overturns the logic. And in being overturned, another logic is built up. But again this is overturned and dissolves in the river of time. Thus, man *is the same on entering and on leaving*—the Japanese have a special attitude to such an image of man. This is made painfully clear to me when I write a novel; for I describe people who possess a particular logic. I equip them with [special] motives. But this logic envelops

the characters like plaster; they become rigid and still, unreal (*usoppachi*) and die. In order to make them into what the Japanese call a "*real*" (*hontōrashii*) *person* one has to begin to break up the logic given at the beginning, during the life, and overthrow it. When this is done then the effect is human.[68]

Mishima gives an example: "One begins to loathe the woman whom one loves. Then one likes her again, feels repelled again, likes her again— when things happen in this way it is felt to be particularly human. I call this the *realism of the transience of all that is earthly* (*shogyō mujōteki riarizumu*)."[69] It would be possible to set up a radial network of connections from this last phrase in Mishima's text to the various concepts, structural principles, and the traditional, and still valid, method of depicting reality which are of importance for shishōsetsu, and to which we have already referred. The concept of *mujōkan,* interpreted here as an affective schema and cultural pattern of action, signifies the same as the dichotomy we have continually emphasized between "genuine" and "artificial."

Mishima confirms that lack of development does not necessarily mean a rigid and inflexible hero.[70] He can be subject to violent changes in his situation in life just as to extreme variations of emotion. It is decisive that these bring about no change of attitude, that the hero remains "the same on entering and leaving."

It is understandable that development in the European, Western sense is unthinkable in shishōsetsu when one realizes that the aim of Japanese personality development is not so much freedom and a feeling of responsibility for an individual who is considered to be autonomous but rather achieving a harmonious unity between oneself and the world, by accepting the world and life as they are. Although this is a somewhat sweeping and global differentiation between the Japanese and the Western image of man, I would maintain that the tendency is correct. The objective of Japanese psychotherapy (of Morita therapy) is similar to *satori,* the inspirational experience of Zen.[71] Both aim at a condition of harmony between the self and the world named *aru ga mama,*[72] an aim that is evident in many shishōsetsu. However, the most famous example of this, Shiga's *An'ya kōro,* is at the same time proof of the fact that there is no change in attitude bound up with the inspirational experience; thus it demonstrates the hero's flexibility but also his lack of development.

One further possible analytical step would be to derive analogous elements in the author's personality from the largely unchanging attitude of the shishōsetsu hero and the corresponding Japanese view of man. We shall not pursue such a difficult question further here, but we should note that there are those who argue for this point of view. Usui Yoshimi's interpretation of Shiga Naoya's life and work is an example. In an essay published in 1955, Usui wrote that Shiga's literature was closely linked to his intuitive, instinctive view of life.[73] Therefore, the following comment on his literature can also be traced to the author's life: "It may seem surprising that for someone who is probably respected more than any other living Japanese writer, there should have been so *little* of what is normally known as *literary development*. In point of depth and width, indeed, hardly any change can be detected from Shiga's first short story, *One Morning*, until his most recent work. Such development as there has been is in the direction of increasing quietness and simplicity."[74] However, as Usui directly admits, "quietness and simplicity" are not new qualities, and former characteristics are not replaced by them. Therefore, there is yet again flexibility without evolution.

THE SHISHŌSETSU READER

SANCTIONED VOYEURISM

Shishōsetsu contain innumerable features which arouse the public's interest in the personality of the author, which obviously refer to his personality, and which, in part, can be understood only if the reader has prior biographical knowledge of the author.[75] Thus, a method of reading is required that the public gladly adopts. There can be no doubt that one important reason for the popularity of the genre is that it sanctions public voyeurism, which seems to be of particular importance in Japan. Anyone who has observed the Japanese mass media will be aware of this as a typical feature.

In order to place my own observations in this matter on a firm footing I shall draw on some principal witnesses. Dennis Keene notes, in a context that appears at first sight to have nothing to do with the genre, since he is making a comparison between the "neosensualist" Yokomitsu Riichi (1898–1947) and André Malraux: "Again the Japanese reader's concern with that personality, the *film star status* given to Akutagawa Ryūnosuke or Dazai Osamu, is not something which has a counterpart of that intensity in the West. On a more vulgar level the obsession of the weeklies with the private lives of screen and T.V. 'talent' seems to be a part of the same tendency."[76] Whether one opens a Japanese newspaper with a circulation of more than 10 million or even an intellectual monthly one is surprised at the large amount of space devoted to society news that is little more than gossip. Each piece of news is presented in such a way that the interest in the private person overshadows or blots out any other news item. Dōke Tadamichi observed something similar as early as 1953: "There is nothing which is so full of gossip (*goshippu*) as Japanese newspapers, magazines, and so forth. From afternoon coffee parties (*idobata kaigi*) to scholarly conferences, the main topics of conversation are rumors about people. Using the words in inverted commas 'private matters' (*watakushigoto, shiji*), that is, on condition that they are not intended for publication, there is great interest in these 'private matters.'"[77] Dōke's explanation for the Japanese "fondness of gossip" is extremely interesting: he sees it against the background of a specific understanding of what is public which cannot be defined as the opposite of the private sphere, as in the West, but instead is limited to the "official" (*official, kanteki*). In his view, many areas of life have reverted to the private sphere from the public, so that "public" life for the average Japanese consists solely of contact with the (dreaded) authorities. According to Dōke, the "privatization" of life has led to a fixation on the purely personal, which he considers to be an important basis of shishōsetsu.[78] It seems to me that this provides an important starting point for an examination of the concept of what is public, similar to, for example, Habermas's *Strukturwandel der Öffentlichkeit,* which would supply literary studies, and shishōsetsu research in particular, with new initiative.

The fact that shishōsetsu satisfied the reader's interest in the author's personality was used early on in the shishōsetsu debate in defense of the genre. For example, Uno Kōji declared that the appeal of shishōsetsu was to be found in "plumbing the depths of the author's human nature,"[79] while Kume Masao claimed that it was "interesting to observe how an author with experience of art and life sees things."[80] According to Toyama Shigehiko, it is because shishōsetsu as an institution officially sanctions the voyeuristic interest in others that is responsible for the genre's popularity: "It is not respectable to eavesdrop on another person's 'ego,' but when we do not understand our own 'ego' properly, then the 'ego' of another takes on the role of a mirror. No one wants to show his own 'ego' to others, but we want to watch another's 'ego' secretly and then correct ourselves accordingly. Such a feeling exists more or less consciously in the hearts of readers of literature. One attraction of shishōsetsu is that the *eavesdropping is officially sanctioned.* It seems to correspond with the same attitude (*shinri*) as that which means that we start reading a record of somebody's life at that point which corresponds with our own age."[81] It is interesting that Toyama supposes a kind of "educational interest," as if the public read literature solely in order to find instruction and advice of use in their own lives. In my opinion there is initially curiosity concerning the writer's private life and this leads to a pseudo-intimacy, which Dōke aptly describes: "Ozaki Kazuo writes that a reader unknown to him knew each of his children so well from his novels that he immediately said 'that is such and such' when he met [the family] for the first time; it is in the nature of shishōsetsu that it lays down such a *pseudo-private personal relationship between author and reader.*"[82]

SHISHŌSETSU AS A MEANS OF IDENTIFICATION

If the following quotation from Sako Jun'ichirō is valid for literature as a whole, then it is certainly valid for shishōsetsu. According to Sako, correct reading implies that the reader allows himself to be influenced by what he reads: "This means that by completely immersing oneself in an author whom one has encountered happily, then, when immersion is so complete that one is always together with the writer, a kind of harmony arises, and this is called influence. This can at times go so far that [the reader's own] attitudes and way of life are completely colored by the views of the author concerned. Only when one is immersed to such an extent can we speak of influence. In this way we can first recognize ourselves."[83] Okuno Takeo supplies us with an example of such devotion to literature in his report on the Dazai fever of his youth.[84]

All the previous observations on author, hero, and reader of shishōsetsu have pointed to a quite astonishing number of homologous structures. It is then hardly surprising that it is easy for shishōsetsu readers to identify with the first-person narrator and through him with the writer of the work. However, certain conditions have to be fulfilled, as Toyama Shigehiko points out:

> There may be some people of poor taste who find it interesting to eavesdrop on anybody at all, but in the long run we look for our opposite. It is not possible that this is unimportant. [Take] a person who has grown up in a wealthy environment, whose career has run smoothly, [whose life] has contained no setbacks and who has become an important personality in the course of his life, if [such a person] left only an outline account of his life it would not arouse much interest. Such a person cannot write a shishōsetsu anyway, but even an autobiography would not be interesting to read.
>
> When we are allowed an insight—and it is into the "ego" of another person—then it should be fairly turbulent, otherwise it is not interesting. This

does not mean that we enjoy another's misfortunes, but, on the other hand, it would be impossible to live if we thought others were happier than ourselves. It is the case that we can live because we think, however badly off I may be, there are people who are even unhappier.[85]

The idea expressed in the last lines of this quotation will be considered in greater detail under the heading of moral support. Obviously, it is inadequate to explain the fact that the reader wants the shishōsetsu hero to be much like himself, only slightly worse off, because of a need to identify with him. The reactions of readers to Hayashi Fumiko's *Hōrōki*, discussed in Part Four show that the feeling of encountering a person with similar problems, the straightforward identification with a similar fate, turns the shishōsetsu into the reader's "friend." However, it nevertheless seems that the public's clear wish for an exaggeration of their own circumstances that is negative is only partly explained by the facility with which one induces identification on the part of the reader by writing in such a style. One could, after all, ask why it would not be possible for this exaggeration to be in a positive direction. Before we turn to this question we must emphasize one further important condition that the reader imposes on shishōsetsu.

THE INCREASED AUTHORITY OF AUTHENTICITY

Throughout this book, a criterion of shishōsetsu that returns continually to the fore is its "genuineness," which is expressed in the structural element factuality and which we defined as the reader's assumption of a mimetic correspondence between non-literary and literary reality.[86]

For the Japanese reader factuality means most basically nothing more than the requirement that the events described in the novel actually happened. The reader's trust in the author goes so far at times that the reality he recalls is modified by the literary description. One example is an episode from Shiga Naoya's short story "Kugenuma yuki" (1912), the description of a family outing undertaken shortly beforehand. In his "Conversations about My Literary Work" ("Sōsaku yodan") Shiga remarks on this: "'Kugenuma yuki' is a piece similar to a diary, an episode from an unsuccessful novel. I faithfully recorded the facts, but there is one place which is not correct, although I was able to write it completely naturally. Since it was so clearly in front of my eyes I wrote it fully conscious [of its fictionality]. Later my second sister, who was there at the time, told me that I had remembered various things very well; but she claimed that she could also remember the other thing well, and that was exactly the invented part I had inserted."[87] This account is, of course, ideally suited to produce an admiring commentary from Akutagawa on Shiga's realism,[88] but it seems to me that it is equally fitting as an example of the possible distortion of recalled events as a result of the claim to factuality and the public's trust.

We should again emphasize here just how important the feeling of dealing with "true events" is for the Japanese reader's enjoyment of the work. Yagi Yoshinori's remark on Miura Tetsuo's "Shinobugawa" brings more aspects to mind, some of which we have already discussed or will consider in more detail later. Here we are particularly interested in the clear statement that the effects of the work are largely based on its factuality: "Thus there definitely is such a person in the world; then I can somehow live—exactly this feeling. For example, Miura Tetsuo's 'Shinobugawa': the 'I' [narrator] and the girl Shino both have a difficult past; the fact that they overcome this and find each other, and that nothing is invented, but that both characters in the work really exist, leads the reader to think: 'How wonderful life is!' The joy of reading a novel and joy of living melt together. This is what makes an excellent shishōsetsu."[89] We see now how significant the "genuineness" principle is, a principle which, as the theoretical *makoto* postulate, we emphasized in Part Three as being one of the most important poetological reasons for the development of the genre. However, we should also note that this principle is not limited to literary theory but represents a cultural code that influences innumerable important areas of life and which we shall discuss in more detail below. Mishima has good reason to speak so clearly of the "Japanese persecution complex," or, more accurately, *idée fixe*, meaning that everything that cannot be directly traced back to fact or which is invented is deemed to be "false" or a "lie" (*uso*).[90]

One should bear in mind that there is a close connection between the artistic value of shishōsetsu and its factuality. Statements made by reviewers revealing that they saw a particular work with new, more sympathetic, eyes once they learned that it was based on real events are evidence of this. One example is Masamune Hakuchō's remark concerning Doppo's literature, already mentioned in Part One. The same is true of Kobayashi Hideo writing about a popular cartoon series by his brother-in-law, Tagawa Suihō.[91] At that moment when the cartoonist revealed that he was portraying himself in the title figure, the dog Norakuro, the cartoons acquired a completely new and much more important meaning. Kobayashi then declared that the popularity the series enjoyed among children stemmed from the fact that they were aware of the autobiographical background much earlier than he was.

However absurd Kobayashi's explanation and his need to see all cartoon figures as incarnations of their creators appears ("It seems clear that Mickey Mouse is Disney himself"),[92] his reaction is nevertheless proof of just how deep the authenticity fixation runs in the Japanese reception of shishōsetsu.

This is true even for one of the authors who consciously tried to depart from conventional literary practice and who are known for their willingness to experiment. Even Ōe Kenzaburō declares that the effect of a work is totally dependent on whether it deals with real experiences when remarking on a shishōsetsu by Kusaka Naoki, in which the author writes about his leprosy, that the book would mean little for him without factuality, would amount to only "mundane syntax" and be unable to stimulate any emotion: "The emotion would not arise if the author were not identical with this 'I' and did not suffer from the Hansen disease."[93]

SHISHŌSETSU AS MORAL SUPPORT

It has been made quite clear, particularly in Parts Four and Five of this book, that the outstanding significance of shishōsetsu in the literary system of communication in modern Japan is, above all, its function as a moral support.[94] It also ought to have become clear by now that this function works analogously for the writer and the reader. We would like therefore to direct our attention to the means by which the support works or, to phrase it differently, how does shishōsetsu "function" and provide the reader with the comforting feeling that he has been "helped"?

In order to discover what this "help" consists of, let us again turn to Toyama Shigehiko's comments: "When we see someone who is entangled [with problems], our hearts soften. We feel more humble. And on the other hand, we feel that life is worthwhile."[95] The similarity of such descriptions of the effects of shishōsetsu is truly remarkable and should be read in conjunction with Yagi Yoshinori's remarks on Miura's "Shinobugawa" since they also emphasize comfort and new hope, all of which finally lead the reader to think: "How wonderful life really is!"[96] Similarly, Akiyama Shun characterizes the inspiration of the shishōsetsu author as a deep sigh which is a source of fresh courage to face life: "To consider one's own pitiful life and say [to oneself]: Ah, even a person like myself will live somehow! That is the [basic] tendency of shishōsetsu."[97] Again, according to Okuno Takeo, such a work is "an eternal champion and salvation for people who were born with a particular character, for people with a weak, beautiful, sad, pure spirit (*tamashii*)."[98] Of what significance is it that the shishōsetsu hero must suffer as much as possible? Toyama Shigehiko expressly emphasizes: "A writer who drives a foreign car, plays golf, and writes shishōsetsu somehow does not fit together. . . . It is inevitable that a shishōsetsu becomes less interesting in direct relation to the improving economic situation of the author."[99] Toyama precedes this statement with an explanation. He characterizes the reader's attitude to the author embodied in the shishōsetsu hero using the example of our behavior towards an acquaintance whom we do not much like. Nevertheless, as soon as we hear that this acquaintance lies ill in bed, we are moved to visit him and wish him a speedy recovery. Magnanimity is mixed with a kind of triumph, which, according to Toyama, is just the same in the case of shishōsetsu: "The private experiences of a poor writer may not produce a particularly good [literary] work, but, when the reader is led to think there are worse things, that such lives even exist, then he has succeeded in creating the *psychology of the visit of condolence*. This produces a feeling of relief for a short time. And that produces the feeling that it was a good book (*omoshirokatta*). It is a moral feeling, but maybe not an artistic (*geijutsuteki*) experience."[100]

The fact that the reader acquires a feeling of relief from this "psychology of the visit of condolence," that is, from the feeling of triumph, was impressively confirmed by the psychologist Minami Hiroshi and illustrated through a selection of texts from different centuries. Numerous works of advice for different social strata, popular philosophical tracts, and so forth recommend a kind of "comparative method"; the reader finds consolation by comparing himself with others worse off than he.[101]

This "there is always someone worse off than I" way of thinking also seems to me to be part of shishōsetsu reception, as confirmed both by Miyagi Otoya's observation that the reader is attracted above all by the martyr pose struck by the author[102] and by the contribution to the discussion by the shishōsetsu scholar Takahashi Hideo. He argues that it is not the hero's strength that fascinates the public but rather his uncertainty, the way he is exposed to danger and ensnared by his destiny with often fatal consequences.[103]

DOCUMENTS ON THE HUMAN CONDITION

One last paradox in shishōsetsu reception remains to be solved, namely how one reconciles the voyeuristic interest in the private person which we spoke of earlier with the "suprapersonal" (*hikoseiteki*) character which, for example, Ōe Kenzaburō ascribes to the genre.[104]

Ōe himself bases this on the "truth" (*shinjitsu*) that here a person is relating experiences which we must all share.[105]

Toyama Shigehiko goes into this matter in more detail:

> There is a particular feeling after having read an excellent shishōsetsu. One acquires a feeling of inner refreshment. How is this possible? I have often asked myself this question. I cannot say for certain, but I have often thought that the reader's ego is sucked up when reading a shishōsetsu. He becomes lighthearted and sees everything lucidly. That is to say, he enters an *impersonal* (*inpāsonaru*) state. A really excellent shishōsetsu makes the reader forget his interest in the author's private life. Not only this, it makes the reader forget his own egoism. Far removed from the life of one individual, small person it makes us think about *human sadness* (*kanashisa*) *as such*. The reader thinks that a shishōsetsu is really good (*omoshiroi*) when he is carried off to the sphere devoid of egoism (*mushi*)![106]

In the "impersonal" state, in which, according to Toyama, the reader of a good shishōsetsu loses interest in the purely private and biographical, he reflects on the human condition. However, the human condition is a sorrowful fate, identical with "sadness" and "pain" (*kanashisa*). This idea is the basis of all shishōsetsu. This attitude is most obvious in the case of Hayashi Fumiko.[107]

The experience of the "suprapersonal" which is connected with shishōsetsu is indeed to be found in a melancholy mood, detached from the world of concrete events. The feeling that human life is something sad, that only misfortune is permanent while happiness is transient has a cathartic effect for the Japanese reader.[108] He feels reconciled to his fate and at one with the world—the state of *aru ga mama* which has already been described as an objective of personal development in Japan. Thus shishōsetsu, as a testament to the human condition, helps the reader to acquire the desirable spiritual equanimity, the passive, resigned feeling of "harmony" (*chōwa*). According to the Japanese view, it is at this level that man achieves the condition of inner purity (*junjō*—pure feelings) in "lack of ego" (*mushi* or *muga*),[109] a condition that represents the highest level of ethical-moral perfection according to the philosopher Watsuji Tetsurō (1889–1960).[110]

---

1. Miura Tetsuo, "Watakushi to shishōsetsu," p. 55.
2. Miura Tetsuo in Akiyama Shun et al, "Shishōsetsu no gensen," p. 6.
3. "Ano koro no jibun no koto" in *Akutagawa Ryūnosuke zenshū*, VI, 311.
4. Cf. ibid.

5. Akiyama Shun et al., p. 11.
6. Cf., e.g., Miura and Akiyama, ibid., Ōe Kenzaburō, "Shishōsetsu ni tsuite," p. 192 and Kanbayashi Akatsuki, "Shishōsetsu no unmei," pp. 43f.
7. "Chosha no kotoba" in *Hayashi Fumiko zenshū*, II, 291.
8. Cited in Ara, p. 23.
9. Cf. Caudill and Doi, p. 389, and Takie Sugiyama Lebra, *Japanese Patterns of Behavior*, p. 229.
10. Cf. Caudill and Doi, p. 390.
11. Ibid. Emphasis in the original.
12. Cf. Ozaki Kazuo, "Shishōsetsu to watakushi," pp. 50f.
13. Cf. Yoshida Seiichi et al., "Shishōsetsu no honshitsu to mondaiten," pp. 61, 64.
14. Miura, "Watakushi to shishōsetsu," pp. 55.
15. Cf. Kanbayashi, p. 44.
16. Cf. Yoshida Seiichi et al., "Shishōsetsu no honshitsu no mondaiten," p. 64.
17. Cited in Kokubo, "Shishōsetsu no seiritsu 1," p. 49.
18. Kanbayashi, p. 48.
19. Cf., e.g., the Shiga quotations in "Fantasized Reality and Realistic Fantasies" (Chapter 16).
20. Kanbayashi, p. 49.
21. Hayashi Fumiko, *Sōsaku nōto*, Foreword (no page numeration).
22. Okuno, "Kaisetsu," in *Shinobugawa*, by Miura Tetsuo, p. 321.
23. On Dazai cf. the bibliographical references in "Writing as a 'Way Out'" (Chapter 16).
24. J. Laplanche and J.-B. Pontalis, *Das Vokabular der Psychoanalyse*, p. 453.
25. Cf. "'Shishōsetsu's Sentimental Esoteric' and Egocentric Speech" (Chapter 16).
26. Cf. Miyagi, p. 47.
27. Cf. Oketani, p. 28.
28. Cf. in particular Doi Takeo, *"Amae" no kōzō*.
29. Cf. Caudill and Doi, p. 407.
30. Doi Takeo proved with his study on the *amae* structure in the literature of Natsume Sōseki (*Sōseki bungaku ni okeru "amae" no kenkyū*) that even an examination of the authors who are not counted among the shishōsetsu writers promises remarkable results—a sign of the far-reaching significance of this concept in Japanese culture.
31. Yamamoto Kenkichi, *Watakushishōsetsu sakkaron*, p. 69.
32. Cited in Morikawa, "Shishōsetsu hōhōka no mondai," p. 13.
33. Eguchi Kiyoshi: "Bundan no taisei to kaku sakka no ichi" (The Main Current of the Literary World and the Positions of the Individual Authors), August 1918 in *Chūgai*, text in *KBHT*, V, 63–81, here p. 72.
34. "Shiga Naoya," in *Kobayashi Hideo zenshū*, IV, 16.
35. Ibid., p. 18.
36. Ibid.
37. "Shiga Naoya shi," *Akutagawa Ryūnosuke zenshū*, V, 134–137, here p. 134.
38. Ibid.
39. Text in *Shiga Naoya zenshū*, VIII, 202. Elision in the original.
40. Sibley, "The Shiga Hero," p. 224.
41. Akiyama et al., p. 11.
42. Cf. Hirano, *Geijutsu to jisseikatsu*, pp. 25f.
43. *Tosha*, literally "vomiting and diarrhea."
44. Ara, p. 23.
45. Ibid.
46. Akiyama et al., p. 10.
47. Kanbayashi, p. 49.
48. Cf. Akiyama et al., p. 10.

49. Cf. Kanbayashi, p. 48.
50. The "crisis of ideals" of which Yagi speaks does not connote any crisis beyond that of the personal realm. The "proletarian" and the "conversion literature" to which Yagi is probably alluding also remain bound to the private, pre-political range of experience.
51. *Roman no zantō* (The Remaining Members of the "Novel" Group, 1947), text in *Ishikawa Tatsuzō sakuhinshū*, VI, 137–214, here p. 138. My emphasis.
52. Dōke Tadamichi, "Shishōsetsu no kiso," pp. 52f.
53. Cf. "The 'Holy Fool'" (Chapter 16).
54. We encounter a decidedly superficial concept of the relationship to society in Sakurai Yoshio, "Shishōsetsu ni tsuite," p. 43. Observations on the (absent) political effect of shishōsetsu of most recent times will follow in Chapter 21.
55. An obvious explanation is produced by the far-reaching author-reader homology and the resulting personal identification of the reader with the first-person narrator, cf. "Shishōsetsu as a Means of Identification" in this chapter below. In this context it is our intention to concentrate on questions of narrative technique.
56. Lotman, p. 391.
57. Cf. "The Narrative Perspective" (Chapter 14).
58. Text in *Shiga Naoya zenshū*, X, 159–161, here p. 159.
59. The introductory sentences from Ishikawa Tatsuzō's *Roman no zantō* mentioned previously may seem to contradict this, but it can be shown that they are not really well-considered thoughts but rather heartfelt sighs intended to emphasize an exceptional existence as an artistic one.
60. More detailed discussion of these characteristics follows in Chapter 20.
61. Cf. "'I Am Proud to Be Decadent!'" (Chapter 16).
62. Cf. "Money, Meals, and Tears" (Chapter 16).
63. Cf. "Giwaku" in *GNBZ*, XIII, 293.
64. Ibid., p. 291.
65. *Hayashi Fumiko zenshū*, II, 217.
66. Cf. Lotman, p. 368.
67. Cf. also I.H.-K., *Mishima Yukios Roman*, p. 206, on Mishima's shishōsetsu criticism.
68. Itō Sei et al., "Nihon no genjitsu to atarashii bungaku no kanōsei," p. 146.
69. Ibid.
70. Cf. Lotman, p. 368.
71. On the secularized inspirational experience as a pattern in Japanese culture cf. I.H.-K., *Mishima Yukios Roman*, pp. 194ff.
72. Caudill and Doi, p. 388.
73. Cf. Usui, "Shiga and Akutagawa," pp. 448f.
74. Ibid., p. 449. Emphasis added.
75. Cf., e.g., "Inter- and Extratextual References to Heighten the *Riariti*" (Chapter 16).
76. Dennis Keene, "Looking at a Foreign Country," p. 285; my emphasis.
77. Dōke, p. 51. Kindaichi, p. 91, also connects the popularity of the shishōsetsu genre with the pronounced Japanese interest in the private person.
78. Cf. Dōke, p. 51. Harutoonian, "Between Politics and Culture," pp. 119ff. contains an important contribution to the semantics and history of the concepts *ōyake* (*kō*) and *watakushi*.
79. Uno Kōji, "Shishōsetsu shiken," p. 21.
80. Cited in Katsuyama, "Taishō-ki ni okeru shishōsetsuron o megutte," p. 71.
81. Toyama Shigehiko, "Shishōsetsu dokusharon," p. 25; emphasis added.
82. Dōke, p. 52; emphasis added.
83. Sako Jun'ichirō, *Bungaku o dō yomu ka*, p. 42.
84. Cf. "'Sublimating Wounds to the Heart'" (Chapter 16).
85. Toyama, pp. 25f.

86. See "Factuality" (Chapter 14).
87. *Shiga Naoya zenshū*, X, 173.
88. Cf. "Shiga Naoya shi," *Akutagawa Ryūnosuke zenshū*, V, 134–137, here p. 135.
89. Akiyama et al., p. 13; emphasis added.
90. Cf. Itō et al., p. 143.
91. Cf. Kobayashi Hideo, "Cartoons."
92. Cf. ibid., p. 215.
93. Ōe, p. 197.
94. Cf. in particular "The Book as the Reader's 'Friend'" (Chapter 16).
95. Toyama, p. 26.
96. Cf. Akiyama et al., p. 13.
97. Ibid., p. 11.
98. Okuno, "Kaisetsu," in *Ningen shikkaku*, by Dazai Osamu, p. 146.
99. Toyama, p. 26.
100. Ibid.; emphasis added.
101. Cf. Minami Hiroshi, *Psychology of the Japanese People,* pp. 64ff.
102. Cf. Miyagi, p. 48.
103. Cf. Takahashi, p. 73.
104. Cf. Ōe, p. 196.
105. Cf. ibid.
106. Toyama, p. 26; emphasis added.
107. Cf. "The Will to Live and the Wish to Die" (Chapter 16).
108. The term *catharsis* is also used in Japanese shishōsetsu research. However, since it is used with various meanings whose explication would require lengthy analysis, I have not made it a subject of this study.
109. Terminological differentiation between *mushi* and *muga*, which would be unavoidable in a philosophical treatise, can be ignored here since we are concerned with characterizing the terms and placing them in their proper relationships in everyday language use. In addition it seems to me that the choice of the expression *mushi* in connection with shishōsetsu is dictated by the lexeme *shi*.
110. Cf., e.g., Takie Sugiyama Lebra, p. 162. More detail on Watsuji in Robert N. Bellah, "Japan's Cultural Identity."

19 · Aspects of Traditionalism

DIARIES AND MISCELLANY LITERATURE

Let us begin this short discussion with an observation from Katō Shūichi: "Few will dispute that the two great mainstreams of tradition in Japanese literature are formed by the short poems that begin with the *Manyōshū* and by the prose diary form that begins with the *Kagerō no Nikki* and extends to the diaries and belles lettres of the Edo period. What happened to these two great currents following the Meiji Restoration? . . . The novelists of 'naturalism,' writing their *watakushi-shōsetsu,* unconsciously returned to the *Kagerō no Nikki.* They represent, rather, an almost complete disappearance of the foreign influences (from Chinese and Western literature) that had affected Japanese literature since the days of the *Manyōshū* and *Kagerō no Nikki.*"[1] In a characteristically grandiose gesture, Katō here links shishōsetsu literature with one of the oldest monuments of so-called diary literature (*nikki bungaku*), *The Gossamer Years* written nearly a thousand years earlier by Michitsuna no haha, a noblewoman from the Heian period. We shall here ignore his surprising assumption that "foreign influences" could suddenly almost completely disappear, influences which (in the case of China) had been important in determining Japanese traditions for a thousand years and which can no longer be separated from native conventions. The "prose diary form" is, at most, held to be a subgroup of prose and, together with miscellany literature (*zuihitsu bungaku*), embodies a form of reported reality as opposed to narrative, "invented," prose (*monogatari*), which is awarded less respect because it is fictional.[2] Could it be that Katō simply adopted these categories from others and that this is the reason he no longer mentions narrative prose?

When Katō states that shishōsetsu authors "unconsciously returned" to diary prose he is referring to a relationship with literary tradition that we called "innovation as renovation."[3] Thus, the "traditionalism" of shishōsetsu is based neither on conscious reference to a specific premodern genre nor to an intentional continuation of traditional literary conventions. It is, instead, the result of the continuity of immanent structural principles of literary art and, more comprehensively, the result of a cultural code that made it possible for diary prose, and correspondingly shishōsetsu literature, to develop as it has. The "traditionalism" in shishōsetsu, of which so much has been made, can therefore, in my opinion, not be explained as a strictly literary textual phenomenon, but only with reference to the total cultural context or to the elements of this context which were valid throughout epochs and which have proved to be decisive for the two genres.

When defining the shishōsetsu genre, we made the above assumption and then collated information that allowed us to form a discriminating view of the traditional references, and we first formulated our definition on the basis of the concepts *mujōkan* and *mono no aware*.[4] In this case we shall proceed the other way round and ask, in view of the numerous references that exist, what connects diary literature to shishōsetsu? The identification of diary literature sets us, however, a difficult task.

In Japan, diary literature (*nikki bungaku*) is understood to be a literary genre in which private experiences are related in the form of a continuous record. This can be a diary of regular, dated notes about the author's life, which the term is customarily understood to mean, or a type of autobiographical novel written retrospectively. *Nikki* literature does not necessarily require a first-person narrator.[5] Originally, Japanese literary scholars spoke of diary literature only from the Heian period until the first quarter of the Kamakura-Muromachi period, that is, from the first known *nikki*, *Tosa nikki*, written by Ki no Tsurayuki (d. 946) in approximately 935, until the fourteenth century. However, in recent times it has become accepted that the genre continues into the present, a view previously held to be unacceptable because, in later epochs, a subgroup of *nikki bungaku*, travel literature (*kikō bungaku*), dominated the field, and separate categories were set up because of the terminological and thematic differences.[6]

The majority of *nikki bungaku* and the most famous examples are characterized by the restriction of the subject matter to the private sphere: "Their vision of what is most significant largely filters out those events that men share in a public context. In other words, Japanese diary literature usually concerns love rather than marriage, death rather than participation in mortal battles, the family rather than public life."[7] The concentration on the private sphere forms undoubtedly an important parallel with shishōsetsu.

Tadokoro Hitoshi, who has examined the "relationship between shishōsetsu and literary tradition" with particular consideration of *nikki* and *zuihitsu,* came to no firm conclusions except that he could determine no direct influence.[8] He sees some connection, as did Itō Sei and Hirano Ken in the reclusive attitudes of shishōsetsu and *zuihitsu* writers and in the way they turned their backs on society.[9]

In my view, the *zuihitsu* genre cannot be conclusively distinguished from diary literature. At most, we can assume an even greater structural openness, since the subject is not constituted primarily by the chronology of a period in the author's life; such a statement is still of little use for an attempt at discerning *zuihitsu.* It is, however, certain that comparing shishōsetsu and *zuihitsu* literature would produce results similar to comparing shishōsetsu with *nikki.* On the other hand, the highly personal perspective commonly held to be a characteristic of *zuihitsu* can also be claimed for diary literature, so that all three genres share both the same narrative perspective and the author's attitude to life.

Tayama Katai was one of the shishōsetsu writers who recognized the close connection between the three most clearly. This is why, in a short essay published in 1925, he called the *Kagerō nikki* a *shinkyō shōsetsu*.[10] I find the passage in which he describes what he considers to be the source of the literary quality of the book particularly interesting, since it shows quite clearly which criteria are of decisive importance for him: "Good ultimately prevails, I thought. I often speak of the genuine (*hontō no mono*)—that's the thing, I thought. It is not a question of declaring the *shinkyō shōsetsu* good or the 'genuine novel' (*honkaku shōsetsu*) as the only valid one. It must be genuine. It must be something one could not keep for oneself but had to write down."[11] Thus, it is again the "genuineness" principle that ennobles both *nikki* and *shinkyō shōsetsu,* the alternative term for shishōsetsu.

The comparison between *nikki* and shishōsetsu has also been taken up by Japanese literary scholars. It appears even in the *Concise Encyclopaedia of Japanese Literature* (*NBS*) where, under the heading *nikki bungaku,* the "content" of *Kagerō nikki* is characterized as a world "which could also be that of a modern shishōsetsu."[12] Nomura Seiichi asks the thought-provoking question: "Is *Kagerō nikki* a 'shishōsetsu'?"[13] His answer is truly Solomon-like: "There is no reason to deny that this work is closest to a 'shishōsetsu' at a time when there was no *Hōjōki* and no *Tsurezuregusa* [famous examples of *zuihitsu* literature]. In comparison (*tatoi*), the theory that *Kagerō nikki* is a shishōsetsu can certainly be argued successfully. That is to say, labeling this work a shishōsetsu of antiquity (*kodaiteki shishōsetsu*) has some scholarly merit."[14] The most exciting aspect for me in comparing *nikki* and shishōsetsu was the importance awarded even at that time to the fact that the author had really experienced the events related. Thus, the dichotomy between "factual/genuine/true" and "invented/artificial/lie" was also constitutive for diary literature. This is shown in the introduction to *Kagerō nikki* in which the author explains that she was directly motivated to write down her own life story by her realization that "innumerable old stories" are nothing more than "invented" (*soragoto*). Her *nikki* was different since she was concerned with a story that she had herself experienced (*mi no ue*).[15] It is hardly possible to imagine a more obvious parallel to the arguments in defense of shishōsetsu!

Even the term *mi no ue* continues to be used today to characterize shishōsetsu as *mi-no-ue-banashi* (stories experienced firsthand)[16] just as it has served to characterize the "different quality"[17] of *nikki* and *monogatari* for thousands of years.

"LYRICISM"

Shishōsetsu is spoken of in connection with lyric literature at least as often as it is in connection with diary and miscellany literature. For many shishōsetsu scholars, the likeness to *haiku* or poetry seems to rest solely on the fact that numerous writers of this genre were also lyric poets.[18] We have already referred to the fact that many Japanese naturalists began their literary careers as poets. Kubota Masabumi, who categorically refused to characterize shishōsetsu as "*tanka*-like poetry" is an exception[19] since lyricism is one of the genre's fundamental characteristics for many scholars and writers,[20] something which is expressed above all in the terminological alternative *shinkyō shōsetsu*.[21]

If we look more closely at what is called "lyricism" in shishōsetsu, it becomes clear that what is meant is the attitude of the *haiku* poets. In this interpretation, which is found as early as 1925 in the case of Kume Masao,[22] and is evident again in 1976 in the writing of Takahashi Hideo,[23] poetic quality is not so much an attribute of the text but rather a special attitude towards life reflected therein. This does not, however, necessarily have to be the case according to the Japanese understanding of the matter, as we shall show below in connection with the concept of *gei*.

We could evade the problem of deciding what the "lyricism" of shishōsetsu actually consists of by referring to the parallels with diary literature established in the previous section; *nikki* usually contains many poems—in the early period with *waka* and *tanka* and later *haikai* and *haiku*—that mark moments of emotional intensity. Miner even goes so far as to suppose that it was the poems that gave *nikki* its artistic character.[24] Indeed, some examples of the genre are considered to be collections of poetry in which the prose text is reduced to the function of a connecting and expository commentary.[25] Shishōsetsu also includes examples in which poems play an important role, for example Hayashi Fumiko's *Hōrōki*, but this observation does not help us a great deal.

There is, however, another way of tracing the "lyricism" in shishōsetsu, using Yoshida Seiichi's study of *tanka, haiku,* and shishōsetsu. We ought to be able to draw certain conclusions concerning the interrelation of the three genres from his work, since it can be assumed that Japanese readers also need some explanation as to the reason for the combination.

Let us proceed directly to Yoshida's central arguments: "One of the peculiarities of shishōsetsu is, of course, that the author forms one part of the novel. Author and novel together produce a work. This is what is *lyrical* about it. In this sense we can say that it comes close to the world of *tanka* and *haiku*."[26] Yoshida's interpretation touches on one of the much discussed theories Käte Hamburger developed in her *Logik der Dichtung*. Her attempt at a typology of genres based on the mode of presentation is the subject of innumerable critical commentaries.[27] However, it seems to me that the definition of poetry and the first-person novel as "non-fictional" genres, as opposed to the "fictional" third-person novel, suggests the direction many shishōsetsu "theoreticians" in Japan aim at without being able to develop the concept so clearly. Hamburger's poetological equation of poetry with the first-person novel is particularly interesting in the light of Yoshida's observation on the way *tanka, haiku,* and shishōsetsu are related. For example, when Hamburger describes the "poetic statement as a statement of reality," "the statement of a genuine subject which can be referred to nothing else other than to this itself,"[28] we see the connection to Yoshida's theories cited above, since he also clearly sees their statement of reality as the characteristic connecting all three genres.

In addition, Ulrich Fülleborn makes it clear that this part of Hamburger's theory is applicable by showing "that sentences which are formally based on a first person writing a letter or diary who is primarily expressing himself, and sentences whose grammatical subject is the lyrical first person of a poem, have a related status in poetological terms and differ in common ways from the narrative sentences of third-person novels."[29] This opens up a new possibility of defining the "lyricism" of shishōsetsu.

NATURE MYSTICISM

When mention is made of the "lyricism," "*haiku* character," and so forth of shishōsetsu, the most frequent association is that of the experience of nature.[30] *Mujōkan* and *mono no aware* as cultural experiences and patterns for action are stimulated above all by the sight of nature, which is also true for modern Japan. In poetry, the change of the seasons, the animal and plant worlds, the countryside, the times of day, and the phases of the moon have remained dominant subjects throughout the centuries. This complex of subjects is not similarly central in terms of its occurrence in shishōsetsu, although we could list many examples in which a description of nature determines the overall impression of a work. For example Takii Kōsaku's shishōsetsu is often called a "landscape novel" (*fūkei shōsetsu*),[31] a designation Takahashi Hideo also applies to works by Ozaki Kazuo and Fujieda Shizuo.[32]

It is more important, however, to discover whether nature in shishōsetsu as a whole has a function analogous to that in the lyrical context than to present a few examples of shishōsetsu which may not be representative. In other words, it is important to show that similar mechanisms are functioning not only within the text but also in production and reception. At the same time, these mechanisms can really be examined only in the context of the overall cultural code, since they are the expression of a Japanese relationship to nature and must be described in philosophical and social-anthropological terms. This section, therefore, forms a transition to the elements of the cultural code which are the subject of the following chapter. By discussing nature within the literary tradition we restrict ourselves to the few aspects which can be directly observed in shishōsetsu and poetry.

Nature in shishōsetsu texts appears in objects and in modes of observation that are familiar to the reader from classical poetry.[33] The subject and its presentation thus confirm the well-known pattern; and there is no feeling of alienation for the reader. One example, the observation made by the first-person narrator in Hayashi Fumiko's *Hōrōki*, is thus completely conventional: The sight of a sunflower in the neighbor's garden arouses feelings of sadness about man's sorrowful fate.

Descriptions of nature in Japanese poetry have at least two levels of meaning—a concrete and a "metaphorical" sense, which is why Brower and Miner speak of a "Janus-headed" allegory.[34] Without naming the symbols in Japanese poetry in detail we can nevertheless recognize that these patterns continue to be effective in shishōsetsu, as, for example, when Kasai Zenzō in "Ko o tsurete" observes some bindweed that grows bigger each day and winds itself around a rope holding an old wooden fence together. The first-person narrator waits in vain for it to produce flowers.[35] Within the framework of a shishōsetsu such a description possesses an associative and symbolic value and a citational character similar to a *haiku*.

Nature is also to a large extent a consoler and a refuge in shishōsetsu. It constitutes a happy alternative to human company, an attitude which obviously links the twentieth-century Japanese reader with the hermit-poets (*inja*) of the middle ages.[36] The "enlightenment" pattern[37] for finding oneself and for the suprapersonal experience of *muga* that I have described above in a different connection presupposes an intense experience of nature. The Japanese topos of the flower as revelation[38] also points in this direction.

Doi Takeo gives a disarmingly simple explanation for the Japanese need to seek refuge in nature: "They become one with nature so to speak and can indulge in the feeling of pure *amae*. From their viewpoint therefore they *feel more human with nature than with humans*."[39] Minami Hiroshi also explains the quietist, escapist character of the Japanese veneration of nature as a traditional means of forgetting life's unpleasantness.[40]

Thus, the mystical union with nature, as it takes place, for example, in the "landscape novels" or in Shiga Naoya's writing, is merely a manifestation of the resigned, fatalistic, and deeply apolitical fundamental outlook on life that characterizes all shishōsetsu. This means that we cannot possibly account for nature mysticism in shishōsetsu by limiting ourselves to strictly literary conventions. Nature mysticism is an aspect which allows us an insight into the complicated structure of elements within the cultural code (made clear by Nakano Hideichirō's ideas on the possibilities of comparative cultural analysis) in anticipation of the next chapter. Nakano exemplifies the interdependence of the three cultural categories he has suggested—cognitive-technical, cathetic-aesthetic, and evaluative-moral—using the example of the Japanese concept of nature:

> The Japanese cognition of nature reflecting sensitively the four seasons (= cognitive) has some influence over the Japanese aesthetic point of view generally called *"mono no aware"* (a delicate feeling towards things especially those easily fading away = cathetic), and also over the Japanese normative way of doing often called *"akirame no yosa"* (to give up something important without reluctance = evaluative). On the contrary, social experience like the *conflict between Giri* (obligation) *and Ninjyo* (human nature) in the feudal period is reflected in the cognition of nature, in terms of *"akirame no yosa,"* and into the aesthetical idea of "imperfectionist," where the consistency of rationalism, for example, complete symmetry, is excluded from the category of beauty. The sympathetic attitude towards nature tends to nurture the basis of religious behavior, of which the ideal is *fusing oneself with Nature* instead of opposing and fighting with her. Thus these three culture elements form a complicated network of relationship.[41]

---

1. Katō, *Form, Style, Tradition,* p. 186.
2. Cf., e.g., Edwin McClellan, "Toson and the Autobiographical Novel," p. 354.
3. Cf. "Innovation as Renovation" (Chapter 3).
4. Cf. "The 'Philosophy'" (Chapter 14).
5. Bruno Lewin takes the semantic incongruity of *nikki* and *diary* into account in this regard by speaking of *memoir literature* (cf. *Japanische Chrestomathie von der Nara-Zeit bis zur Edo-Zeit,* p. 6). However, since this term has now come to have a specific meaning in literary studies as a line of demarcation within autobiography (cf. Neumann, pp. 12ff., also Müller, pp. 21ff. and Sloterdijk, pp. 17f.), I shall continue with the literal translation of *nikki bungaku.* The semi-tautological character of the term *diary literature* should ideally produce an effect of alienation to make it clear that *diary* and *diary literature* are not identical. Edward Seidensticker, *The Gossamer Years,* p. 7, refers to *Kagerō nikki* in the foreword to his translation as "a combined autobiography-diary."
6. Cf. Earl Miner, *Japanese Poetic Diaries,* pp. 12ff.
7. Ibid., p. 4.
8. Cf. Tadokoro Hitoshi, "Shishōsetsu to dentō bungaku to no kankei," p. 75.
9. Cf. ibid., pp. 76f. On this aspect seen from a strictly linguistic point of view, cf. also Hara Shirō, "Kindai sakka kara gendai sakka e," particularly p. 8. On the "recluse" in Satō Haruo cf. Yoshida Seiichi, *Gendai bungaku to koten:* "Satō Haruo to inja bungaku," pp. 174–200.
10. "Sōshun," cited in Miyazaki Sōhei, "Kindai sakka no 'Kagerō nikki' kan," p. 160.
11. Cited in ibid., p. 161.
12. Imai Takauji in *NBS,* p. 883.
13. Cf. Nomura Seiichi, "'Kagerō nikki' wa 'shishōsetsu' ka."
14. Ibid., p. 112.
15. The text edition used is in *NKBZ,* vol. IX: *Tosa nikki, Kagerō nikki,* here p. 125. Cf. for more details on this passage Tamai Kōsuke, *Nikki bungaku no kenkyū,* pp. 120ff.

16. Cf., e.g., Senuma, "Shishōsetsuron no keifu," p. 25.
17. "I.e. the nature, the concrete quality of the difference which exists between real events and the literary work—and that between two or more works on the other hand" (Strohschneider-Kohrs, p. 26).
18. Cf. Yamamoto, *Watakushishōsetsu sakkaron,* pp. 132ff. for the example of the shishōsetsu writer and *haiku* poet Takii Kōsaku.
19. Cf. Kubota Masabumi, "Shishōsetsu to tankateki jojō."
20. Cf., e.g., Takami Jun in Yoshida Seiichi et al., p. 64.
21. Cf. "The Dispute over Shishōsetsu" (Chapter 11).
22. Cf. ibid. for more detail.
23. Cf. Takahashi, pp. 16ff.
24. Cf. Miner, *Japanese Poetic Diaries,* p. 16.
25. Cf. ibid., p. 53.
26. Yoshida Seiichi, *Kanshō to hihyō,* p. 112; emphasis on *lyrical* added.
27. Cf. the bibliographical references in Müller, p. 57, note 8.
28. Käte Hamburger, *Die Logik der Dichtung,* p. 216.
29. Ulrich Fülleborn: "Bemerkungen zum Thema Prosalyrik und Roman" (Comments on the Subject of Prose-Poetry and the Novel), in Hinck, pp. 93–103, here p. 95.
30. Cf., e.g., Takahashi, pp. 16ff.
31. Cf. Akiyama et al., p. 11 and Fujieda Shizuo in *NBS,* heading "Takii Kōsaku," p. 719.
32. Cf. Takahashi, p. 18.
33. In this framework I justify my use of global expressions such as *classical poetry* or *Japanese poetry* by referring to observations such as are found in Brower and Miner, "Formative Elements in the Japanese Poetic Tradition."
34. Cf. ibid, p. 132.
35. Cf. Kasai Zenzō, *Ko o tsurete,* p. 4.
36. Cf., e.g., Takahashi, p. 78.
37. Cf. I.H.-K., *Mishima Yukios Roman,* pp. 195ff.
38. Cf. ibid., p. 196.
39. Doi Takeo, "Omote and ura," p. 260; emphasis added.
40. Cf. Minami, pp. 56ff.
41. Nakano Hideichirō, "A Framework of Comparative Culture Analysis," p. 67; emphasis added.

20 · The Cultural Code

THE *MAKOTO* PRINCIPLE

Our attempt to describe some elements of the cultural code, which is of constitutive importance for the shishōsetsu genre, is brief and selective and may lead to demands for greater detail. Also, the list of elements is not complete. Let us, however, repeat that our intention is to place the context of shishōsetsu within a larger, comprehensive cultural framework, something that has not previously been undertaken,[1] and to sketch the outline which can be filled in only by more specialized studies in this field.

We were confronted by the term *makoto* for the first time as the Japanese reading for the character *jitsu* in the dichotomy of "real/genuine/true" versus "invented/artificial/lie" in the explanation of the literary-theoretical premises necessary for the understanding of shishōsetsu and for traditional poetics. We also have seen that the principle of "genuineness" has a long tradition in literature. The concept that appears in a literary context must be seen in connection with the all-encompassing philosophical, aesthetic, and ethical-moral base which I shall call the *makoto* principle. It is the element from which those others, which we shall consider in the following sections, can be derived, a central principle, therefore, that molds patterns of thought and action in Japanese culture.

In his study of Japanese heroes from the fourth to the twentieth centuries (*The Nobility of Failure,* 1975), Ivan Morris also has recourse to this *makoto* principle as the key to understanding the Japanese veneration of the tragic, failed hero. In the glossary of his book he defines it as follows: "Makoto: 'Sincerity,' the cardinal quality of the Japanese hero, denoting purity of motive, rejection of self-serving, 'practical' objectives, and complete moral fastidiousness."[2] Before we show how the above *makoto* principle has influenced shishōsetsu, it would be appropriate here to discuss briefly the concept of art in shishōsetsu, since it will become clear that we can then judge the central significance of the *makoto* principle much better.

The traditional concept of *gei* is the basis of shishōsetsu, one of those famous terms considered so obvious that no one would consider defining them. The reason for such neglect also lies in the Japanese conviction that definitions are of no value in increasing knowledge and that something as comprehensive as *gei* or *geidō* (the path of art)[3] cannot be subjected to such treatment anyway. In addition: "Westerners pursue the theory of art, but the Japanese practice art." (*Gei o ronzuru no wa seiyōjin de aru ga gei o tanren suru no wa Nihonjin de aru.*)[4] This statement from Niizeki Ryōzō, which I have only inadequately translated, deliberately leaving out some important associations, is intended to illustrate the mystification surrounding the Japanese *gei* concept. Putting it differently, *gei* precludes any theoretical examination, according to the Japanese understanding of it, because it itself denies theory.

In my opinion, the core of the understanding of art is to be found in a Japanese ideal of dilettantism which sees its "objective" or purpose in the pursuit itself. *Gei* serves primarily to cultivate and purify the individual, ethically and morally, but at the same time the ideal pursuit of *gei* demands "purity" as a precondition. It cannot, therefore, be considered independent of life.

The following selection of quotations from source and secondary literature on shishōsetsu documents the fact that the *gei* concept, as presented, for example, in the figure of the *haiku* poet Bashō (1644–1694), also characterizes the genre under study here. On the relationship between life and art, Uno Kōji asserts: "Writing literature is, expressing it in a complicated way, life."[5] And the critic Hasegawa Ken notes: "I want to emphasize the well-known truth that only a good life can produce good literature."[6]

Shishōsetsu as *gei* demands a certain degree of maturity, in contrast to "fictional" literature. Thus, the writer Shimamura Toshimasa (b. 1912) confessed that he would have to be satisfied with writing "fiction" being as yet incapable of undertaking a shishōsetsu.[7] The same point is emphasized by the critic Asami Fukashi, who maintains that the writer's personal development is the precondition for the production of really good literature.[8]

The opposite view is also valid, fully in agreement with the *gei* concept: "Both the authors themselves and the critics say that shishōsetsu amounts to a school of life (*jinsei shugyō*)."[9] However, in view of the professionalization of shishōsetsu, one fears for the purity of motivation that is a precondition for the Japanese concept of dilettantism. Such anxiety was expressed recently, for example, by Kawasaki Chōtarō,[10] but it was also a subject of discussion in the early phase of the shishōsetsu debate, vide Ikuta Chōkō's remarks made in 1924. He accuses the shishōsetsu writers of adapting art to suit life rather than adapting life to suit art as the famous *haiku* poets did.[11]

We would continue with more quotations, but it seems to me that the underlying tendency is already quite clear. The *gei* concept also explains the shift of critical attention from the literary work to the creative process itself. Not the result but the attitude of the writer is judged, a method we have already observed on several occasions[12] and which we could illustrate with numerous examples. We shall, however, include only one, from the Kasai reception. On the publication of "Ko o tsurete" the critic Nakamura Kogetsu wrote in August 1918: "What has to be judged in this work is the life of Mr. Kasai himself. . . . His attitude to writing is, as the attitude of an author, impeccable."[13] The ultimate consequence of this understanding of art would be to do without the end result of the process that is being judged—the literary work; indeed, shishōsetsu reception provides impressive examples of this. Thus, for example, continuing the idea that crises are necessary for artistic creativity, Yagi Yoshinori writes: "And after Shiga had overcome his crisis he lost, to put it bluntly, the material to write. Putting it another way, he no longer needed to write *shōsetsu* . . . However, the fact that a person with such a strong character as Shiga Naoya completely stopped writing and merely existed gives us courage. *His very existence made us sense art.*"[14]

Let us return to the *makoto* principle. It is almost superfluous to point out its central importance for shishōsetsu and is quite obvious in the view of art illustrated above. Within the framework of this understanding, the literary work is nothing more than a reflection of the artist's personal development in the sense of the *makoto* principle, something that includes sincerity and the "purity" which should be interpreted on the basis of the Shinto *kiyoshi* ideal.[15] Only now do we fully understand the almost religious ardor of Akutagawa's admiration of Shiga,[16] in whom he considered this "purity" to be perfected.

"Purity" of motivation, as demanded by the *makoto* principle, consists of selfless devotion to a thing that does not promise any direct personal advantage. Even when the target proves to be unattainable and any attempts to achieve it are seen to be useless, the attempt is still judged by the "pure" motive; any outward appearance of failure is unimportant. The kamikaze pilots of World War II are a particularly extreme form of such spiritualism. Admiral Ōnishi, who was the real organizer of the kamikaze project, maintained that it was the noble spirit of the young men who sacrificed themselves that would save their fatherland from destruction, even if the war itself might be lost.[17]

The same ideal of heroism is to be found everywhere in shishōsetsu. The suspicion, usually suppressed but always resurfacing, that the authors of the "decline" type of shishōsetsu merely staged their suffering[18] indicates the problems shishōsetsu writers experienced in claiming a "pure" motive for themselves. The problem is only poorly concealed by the myth of life or personal sacrifice for the sake of art.[19] These attitudes prove at any rate that shishōsetsu is judged by the same standards, those determined by the *makoto* principle. One notes the case of the failure and senselessness that ennoble the Japanese hero. The same effect is apparent in shishōsetsu, where the despairing, often obstinate, and completely impractical hero provides evidence of his "pure" motivation through these very characteristics and enjoys the special sympathy and admiration of the public. He is the "holy fool."[20]

EMPIRICISM

The way the terms *real, genuine,* and *true* are implicitly equated with each other in the *jitsu/makoto* concept is a logical consequence of the "radically empirical trait of Japanese culture."[21] There is a far-reaching general agreement about these characteristics in the systematic and comparative studies on Japanese cultural typology.[22] Empiricism as a theory of knowledge should be categorized with Japanese monism, according to which "the ultimate truth exists in nature and the realities of our lives."[23] Starting with the basic assumption that truth can be grasped only inductively, in the individual phenomenon, then concrete experience becomes the most important source of knowledge. Empiricism also explains the condition of factuality which is so central for the shishōsetsu genre—knowledge can be gained only on the basis of real experience—and ultimately why *riariti,* the effect of "genuineness" founded on factuality, guarantees the high literary value of a work.

We should not forget to point out the close relationship between religious and aesthetic values in this context: "The main concern of Japanese religions, especially Buddhism, has not been so much with the good and evil of man's conduct as with the attitude of man, that is, how he accepts the given environment. In other words, they put stronger emphasis on the mental aspect of man than on the behavioral aspect. They instruct man how to reach *a tranquil and balanced state of mind.* Then man can *see things just as they are,* without any disturbance or bias in his mind. Such mental emphasis on the part of religion makes its *relationship to aesthetic value* very close."[24] These remarks can be directly linked to the observations we made concerning the shishōsetsu hero, his "lack of development" and his effect on the reader. If it is true that one central concern of the pursuit of religion and art—whereby religion, in the Japanese context, largely dispenses with the ethical aspect[25]—is achieving the condition of *aru ga mama,* the harmony between self and the world, then the phenomenon of shishōsetsu does indeed reflect this desire in several ways. It does so on the textual level and in the author's biography, but most notably in the specific relationship between life and the work of art, since the process of creation is itself considered to be an aesthetic and quasi-religious process (*shugyō*).[26] The *makoto* principle can constantly be glimpsed behind our discussions, and they repeatedly tie in with comments made in different contexts.

We have the opportunity here of making an astonishing discovery. When René Wellek and Austin Warren, in their *Theory of Literature,* inveigh quite justifiably against biographism in literary studies and claim, quite plausibly, that "there is no relation between 'sincerity' and value as art,"[27] then it seems obvious that their statement fails to possess the absolute validity they probably attributed to it. In Japan—and this is still true to a large degree today—"sincerity" or *riariti* is a condition of the artistic character of a literary work, which in turn makes clear just how dependent "literary values" are on social and historical implications. (This statement does not, however, signify approval of the excessive biographism of Japanese literary studies. That predilection is certainly rooted in this artistic ideal which continues to exist today, a fact we recognized without necessarily applauding it.)

Our observation on biographism contains a minute indication of how exciting and rewarding comparative studies could be for literary studies generally, particularly the comparison of such different systems as Western and Japanese literature. At the same time, it is a warning that what we examine should be judged by its own criteria and not by our own.

Having provided an outline of empiricism in shishōsetsu and its reception by referring to the connection between aesthetic and religious evaluative categories, we shall now draw attention to the fact that the extreme "respect for empirical reality"[28] can already be detected in classical Japanese literature.

Thus, the *Kokon chomonjū* (Stories Heard from Writers Old and New), a major collection of *setsuwa* (brief narratives) from the early Kamakura period (1254) compiled by Tachibana no Narisue (c. 1205–?) tells of a lady of the Court who wrote a poem about the pain caused by an unfaithful lover. She had however to wait several years until she actually experienced a love affair and its aftermath for the poem to win its factuality.

Another famous example is the story of the poet who wrote a travel poem and attempted to increase its "genuineness" by hiding for a time at home, so that he was thought to be traveling; he also made sure to acquire the necessary tan to make the poem seem even more authentic.

Brower and Miner cite this anecdote as an example of the attitudes of the early classical period, which insisted on the autobiographical authenticity of the poetry of experience, while the middle classical period allowed for a greater distance between the poet and the lyrical "I."[29] In my opinion, this change does not prove that the "genuineness" principle had become invalid; it can be explained instead by more obvious reasons, as Brower and Miner confirm. To the extent that the activity of writing poetry was subsequently forced to adopt conventional forms, as one can infer from the poetry competitions and works written to order, poetry was bound to lose its character as the spontaneous expression of the subject's feelings. This need not necessarily mean a final relinquishment of the empirical artistic ideal however. Important aspects of the overriding *makoto* principle continue to retain their authenticity in our own time.

THE MYTH OF IMMEDIACY

In the discussion on the shishōsetsu author, we have already mentioned the Japanese idea of a kind of *écriture automatique*.[30] At this stage, it is possible for us to place the demand, on the basis of the information we have about the *makoto* principle, for a quasi-subconscious, spontaneous mode of writing in a wider context since we recognize now that we are not dealing, according to the Japanese view, with one of several possibilities in writing, but with the only one that is conceivable within the framework of the *makoto* principle.

Seen from the point of view of literary studies, one cannot really claim that there exists a genuine, "original" writing, since each text is overdetermined by a process of selection and construction. However, we saw in the context of literary technique, as when Shiga Naoya created the "illusion of immediate writing," that neither the author nor the public wanted to admit as much.[31] When all concerned are convinced that reality can be depicted "just as it is" through literary means, they are also prepared to believe in "immediate" narrative. We are obliged to define this as an illusion although, at the same time, we recognize that it is too deeply rooted to be considered a mere literary convention. The *makoto* principle demands such spontaneity.

Having established the principle of immediacy, we find that it protects the work from all criticism, since that which has been created in the spirit of *makoto*—and that is the only relevant issue—cannot be bad in the "artificial" sense. Thus, Shiga Naoya defended one of his works against criticism by saying that he wrote it to the best of his abilities (*ryōshin ni shitagatte*), that he described things exactly as he saw them, and that this could only produce a good work.[32]

Japanese writers take the requirements of absolute spontaneity and sincerity very seriously. They are prepared, for example, to supply information about the quantitative relationship between fiction and "amount of reality" in their novels. It is, in my opinion, a testament to the power of convention that demands absolute sincerity that Kawabata Yasunari, during the filming of his short story "Izu no odoriko" (The Izu Dancer, 1926) in 1933 admitted hesitating for days as to whether he should make public the fact that the relatives accompanying the dancing girl suffered from a disfiguring disease, something he had also found difficult to keep secret when writing the book.[33] The rule is validated by the fact that breaking it makes the author obliged to confess his "sin."

The information Shiga Naoya supplied about his writing is particularly interesting on the subject of how a Japanese writer tries to do justice to the demands for immediacy. He provides clear evidence of his anxiety that readers will not believe particular scenes and repeatedly gives reassurances as to their authenticity.[34]

Finally, literary immediacy as Shiga understood it also implies transposing oneself consciously into the time which is being described—however paradoxical this may sound. This does not only mean that it was very difficult for him to describe a summer scene in the middle of winter,[35] but also that he goes so far as to refuse to use knowledge he did not actually possess at the time being described, even if it is only a matter of the correct names for particular objects. For example, when a reader informed him of the name of an insect he had only described in *An'ya kōro*, without being able to name it, Shiga retorted that he was quite aware of the name when writing the novel, but that he wanted to reproduce his ignorance at the time described since, "I wanted spontaneously (*massugu*) to tell of the author's feelings at that time."[36] In a different context he uses the same argument to explain an incorrect geographical name.[37]

The scholar Miyoshi Yukio has said that the first example illustrates a case of confusion. The author and his hero, Tokitō Kensaku, are two different people, so that it is quite possible for Kensaku to have knowledge of things which the author did not know in that situation.[38] For me this discussion, apart from illustrating the desire for immediacy and authenticity, also proves that *An'ya kōro* is a "genuine" shishōsetsu, something always under discussion. What could be clearer evidence than the apparent confusion of the author with the focus figure? The author identifies with the hero. However, in order to prove this, a degree of discrimination is necessary and Miyoshi is ahead of the majority of his Japanese colleagues in being able to see these relationships!

IRRATIONALISM AND FATALISM

A form of dualism subconsciously controls Japanese thinking, although the term itself is usually denied, since dualism is considered to be Western. It is the dichotomy of intellect versus feeling, of idea, philosophy, and thought (*idē, kannen, shisō*, and so forth) versus heart, emotion, sense and the "voice of one's physical being" (*kokoro, nikusei*, and so forth). We cannot discuss the historical dimensions of such dualism here, but the connections between the emotional side and the *makoto* principle are obvious. The sharpness of the dualism in Japanese thinking since the Meiji period is based, in my opinion, on the permanent confrontation between Japanese and Occidental thought which has preoccupied Japanese intellectuals. The expression *sharpness* implies clarity and connotates a pain which is combined with the experience of this dualism. Having seen with what grim fanaticism a large number of leading Japanese intellectuals attempt to present all that is committed to rationalism and entails a cognitive process as "skillful but empty," "clever but without substance," it is possible to understand that this must stem from a deeply-rooted complex of "non-Aristotelian" as opposed to "Aristotelian" thought.

Let us place the contrast of intellect (–) versus feeling (+) in relation to the *makoto* principle. Emotion is considered to be the core of man's nature while everything cognitive is held to be relatively external and even dispensable. The theory of art constructed on the concept of *mono no aware* conforms to this view. It can be traced back to the beginnings of Japanese poetic theory in the famous foreword to the poetry anthology *Kokin wakashū* (Collection of Ancient and Modern Japanese Poems, compiled from 905 to c. 914). Here Ki no Tsurayuki interprets poetry as the outpourings of *kokoro*, of human nature in the sense of the emotional aspect,[39] a view which, with somewhat different terminology, was again argued in the 1970s.

In *The Structure of "Mujō,"* 1976, Isobe Tadamasa is concerned with proving the validity and practical use of traditional theories for the present. His statements that a poem (*uta*) is the result of a spontaneous expression of feeling, a result of being unable to suppress emotions any longer, sounds anachronistic to Western readers[40] and awakens associations with Ki no Tsurayuki's foreword to the *Kokin wakashū* and his *Tosa nikki*, in which he defines art as something created when the poet can no longer bear to hem in his feelings (*omofu koto ni tahenu toki no waza*).[41] Prince Genji, the mouthpiece of the author Murasaki Shikibu (978–c. 1015), expresses a similar opinion in the chapter "Hotaru" of *Genji monogatari* (The Tale of Genji, completed c. 1010). He explains that the reason for writing is that the poet is so moved by the things he experiences that he wants to pass them on to others.[42]

The statements made by shishōsetsu authors about their work are nearly the same as those above, for example when Tayama Katai presented "genuine" literature as something "one could no longer keep to oneself but had to write down"[43] or when Miura Tetsuo described his motivation for writing as impatience, "spitting out as quickly as possible" something which had been plaguing him for years.[44]

It is certainly not the intention here to conflate statements made over the course of several centuries into one handy package and claim that they are all identical; that would be unhistorical, since we may have ignored completely the possibly widely diverging implications of these quotations. However, we can confidently state that they are manifestations of one constant theme in the Japanese theory of literature in which an expressive impulse is attributed to an emotional effect.[45] The first parts of this section are nothing other than the illustration of this principle through the example of shishōsetsu.

In accordance with the Japanese idea that the poetic impulse should unearth "feeling" (*ninjō*), which is the "pre-logical" as it were, shishōsetsu is expected to reveal "the form of *kokoro*" (*kokoro no sugata*).[46] Works from recent times are regrettably often felt to be based on "ideas" (*kannen*); they produce a feeling (!) of having been "constructed in the head" instead of expressing the "voice of one's physical being" (*niku no koe*).[47] Such irrationalism and anti-intellectualism is based on the idea described above in relation to artistic theory: "Deep, significant, stirring truth, according to most Japanese thinkers, is reached by transcending the intellect and going beyond the limitations of rational reason, plunging with our entire being, body and soul, into the quest."[48] The following is a relevant example of this in relation to shishōsetsu. In the 1977 discussion on "The Sources of Shishōsetsu," Yagi Yoshinori expressed the opinion that if free rein were given to the Japanese literary taste the end result would inevitably be a shishōsetsu; the critics constantly attacked the lack of "philosophy" or "intellectualism" (*shisō*), but "the Japanese are people who basically do not need a philosophy."[49] He considers that which he terms the conflict of "ideas" in Occidental literature to be nothing more than stylistic adornment and refinement to satisfy the baroque taste of Westerners. On the other hand, he feels the following is true for the Japanese: "When we become one with nature, when this is the case, then the despairing battle between crime and punishment, between the good and God as [fought out] by the characters in Dostoevski's works is unnecessary."[50] According to Yagi, Japanese art has cultivated simplicity and can therefore do without decorative "intellectualism" or "philosophy." It is satisfied with the beauty expressed in the simple, direct—and that means emotional—"I."[51]

It becomes clear here just how indebted shishōsetsu literature is to traditional and current Japanese irrationalism which is notable in almost every sphere of life. For example, when Kimura Shōzaburō, Professor of Western History at Tokyo University, states that foreign criticism of the large Japanese balance-of-payments surplus is based on "incorrect attitudes" towards Japan, this is not a diversionary tactic but a manifestation of the Japanese way of looking at things, which he himself explains in his article. The following quotation clarifies patterns of thought that are also the basis of shishōsetsu production and reception:

As soon as a society enters a systematized form it is no longer necessary for the individual to live defensively. The result is a transition of the focus of interest from the rational to the emotional. This is the inevitable product of an industrialized society. This tendency can be recognized in the society of the peoples of Europe and the United States. In this sense it seems to me that Western society is unintentionally coming closer to Japan.

One may safely say that the recent difficulties in the industrial sector are based on differences in the way of life and thinking between the two worlds of the East and West.[52]

We are here witnessing an interesting process in which those who are products of European culture see a mirror image of themselves. Just as we are bound to find the Dostoevski interpretation completely inadequate and see no connection between balance-of-payment surpluses and the Japanese tendency "to adopt things which come from the East or West,"[53] so would the Japanese reject receiving a shishōsetsu based on European categories of thought. We are dealing with two radically different discourses; characterizing the Japanese as irrational of course reflects an Occidental perspective, since irrational can be defined only in terms of "rational."

We also become conscious of the dependency of our system of values on such basic axioms upon comparison with another value system. It becomes clear from the Kimura text (which we can fully appreciate only with difficulty) that he places the "emotional" aspect of Japanese culture higher than the "rational," not so fully "systematized" Western societies who are gradually catching up with Japan. The same pattern is revealed in the statement from Niizeki Ryōzō cited earlier on the concept of art: "Westerners pursue the theory of art, but the Japanese practice art,"[54] since, when "theory" is considered to be a superfluous practice given that the nature of things can be revealed only intuitively and through personal experience, then "practicing" (*tanren*) art is obviously superior. Yagi Yoshinori indeed says exactly the same when arguing that even Dostoevski's literature can be reduced to the same central core as the shishōsetsu by Chikamatsu Shūkō or Kasai Zenzō. Shishōsetsu embodies the "real" nature, the "lowest motive force" (*ichiban kihon no bane*); everything else, even the "despair of life" (also considered intellectual) are mere additions, questions of style (*sutairu*) which do not touch the core.[55]

It would of course be foolish to conclude that rationality has been completely excluded from Japanese life. It merely assumes a different role and has a much more limited function; it is an "instrumental rationality" designed to solve practical problems. On the other hand, the leading principles in the system of thought and in the confrontation with existential questions are "intuition over rationality, particulars over universals, the concrete over the abstract, symbols rather than definitions."[56]

That which strikes us, seen from a Western point of view, as to a large extent fatalistic in shishōsetsu can also be explained by these attitudes. The shishōsetsu hero is a victim of his own moods and feelings; he believes himself to be completely at the mercy of life and can only react, and is not even capable of gauging the consequences of his actions.[57] Since he is not interested in winning insight into his situation (this would be "rationalistic"), he can also see no difference between what he has himself brought about and what is caused by his social situation. Painful experiences are also, on the one hand, self-pityingly bemoaned as unavoidable fate while, on the other, they are the cause of sentimental *mujō* feelings, that is, they lose their concreteness and are aesthetically exaggerated. That his wife and children are starving is not grounds for thought about causality for the shishōsetsu hero. Nor does it lead him to look for concrete possibilities of altering the situation. But it is an excuse to get thoroughly drunk and then to lament the misery of mankind.[58]

The fatalism that is dominant in shishōsetsu is characterized by *akirame* behavior, held to be a positive virtue in Japan as resignation in the face of an unavoidable fate (*un*). Many things are attributed to fate that a Westerner would consider to be within the scope of what can be changed and influenced or to be matters of personal responsibility. However, in Japan a capacity for *akirame*, of unconditional resignation, is considered to be a sign of human maturity and wisdom and is closely connected with the Buddhist *satori* ideal.[59] To this extent, the aesthetic abstraction of the concrete situation conforms with the ideal picture of the mature Japanese personality, since it is the outward indication of achieving the condition of "selflessness" (*muga, mushi*).[60]

As Joseph Spae points out, however, *akirame* does not imply pessimism but an acceptance of things "as they really are"[61] which brings with it relief or, to quote Toyama Shigehiko, "refreshment."[62] The fact that social experiences acquire the status of unavoidable natural events in this context is an observation that we have already recorded on several occasions.[63] If nature and human society are thought of as alternatives, then the same traditional ideal of conformity rather than intervening is valid for both. The personal fulfillment, in the Japanese sense, which shishōsetsu heroes experience is to be found in the choice of one of these alternatives—consequently we cannot speak of escapism—and in the harmonious absorption into at least one of these "worlds."

---

1. There are some important and interesting studies in which Japanese literature is examined from a social-psychological or cultural-political point of view, including studies by Maruyama Masao, Wagatsuma Hiroshi or Arima Tatsuo's analysis, *The Failure of Freedom*, held in considerable disdain by Sibley, of the position of the intellectual community up to the eve of World War II, but in these cases the literature is merely used as material for arguments in discourse outside that of literary scholarship.
2. Ivan Morris, *The Nobility of Failure*, p. 472.
3. Cf. Horst Hammitzsch, "Zum Begriff 'Weg' im Rahmen der japanischen Künste," on the term *dō*.
4. Niizeki Ryōzō, "Nihon geidōron," p. 301.
5. Cited in Yamamoto, *Watakushishōsetsu sakkaron,* p. 91.
6. Cited in Tsuruta, p. 18.
7. Akiyama et al., p. 5.
8. Asami Fukashi, "'Shishōsetsu' kaishaku no hensen," p. 12.
9. Yoshida Seiichi, *Kanshō to hihyō,* p. 113.
10. Cf. Kawasaki Chōtarō, "Shishōsetsu ni tsuite," p. 54.
11. "Nichijō seikatsu o henjū suru akukeikō" (On the Bad Tendency of Overemphasizing Everyday Life), July 1924, text in Hirano et al., pp. 97–108, here p. 107.
12. Cf. also Akutagawa's essay on Shiga with his criterion of "moral purity," in *Akutagawa Ryūnosuke zenshū,* V, 134–137.
13. "Shinshin sakka o hyōsu" (Reviewing a New-Generation Author, published in *Yūben*), cited in Ōmori, p. 113.
14. Akiyama et al., p. 10; emphasis added.
15. Cf. Joseph Spae, *Shinto Man,* p. 20.
16. Cf. "Self-Revelation as a Moral Act" (Chapter 18).
17. Cf. Morris, *The Nobility of Failure,* pp. 284, 443.
18. Cf. "The Institutionalized Outsider" (Chapter 18).
19. Cf., e.g., also Yamamoto, *Watakushishōsetsu sakkaron,* pp. 61f.
20. Cf. "The 'Holy Fool'" (Chapter 16), and "The Institutionalized Outsider" (Chapter 18).
21. Kishimoto Hideo: "Some Japanese Cultural Traits and Religions," in Charles A. Moore, ed., *The Japanese Mind,* pp. 110–121, here pp. 115, 120. In similar vein also Kawashima Takeyoshi, ibid., p. 262 and Nakamura Hajime, ibid., p. 194.
22. Cf., e.g., the conclusive analysis by Fosco Maraini, "Japan and the Future."
23. Suzuki Daisetz, cited in ibid., p. 22.
24. Cf. Kishimoto Hideo in Moore, p. 117; emphasis added.
25. Cf. also the observations made by James T. Araki, "Ideals and Values of Young People in Japan," pp. 99f.: "What definitely distinguishes the Japanese from the Europeans is that the need they feel for religion is related to sentiments, sensibility and sometimes even sensuality, but never to morality."
26. Cf. "The *Makoto* Principle" in this chapter, and the Katai quotations in Senuma, "Shishōsetsu to shinkyō shōsetsu," p. 16.
27. René Wellek and Austin Warren, *Theory of Literature,* p. 80.
28. Senuma, "Shishōsetsu to shinkyō shōsetsu," p. 16.
29. Cf. Brower and Miner, *Japanese Court Poetry,* pp. 299f.

30. Cf. "Shishōsetsu as an 'Automatic Text'" (Chapter 18).
31. Cf. "Shishōsetsu Narrative Strategies" (Chapter 16).
32. Cf. Itō et al., p. 137.
33. Cf. Enomoto Takashi, "Kawabata Yasunari 'Izu no odoriko,'" p. 87.
34. Cf., e.g., "Zokuzoku sōsaku yodan" (Conversations about My Literary Work, Second Sequel, 1955), *Shiga Naoya zenshū,* X, 199–208, here p. 202.
35. Cf. "Zoku sōsaku yodan," ibid., pp. 181–198, here p. 186.
36. "Nakamura Shin'ichirō kun no gimon ni tsuite," ibid., p. 161.
37. "Zoku sōsaku yodan," ibid., p. 191.
38. Miyoshi, *Sakuhinron no kokoromi,* p. 112.
39. In common use *kokoro* means, in its most general sense, the unity of intellect, feeling and will (cf. *Kōjien*). However, secondary meanings and connotations, and the immediate context in which *kokoro* is often found, bring about a definite displacement in the direction of "feeling."

    For more detail on Ki no Tsurayuki's poetic theory cf., e.g., Ueda, *Literary and Art Theories in Japan,* pp. 1f.
40. Cf. Isobe, p. 106.
41. Cf. Earl Miner, "Toward a New Conception of Classical Japanese Poetics," p. 105 and Ueda, *Literary and Art Theories in Japan,* pp. 25f.
42. Cf. Miner, "Toward a New Conception," p. 107.
43. Cf. "Diaries and Miscellany Literature" (Chapter 19).
44. Cf. "*Kakitagaru Byō*" (Chapter 18).
45. Cf. Miner, "Toward a New Conception," p. 106.
46. Akiyama et al., p. 13.
47. Cf. ibid., p. 10.
48. Maraini, p. 41.
49. Akiyama et al., p. 8.
50. Cf. ibid.
51. Cf. ibid.
52. Kimura Shōzaburō, "Gespräch zwischen Ost und West steht erst am Anfang," pp. 12f.
53. Ibid., p. 11.
54. Niizeki, p. 301.
55. Cf. Akiyama et al., p. 11. An analogous phenomenon is Saeki's comparison of Takii Kōsaku with the *nouveau roman,* cf. Saeki et al., p. 159.
56. Maraini, p. 73. Cf. ibid., pp. 39ff. on "instrumental rationality."
57. Cf. "Inner Voices and Higher Powers" and "Good and Bad Moods" (Chapter 16).
58. This pattern is extremely widespread. Among the examples given in Part Four we find it, for example, in Kasai Zenzō and, in a slightly different form, in Dazai Osamu.
59. Cf. Takie Sugiyama Lebra, p. 167.
60. Cf. "Nature Mysticism" (Chapter 19).
61. Cf. Spae, p. 34.
62. Cf. Toyama, p. 26.
63. Cf., e.g., "Nature Mysticism" (Chapter 19), and I.H.-K., "Innovation als Renovation," p. 366.

21 · Shishōsetsu— A Critical Assessment

In the previous sections we have presented the most important elements of the shishōsetsu discussion both in their interdependence and as they refer to the wider cultural code. Selected quotations from the essay of the famous literary critic Akiyama Shun entitled "The Simple Life" ("Kantanna seikatsu," 1969) will show how relevant and widespread this discussion still is at present. At the same time, these quotations will provide evidence of the central importance of the questions we have discussed in connection with shishōsetsu, and prove what an exemplary character an examination of this genre has in raising questions of fundamental interest to modern Japan.

> As a simple man living this simple life, I have a longing to talk [*shaberu*]. Man is a talking animal. He seeks in talking some loathsome and irresistible pleasure. . . .
> . . . What does he talk about? Invariably, it is himself he wants to talk about. . . .
> Everybody talks in this way. . . .
> . . . I am at this moment seized with an intense desire to talk. It is a disease, no doubt about it. But it is a disease which makes you shudder with a sensation of pleasure. . . .
> I am living extremely simply. . . . You have to keep a constant watch on yourself, remaining always in doubt as to what simplicity is. This effort is probably rather ridiculous, a somewhat futile and useless activity. I must admit that I myself am not entirely clear about the purpose and reason behind this activity. All the same, I do intend to live extremely simply. The words "live simply" are carved on my skull with a sort of necessity [*hitsuzen*], a witness, as it were, of the essence of this existence, me; or like solemn words of command. . . .

> I know only simple things. That is to say, all that I understand about living things is the simple fact that they are alive. . . .
>
> We are told that we have a genuine inclination to love nature, that it is a part of our disposition to want to be assimilated to nature, to want to think of ourselves as part of nature. In my opinion this basic motive force does direct our spirit to nature, but this is not because of our love of nature, but because of our dislike of man. I believe that this force in us has its centre in our unrelenting dislike of man. . . .
>
> This desire to be assimilated to nature, then, to think of oneself as a part of nature, to live like a corpse seems far removed from that other order of life which looks for complexity, enlarging and deepening of the self. What this order sees as the ultimate ground of man will be something like god or the totality of history. . . .
>
> For someone like myself, society is a frightening thing. . . .
>
> Have you ever dreamed that you met some really frightening, cruel, uncanny being, truly evil, filled with hate for you, terrifying, and which came towards you as if you were its prey? I feel something of this kind of animosity in the character of society. . . .
>
> . . . It is the simple man's form of life which provides a radical criticism of society, for the simple man can say: "I have no need of society."
>
> I want to disown many of the human realities which the character of society allows men to set up. I want to deny that I have my own parents or that I desire to have my own children. . . .
>
> I do not understand what it is like to love someone. I do not know what it is like to trust someone. I do not even know what it is like to cooperate with someone. I do not trust doctors. . . .
>
> What occurs to me at this point is that we have two different ways of using words, the one when we address them to others, the other when we direct them to ourselves. The words we use to ourselves are simple, those we direct to others are complicated. The simple man is the man who has lost the ability to say anything except to himself, so he comes to lose the ability readily to understand talk of the other, complicated kind. . . .
>
> . . . I do not fight this society, but neither am I at peace with it. I feel that I am somewhere else, rather far away. To be precise, I am a man who wants to live a life hidden from society.[1]

This essay reads like a summary of the basic ideas, concepts and structural principles of shishōsetsu. The "writing disease," the expressive aspect of literary theory, egocentrism, autism, anti-intellectualism and empiricism are to be found here just as are the *makoto* principle, theatricality, and sweepingly vague abstraction, the rejection of society and history, the alternatives of nature and society, and their reduction to the immediate personal environment.

I do not wish to go into the consequences this has for Akiyama's recognition as an intellectual, a member of the younger generation who has been awarded several literary prizes. However, it is worth mentioning in this context that Akiyama is one of the spokesmen and leading figures of the literature of the late 1960s and the 1970s called *naikō no sedai* (introverted generation).[2] A separate study would be needed to clarify the relationship between this multifarious Japanese variety of a "new sensitivity" and shishōsetsu. But it seems that the "introverted generation" has succeeded to the estate of shishōsetsu, not only in the eyes of the critics and the public;[3] the writers themselves feel they are bound to this tradition.[4] Of course, the term *shishōsetsu* continues to exist, and we can concur with the Japanese predictions[5] which say that the genre will not disappear from the literary scene in the foreseeable future.

Predictions are not, however, part of literary studies, so that we are at least obliged to give an explanation for the persistence of shishōsetsu. Assuming that literature is to a large degree "dependent on the social reality in which it is generated,"[6] we can formulate the following theory: As long as the elements of the cultural code which are of constitutive importance for shishōsetsu and the communicative function of literature in the socio-cultural context as a whole do not change significantly, shishōsetsu will retain its importance.

Inversely, we can also put forward a thesis that stresses the implications of the characteristic, vertical social structure (*tate shakai*)[7] of Japan and also of the conception that a large part of the intellectuals in society have of themselves for the genre. It should be clear from the discussions in the last part of this book that setting literature in the context of the socio-cultural system as a whole is not tantamount to indulgence in naive sociologism and reductionism. It is instead an essential analytical step after one has recognized the limits to an exclusively literary study.

We should not forget to point out that the cultural code that is relevant for shishōsetsu is only part of the complete socio-cultural system, made up of numerous competing values and norms. It is by no means a homogeneous unit, as is, for example, the "literary tradition" with which shishōsetsu has so often been associated in an all too general manner.[8] As a result, shishōsetsu was and is criticized by those groups within Japanese society who are not, or not fully, bound to the code described.

The first wave of criticism began in the 1920s with the increasing influence of Marxist-oriented literati,[9] and there was a second high point of shishōsetsu criticism after World War II. The arguments were predominantly similar, but the discussion became increasingly violent on the part of the opponents in the 1950s. Shishōsetsu was accused of spiritual meanness, social abstinence and "hermit-like isolation" (Kuwabara

Takeo),[10] "privatism," and "passive conformity," retreating from public responsibility (Maruyama Masao) and the name of the genre was given derogatively a purely symbolic meaning.[11] Sugiura Minpei's attack, conforming with the communist party line, on the genre concluded with an indiscriminate condemnation of the shishōsetsu writers as members of the "parasitic landowning class."[12] Takeuchi Yoshimi, on the other hand, places the problem within a larger framework: "The problem of shishōsetsu is by no means only a literary problem but much more the problem of the nature (*seikaku*) of Japanese 'modernity.'"[13] The most truly radical criticism has been expressed by Tamiya Torahiko: "If shishōsetsu is distorted (*ibitsu*), then it is because the society which produced it was distorted. I think it is not right to reject this society's product, shishōsetsu, without wanting to change the distortion of the society."[14] The views represented here, which are expressed less often in Japan nowadays, correspond to the ideological critical point of view that is also applied outside Japan. Tamiya's extension of the criticism to the society as a whole makes clear that this point of view is based on different standards and even a completely different system of values than the traditional ways of thinking on which shishōsetsu production and reception are based.

The observation of a coexistence between different value systems in modern Japan is, of course, by no means new. Since the Meiji Restoration the West-East culture conflict of, with a somewhat different emphasis, the struggle between tradition and modernization has remained probably the most important subject in Japan. As far as shishōsetsu is concerned, William Caudill's statements that "modernization" is effective primarily in the public and social field, while private life remains largely conservative-traditional,[15] is of interest, since it offers an explanation for the persistence of shishōsetsu as a literary genre bound to the traditional value system, which is also inclined to allow the individual reader to reexperience the work on a predominantly emotional level.

This fact leads to a further thesis: Shishōsetsu can have no critical or emancipatory effect owing to its personally oriented nature and the emotional identification of the reader with the focus figure. This is why those representatives of proletarian literature who write shishōsetsu[16] are bound to fail, in my opinion, since they cannot put their message across using this genre. A more relevant case today is that of the authors who are categorized as progressive and who employ the shishōsetsu pattern, although they would certainly deny this. Amongst others are, for example, Kurahashi Yumiko (b. 1935), Kaikō Ken (b. 1930), and Shibata

Shō (b. 1935), who told me personally that he never intended to write a shishōsetsu. However, anybody who writes a novel in the Japan of the 1960s in which the first-person narrator shares the same age, sex, profession, surroundings, and attitudes with the author must expect that the work will be received as a shishōsetsu. It may be inviting to exploit the numerous advantages the pattern has due to its familiarity and effectiveness. However, to deny doing so is, in my opinion, merely a clumsy way of distancing oneself from traditional shishōsetsu.

A European writer would probably answer this question by saying that he was consciously making use of the shishōsetsu pattern but to a different end or, perhaps, to illustrate the value of the genre for different purposes and effects. If that is the intention of these authors, however, the specific limitations of shishōsetsu still hold true. It undermines all new intentions by the fact that its effectiveness is bound to the emotions. Shishōsetsu does not challenge the reader to adopt a critical position nor to think further about the subject, since there is no room for thought when everything is concentrated on feeling. Put another way, critical or emancipatory experiences, as we know them in the Western Enlightenment view of man, are alien to the discourse of and around shishōsetsu.

A critical evaluation of shishōsetsu must be based on an examination of numerous individual examples, each considered in relation to its own historical period. Only when, on the basis of the examples, homologous structures in the "global semantic systems of the socio-cultural communication system"[17] become visible within the corresponding historical moments can one evaluate the genre as a whole. The present study constitutes a preparatory attempt at an assessment.

I hope that the method adopted here of considering literature in its context, reconstructing the discourse, and reflecting the relevant research within its contextual limitations has proved to be practicable and meaningful. Only such an approach can sharpen our senses to the discrepancy, of which we have gradually become aware, between our trusted Western values and the differing cultural understanding which manifests itself in the work as the "cultural unconscious."[18] I am convinced that the special value and the real justification of non-Japanese "Japanology" lies in the possibility of seeing this more clearly than Japanese scholars, who are unable to attain a broader perspective simply because they are trapped within these structures.

1. Akiyama Shun, "Kantanna seikatsu," pp. 59–68. Quoted from Joseph and Chihoko Moran's English translation, "The Simple Life," pp. 184–201.
2. Cf. I.H.-K. "Die nicht existenten Probleme der modernen japanischen Literaturgeschichtsschreibung," on the term *naikō no sedai*.
3. Cf., e.g., the readers' contributions "Dokusha no pēji" in the August 1978 edition of *Kaishaku to kanshō* on the subject of "Literature since the Introverted Generation," pp. 176–180.
4. Cf., e.g., Ogawa Kunio and Furui Yoshikichi, "Genkei e no shikō."
5. Cf. the evidence in note 6, Chapter 18.
6. Hans Dieter Zimmermann, p. 133.
7. Cf. Nakane Chie, *Japanese Society*.
8. Cf. "The 'Philosophy'" (Chapter 14).
9. Cf. Chapter 11.
10. Cf. the quotation in Miyoshi Yukio, *Nihon bungaku no kindai to hankindai*, p. 237.
11. Cf. Maruyama Masao, "Patterns of Individuation and the Case of Japan," pp. 508, 512.
12. Sugiura Minpei, "Kiseisha no bungaku," p. 58.
13. Takeuchi, p. 69.
14. Tamiya Torahiko, "Shishōsetsu no unmei," p. 60.
15. Cf. William Caudill, "The Influence of Social Structure and Culture on Human Behavior in Modern Japan," particularly p. 242.
16. Cf., e.g., Tokunaga Sunao, "Soto kara uchi e," and Kurahara Korehito, "Shishōsetsu shikan" on this.
17. Schulte-Sasse and Werner, p. 233.
18. Pierre Bourdieu, *Zur Soziologie der symbolischen Formen*, p. 115.

Bibliography
*Appendix to
the Bibliography*
Index

Bibliography

PRELIMINARY REMARKS

Shishōsetsu-related secondary literature (cf. the way we defined it in Chapter 7) is marked by an asterisk. Titles not accessible or not consulted as well as titles published after 1980 are listed in the Appendix to the Bibliography.

Bibliographical entries pertaining to one name are arranged in the following order: sole author/editor (in chronological order), followed by several authors/editors (in chronological order). The Collected Works (*zenshū*) appears as the last item.

General works of reference appear only in the notes.

Abe Akio. *Kokubungaku gaisetsu.* 15th ed. Tokyo: Tōkyō daigaku shuppankai, 1976 (1959).
*Aeba Takao. "Dazai Osamu ni okeru 'watakushi' no hyōgen," *KKK,* December 1977, 6–13.
*———. "'Watakushi' no fukami ni mukatte: Shōwa gojūichi nendo no bungaku," *Bungakukai,* January 1977, 214–226.
———. *Hihyō to hyōgen: Kindai Nihon bungaku no "watakushi"* Tokyo: Bungei shunjū, 1979.
Agawa Hiroyuki. *Shiga Naoya no seikatsu to sakuhin.* Tokyo: Sōgeisha, 1955.
Akatsuka Yukio. "Senpyō to jushō sakka no unmei: Dai yonjūyon kai: Shinobugawa, Miura Tetsuo," *Akutagawa shō jiten.* KKK (special edition), January 1977, 127–128.
Akiyama Shun. "Kantanna seikatsu," *Kikan geijutsu,* October 1969, 58–68.
———. "The Simple Life." Tr. Joseph and Chihoko Moran. In Yukio Mishima, and Geoffrey Bownas, eds., *New Writing in Japan.* Harmondsworth: Penguin, 1972.
*———. "Shiga Naoya no 'watakushi' ni tsuite," *KBG,* March 1976, 64–68.
*———, Yagi Yoshinori, Shimura Toshimasa, et al. "Shishōsetsu no gensen," *Waseda bungaku,* July 1977, 4–15.
Akutagawa Ryūnosuke zenshū. Vols. I–VIII. Tokyo: Shinchōsha, 1964.

Anderegg, Johannes. *Fiktion und Kommunikation: Ein Beitrag zur Theorie der Prosa.* 2nd ed. with an afterword. Göttingen: Vandenhoeck & Ruprecht, 1977 (1973).
*Ara Masahito. "Shishōsetsuron," *Bungakukai,* September 1952, 23–30.
Arakawa Sōbei. *Kadokawa gairaigo jiten.* 31st ed. Tokyo: Kadokawa shoten, 1970 (1967).
Araki, James T. "Ideals and Values of Young People in Japan," *International Journal of Adult and Youth Education* 16:91–100 (1964).
Arima Tatsuo. *The Failure of Freedom: A Portrait of Modern Japanese Intellectuals.* Cambridge: Harvard University Press, 1969.
*Ariyama Mitsuhiro, Sugimoto Yuki, and Mawatari Kenzaburō. *Meiji bungaku kara Shōwa bungaku made: Kindai Nihon bungakushi.* Tokyo: Monshō no kai, 1966.
*Asami Fukashi. "'Shishōsetsu' kaishaku no hensen," *KBG,* March 1966, 10–14.
Axthelm, Peter M. *The Modern Confessional Novel.* 3rd ed. New Haven, London: Yale University Press, 1974 (1967).

Barnlund, Dean C. *Public and Private Self in Japan and the United States: Communicative Styles of Two Cultures.* Tokyo: Simul Press, 1975.
Bellah, Robert N. "Japan's Cultural Identity: Some Reflections on the Work of Watsuji Tetsurō." In John A. Harrison, ed., *Japan. Enduring Scholarship Selected from the Far Eastern Quarterly—The Journal of Asian Studies, 1941–1971: 30th Anniversary Commemorative Series,* vol. II. Tucson: University of Arizona Press, 1972 (1965).
Ben-Dasan, Isaiah. *Nihonjin to Yudayajin.* 9th ed. Tokyo: Kadokawa shoten, 1971 (Yamamoto shoten, 1970).
Benl, Oscar. "Naturalism in Japanese Literature," *MN* 9.1:1–33 (1953).
Berger, Peter L., and Thomas Luckmann. *Die gesellschaftliche Konstruktion der Wirklichkeit: Eine Theorie der Wissenssoziologie.* Frankfurt/M.: S. Fischer, 1970 (1969).
Berger, Willy R. "Probleme und Möglichkeiten vergleichender Gattungsforschung." In Horst Rüdiger, ed., *Die Gattungen in der Vergleichenden Literaturwissenschaft.* Berlin, New York: De Gruyter, 1974.
Berndt, Jürgen, "Einiges zur Problematik bei Betrachtungen der modernen japanishen Literatur." *25th International Congress of Orientalists, Moscow 1960,* vol. V. Moscow, 1963.
Bormann, Alexander von. "Ansatz und Reichweite einer historischen Gattungssemantik am Beispiel des (naturalistischen) Trauerspiels." In Walter Hinck, ed., *Textsortenlehre, Gattungsgeschichte.* Heidelberg: Quelle & Meyer, 1977.
Borton, Hugh. *Japans Modern Century.* New York: Ronald Press, 1955.
Bourdieu, Pierre. *Zur Soziologie der symbolischen Formen.* Frankfurt/M.: Suhrkamp, 1974 (1970).
Bowring, Richard. "The Background to 'Maihime,'" *MN* 30.2:167–176 (1975).
Brower, Robert H., and Earl Miner. *Japanese Court Poetry.* Stanford: Stanford University Press, 1961.
———, and Earl Miner. "Formative Elements in the Japanese Poetic Tradition." In John A. Harrison, ed., *Japan. Enduring Scholarship Selected from the Far*

Eastern Quarterly—The Journal of Asian Studies, 1941–1971: 30th Anniversary Commemorative Series, vol. II. Tucson: University of Arizona Press, 1972 (1957).
Bungei yōgo no kiso chishiki, comp. Hasegawa Izumi, and Takahashi Shintarō. *KKK* (special edition), March 1976.
Büschen, Ilka. *Sentimentalität: Überlegungen zur Theorie und Untersuchungen an mittelhochdeutschen Epen.* Stuttgart: Kohlhammer, 1974.

Caudill, William A. "Japanese Value Orientations and Culture Change," *Ethnology* (Pittsburgh) 1:53–91 (1962).
———. "The Influence of Social Structure and Culture on Human Behaviour in Modern Japan," *Journal of Nervous and Mental Disease* 157.4:240–257 (1973).
———, and Takeo Doi. "Interrelations of Psychiatry, Culture and Emotion in Japan." In Iago Galdston, ed., *Man's Image in Medicine and Anthropology.* New York: International University Press, 1963.
Chiba Kameo. "The Japanese Psychology as Seen Through Current Literature," *Japan Today and Tomorrow.* Osaka: Osaka Mainichi Pub. Co., 1931/32:2–3.
———. "Recent Literature Tendencies," *Open Court* 47:197–216 (April–May 1933).
*Chiba Masaaki. "Dazai Osamu sakkaron jiten: shishōsetsu," *Dazai Osamu hikkei. Bessatsu KBG,* 7:36–37 (September 1980).

Dazai Osamu. *No Longer Human.* Tr. Donald Keene. Tokyo, Rutland: Tuttle, 1981 (translation first published 1958).
Dazai Osamu zenshū. Vols. I–XII. Tokyo: Chikuma shobō, 1955–1964.
De Vos, George A. *Socialization for Achievement: Essays on the Cultural Psychology of the Japanese.* With contributions by Wagatsuma Hiroshi, William Caudill, and Mizushima Keiichi. Berkeley, Los Angeles, London: University of California Press, 1973.
Doi Takeo. *"Amae" no kōzō.* 13th ed. Tokyo: Kōbundō, 1971.
———. "Omote and Ura: Concepts Derived from the Two-Fold Structure of Consciousness," *Journal of Nervous and Mental Disease* 157.4:258–261 (1973).
———. *Sōseki bungaku ni okeru "amae" no kenkyū.* 9th ed. Tokyo: Kadokawa shoten, 1977 (1972).
Dōke Tadamichi. "Shishōsetsu no kiso," *Bungaku,* December 1953, 49–55.

Eco, Umberto. *Einführung in die Semiotik.* Munich: Fink, 1972.
Eimermacher, Karl. "Zum Problem einer naturwissenschaftlichen Metasprache," *Sprache im technischen Zeitalter* 48:255–277 (1973).
*Enomoto Takashi. "Shishōsetsu, shinkyō shōsetsu," *KBG* (special edition), June 1968, 45–47.
———. "Tayama Katai 'Shōsetsu sahō,'" *KKK,* April 1976, 142–143.
*———. "'Watakushi' no fukkatsu," *KKK,* September 1977, 58–64.
———. "Kawabata Yasunari 'Izu no odoriko,'" *KKK,* April 1978, 84–87.
Erben, Johannes. *Abriß der deutschen Grammatik.* 7th ed. Berlin: Akademie-Verlag, 1964 (1958).

Etō Jun. "An Undercurrent in Modern Japanese Literature," *Journal of Asian Studies* 23:433–445 (1964).
———. "Modern Japanese Literary Criticism," *JQ* 12.2:177–186 (1965).

Fairbank, John K., Edwin O. Reischauer, and Albert M. Craig. *East Asia: Tradition and Transformation.* London: Allen & Unwin, 1973.
Foucault, Michel. "Was ist ein Autor?" In his *Schriften zur Literatur.* Munich: Nymphenburger Verlagsbuchhandlung, 1974 (1969).
Fowler, Edward. "Death and Divine Indifference in 'Dwelling by the Moat,'" *MN* 32.2:230–234 (1977).
Fuji Jintaro, ed. *Outline of Japanese History in the Meiji Era.* Tokyo: Ōbunsha, 1958 (Reprint ed., 1969).
Fujieda Shizuo. "Shi-shishōsetsu," *Subaru,* June 1973, 186–191.
Fukuda Rikutarō. "Japanese Writers: No Longer Insular?" In François Jost, ed., *Actes du 4e Congrès de l'Association Internationale de Littérature Comparée, Fribourg 1964,* vol. II. The Hague: Mouton, 1966.
———, and Muramatsu Sadataka, eds. *Bungaku yōgo kaisetsu jiten.* 3rd ed. Tokyo: Tōkyōdō, 1977 (1971).
*Furui Yoshikichi. "Shishōsetsu o motomete." Review of *Tokuda Shūsei no bungaku,* by Noguchi Fujio. *Asahi jānaru,* 4 April 1980, 61–63.
Furuki Akira. "Kaisetsu: Shiga Naoya kenkyū gaishi." In Nihon bungaku kenkyū shiryō kankōkai, eds., *Shiga Naoya.* Tokyo: Yūseidō shuppan, 1970.
Furuki Tetsutarō. *Taishō no sakka.* Tokyo: Ōfūsha, 1967 (reprint ed.).
Futabatei Shimei zenshū. Vols. I–XVII. Tokyo: Iwanami shoten, 1953–1954.

Gehlen, Arnold. *Die Seele im technischen Zeitalter: Sozialpsychologische Probleme in der industriellen Gesellschaft.* Reinbek: Rowohlt, 1976 (1957).
Gendai bungakuron taikei. Comp. Aono Suekichi, Itō Sei, et al. Vols. I–VIII. Tokyo: Kawade shobō, 1953–1956.
Gendai Nihon bungaku daijiten. Ed. Hisamatsu Sen'ichi, et al., zōtei shukusatsuban. Tokyo: Meiji shoin, 1968.
Gendai Nihon bungaku ronsōshi. Comp. Hirano Ken, Odagiri Hideo, et al., 5th ed. Vols. I–III. Tokyo: Miraisha, 1964 (1956).
Gendai Nihon bungaku taikei. Ed. Takenouchi Shizuo. Vols. I–LXXXXVII. Tokyo: Chikuma shobō, 1968–1973.
Gluck, Jay, ed. *Ukiyo: Stories of 'The Floating World' of Postwar Japan.* New York: Universal Library, 1963.
Goldstein, Bernice Z. and Tamura Kyoko. *Japan and America: A Comparative Study in Language and Culture.* Rutland, Tokyo: Tuttle, 1975.
Günther, Hans. "Die Konzeption der literarischen Evolution im tschechischen Strukturalismus." In Jens Ihwe, ed., *Literaturwissenschaft und Linguistik: Eine Auswahl: Texte zur Theorie der Literaturwissenschaft,* vol. I. Frankfurt/M.: Athenäum-Fischer-Taschenbuch-Verlag, 1972 (1971).

Habermas, Jürgen. *Strukturwandel der Öffentlichkeit: Untersuchungen zu einer Kategorie der bürgerlichen Gesellschaft.* 5th ed. Neuwied, Berlin: Luchterhand, 1971 (1962).

Hamburger, Käte. *Die Logik der Dichtung.* 2nd, strongly altered ed. Stuttgart: Klett, 1968.
Hammitzsch, Horst. "Zum Begriff 'Weg' im Rahmen der japanischen Künste," *NOAG* 82:5–14 (1957).
Hane, Mikiso. *Japan: A Historical Survey.* New York: Charles Scribner's Sons, 1972.
Hara Shirō. "Kindai sakka kara gendai sakka e: Sono buntai no suii," *KKK,* April 1976, 6–16.
Harootunian, Harry D. "Between Politics and Culture: Authority and the Ambiguities of Intellectual Choice in Imperial Japan." In Bernard S. Silberman, and H. D. Harootunian, eds., *Japan in Crisis: Essays in Taisho Democracy.* Princeton: Princeton University Press, 1974.
*Hasegawa Izumi. "Meiji Taishō Shōwa shishōsetsu sanjūgo sen," *KKK,* December 1962, 77–91.
———. "Mori Ōgai," *JQ* 12.2:237–244 (1965).
———. "Shishōsetsu to jiden bungaku," *KBG,* March 1966, 59–64.
———. *Kindai Nihon bungaku shichōshi.* 4th ed. Tokyo: Shibundō, 1967 (1961).
———. *Kindai bungaku kenkyūhō.* 3rd ed. Tokyo: Meiji shoin, 1971 (1966).
———, ed. *Bundanshi jiten.* Tokyo: Shibundō, 1972.
———. *Bungaku no kyokō to jitsuzon.* Tokyo: Shibundō, 1977.
Hashimoto Yoshi. "'Futon' ni kansuru memo." In Nihon bungaku kenkyū shiryō kankōkai, eds., *Shizenshugi bungaku.* Tokyo: Yūseidō shuppan, 1975 (1959).
Hayashi Fumiko. *Sōsaku nōto.* Tokyo: Kantōsha, 1947.
Hayashi Fumiko zenshū. Ed. Satō Yoshio. Vols. I–XXIII. Tokyo: Shinchōsha, 1951–1953.
Hempfer, Klaus W. *Tendenz und Ästhetik: Studien zur französischen Verssatire des 18. Jahrhunderts.* Munich: Fink, 1972.
———. *Gattungstheorie: Information und Synthese.* Munich: Fink, 1973.
Hermand, Jost. "Probleme der heutigen Gattungsgeschichte," *Jahrbuch für internationale Germanistik* 2:85–94 (1970).
*Hibbett, Howard. "The Portrait of the Artist in Japanese Fiction," *Far Eastern Quarterly* 14:347–354 (1954/55).
———. "Sōseki and the Psychological Novel." In Donald H. Shively, ed., *Tradition and Modernization in Japanese Culture.* Princeton: Princeton University Press, 1972.
*———. "Introspective Techniques in Modern Japanese Fiction." In A. R. Davis, ed., *Search for Identity.* Sydney: Angus & Robertson, 1974.
———, ed. *Contemporary Japanese Literature: An Anthology of Fiction, Film, and Other Writing since 1945.* New York: Knopf, 1977.
Hijiya-Kirschnereit, Irmela. "Kritische Bemerkungen zur japanischen Literaturkritik." In Abteilung für Ostasienwissenschaften, Ruhr-Universität Bochum, eds., *Ostasienwissenschaftliche Beiträge zur Sprache, Literatur, Geschichte, Geistesgeschichte, Wirtschaft, Politik und Geographie.* Wiesbaden: Harrassowitz, 1974.
———. *Mishima Yukios Roman "Kyōko-no ie": Versuch einer intratextuellen Analyse.* Wiesbaden: Harrassowitz, 1976.
———. "Abe Kōbō und der Nouveau Roman," *NOAG* 121/122:39–52 (1977).

———. Review of Masao Miyoshi, *Accomplices of Silence: The Modern Japanese Novel. NOAG* 121/122:151–160 (1977).
*———. "Innovation als Renovation: Zur literarhistorischen Bedeutung von Tayama Katais Erzählung 'Futon,'" *Bochumer Jahrbuch zur Ostasienforschung* 1:348–373 (1978).
———. "Die nicht existenten Probleme der modernen japanischen Literaturgeschichtsschreibung." In Fritz Opitz, and Roland Schneider, eds., *Referate des IV. Deutschen Japanologentags in Tübingen.* Mitteilungen der Gesellschaft für Natur- und Völkerkunde Ostasiens, vol. LXXIII. Hamburg, 1978.
———. "Theoriedefizit und Wertungswut: Die nicht existenten Probleme der modernen japanischen Literaturgeschichtsschreibung (2)," *Bochumer Jahrbuch zur Ostasienforschung* 2:286–306 (1979).
———. Review of William F. Sibley, *The Shiga Hero. JJS* 7.1:142–149 (1981).
———. "Wissenschaft als Kunst: Zur Anatomie einer aktuellen Kontroverse in der japanischen Philologie," *Bochumer Jahrbuch zur Ostasienforschung* 4:144–165 (1981).
Hinck, Walter, ed. *Textsortenlehre—Gattungsgeschichte.* Heidelberg: Quelle & Meyer, 1977.
Hinuma Rintarō. *Junbungaku to taishū bungaku no aida.* Tokyo: Kōbundō shinsha, 1967.
*Hirano Ken. *Junbungaku ronsō igo.* Tokyo: Chikuma shobō, 1972.
*———. *Geijutsu to jisseikatsu.* 14th ed. Tokyo: Shinchōsha, 1976 (1958).
———, Odagiri Hideo, and Yamamoto Kenkichi, eds. *Gendai bungaku ronsōshi.* 17th ed., vol. I. Tokyo: Miraisha, 1975 (1956).
*Hiraoka Tokuyoshi. "Shishōsetsu no suitai to tensei," *KBG,* July 1975, 149–155.
*Hiraoka Toshio. "Shishōsetsu no kyokōsei," *KBG,* March 1966, 81–87.
———. "Sengo no bungakushi-zō to Tōkoku-zō," *Bungaku,* September 1969, 12–24.
———. "Ken'yūsha ni okeru Kōyō," *KKK,* May 1978, 35–41.
Hisamatsu Sen'ichi. *The Vocabulary of Japanese Literary Aesthetics.* Tokyo: Asian Cultural Centre for Unesco, 1963.
———, ed. *Zōho shinpan Nihon bungakushi.* Vols. VI and VII (*Kindai,* I and II). Tokyo: Shibundō, 1975.
———. *The Biographical Dictionary of Japanese Literature.* Tokyo, New York, San Francisco: Kodansha International, 1976.
Hopper, Helen M. "Mori Ōgai's Response to Suppression of Intellectual Freedom, 1909–12," *MN* 29.4:381–414 (1974).
*Hoshō Masao. "Senjika ni okeru shishōsetsu sakka," *KBG,* March 1966, 46–53.

Ikari Akira. "Tayama Katai to Mōpassan." In Nihon bungaku kenkyū shiryō kankōkai, eds., *Shizenshugi bungaku.* Tokyo: Yūseidō shuppan, 1975.
*Inagaki Tatsurō. "Shishōsetsu to shōsetsu janru," *Bungaku,* December 1953, 38–41.
*———. "Shishōsetsu." In Nihon bungaku kyōkai, eds., *Nihon no shōsetsu,* vol. II (*Nihon bungaku kōza,* vol. V). Tokyo: Tōkyō daigaku shuppankai, 1955.
*———. "Shishōsetsu o megutte," *KBG,* March 1966, 8–10.
*Ino Kenji. *Zōho kindai Nihon bungakushi kenkyū.* Tokyo: Miraisha, 1964.

Inoue Hiroshi. *Nihon bungakushi shōjiten.* Tokyo: Meiji shoin, 1969.
Inukai Ren. "Tayama Katai to Kagerō nikki," *KKK,* February 1967, 26–28.
*Irisawa Yasuo. "Nakamura Shin'ichirō no shōsetsu ni okeru 'watakushi,'" *KKK,* May 1977, 6–9.
Iser, Wolfgang. *Der Akt des Lesens: Theorie ästhetischer Wirkung.* Munich: Fink, 1976.
Ishida Tadahiko. "Rohan no naka no 'fūryū,'" *KKK,* May 1978, 63–69.
Ishikawa Tatsuzō sakuhinshū. Vols. I–XII. Tokyo: Shinchōsha, 1957–1958.
Isobe Tadamasa. *"Mujō" no kōzō.* Tokyo: Kōdansha, 1976.
*Isogai Hideo. "Shishōsetsu no seiritsu to henshitsu," *KBG,* July 1967, 48–54.
———. "Shōwa bungaku no sei to fu: Hyōka no kijiku o megutte," *Shōwa no bungaku,* vol. I. (*Gendai bungaku kōza,* vol. V). *KKK* (bessatsu), November 1974, 113–140.
*———. "Inoue Yasushi to shishōsetsu," *KBG,* March 1975, 81–86.
Itagaki Naoko. "Kaisetsu." In Hayashi Fumiko, *Hōrōki.* 77th ed. Tokyo: Shinchōsha, 1977 (1947).
Itō Sei. "Rise of Naturalism (Modern Japanese Literature V)," *JQ* 2.4:509–515 (1955).
———. "Modes of Thought in Contemporary Japan," *JQ* 12.4:501–514 (1965).
*———. *Shōsetsu no hōhō.* 16th ed. Tokyo: Kawade shobō, 1971 (1957).
———, Hotta Yoshie, Takeda Taijun, and Mishima Yukio. "Nihon no genjitsu to atarashii bungaku no kanōsei" (zadankai), *Sekai,* April 1956, 134–152.
Itō Sei zenshū. Ed. Senuma Shigeki. Vols. I–XIV. Tokyo: Kawade shobō, 1955–1956.
Iwanaga Yutaka. *Tayama Katai kenkyū.* Tokyo: Hakuyōsha, 1956.

Jansen, Marius B. "The Meiji Restoration." In David Wurfel, ed., *Meiji Japan's Centennial: Aspects of Political Thought and Action.* Lawrence, Manhattan, Wichita: University Press of Kansas, 1971.
Jauß, Hans Robert. "Theorie der Gattungen und Literatur des Mittelalters." In Hans Robert Jauß, and Erich Köhler, eds., *Grundriß der romanischen Literaturen des Mittelalters,* vol. V. Heidelberg: Winter, 1972.
Jolles, André. *Einfache Formen.* 2nd ed. Darmstadt: Wissenschaftliche Buchgesellschaft, 1958 (1930).

Kakeda Katsumi. "Hametsugata sakka no seishin byōri: Dazai Osamu no hito to sakuhin o chūshin ni" (1958), *Gendai no esupuri* 51, July 1971, 210–222.
*Kamei Hideo. "'Watakushi' satei no shomondai: Bungaku ni okeru 'watakushi,'" *Bungakushi no shomondai* (*Gendai bungaku kōza,* vol. VIII). *KKK* (bessatsu), January 1975, 112–137.
———. "Kaisetsu." In Hirano Ken, *Geijutsu to jisseikatsu.* 14th ed. Tokyo: Shinchōsha, 1976 (1964).
*Kamei Katsuichirō. "Shishōsetsu ni tsuite no kansō," *Kanshō to kenkyū: Gendai Nihon bungaku kōza,* vol. X (*Hyōron zuihitsu* 3, *Shōwa-ki*). Tokyo: Sanseidō, 1963.
Kamiya Tadataka. "'Shakaika shita watakushi' no tassei," *KKK,* March 1977, 116–122.

*Kanbayashi Akatsuki. "Shishōsetsu no unmei," *Bungei,* January 1947, 43–49.
Karaki Junzō. *Mujō.* Tokyo: Chikuma shobō, 1973 (1964).
*Karatani Yukihito [Kōjin]. "Shishōsetsu no keifugaku," *KBG,* December 1978, 116–121.
Kasai Zenzō. *Ko o tsurete.* Tokyo: Shinchōsha, 1919.
*Katō Shūichi. "IN EGOISTOS," *Kanshō to kenkyū: Gendai Nihon bungaku kōza,* vol. X (*Hyōron zuihitsu* 3, *Shōwa-ki*). Tokyo: Sanseidō, 1963.
———. "Japanese Writers and Modernization." In Marius B. Jansen, ed., *Changing Japanese Attitudes Toward Modernization.* Princeton: Princeton University Press, 1965.
———. *Form, Style, Tradition: Reflexions on Japanese Art and Society.* Berkeley, Los Angeles, London, Tokyo: University of California Press, 1971.
Katsumoto Seiichirō. "'Haru' o toku kagi." Nihon bungaku shiryō kankōkai, eds., *Shimazaki Tōson.* 3rd ed. Tokyo: Yūseidō shuppan, 1973 (1951).
*Katsuyama Isao. "Shoki shishōsetsuron ni tsuite: Shishōsetsuron-shi josetsu," *Kokugo to kokubungaku,* December 1953, 46–55.
*———. "Shishōsetsu, shinkyō shōsetsu." In Kindai bungaku kondankai, eds., *Kindai bungaku kenkyū hikkei.* 2nd ed. Tokyo: Gakutōsha, 1965 (1961).
*———. "Taishō-ki ni okeru shishōsetsuron o megutte," *KBG,* February 1965, 68–74.
*———. "Taishō-ki ni okeru shishōsetsu no keifu," *KBG,* March 1966, 32–37.
*———. "Uno Kōji ni okeru shi to yume," *Taishō no bungaku* (*Gendai bungaku kōza,* vol. IV). *KKK* (bessatsu), May 1975, 124–145.
Kawai Hiroshi. "Dazai Osamu no byōshi" (1963), *Gendai no esupuri* 51, July 1971, 233–237.
Kawakami Tetsutarō. "Kaisetsu." In Nakamura Mitsuo, *Fūzoku shōsetsuron.* 14th ed. Tokyo: Shinchōsha, 1970 (1958).
*Kawasaki Chōtarō. "Shishōsetsu ni tsuite," *KKK,* December 1962, 52–54.
Kawauchi Mitsuharu. "Akutagawa shō sakuhin jiten: dai yonjūyon kai: Shinobugawa, Miura Tetsuo," *Akutagawa-shō jiten. KKK* (enlarged special ed.), January 1977, 320–321.
Kazamaki Keijirō. *Sakuhin o chūshin to shita Nihon bungakushi.* Tokyo: Kadokawa shoten, 1965.
Keene, Dennis. "The Shinkankakuha: A Japanese Literary Movement of the Nineteen Twenties," *Transactions of the International Conference of Orientalists in Japan* (The Toho Gakkai) 16:36–52 (1971).
———. "Flaubert and Yokomitsu: Does Stylistic Influence Take Place?" *Transactions of the International Conference of Orientalists in Japan* (The Toho Gakkai) 17:39–72 (1972).
———. "Looking at a Foreign Country: Yokomitsu and Malraux." In The Japan P.E.N. Club, eds., *Studies on Japanese Culture,* vol. I. Tokyo, 1973.
Keene, Donald. "Japanese Literature and Politics in the 1930s," *JJS* 2.2:225–248 (1976).
Kenmochi Takehiko. "Kōyō: sono sakuhin," *KKK,* May 1978, 157–160.
Kikuchi Kan. *History and Trends of Modern Japanese Literature.* Ed. Kokusai bunka shinkōkai. Tokyo: Kokusai bunka shinkōkai, 1936.
Kikuchi Kan zenshū. Vols. I–III. Tokyo: Kaizōsha, 1931–1932.

Kikuta Shigeo. "Chūko nikki, zuihitsu kenkyū no gendankai," *KBG,* May 1967, 37–45.
Kimura Ki. "Kōyō, Rohan, Ichiyō no kyōtsūsei to idōsei," *KKK,* May 1978, 6–14.
Kimura Shozaburo. "Gespräch zwischen Ost und West steht erst am Anfang," *Neues aus Japan* 258.1:11–13 (1979).
*Kimura Yukio. "Shishōsetsu to shakaisei," *KBG,* March 1966, 87–92.
Kindai bungaku hyōron taikei. Comp. Yoshida Seiichi, and Asai Kiyoshi. Vols. I–X. Tokyo: Kadokawa shoten, 1971–1975.
Kindaichi Haruhiko. *Nihonjin no gengo hyōgen.* Tokyo: Kōdansha, 1975.
Kobayashi Hideo. "Cartoons," *JQ* 12.2:212–215 (1965).
———. *X e no tegami, Watakushishōsetsuron.* 18th ed. (revised 8th ed., 1970). Tokyo: Shinchōsha, 1976.
Kobayashi Hideo zenshū. Vols. I–XII. Tokyo: Shinchōsha, 1967–1968.
Kobayashi Ichirō. "Katai bungaku o sasaete iru mono: Nihon shizenshugi bungaku no seikaku." In Nihon bungaku kenkyū shiryō kankōkai, eds., *Shizenshugi bungaku.* Tokyo: Ōfūsha, 1975 (1960).
———. *Tayama Katai kenkyū: Tatebayashi jidai.* Tokyo: Ōfūsha, 1976.
Kohl, Stephen W. "Shiga Naoya: A Critical Biography." Ph.D. dissertation, University of Washington, 1974.
*———. "Shiga Naoya and the Literature of Experience," *MN* 32.2:211–217 (1977).
Köhn, Lothar. *Entwicklungs- und Bildungsroman: Ein Forschungsbericht.* Stuttgart: Metzler, 1969.
*Kojima Nobuo, Hirano Ken, and Yasuoka Shōtarō. "Bungaku ni okeru 'watakushi' to wa nani ka" (zadankai), *Bungei,* November 1968, 234–255.
*Kokubo Minoru. "Shishōsetsu no seiritsu 1," *Kokubungaku* (Kansai daigaku) 14, June 1955, 49–62.
*———. "Shishōsetsu no seiritsu 2," *Kokubungaku* (Kansai daigaku) 15, December 1955, 37–52.
Kokugogaku jiten. 23rd ed. Comp. Kokugo gakkai. Tokyo: Tōkyōdō, 1973 (1955).
*Kōno Toshirō. "Shishōsetsu ni okeru Shirakaba-ha no yakuwari," *KBG,* March 1966, 26–32.
*———. "Joryū bungaku ni okeru 'watakushi,'" *KBG,* July 1976, 65–69.
———. "Satomi Ton 'Kimi to watakushi to': Shiga Naoya banare ni tsuite," *Waseda bungaku,* July 1977, 19–21.
———, Miyoshi Yukio, Takeuchi Ten'yū, and Hiraoka Toshio, eds., *Meiji no bungaku.* Tokyo: Yūhikaku, 1972.
——— et al., eds. *Taishō no bungaku.* Tokyo: Yūhikaku, 1972.
——— et al., eds. *Shōwa no bungaku.* Tokyo: Yūhikaku, 1972.
Kōnoshi Takamitsu. "Genji monogatari no isō: Genji monogatari bukkyō shisō no mondaiten," *Genji monogatari,* vol. I. (*Kōza Nihon bungaku*). *KKK* (bessatsu), May 1978, 114–133.
Kōsaka Masaaki. "The Status and Role of the Individual in Japanese Society." In Charles A. Moore, ed., with the assistance of Aldyth W. Morris, *The Status of the Individual in East and West.* Honolulu: University of Hawaii Press, 1968.

———, ed. *Japanese Thought in the Meiji Era*. Reprint ed. Tr. and adapted by David Abosh. Tokyo, 1969 (Pan-Pacific Press, 1958).
Kōyō zenshū. Vols. I–IV. Tokyo: Hakubunkan, 1906–1913.
Kressler, O. "Mono no aware: Interpretation bei Motoori Norinaga und die Rasa-Lehre der altindischen Poetik." Mitteilungen der Gesellschaft für Natur- und Völkerkunde Ostasiens, vol. XXV/B. 98–111 (1935).
*Kubota Masabumi. "Shishōsetsu to tankateki jojō," *KBG*, March 1966, 71–74.
Kume Masao. "Watakushishōsetsu to shinkyō shōsetsu." In *Kume Masao zenshū*, vol. XIII. Tokyo: Heibonsha, 1930 (1925).
*Kurahara Korehito. "Shishōsetsu shikan," *Bungaku*, December 1953, 73–76.

LaFleur, William R. "Death and Japanese Thought: The Truth and Beauty of Impermanence." In Frederick Holck, ed., *Death and Eastern Thought: Understanding Death in Eastern Religions and Philosophies*. Nashville, New York: Abingdon, 1974.
Lämmert, Eberhard. *Bauformen des Erzählens*. 4th ed. Stuttgart: Metzler, 1970 (1955).
Lane, Richard. "Saikaku and the Modern Japanese Novel." In Edward Skrzypczak, ed., *Japan's Modern Century* (special issue of *MN*). Tokyo, Rutland: Tuttle, 1968.
Laplanche, J., and J. B. Pontalis. *Das Vokabular der Psychoanalyse*. 2 vols. Frankfurt/M.: Suhrkamp, 1973.
Lebra, Takie Sugiyama, and William P. Lebra. *Japanese Culture and Behaviour: Selected Readings*. Honolulu: University of Hawaii Press, 1974.
———. *Japanese Patterns of Behaviour*. Honolulu: University of Hawaii Press, 1976.
Lecke, Bodo. *Das Stimmungsbild: Musikmetaphorik und Naturgefühl in der dichterischen Prosaskizze 1721–1780*. Göttingen: Vandenhoeck & Ruprecht, 1967.
Lejeune, Philippe. "Le pacte autobiographique," *Poétique* 14:137–162 (1973).
Lewin, Bruno. *Futabatei Shimei in seinen Beziehungen zur russischen Literatur*. Hamburg: Gesellschaft für Natur- und Völkerkunde Ostasiens, 1955.
———. *Japanische Chrestomathie von der Nara-Zeit bis zur Edo-Zeit*, vol. I (*Kommentar*). Wiesbaden: Harrassowitz, 1965.
———. "Denkweise und sprachlicher Ausdruck in Japan." In *Das Gespräch*. Hannover: Friedrich-Rauch-Institut, 1967.
———, ed. *Japanische Literaturwissenschaft: Fachtexte*. Wiesbaden: Harrassowitz, 1981.
Linhart, Ruth. *Ishikawa Takuboku und der japanische Naturalismus: Ein Beitrag zur Ergänzung des Takuboku-Bildes in der japanischen Literaturgeschichte*. Vienna: Institut für Japanologie an der Universität Wien, 1971.
———. "Some Analogies and Differences of Japanese and German Naturalism." In The Japan P.E.N. Club, eds., *Studies on Japanese Culture*, vol. I. Tokyo, 1973.
Linke Literatur in Japan: 1912–1923. Munich: University of Munich (Seminar für Japanologie), 1973.
Lockemann, Wolfgang. "Textsorten versus Gattungen oder ist das Ende der Kunstwissenschaft unvermeidlich?" *Germanisch-Romanische Monatsschrift* 24: 284–304 (1974).

Lotman, Jurij M. *Die Struktur literarischer Texte.* Munich: Fink, 1972.
Luther, Wilhelm. *Sprachphilosophie als Grundwissenschaft: Ihre Bedeutung für die wissenschaftliche Grundlagenbildung und die sozialpolitische Erziehung.* Heidelberg: Quelle & Meyer, 1970.

Maeda Ai. *Kindai dokusha no seiritsu.* Tokyo: Yūseidō shuppan, 1973.
Maraini, Fosco. "Japan and the Future: Some Suggestions from Nihonjinron Literature." In Gianni Fodella, ed., *Social Structures and Economic Dynamics in Japan up to 1980.* Series on East Asian Economy and Society, vol. I. Milan: Luigi Bocconi University (Institute of Economic and Social Studies for East Asia), 1975.
*Maruyama Masao. "From Carnal Literature to Carnal Politics." In Maruyama Masao, *Thought and Behaviour in Modern Japanese Politics,* ed. Ivan Morris. London, New York: Oxford University Press, 1963.
———. "Patterns of Individuation and the Case of Japan: A Conceptual Scheme." In Marius B. Jansen, ed., *Changing Japanese Attitudes Toward Modernization.* Princeton: Princeton University Press, 1965.
Masamune Hakuchō. "Iwano Hōmei." In *Iwano Hōmei, Chikamatsu Shūkō shū* (*Gendai Nihon bungaku zenshū,* vol. XIII). Tokyo: Chikuma shobō, 1954.
Masamune Hakuchō zenshū. Vols. I–XIII. Tokyo: Shinchōsha, 1976.
Mathy, Francis. "Mono no aware," *Occasional Papers* 11 (*Japanese Culture* II). East Lansing: Michigan State University, 1969.
———. *Shiga Naoya.* New York: Twayne, 1974.
*Matsubara Shin'ichi. *"Gusha" no bungaku.* Tokyo: Tōjusha, 1974.
Matsuda Michio. *Nihon chishikijin no shisō.* 11th ed. Tokyo: Chikuma shobō, 1973.
Matsumoto Shigeru. *Motoori Norinaga: 1730–1801.* Cambridge: Harvard University Press, 1970.
*Matsumoto Tōru. "'Kindaiteki jiga' to gendai bungaku," *KKK,* December 1979, 32–39.
*Matsumoto Tsuruo. "Bungaku, shishōsetsu to jiko shōshitsu no jidai," *Kikan sōzō* 2.1:231–238 (1977).
*———. "Kindai bungei yōshiki nōto (1): Shishōsetsushi shomondai to Shimao Toshio," *Kenkyū nenpō* (Nihon daigaku bunri gakubu) 28.2:32–45 (1980).
May, Ekkehard, and Karl Maurer. "Eine japanische 'Theorie der Prosa'? Ryūnosuke Akutagawas Essays zur 'historischen Erzählung' und zur 'Erzählung ohne geschichtenähnliche "Geschichte,"'" *Poetica* 4.2:251–266 (1971).
*McClellan, Edwin. "The Impressionistic Tendency in Some Modern Japanese Writers," *Chicago Review* 17.4:48–60 (1965).
———. *Two Japanese Novelists: Sōseki and Tōson.* Chicago, London: University of Chicago Press, 1969.
*———. "Tōson and the Autobiographical Novel." In Donald H. Shively, ed., *Tradition and Modernization in Japanese Culture.* Princeton: Princeton University Press, 1971.
*———. "Some General Comments on Shishōsetsu." In The Japan P.E.N. Club, eds., *Studies on Japanese Culture,* vol. I. Tokyo, 1973.
Meiji bungaku zenshū. Vols. I–LXXXXVII. Tokyo: Chikuma shobō, 1965–1974.

Melanowicz, Mikolaj. "Narrator and Character in Japanese Prose: A Discussion Based on Tanizaki Jun'ichirō's Work," *Zagadnienia rodzajów literackich* 19.2: 63–83 (1976).

Minami Hiroshi. *Psychology of the Japanese People.* Tr. Albert R. Ikoma. Tokyo: University of Tokyo Press, 1971 (1953).

Miner, Earl. "Toward a New Conception of Classical Japanese Poetics." In The Japan P.E.N. Club, eds., *Studies on Japanese Culture*, vol. I. Tokyo, 1973.

———. Introduction to *Japanese Poetic Diaries.* Berkeley, Los Angeles: University of California Press, 1976 (1969).

*Miura Tetsuo. "Watakushi to shishōsetsu," *KKK,* December 1962, 54–56.

———. *Shinobugawa.* 31st ed. Tokyo: Shinchōsha, 1977 (1965).

*Miyagi Otoya. "Shishōsetsu no shinrigaku: Kasai Zenzō o yonde," *Bungaku,* December 1953, 42–48.

Miyauchi Yutaka. "Kobayashi Hideo to gendai hihyō," *KKK,* August 1975, 62–65.

Miyazaki Sōhei. "Kindai sakka no 'Kagerō nikki' kan," *KKK,* September 1978, 157–168.

*Miyoshi Yukio. "Shishōsetsu ni wa donna tēma ga aru ka," *KKK,* December 1962, 49.

———. *Mori Ōgai.* 2nd ed. (*Kindai bungaku chūshaku taikei*). Tokyo: Yūseidō shuppan, 1966.

*———. "Shōwa ni okeru shishōsetsu sakka," *KBG,* March 1966, 43–64.

*———. *Sakuhinron no kokoromi.* 4th ed. Tokyo: Shibundō, 1970 (1967).

*———. *Nihon bungaku no kindai to hankindai.* Tokyo: Tōkyō daigaku shuppankai, 1972.

*———. *Nihon no kindai bungaku.* 2nd ed. Tokyo: Hanawa shobō, 1976 (1972).

———, ed. *Nihon kindai bungaku kenkyū hikkei.* 2nd ed. Tokyo: Gakutōsha, 1977.

———. "Dazai Osamu: Hito to bungaku," *Dazai Osamu hikkei. Bessatsu KBG,* 7:6–8 (September 1980).

*———, Takahashi Hideo, and Yoshida Hiroo. "Kyōdō tōgi: 'Watakushishōsetsuron' o megutte," *KBG,* February 1980, 60–81.

Möhrmann, Renate. *Der vereinsamte Mensch: Studien zum Wandel des Einsamkeitsmotivs im Roman von Raabe bis Musil.* Bonn: Bouvier, 1974.

Moore, Charles A., ed. *The Japanese Mind: Essentials of Japanese Philosophy and Culture.* Honolulu: University of Hawaii Press, 1967.

Mori Ōgai zenshū. Vols. I–VIII. Tokyo: Chikuma shobō, 1965.

*Morikawa Tatsuya. "Shishōsetsu hōhōka no mondai: Futatabi shishōsetsuron o," *Kindai bungaku,* August 1961, 1–17.

*———. "Bungaku wa hirakareru: 'Kūkyo' no naka de, bungaku wa ima . . . : Shinsedai no tachiba to hachijū nendai," *Subaru* 2.4:190–198 (1980).

*Morishige, Alyce Hisae Kawazoe. "The Theme of the Self in Modern Japanese Fiction: Studies on Dazai, Mishima, Abé, and Kawabata." Ph.D. dissertation, Michigan State University, 1970.

Morris, Ivan, ed. *Modern Japanese Stories: An Anthology.* Tokyo, Rutland: Tuttle, 1962.

———. *The Nobility of Failure: Tragic Heroes in the History of Japan.* London: Secker & Warburg, 1975.

———. "Japanese Heroes and Hero Worship," *The Japan Foundation Newsletter* 4.3:8–12 (1976).

Morrison, John W. *Modern Japanese Fiction.* Salt Lake City: University of Utah Press, 1955.
Müller, Klaus-Detlef. *Autobiographie und Roman: Studien zur literarischen Autobiographie der Goethezeit.* Tübingen, 1976.
Nakai Yoshiyuki. "Ōgai's Craft: Literary Techniques and Themes in 'Vita Sexualis,'" *MN* 35.2:223–240 (1980).
*Nakamura Mitsuo. "Shishōsetsu ni tsuite," *Bungakukai,* September 1935, 70–92.
———. "Tayama Katai ron." In Yoshida Seiichi et al., eds. *Tōson, Katai (Kokugo kokubungaku kenkyūshi taisei,* vol. XIII). Tokyo: Sanseidō, 1960 (1945).
———. *Nihon no kindai shōsetsu.* 23rd ed. Tokyo: Iwanami shoten, 1969 (1954).
*———. *Fūzoku shōsetsuron.* 14th ed. Tokyo: Shinchōsha, 1970 (1958).
———. *Nihon no gendai shōsetsu.* 4th ed. Tokyo: Iwanami shoten, 1970 (1968).
———. *Shōsetsu nyūmon.* 23rd ed. Tokyo: Shinchōsha, 1977 (1959).
*———. "Taishō bungaku no shūen," *Asahi jānaru,* 10 June 1977, 42–44.
*———. "'Hanashi no nai shōsetsu' o megutte," *Asahi jānaru,* 17 June 1977, 42-44.
*———. "Shishōsetsu e no kuppuku," *Asahi jānaru,* 24 June 1977, 42–44.
Nakamura Murao. "Honkaku shōsetsu to shinkyō shōsetsu to," *Shinshōsetsu,* January 1924, 18–24.
*Nakamura Shin'ichirō. "Shishōsetsu to jikken shōsetsu," *Bungakukai,* April 1961, 5–7.
*Nakamura Yū. "Taishō-ki shishōsetsu ni matsuwaru oboegaki (1)," *Gakuen* 445.1: 165–174 (1977).
Nakane Chie. *Japanese Society.* Harmondsworth: Penguin, 1973 (Weidenfeld & Nicholson, 1970).
Nakano Hideichirō. "A Framework of Comparative Culture Analysis: Japanese Normative Culture Reconsidered," *Kwansei Gakuin University: Annual Studies* 21:65–76 (1972).
Naruse Masakatsu. *Shōwa bungaku jūyon kō.* Tokyo: Yūbun shoin, 1966.
Neumann, Bernd. *Identität und Rollenzwang: Zur Theorie der Autobiographie.* Frankfurt/M.: Athenäum, 1970.
"New Phases in Japanese Literature: Proletarian, Bourgeois, Modern and Storytelling Groups," *Present-Day Nippon: Annual English Edition* (Osaka), 1931.
Nihon kindai bungaku taikei. Ed. Itō Sei et al. Vols. I–LX. Tokyo: Kadokawa shoten, 1969–1971.
Nihon kokugo daijiten. Ed. Nihon daijiten kankōkai. Vols. I–XX. Tokyo: Shōgakkan, 1972–1976.
Nihon koten bungaku taikei. Vols. I-C. Tokyo: Iwanami shoten, 1957–1967.
Nihon koten bungaku zenshū. Ed. Akiyama Ken, Ichiko Teiji, et al. Vols. I–LI. Tokyo: Shōgakkan, 1971–1975.
Niizeki Ryōzō. "Nihon geidōron." In Niizeki Ryōzō, *Nihon engekiron.* Tokyo: Unebi shobō, 1942.
*Nishimura Kōji. "Jiden bungaku: Igirisu no baai," *KKK,* December 1962, 20–24.
Nitobe Inazo et al. *Western Influences in Modern Japan.* Chicago: University of Chicago Press, 1931.
Noda Utarō. *Mori Ōgai.* 7th ed. Tokyo: Chikuma shobō, 1964 (1957).

*Nomura Seiichi. "'Kagerō nikki' wa 'shishōsetsu' ka," *KKK*, September 1978, 103–113.

Ōba Shunsuke. *Nihon bungaku no keitō.* Tokyo: Ashi shobō, 1965.
O'Brien, James A. *Dazai Osamu.* New York: Twayne, 1975.
*Odagiri Hideo. *Shishōsetsu, shinkyō shōsetsu.* 2nd ed. (*Iwanami kōza Nihon bungakushi,* vol. XII). Tokyo: Iwanami shoten, 1960 (1958).
———. "Japanese Literature in 1979," The Japanese P.E.N. Club, eds., *Japanese Literature Today* 5.3:1–14 (1980).
*Ōe Kenzaburō. "Shishōsetsu ni tsuite," *Gunzō,* September 1961, 192–197.
*Ogasawara Masaru. "Taishō-ki ni okeru 'watakushi'-shōsetsu no ron ni tsuite," *Kokugo kokubun kenkyū,* November 1958, 63–84.
*———. "Shishōsetsu no seiritsu to hensen: chūshakuteki oboegaki," *KKK,* December 1962, 34–42.
*———. "'Junbungaku' no mondai: 'Junsui shōsetsuron' zengo," *Bungaku,* September 1969, 25–45.
*———. "Shishōsetsu no biishiki: Sono kyokuhoku," *KKK,* November 1969, 32–37.
*———. "Shishōsetsu no seiritsu o megutte." In Ogasawara Masaru, *Shōwa bungaku shiron.* Tokyo: Yagi shoten, 1970.
Ogata Akiko. "'Futon' zenya: 'Onna kyōshi' kara 'Shōjobyō' made," *Bungei to hihyō* 4.6:43–52 (1976).
———. "'Futon' shiron," *Kokubungaku kenkyū* (Waseda daigaku) 60.10:41–53 (1976).
*Ogawa Kunio, and Furui Yoshikichi. "Genkei e no shikō" (taidan), *KKK,* March 1977, 14–32.
*Okaya Kōji. "Misheru Rerisu no 'watakushi,'" *Waseda bungaku,* July 1977, 28–30.
Okazaki Yoshie. *Japanese Literature in the Meiji Era.* Tr. and adapted by V. H. Viglielmo. Tokyo: Ōbunsha, 1955.
Oketani Hideaki. *Gyōshi to hōkō,* vol. I. 2nd ed. Tokyo: Tōjusha, 1973 (1971).
*Ōkōchi Shōji. "Jiga no kyoten to shite no nichijō: Kuroi Senji to Furui Yoshikichi no sakuhin o megutte," *KKK,* September 1977, 120–126.
Ōkubo Kanji. "Geruharuto Hauputoman." In Fukuda Mitsuharu et al., eds., *Ōbei sakka to Nihon kindai bungaku,* vol. IV (*Doitsu hen*). Tokyo: Kyōiku shuppan sentā, 1974.
Ōkubo Tadatoshi. "Dazai Osamu e no buntaironteki sekkin: 'Ningen shikkaku' no buntaiteki tokuchō." In Nihon bungaku kenkyū shiryō kankōkai, eds., *Dazai Osamu.* Tokyo: Yūseidō shuppan, 1970.
*Ōkubo Tsuneo. "Shizenshugi to shishōsetsu," *KBG,* March 1966, 20–26.
———. "'Futon,' Tayama Katai: bungakushiteki ichizuke," *KBG,* July 1968, 125–129.
*———. "'Dai san no shinjin' to katei shōsetsu," *KBG,* June 1973, 132–139.
*———. *Iwano Hōmei no jidai.* Tokyo: Tōjusha, 1973.
———. "Senchū, sengo no Kobayashi Hideo," *KBG,* August 1975, 56–61.
———, and Yoshida Hiroo, eds. *Gendai sakka jiten.* Tokyo: Tōkyōdō, 1973.
Okuno Takeo. *Dazai Osamu ron.* 28th ed. Tokyo: Kadokawa shoten, 1976 (1960).

*———. *Nihon bungakushi: Kindai kara gendai e.* 10th ed. Tokyo: Chūō kōronsha, 1976 (1970).
———. "Kaisetsu." In Dazai Osamu, *Ningen shikkaku.* 71st ed. Tokyo: Shinchōsha, 1977 (1972).
———. "Kaisetsu." In Miura Tetsuo, *Shinobugawa.* 31st ed. Tokyo: Shinchōsha, 1977 (1965).
Olney, James. *Metaphors of Self: The Meaning of Autobiography.* Princeton: Princeton University Press, 1972.
*Ōmori Sumio. "Kasai Zenzō to shishōsetsu," *Taishō no bungaku* (*Gendai bungaku kōza,* vol. IV). *KKK* (bessatsu), May 1975, 103–123.
Ōnishi Tadao. "Mōpassan to sono Nihon e no eikyō." In Kawauchi Kiyoshi, ed., *Shizenshugi bungaku.* Tokyo: Keisō shobō, 1962.
*Ōoka Shōhei, and Nakano Kōji. "Tokubetsu taidan: Jiko kenshō no bungaku," *Bungakukai,* May 1979, 222–235.
*Ōta Seiichi. "Zangemichi to shite no shishōsetsu no keifu," *Bungaku,* February 1961, 46–53.
*Ozaki Kazuo. "Shishōsetsu to watakushi," *KKK,* December 1962, 50–52.
Ozaki Kōyō. See *Kōyō zenshū.*

Pascal, Roy. *Die Autobiographie: Gehalt und Gestalt.* Stuttgart, Berlin, Cologne, Mainz: Kohlhammer, 1965 (1960).
Posner, Roland. "Strukturalismus in der Gedichtinterpretation." In Jens Ihwe, ed., *Literaturwissenschaft und Linguistik: Eine Auswahl: Texte zur Theorie der Literaturwissenschaft.* Vol. I. Frankfurt/M.: Athenäum-Fischer-Taschenbuch-Verlag, 1972 (1971).
Powell, Irena. "Itō Sei's Concept of Hōki and Chōwa in Modern Japanese Literature." In The Japan P.E.N. Club, eds., *Studies on Japanese Culture,* vol. I. Tokyo, 1973.
*Power, J. B. "Shiga Naoya and the Shishōsetsu." In A. R. Davis, ed., *Search for Identity.* Sydney: Angus & Robertson, 1974.
Putzar, Edward. *Japanese Literature: A Historical Outline.* Tucson: University of Arizona Press, 1973.
Pyle, Kenneth B. *The New Generation in Meiji Japan: Problems of Cultural Identity, 1885–1895.* Stanford: Stanford University Press, 1969.

Richter, Frederick. "Tayama Katai and Two Narrative Modes of Japanese Literary Naturalism," *Literature East and West* 15.4 and 16.1 and 2:773–789.
Rimer, J. Thomas. *Mori Ōgai.* New York: Twayne, 1975.
Roggendorf, Joseph. "Shimazaki Tōson: A Maker of the Modern Japanese Novel," *MN* 7.1:40–66 (1951).
Romberg, Bertil. *Studies in the Narrative Technique of the First-Person Novel.* Stockholm: Almquist & Wiksell, 1962.
Ryan, Marleigh Grayer. *Japan's First Modern Novel: Ukigumo of Futabatei Shimei: Translation and Critical Commentary.* New York, London: Columbia University Press, 1967.
———. *The Development of Realism in the Fiction of Tsubouchi Shōyō.* Seattle, London: University of Washington Press, 1975.

*———. "Modern Japanese Fiction: Accommodated Truth," *JJS* 2.2:249–266 (1976).

*Saegusa Hiroto. "Shishōsetsu no 'watakushi' no minamoto," *Bungaku,* December 1953, 62–65.

Saegusa Yasutaka. *Nihon romanha no gunzō.* Tokyo: Yūshindō, 1967.

*Saeki Shōichi. "Kindai Nihon no jiden (1): Watakushigatari no riariti," *Gunzō,* January 1980, 326–336.

*———, Ueda Miyoji, Isoda Kōichi, and Aeba Takao. "Kyōdō tōgi 'Shishōsetsu,'" *Bungakukai,* February 1980, 148–175.

Saitō Kiyoe. *Nihon bungei shichōshi.* Tokyo: Nan'undō Ōfūsha, 1963.

———. "Kokubungaku no janru." In *Nihon bungaku kenkyū no shomondai* (*Kōza Nihon bungaku,* vol. XII). Tokyo: Sanseidō, 1969.

Sakagami Hiroichi. "Bungaku o ajiwau yomikata." In Hirai Masao, and Ōkuma Gorō, eds., *Jōhōka jidai no kotoba no seikatsu. KKK* (bessatsu), April 1976, 66–97.

Sakita Susumu. "'Kamen no kokuhaku' shiron: 'Kamen' to 'kokuhaku' no nazo o megutte," *Kanazawa daigaku gogaku, bungaku kenkyū* 9.1:12–17 (1979).

Sako Jun'ichirō. *Bungaku o dō yomu ka.* 39th ed. Tokyo: Shakai shisōsha, 1976 (1958).

*Sakurai Yoshio. "Shishōsetsu ni tsuite," *Mito hyōron* 9.11:39–46 (1979).

Sasabuchi Tomoichi. *Meiji Taishō bungaku no bunseki.* Tokyo: Meiji shoin, 1970.

*Sasaki Kiichi. "Shishōsetsu, shinkyō shōsetsu." In Nihon kindai bungakukan, eds., *Nihon kindai bungakushi.* Tokyo: Yomiuri shinbunsha, 1966.

Satō Etsuko. "Kobayashi Hideo ni okeru 'Shiga Naoya': Hihyō no 'watakushi' ni tsuite," *Nihon bungaku nōto* 3.9:1–21 (1976).

Satō Haruo. "Kaisetsu." In *Tayama Katai zenshū,* vol. XIV. Tokyo: Bunsengaku shoten, 1974.

*Satō Kōichi. "Ihi romān," *KKK,* December 1962, 10–14.

*Satō Masaru. "Puroretaria bungaku ni okeru shishōsetsu," *KBG,* March 1966, 37–43.

*Satō Yasumasa. "Shishōsetsu no keifu: Shiga Naoya o koeru mono," *KKK,* March 1977, 90–97.

*———. "Jiishiki no kussetsu: 'Hōyō kazoku' o jiku to shite," *KKK,* September 1977, 65–72.

Schamoni, Wolfgang. "Die Entwicklung der Romantheorie in der japanischen Aufklärungsperiode," *NOAG* 118:9–39 (1975).

Schlötke-Schröer, Charlotte, "Selbstaussage und Kulturproblematik im französischen Roman des 19. Jahrhunderts." In G. Reichenkron, and E. Haase, eds., *Formen der Selbstdarstellung: Analekten zu einer Geschichte des literarischen Selbstportraits: Festgabe für Fritz Neubert.* Berlin: Duncker & Humblot, 1956.

Schmidt, Carl P. "The Modern Japanese Novel: Form and Feeling," *Asia* 22:53–71 (1971).

Schmidt, Siegfried J. *Ästhetizität.* Munich: Bayerischer Schulbuch-Verlag, 1971.

———. "Ist Fiktionalität eine linguistische oder eine texttheoretische Kategorie?"

In Elisabeth Gülich, and Wolfgang Raible, eds., *Textsorten.* Frankfurt/M.: Athenäum, 1972.
Schober, Wolfgang Heinz. *Erzähltechniken in Romanen: Eine Untersuchung erzähltechnischer Probleme in zeitgenössischen deutschen Romanen.* Wiesbaden: Athenaion, 1975.
Schulte-Sasse, Jochen, and Renate Werner. *Einführung in die Literaturwissenschaft.* Munich: Fink, 1977.
Seidensticker, Edward G. "Strangely Shaped Novels: A Scattering of Examples." In Joseph Roggendorf, ed., *Studies in Japanese Culture.* Tokyo: Sophia University Press, 1963.
———. Introduction to *The Gossamer Years: The Diary of a Noblewoman of Heian Japan.* Tokyo, Rutland: Tuttle, 1964.
———. "The Unshapen Ones," *JQ* 11.1:64–69 (1964).
———. *Kafū the Scribbler: The Life and Writings of Nagai Kafū, 1879–1959.* Stanford: Stanford University Press, 1965.
———. "Kafū and Tanizaki," *JQ* 12.3:491–494 (1965).
———. "The 'Pure' and the 'In-Between' in Modern Japanese Theories of the Novel," *HJAS* 26: 174–186 (1966).
———. "Kobayashi Hideo." In Donald H. Shively, ed., *Tradition and Modernization in Japanese Culture.* Princeton: Princeton University Press, 1971.
*Senuma Shigeki. "Shishōsetsuron no keifu," *KKK,* December 1962, 25–33.
*———. "Shishōsetsu to shinkyō shōsetsu," *KBG,* March 1966, 14–20.
Shea, G. T. *Leftwing Literature in Japan: A Brief History of the Proletarian Literary Movement.* Tokyo: Hōsei University Press, 1967.
Shiga Naoya zenshū. Vols. I–XVII. Tokyo: Iwanami shoten, 1955–1956.
Shimazaki Toshiki, and Fukumizu Yasuo. "Seishin igaku kara mita Dazai Osamu," *Gendai no esupuri* 51, July 1971, 223–232 (1960).
Shimazaki Tōson zenshū. Vols. I–XXXI. Tokyo: Chikuma shobō, 1956–1958.
Shinchō Nihon bungaku shōjiten. Ed. Itō Sei et al. 5th ed. Tokyo: Shinchōsha, 1975 (1968).
Shinoda Hajime. *Nihon no gendai shōsetsu.* Tokyo: Shūeisha, 1980.
*Shirai Kōji. "Roman perusoneru ni tsuite," *KKK,* December 1962, 15–19.
Shively, Donald H. Review of *World Within Walls,* by Donald Keene. *JJS* 4.1:37–44 (1978).
*Shōno Junzō. "Hōhō to shite no shishōsetsu," *KKK,* December 1962, 56–58.
Sibley, William F. "Naturalism in Japanese Literature," *HJAS* 28:157–169 (1968).
*———. "The Shiga Hero." Ph.D. dissertation, University of Chicago, 1971.
*———. *The Shiga Hero.* Chicago: University of Chicago Press, 1979.
Silberman, Bernard S., ed. *Japanese Character and Culture: A Book of Selected Readings.* Tucson: University of Arizona Press, 1962.
Sloterdijk, Peter. *Literatur und Organisation von Lebenserfahrung: Autobiographien der Zwanziger Jahre.* Munich: Hanser, 1978.
Smit, Harvey A. "The Center of Value in Japanese Society," *Japan Christian Quarterly* 39:15–22 (1973).
Smith, Robert J., and Richard K. Beardsley, eds. *Japanese Culture: Its Development and Characteristics.* London: Johnson, 1963 (1962).
Sōma Tsuneo. *Nihon shizenshugiron.* Tokyo: Yagi shoten, 1970.

Spae, Joseph J. *Shinto Man.* Tokyo: Oriens Institute for Religious Research, 1972.
Staiger, Emil. *Grundbegriffe der Poetik.* 7th ed. Zurich, Freiburg: Atlantis Verlag, 1966 (1946).
Stanzel, Franz. *Die typischen Erzählsituationen im Roman: Dargestellt an Tom Jones, Moby Dick, The Ambassadors, Ulysses u.a.* Wien: Braumüller, 1963 (1955).
Strohschneider-Kohrs, Ingrid. *Literarische Struktur und geschichtlicher Wandel: Aufriß wissenschaftsgeschichtlicher und methodologischer Probleme.* Munich: Fink, 1971.
*Strong, Kenneth. "Downgrading the 'Kindai Jiga': Reflections on Tōson's 'Hakai' and Subsequent Trends in Modern Literature." In The Japan P.E.N. Club, eds., *Studies on Japanese Culture,* vol. I. Tokyo, 1973.
*Sugiura Minpei. "Kiseisha no bungaku," *Bungaku,* December 1953, 56–59.

Tachibana Yutaka. "Dazai Osamu no buntai: 'Ningen shikkaku' no kudokuten no zensū chōsa," *KKK,* December 1977, 152–160.
*Tadokoro Hitoshi. "Shishōsetsu to dentō bungaku to no kankei," *KBG,* March 1966, 74–80.
*Takahashi Hideo. *Gensō to shite no "watakushi": Shishōsetsu sakkaron.* Tokyo: Kōdansha, 1976.
Taketomo Torao. "Modern Japanese Fiction," *Asia* 21.7:632–640 (1921).
*Takeuchi Yoshimi. "Shishōsetsu ni tsuite," *Bungaku,* December 1953, 66–69.
Tamai Kōsuke. *Nikki bungaku no kenkyū.* Tokyo: Hanawa shobō, 1965.
*Tamiya Torahiko. "Shishōsetsu no unmei," *Bungaku,* December 1953, 59–62.
Tanikawa Tetsuzō. *Shiga Naoya no sakuhin.* 2 vols. Tokyo: Sanryū shobō, 1942.
Tanizaki Jun'ichirō zenshū. Vols. I–XXVIII. Tokyo: Chūō kōronsha, 1966–1968.
Tanizawa Eiichi. "Dazai Osamu 'Ningen shikkaku' no kōsei." In Nihon bungaku kenkyū shiryō kankōkai, eds., *Dazai Osamu.* Tokyo: Yūseidō shuppan, 1970.
Tayama Katai. *Meiji no shōsetsu: Shizenshugi to shajitsushugi* (*Nihon bungaku kōza,* vol. XI). Tokyo: Shinchōsha, 1931.
Tayama Katai zenshū. Vols. I–XVI. Tokyo: Bunsendō, 1973–1974.
*Terada Tōru. "Shishōsetsu oyobi shishōsetsuron." In *Iwanami kōza "Bungaku,"* vol. V. Tokyo: Iwanami shoten, 1954.
Teruoka Yasutaka. "Junbungaku to taishū bungaku: Sono rūtsu o saguru," *Buntai* 5, September 1978, 99–103; *Buntai* 6, December 1978, 121–126; *Buntai* 7, March 1979, 90–100.
Todorov, Tzvetan. "Die Kategorien der literarischen Erzählung." In Heinz Blumensath, ed., *Strukturalismus in der Literaturwissenschaft.* Cologne: Kiepenheuer & Witsch, 1972.
———. *Poetik der Prosa.* Frankfurt/M.: Athenäum, 1972.
———. "Poetik." In François Wahl, ed., *Einführung in den Strukturalismus.* Frankfurt/M.: Suhrkamp, 1973.
*Tokunaga Sunao. "Soto kara uchi e, uchi kara soto e: Keiken to shite," *Bungaku,* December 1953, 69–73.
*Torii Kunio. "Sengo ni okeru shishōsetsuteki ishiki," *KBG,* March 1966, 53–58.
*———. "Senzen shishōsetsu to no renzoku to danzetsu," *KBG,* August 1977, 85–92.

*Toyama Shigehiko. "Shishōsetsu dokusharon," *Waseda bungaku,* July 1977, 25–27.
Tsurumi Kazuko. *Social Change and the Individual: Japan before and after Defeat in World War II.* Princeton: Princeton University Press, 1970.
Tsurumi Yusuke. *Present-Day Japan.* New York: Columbia University Press, 1926.
*Tsuruta Kin'ya. "Akutagawa Ryūnosuke and I-Novelists," *MN* 25:13–27 (1970).
Tynjanov, Jurij. "Über die literarische Evolution." In Jurij Striedter, ed., *Russischer Formalismus: Texte zur allgemeinen Literaturtheorie und zur Theorie der Prosa.* Munich: Fink, 1971 (1927).

Ueda Makoto. *Literary and Art Theories in Japan.* Cleveland: Press of Western Reserve University, 1967.
———. *Modern Japanese Writers and the Nature of Literature.* Stanford: Stanford University Press, 1976.
Uno Kōji. "Shishōsetsu shiken," *Shinchō,* October 1925, 18–23.
———. "Chikamatsu Shūkō." *Iwano Hōmei, Chikamatsu Shūkō shū* (*Gendai Nihon bungaku zenshū,* vol. XIII). Tokyo: Chūō kōronsha, 1954 (1947).
Uno Kōji zenshū. Vols. I–XII. Tokyo: Chūō kōronsha, 1968–1969.
Usui Yoshimi. "Shiga and Akutagawa," *JQ* 2.4:447–452 (1955).
———. *Kindai bungaku ronsō.* 3rd ed. Vol. I. Tokyo: Chikuma shobō, 1957 (1956).
*———. *Shōsetsu no ajiwaikata.* 14th ed. Tokyo: Shinchōsha, 1976 (1967).

Varley, H. Paul. *Japanese Culture: A Short History.* London: Faber & Faber, 1973.

Wada Kingo. *Shimazaki Tōson.* Tokyo: Meiji shoin, 1966.
*———. "Shishōsetsu sakka ni okeru geijutsu to jisseikatsu," *KBG,* March 1966, 93–98.
———. "Tayama Katai to 'Kagerō nikki,'" *KKK,* February 1967, 29–34.
———. "'Heimen byōsha'-ron no shūhen," *Tayama Katai shū* (*Meiji bungaku zenshū,* vol. LXVII). Tokyo: Chikuma shobō, 1968.
*———. "Shishōsetsu no seiritsu to tenkai," *Sanseidō kōza Nihon bungaku,* vol. X (*Kindaihen* II). Tokyo: Sanseidō, 1969.
———. "Tayama Katai shū kaisetsu," *Tayama Katai shū* (*Nihon kindai bungaku taikei,* vol. XIX). Tokyo: Kadokawa shoten, 1972.
Wagatsuma Hiroshi, and George A. De Vos. "Alienation and the Author: A Triptych on Social Conformity and Defiancy in Japanese Intellectuals." In G. A. De Vos, *Socialization for Achievement.* Berkeley, Los Angeles, London: University of California Press, 1973.
Wakizaka Mitsuru. "Kobayashi Hideo no hōhō to shisōsei." In Nihon bungaku kenkyū shiryō kankōkai, eds., *Kobayashi Hideo.* Tokyo: Yūseidō shuppan, 1977.
Waldmann, Günter. *Theorie und Didaktik der Trivialliteratur: Modellanalysen—Didaktikdiskussion—literarische Wertung.* Munich: Fink, 1973.
———. *Kommunikationsästhetik 1: Die Ideologie der Erzählform: Mit einer Modellanalyse von NS-Literatur.* Munich: Fink, 1976.
Weisstein, Ulrich. "Influences and Parallels: The Place and Function of Analogy

Studies in Comparative Literature." In Beda Allemann, and Erwin Koppen, eds., in cooperation with Dieter Gutzen, *Teilnahme und Spiegelung: Festschrift für Horst Rüdiger.* New York, Berlin: De Gruyter, 1975.

Wellek, René, and Austin Warren. *Theory of Literature.* Harmondsworth: Penguin, 1978 (1949).

The World of Japanese Fiction. Ed. and with an introduction and headnotes, Hakutani Yoshinobu, and Arthur O. Lewis. New York: Dutton, 1973.

Wuthenow, Ralph-Rainer. *Das erinnerte Ich: Europäische Autobiographie und Selbstdarstellung im 18. Jahrhundert.* Munich: Beck, 1974.

*Yahagi Katsumi. *Denki to jiden no hōhō.* Tokyo: Shuppan nyūsusha, 1971.

*Yakushiji Noriaki. "Shishōsetsu no hitei: Sono rekishiteki keika o megutte," *KKK,* September 1977, 30–35.

*Yamagata Hiroshi. "Shishōsetsu ni okeru 'watakushi' no ichi," *Bungaku,* September 1977, 67–80.

*Yamamoto Kenkichi. "Shishōsetsu zakkan," *KKK,* December 1962, 43–45.

*———. "Shishōsetsu sakkatachi." In Nihon kindai bungakukan, eds., *Nihon no kindai bungaku.* Tokyo: Yomiuri shinbunsha, 1964.

*———. *Watakushishōsetsu sakkaron.* Tokyo: Shinbisha, 1966.

Yanagida Izumi. *Tayama Katai no bungaku,* vol. I (*Katai bungaku no botai*). Tokyo: Shunjūsha, 1957.

———. *Tayama Katai no bungaku,* vol. II (*Shōnen Katai no bungaku*). Tokyo: Shunjūsha, 1958.

Yanagida Kunio *Japanese Manners and Customs in the Meiji Era.* Tr. and adapted by Charles S. Terry. Tokyo: Ōbunsha, 1957.

Yasuoka Shōtarō. *Shiga Naoya shiron.* Tokyo: Bungei shunjūsha, 1968.

———. "Kaisetsu." In Shiga Naoya, *Wakai.* 46th ed. Tokyo: Shinchōsha, 1976.

*Yazaki Dan. "Kindai jiga no Nihonteki keisei (jō)," *Shōwa jūnendai* (*Shōwa hihyō taikei,* vol. II). Tokyo: Banchō shobō, 1968.

Yōrei ni miru kindai bungakushi yōgo jiten. KKK 7 (enlarged special ed., July 1970).

*Yoshida Hiroo. "Shishōsetsuron no keifu," *KBG,* March 1966, 65–71.

*———. "Watakushishōsetsuron," *Kobayashi Hideo* (*Kindai bungaku kanshō kōza,* vol. VII). Tokyo: Kadokawa shoten, 1966.

*———. "'Shishōsetsuron' zengo," *Kōza Nihon bungaku no sōten,* vol. VI (*Gendaihen*). Tokyo: Meiji shoin, 1969.

———. "Sengo hihyō e no hansatei," *KBG,* June 1973, 105–112.

*———. "'Watakushishōsetsuron' zengo," *Shōwa no bungaku* I (*Gendai bungaku kōza,* vol. V). KKK (bessatsu), November 1974, 141–166.

———. "Kobayashi Hideo no 'Shiga Naoya.'" In Nihon bungaku kenkyū shiryō kankōkai, eds., *Kobayashi Hideo.* Tokyo: Yūseidō shuppan, 1977.

*Yoshida Seiichi. *Shizenshugi no kenkyū.* Vol. I–II. Tokyo: Tōkyōdō, 1955–1958.

———. *Kanshō to hihyō.* 2nd ed. Tokyo: Shibundō, 1964 (1962).

———. *Hyōshaku: Gendai hyōron, zuisō.* Tokyo: Ōbunsha, 1968.

———. *Gendai bungaku to koten.* 2nd ed. Tokyo: Shibundō, 1971 (1960).

———, Ishimaru Hisashi, and Iwanaga Yutaka, eds. *Tōson, Katai* (*Kokugo kokubungaku kenkyūshi taisei,* vol. XIII). Tokyo: Sanseidō, 1960.

*———, Nakamura Mitsuo, Takami Jun, and Hirano Ken. "Shishōsetsu no honshitsu to mondaiten," *KKK,* December 1962, 60–72.

Yoshitake Yoshinori. *Kindai bungaku no naka no Seiō: Kindai Nihon yakuanshi.* Tokyo: Kyōiku shuppan sentā, 1974.

Zimmermann, Friedrich Wilhelm. "Episches Präteritum, Episches Ich und Epische Normalform," *Poetica* 4: 306–324 (1971).

Zimmermann, Hans Dieter. *Vom Nutzen der Literatur: Vorbereitende Bemerkungen zu einer Theorie der literarischen Kommunikation.* Frankfurt/M.: Suhrkamp, 1977.

Zōho kaitei Nihon bungaku daijiten. 7th ed. Vols. I–VII and 1 suppl. Tokyo: Shinchōsha, 1963 (1950–1952).

Appendix to the Bibliography

List of titles concerning shishōsetsu research which were not consulted in this work, either because of inaccessibility or because they appeared between 1981 and 1988. Incomplete data are due to the sources.

Aeba Takao. "'Watakushi' o koeru mono," *KKK,* September 1971, 43–50.
———. "'Watakushi'-shōsetsu to wa nani ka: Nihon no shinsei to no kakawari," *Bungakukai,* February 1982, 164–181.
Ara Masahito. "Taishō bungaku no tenbō." In Hisamatsu Sen'ichi et al., *Gaisetsu gendai Nihon bungakushi.* Tokyo: Kaname shobō, 1951.

Dazai Osamu. *Return to Tsugaru: Travels of a Purple Tramp.* Tr. James Westerhoven. New York: Kōdansha, 1985.

Fowler, Edward Blair. "Fiction and Reality in the Modern Japanese Novel." Ph.D. dissertation, University of California, Berkeley, 1981.
———. *The Rhetoric of Confession: Shishōsetsu in Early Twentieth Century Japanese Fiction.* Berkeley, Los Angeles, London: University of California Press, 1988.
———[Teddo Faurā]. "Shishōsetsu no miryoku," *Shinchō,* October 1985, 256–257.
Fukuda Tsuneari. *Sakka no taido.* Tokyo: Chūō kōronsha, 1947.

Hasumi Shigehiko. "*Shishōsetsu" o yomu.* Tokyo: Chūō kōronsha, 1979.
———. "*Shishōsetsu" o yomu.* Tokyo: Chūō kōronsha, 1985 (expanded version of 1979).
Hijiya-Kirschnereit, Irmela. "The stubborn persistence of a much abused genre: On the popularity of 'shishōsetsu' in contemporary Japanese literature." In Gordon Daniels, ed., *Europe interprets Japan.* Tenterden: Paul Norbury, 1984.
———. "The Darkness at the Foot of the Lighthouse: Recent Research on *Shishōsetsu*" (review of *The Rhetoric of Confession,* by Edward Fowler), *MN* 44, 3:337–345 (1989).

Inagaki Tatsurō. *Kindai Nihon bungaku no fūbō.* Tokyo, 1957.
Inaka Etsuko. "Kobayashi Hideo no 'Watakushishōsetsuron': Shakaika shita 'watakushi' no kanōsei," *Nihon kindai bungaku,* October 1980.
Ishizaka Mikimasa. "Hirano kōshiki, Itō riron no sōgō shintō: Shishōsetsuron no kōsō oyobi sono kanōsei o megutte," *Bungei kenkyū: Meiji daigaku bungakubu kiyō* 36:72–92 (1976).
———. "Shisō, jisseikatsu ronsō no bungakuteki igi: Shishōsetsu no kōsō oyobi sono kanōsei o megutte," *Bungei kenkyū: Meiji daigaku bungakubu kiyō* 39: 118–139 (1978).
———. "Shishōsetsuron no kōsō (1): 'Shishōsetsu' gainen no shomondai," *Ronkyū* 2 (August 1981).
———. "Shishōsetsuron no kōsō (2): Shishōsetsu no seikaku no mondai," *Ronkyū* 3 (July 1982).
———. "Shishōsetsuron no kōsō (3): Shishōsetsu sonritsu no kihon jōken," *Ronkyū* 4 (December 1982).
———. "Shishōsetsuron no kōsō (4): Shishōsetsu no hihyō to riron," *Ronkyū* 5 (July 1983).
———. "Shishōsetsuron no kōsō (5): 'Geijutsu to jisseikatsu' ron no mondai," *Ronkyū* 6 (December 1983).
———. "Shishōsetsuron no kōsō (6): 'Shōsetsu no hōhō' no kōsō: Shishōsetsuron no aratana shiten o motomete," *Ronkyū* 7 (December 1984).
———. "Shishōsetsu, Marukishizumu bungaku dōkonsetsu: Itō Sei no 'Bungakushi'-zō no mondai," *Ronkyū* 8 (December 1985).
———. *Shishōsetsu no riron: Sono hōhō to kadai o megutte.* Tokyo: Yachiyo shuppan, 1985.
Isoda Kōichi. *Sengoshi no kūkan.* Tokyo: Shinchōsha, 1983.
Itō Sei. *Shōsetsu no ninshiki.* Tokyo: Kawade shobō, 1985.

Kanbayashi Akatsuki et al. "'Watakushishōsetsu'-ron," *Shinchō,* May 1942, 40–51.
Kashiwara Osamu. "'Watakushi' to shishōsetsu: Taishō makki bungaku no kōzō e no ichi shiten: Ono Susumu kyōju tsuitō," *Yamaguchi kokubun,* March 1981, 69–80.
Katsumata Hiroshi. "Kobayashi Hideo 'Watakushishōsetsuron' no mondai," *Shōwa bungaku kenkyū* 8 (January 1984).
Katsuyama Isao. *Taishō, shishōsetsu kenkyū.* Tokyo: Meiji shoin, 1980.
Kitada Reiichirō. "Hachijū nendai no bungaku o kangaeru," *Shin Nihon bungaku,* March 1980, 63–67.
Kitagawa Tsuneo. *Shishōsetsu no rinen.* Tokyo, 1983.
———. "Shishōsetsu sakka no rinri," *Ōtani gakuhō,* February 1983, 26–34.
Kodama de Larroche, Christine. *Les cercles d'un regard: Le monde de Kajii Motojirō.* Paris: Maisonneuve & Larose, 1987.
Kōno Toshirō, ed. "Kindai bungakushi ni okeru 'watakushi' no ninshiki," *KKK,* September 1971, 125–142.
Kuwabara Takeo. "Nihon gendai shōsetsu no jakuten." In his *Gendai Nihon bunka no hansei.* Tokyo: Hakujitsu shoin, 1947.

Lyons, Phyllis I. "Art *Is* Me: Dazai Osamu's Narrative Voice As a Permeable Self," *HJAS* 41: 93–110 (1981).

Maruyama Shizuka. "Gendai shōsetsu." In his *Gendai bungaku kenkyū*. Tokyo: Tōkyō daigaku shuppankai, 1956.
Matsubara Shin'ichi. "Hōhō to shite no 'watakushi,'" *KKK*, September 1971, 30–36.
Matsumoto Tōru. "Kihon no shōsetsu: Ōe Kenzaburō, Nakagami Kenji no kinsaku o chūshin ni," *Bungakukai*, December 1989, 220–232.
Matsumoto Tsuruo. "Dazai Osamu, Tanaka Hidemitsu, Shimao Toshio: Shishōsetu," *Nijimasu* 6:74–93 (December 1980).
Matsuzaka Toshio. "Ichiyō no shōsetsusei," *KKK*, November 1974, 99–107.
Mito Reed, Barbara E. "Chikamatsu Shūkō: An Inquiry into Narrative Modes in Modern Japanese Fiction," *JJS* 14.1: 59–76 (1988).
Miyoshi Masao. "Against the Native Grain: Reading the Japanese Novel in America." In Peter H. Lee, ed., *Critical Issues in East Asian Literature: Report on an International Conference on East Asian Literature*. Seoul: International Cultural Society of Korea, 1983.
Miyoshi Yukio. "Kindai bungaku ni okeru 'watakushi': Sobyō," *KKK*, September 1971, 10–14.
Morikawa Tatsuya. "Jitsuzon to shite no 'watakushi,'" *KKK*, September 1971, 37–42.
Munakata Kazushige. "Taishō kyū (1920) nen no 'shishōsetsu' ron: Sono hottan o megutte," *Waseda daigaku kyōiku gakubu gakujutsu kenkyū kokugo kokubungaku hen* 32:47–58 (1983).
Muramatsu Sadataka. "Ichiyō nikki no bungeisei: Shishōsetsuteki kōsei no imi suru mono," in Satō Yasumasa, ed., *Nikki to bungaku*, Haikō jogakuin daigaku kōkai kōza ronshū 17. Tokyo: Kasama shoin, 1985.

Nakajima Makoto. "Gendai bungaku no hitotsu no hōkō," *Shin Nihon bungaku*, March 1980.
Nakamura Mitsuo. "Junsui shōsetsuron ni tsuite: Bungei jihyō," *Bungakukai*, May 1935.
———. "Shishōsetsu ni tsuite II." In his *Bungakuron*. Tokyo: Chūō kōronsha, 1942.
———. "Bungaku wa henshitsu shita ka," *Gunzō*, June 1961.
——— and Minakami Tsutomu. "Taidan kaisetsu: Shishōsetsu no keifu." In Nihon pen kurabu, eds., *Shishōsetsu meisakusen*. Tokyo: Shūeisha, 1980.
Nihon pen kurabu, eds., *Shishōsetsu meisakusen*. Tokyo: Shūeisha, 1980.
Nishida Masayoshi. *Shishōsetsu saihakken*. Tokyo: Ōfūsha, 1973.
———. *Shishōsetsu saihakken: Shishōsetsu no riron*. Tokyo: Yachiyo shuppan, 1985.
Novák, Miroslav. "Watakushi shōsetsu: The Appeal of Authenticity," *Acta Universitatis Carolinae, Philologica* 2 (Orientalia Pragensia II): 27–43 (1962).

Ogasawara Masaru. "Shishōsetsu ni okeru 'watakushi': Mondai no kiten, Itō Sei no hōhō ni karamete," *KKK*, September 1971, 23–30.
Okada Hideko. "Shishōsetsu seiritsu ni tsuite no kazoku yakuwariteki kōsatsu:

Shiga Naoya o chūshin ni," *Hōsei daigaku kyōyōbu kiyō* 19:93–112 (March 1971).
Oketani Hideaki. "Kindaiteki jiga to kojinshugi," *KKK,* September 1971, 16–23.
Ōmori Sumio. "'Watakushishōsetsuron' mokuroku," *Watakushishōsetsu kenkyū* 1: 25–49 (May 1972).
———. *Watakushishōsetsu sakka kenkyū.* Tokyo: Meiji shoin, 1982.
Ōnuki Tōru. "Jiden ni okeru 'jiko naru mono' ni tsuite no ichi kōsatsu." In *Hikaku bungaku bunka ronshū* 1. 1985.
Ōtaku Taeru. "Shishōsetsuron no seiritsu o megutte," *Gunzō* (1962).

Saeki Shōichi. *Nihon no "watakushi" o motomete.* Tokyo: Kawade shobō shinsha, 1974.
———. "Monogatari no naka no 'watakushi': Dai ni no katarite no tanjō," *Subaru,* September 1975, 214–226.
——— et al. "'Shishōsetsu' (kyōdō tōgi)," *Bungakukai,* February 1980, 148–175.
———. *Kindai Nihon no jiden.* Tokyo: Kōdansha, 1981.
———. "The curious relationship between biography and autobiography in Japan." In Anthony M. Friedson, ed., *New Directions in Biography.* Honolulu: University of Hawaii Press, 1981.
———. *Jiden bungaku no sekai.* Tokyo: Asahi shuppansha, 1983.
———. *Jiden no seiki.* Tokyo: Kōdansha, 1985.
——— and Shinoda Hajime. "Taidan: Jiden to nonfikushon," *Gunzō,* October 1985.
Saitō Akira. "'"Rein tsurī" o kiku onnatachi' o yomu: Ichininshō to shite no boku no sonzai o chūshin ni," *Monogatari bungaku ronkyū* 7.3: 39–42 (1983).
Saitō Shinji. "Ippen no shishōsetsu to shite," *Tanka* 35 (March 1988).
Sasaki Ryōko. "Shishōsetsu ni tsuite: Nihon to Furansu no shishōsetsu rinen no hikaku kara," *Tōkyō joshi daigaku fuzoku hikaku bunka kenkyūjo kiyō* 41:71–86 (1981).
Satō Saburō. "Shimazaki Tōson: Kokuhaku to jihaku no isō: Ushimatsu to kindai seishin," *Kokusai kankei kenkyū* (Nihon daigaku) 8.2 (November 1988).
Shimao Toshio. *"The Sting of Death" and Other Stories.* Translated, with an introduction and interpretive comments by Kathryn Sparling. (Michigan Papers in Japanese Studies 12). Ann Arbor: Center for Japanese Studies, University of Michigan, 1985.
Shinoda Hajime et al. "Nihon bungaku no genzai (kyōdō tōgi)," *Bungakukai,* January 1982, 302–326.
——— et al. "Nihon bungaku no genzai: 1984 nen (kyōdō tōgi)," *Bungakukai,* January 1985, 234–266.
Shishōsetsu. Ed. Nihon bungaku kenkyū shiryō kankōkai. Tokyo: Yūseidō shuppan, 1983.
Sōma Shōichi. "Dazai bungaku to shishōsetsu no mondai," *Dazai Osamu kenkyū* 10 (September 1969).
Sone Hiroyoshi. "Sensōka no Itō Sei no hyōron: Shishōsetsukan no hensen o chūshin ni," *Gobun* (Nihon daigaku) 62 (1985).

Takahashi Tadashi. "Ōmachi Keigetsu to shishōsetsu," *Kōdai kokugo kyōiku* 28.12: 19–26 (1980).
Tanizawa Eiichi. *Taishō-ki no bungei hyōron*. Tokyo: Haniwa shobō, 1959.
———. "Shishōsetsu no keifu." In his *Kindai Nihon bungakushi no kōsō*. Tokyo: Shōbunsha, 1964.
Terada Tōru. "Shinkyō shōsetsu, shishōsetsu." In *Nihon bungaku kōza* 6 (*Kindai no bungaku*). [Before 1954].

Walker, Janet. *The Japanese Novel of the Meiji Period and the Ideal of Individualism*. Princeton: Princeton University Press, 1979.
———. Review of *The Saga of Dazai Osamu*, by P. Lyons, and *Return to Tsugaru*, by Osamu Dazai, tr. J. Westerhoven, *JJS* 13.2:457–464 (1987).

Yagi Yoshinori. "Shishōsetsu no naka no watakushi," *Shinchō*, December 1983, 220–221.
Yamada Akio. "Watakushishōsetsu no mondai," *KKK*, January 1965, 43–47.
Yamamoto Kenkichi. *Watakushishōsetsu sakkaron*. Tokyo: Fukutake shoten, 1983.
Yamamuro Shizuka. "Kamura Isota no baai: Gendai to shishōsetsu." In his *Genzai no bungaku no tachiba*. Tokyo: Akatsuka shobō, 1939.
Yanagisawa Takako. "Shishōsetsu no kenkyū no koto nado," *Nihon kindai bungaku*, October 1982, 209–214.
Yasuoka Shōtarō. "Gendai ni okeru watakushishōsetsu," *Mita bungaku*, October 1971, 28–34.
Yazaki Dan. *Kindai jiga no Nihonteki keisei*. Tokyo: Kamakura shobō, 1943.
Yoshida Seiichi. "Watakushishōsetsu no mondai ni tsuite," *KKK*, July 1947, 19–24.
———. *Meiji Taishō bungakushi*. 5th ed. Tokyo: Tōkyō shūbunkan, 1948.

Index of Persons and Works

The literary works discussed—in cases where the author's works have been treated at length—are listed under the name of the author.

Several titles of premodern, in some cases anonymous, Japanese works are included in the subject index as well.

Abe Akio, 193
Abe Kōbō, 41, 143
Aeba Takao, 77, 105, 106, 109, 119, 126, 127, 267
Agawa Hiroyuki, 257
Akatsuka Yukio, 259, 260
Akiyama Shun, xviii, 104, 109, 125, 290, 292, 293, 295, 305, 319, 320, 321–323, 326
Akutagawa Ryūnosuke, xi, 100, 102–103, 109, 140, 145, 150, 155–156, 184, 212, 229, 269–270, 274, 285, 289, 309, 319; "Ano koro no jibun no koto," 225, 258, 292; *Aru ahō no isshō*, 145; "Gakikutsu nichiroku," 258; "Haguruma," 103; "Jigokuhen," 103
Althusser, Louis, xiii
Anderegg, Johannes, 173
Andō Hiroshi, xviii
Aono Suekichi, 155, 159
Ara Masahito, 9, 108, 126, 275–276, 293
Arakawa Sōbei, 165

Araki, James T., 319
Arima Tatsuo, 30, 158, 319
Arishima Takeo, 93, 140, 148, 150
Ariyama Mitsuhiro, 9, 98, 127
Artsybashev, Mikhail P., 234
Asami Fukashi, 308, 319

Baba Kochō, 52, 54
Balint, Michael, 274
Balzac, Honoré de, 153; *Human Comedy*, 153
Bannfield, Ann, 121
Barrès, Maurice, 81
Barthes, Roland, 98
Bashō, 308
Baudelaire, Charles, 241
Bellah, Robert N., 295
Ben-Dasan, Isaiah, 92
Benl, Oscar, 30
Berger, Peter L., 7, 9
Berndt, Jürgen, 20
Bismarck, Otto von, 203
Booth, Wayne, 246
Bormann, Alexander von, 200

Borton, Hugh, 19
Bourdieu, Pierre, 326
Bourget, Paul, 33
Bovet, E., 167
Bowring, Richard, 122, 128, 143
Brower, Robert H., 189, 194, 303, 305, 312, 319
Browning, Robert, 203
Brunetière, Ferdinand, 167, 168
Bühler, Karl, 186
Büschen, Ilka, 193
Byron, George Gordon Lord, 18

Caudill, William, 20, 270–271, 293, 294, 324, 326
Chekhov, Anton P., 234
Chiba Masaaki, 104
Chikamatsu Shūkō, 58, 61, 117, 121, 140, 141, 221, 233, 254, 317; "Giwaku," 90, 208–212, 281–282; "Wakaretaru tsuma ni okuru tegami," 139, 209–210; "Yuki no hi," 208
Collins, William Wilkie, 32
Comte, Auguste, 38
Constant, Benjamin: *Adolphe*, 79, 86, 117

Da Vinci, Leonardo, 202–203, 234
D'Annunzio, Gabriele, 33; *L'innocente*, 39
Darwin, Charles, 24, 30, 36, 38, 46
Dazai Osamu, 99, 101, 104, 120, 253, 254, 255, 258, 276, 285, 287, 320; "Dōke no hana," 241, 242; *Human Lost*, 242; *Ningen shikkaku*, 200, 237–247; "Omoide," 241; *Shayō*, 104
De Vos, George A., 259
Dickens, Charles, 32
Disney, Walt, 290
Doi Takeo, 270–271, 273, 293, 294, 303, 305
Dōke Tadamichi, 109, 277–278, 286, 287, 294
Dostoevski, Fedor M., 27, 316, 317; *Crime and Punishment*, 25, 51, 153
Dumas, Alexandre, 32

Eagleton, Terry, xviii
Eco, Umberto, 8, 19
Eguchi Kiyoshi, 141, 145, 293
Eimermacher, Karl, 115, 127
Emerson, Ralph Waldo, 18, 26, 203
Endō Shūsaku, xi
Enomoto Takashi, 54, 77, 144, 320
Erben, Johannes, 218
Etō Jun, 85, 92, 96, 145

Fairbank, John K., 20
Flaubert, Gustave, 21, 33, 89; *L'éducation sentimentale*, 23; *Madame Bovary*, 24, 35, 82, 87, 153
Foucault, Michel, xii–xiii, 98, 111
Fowler, Edward B. xii, 121–122, 128
Frege, Gottlob, 267
Fujieda Shizuo, 8, 116, 302, 305
Fujii, James A., xiii, xviii
Fukuda Rikutarō, 162, 167
Fukuda Tsuneari, 119
Fukumizu Yasuo, 259
Fukuzawa Yukichi, 16; *Bunmeiron no guiryaku*, 16; *Gakumon no susume*, 16
Fülleborn, Ulrich, 302, 305
Funabashi Seiichi, 248
Furui Yoshikichi, 106, 326
Furuki, Akira, 258
Futabatei Shimei, 16, 21, 28, 32, 45, 60; *Heibon*, 65–66; *Sono omokage*, 65; *Ukigumo*, 16–17, 20, 27, 32, 50, 65, 116

Gálik, Marián, xviii
Genette, Gérard, xii, 121
Gide, André, 81, 82; *Journal*, 258
Gladstone, William E., 203
Gluck, Jay, 194
Goethe, Johann Wolfgang von, 153; *Clavigo*, 134; *Die Leiden des jungen Werthers*, 79–80, 92, 134, 234; *Wilhelm Meisters Lehr- und Wanderjahre*, 134
Goncourt, Jules Huot de, 21, 69
Gorki, Maksim, 33
Grass, Günter: *The Tin Drum*, 112

Grimmelshausen, Hans Jakob Christoffel von: *Simplicissimus*, 112
Günther, Hans, 200

Habermas, Jürgen, 286
Haeckel, Ernst, 33, 46
Hagiwara Kyōjirō, 234
Halbe, Max, 33
Hamburger, Käte, 301–302, 305
Hammitzsch, Horst, 319
Hamsun, Knut, 234, 281; *Hunger*, 234
Hara Shirō, 304
Hara Tamiki, 126, 275–276
Hartl, R., 168
Hartleben, Otto Erich, 33
Hartmann, Eduard von, 18, 134
Harutoonian, Harry D., 294
Hasegawa Izumi, 92, 101, 112, 127, 143, 168
Hasegawa Ken, 308
Hasegawa Tenkei, 26, 30, 41; "Genmetsu jidai no geijutsu," 30; "Genjitsu bakuro no hiai," 30
Hashimoto Yoshi, 101
Hasumi Shigehiko, 116
Hauptmann, Gerhart, 33, 41, 46–48; *Einsame Menschen*, 41, 46–48, 49, 53–54, 66, 69; *Die versunkene Glocke*, 41
Hayama Sankichi, 144
Hayama Yoshiki, 100
Hayashi Fumiko, 258, 272, 281, 292, 293; *Hōrōki*, 230–237, 253, 270, 282, 288, 301, 303
Hayashi Mariko, xi
Hempfer, Klaus W., 8, 173, 192, 200
Heraclitus, 189
Heyse, Paul, 66, 143
Hibbett, Howard, 75, 77, 108, 109, 125, 126, 127, 173, 192
Higuchi Ichiyō, 19, 21, 123; *Takekurabe*, 19, 20
Hijiya-Kirschnereit, Irmela, xiv, xviii, xix, 8, 19, 41, 53, 54, 78, 124, 126, 127, 128, 143, 168, 193, 256, 294, 305, 320, 326
Hinck, Walter, 173, 267, 305

Hirabayashi Hatsunosuke, 154
Hirabayashi Taiko, 234
Hirano Ken, 2, 8, 89–91, 93, 96, 97, 99, 102, 104, 109, 118, 119, 124, 125, 126, 143, 144, 145, 150, 152, 157, 158, 208, 223, 247, 256, 274, 293, 299, 319
Hiraoka Tokuyoshi, 222, 257
Hiraoka Toshio, 40, 109
Hirotsu Kazuo, 118, 148
Hisamatsu Sen'ichi, 8, 41, 69, 145, 200, 256
Hōjō Tamio, 102
Holz, Arno, 135, 143
Honma Hisao, 140, 145
Hopper, Helen M., 144
Hoshō Masao, 98
Hugo, Victor, 32; *Le dernier jour d'un condamné*, 257; *Les misérables*, 32
Huysmans, Joris-Karl, 33, 141; *La cathédrale*, 145; *Là-bas*, 145

Ibsen, Henrik, 33, 66
Ibuse Masuji, 105, 251
Ihara Saikaku. *See* Saikaku
Ikari Akira, 41
Ikuta Chōkō, 153, 309
Ikuta Shungetsu, 152
Imai Takauji, 304
Inagaki Tatsurō, 9, 77, 95, 139, 143, 164, 271
Ingarden, Roman, 167
Ino Kenji, 98
Inoue Yasushi, 105
Inukai Ren, 110
Iser, Wolfgang, 266, 267
Ishibashi Ningetsu, 133
Ishida Tadahiko, 40
Ishikawa Takuboku, 32
Ishikawa Tatsuzō, 277; *Roman no zantō*, 294
Ishimaru Hisashi, 53
Ishizaka Mikimasa, 118–119, 128
Isobe Tadamasa, 190, 194, 315, 320
Isoda Kōichi, xi, 123
Isogai Hideo, 95, 105
Itagaki Naoko, 232, 235–236, 258

Itō Jinsai. *See* Jinsai
Itō Sei (Hitoshi), 30, 83–86, 87, 89, 90, 91, 92, 93, 99, 102, 119, 152, 283, 294, 295, 299, 320
Iwanaga Yutaka, 32, 40, 53
Iwano Hōmei, 26, 27, 30, 177; "Dokuyaku o nomu onna," 192; "Hōrō," 139, 207; "Shinpiteki hanjūshugi," 203; "Tandeki," 139, 201–208, 211, 234, 281
Izumi Kyōka, 100

Jansen, Marius B., 19
Jauß, Hans Robert, 126, 173
Jinsai, 136
Jolles, André, 173
Joyce, James, 82; *Ulysses*, 91

Kaikō Ken, 324
Kajii Motojirō, 102, 120
Kakeda Katsumi, 259
Kakinomoto no Hitomaro, 193
Kamei Hideo, 91, 92, 93
Kamiya Tadataka, 92
Kamo no Chōmei, 189; *Hōjōki*, 189, 300
Kamura Isota, 102, 110–111, 118, 273
Kanbayashi Akatsuki, 102, 108, 126, 271, 272, 276, 277, 293, 294
Karaki Junzō, 193, 194
Karatani Kōjin (Yukihito), xiii, xviii, 111, 127
Karatani Yukihito. *See* Karatani Kōjin
Kasai Zenzō, 102, 103, 110–111, 114, 117, 118, 121, 124, 253, 273, 305, 317, 320; "Ko o tsurete," 215, 220–223, 236, 253, 273, 303, 309
Katagami Noboru. *See* Katagami Tengen
Katagami Tengen (Noburu), 61, 148
Katai. *See* Tayama Katai
Katō Shūichi, 126, 297–298, 304
Katsumoto Seiichirō, 67, 69
Katsuyama Isao, 77, 96, 98, 103, 116–117, 119, 144, 145, 158, 294
Kawabata Yasunari, 109, 247, 260; "Izu no odoriko," 183–184, 260, 313
Kawai Hiroshi, 259
Kawakami Hajime, 148

Kawakami Tetsutarō, 92
Kawasaki Chōtarō, 102, 108, 113, 117, 309, 319; *Katabutori no onna*, 101
Kawashima Takeyoshi, 319
Kawauchi Mitsuharu, 259
Kayser, Wolfgang, 167
Kazamaki Keijirō, 259
Keene, Dennis, 27, 29, 30, 285, 294
Keene, Donald, 200, 259
Ki no Tsurayuki, 298, 320; *Kokin wakashū*, 315; *Tosa nikki*, 298, 315
Kikuchi Kan (Hiroshi), 127, 142, 149, 154, 162, 163, 164; "Tomo to tomo to no aida," 223–230
Kimura Ki, 24, 29
Kimura Shōzaburō, 316–317, 320
Kimura Yukio, 109
Kindaichi Haruhiko, 257, 294
Kinoshita Naoe, 19
Kishimoto Hideo, 319
Kitada Reiichirō, 123
Kitamura Tōkoku, 18, 32, 33, 116, 135
Kiyama Shōhei, 102
Kiyooka Takayuki, 105
Kō Haruto, 117
Kobayashi Chishō, 194
Kobayashi Hideo, 1, 8, 79–83, 84, 86, 87, 88–89, 91, 92, 96, 97, 109, 115, 117, 119, 127, 187, 219, 274, 289, 295
Kobayashi Ichirō, 40, 54
Kobayashi Takiji, 102
Kōda Rohan, 28, 32, 100; *Fūryūbutsu*, 32
Kodama de Larroche, Christine, 120
Kohl, Stephen W., 103, 127, 257
Kojima Masajirō, 133
Kojima Nobuo, 109, 124
Kokubo Minoru, 9, 77, 95, 145, 158, 293
Kōno Toshirō, 98, 164, 257, 258
Kōnoshi Takamitsu, 193
Kōsaka Masaaki, 20, 28, 30
Kosugi Tengai, 21–23, 26; *Hatsusugata*, 21–23; *Hayariuta*, 22, 23
Kressler, O., 194
Kubokawa Tsurujirō, 124
Kubota Masabumi, 110, 300, 305

Kuga Katsunan, 18
Kume Masao, 95, 112, 141, 142, 150, 152, 153–154, 155, 158, 162, 164, 181, 224–227, 286, 300; "Bosan," 225; "Haisha," 225; "Hasen," 225; "Hotarugusa," 225; "Ryōyū akuyū," 225; "Warei," 225
Kunikida Doppo, 26, 27, 32, 33, 34, 45, 60, 109, 136, 289; *Dopposhū*, 45; *Unmei*, 136; "Unmeironsha," 60
Kurahara Korehito, 326
Kurahashi Yumiko, 324
Kuroda, S.-Y., 121
Kurumizawa Kōshi, 128
Kusaka Naoki, 290
Kuwabara Takeo, 323

Lacan, Jacques, xiii
LaFleur, William, 194
Laistner, Ludwig, 143
Lämmert, Eberhard, 173, 267
Lane, Richard, 20, 127
Laplanche, J., 293
Lawrence, David Herbert: *Lady Chatterley's Lover*, 91
Lebra, Takie Sugiyama, 293, 295, 320
Leiris, Michel, 112
Lejeune, Philippe, 193
Lewin, Bruno, 20, 40, 69, 92, 194, 304
Lockemann, Wolfgang, 173, 192
Loti, Pierre, 33
Lotman, Jurij M., 19, 279, 283, 294
Luckmann, Thomas, 7, 9
Luther, Wilhelm, 92
Lyons, Phyllis I., 120, 128

Maedakō Hiroichirō: *Shijūnisai no genzai made*, 112
Maeterlinck, Maurice, 26, 33, 66, 203
Makino Shin'ichi, 117
Malraux, André, 285
Mann, Thomas, 89
Maraini, Fosco, 319, 320
Maruyama Banka, 51
Maruyama Masao, 85, 319, 324, 326
Masamune Hakuchō, 26, 33, 34, 41, 51, 60, 61, 62, 63, 64, 68, 69, 208, 256, 289; "Doko e," 139; "Doro ningyō," 139; "Shizenshugi seisuishi," 40, 54, 62, 69, 192, 256
Mathy, Francis, 103, 194
Matsubara Shibun, 61
Matsubara Shin'ichi, xi, xviii, 77, 102, 103, 106–107, 119, 126, 212, 256, 278
Matsumoto Shigeru, 144, 193
Matsumoto Tōru, 128
Matsumoto Tsuruo, 99, 105, 125, 126
Matsuo Bashō. *See* Bashō
Matsuoka Yuzuru, 224–227; "Yūutsuna aijin," 225
Matsuzaka Toshio, 128
Maupassant, Guy de, 21, 33, 41; *Bel ami*, 23
Maurer, Karl, 157
May, Ekkehard, 157
Mayama Seika, 26
McClellan, Edwin, 101, 108, 109–110, 119, 304
Merezhkovskiy, Dmitriy S.: *Leonardo da Vinci*, 202, 281
Michitsuna no haha, 297; *Kagerō (no) nikki*, 297, 299–300, 304
Minakami Tsutomu, 117
Minami Hiroshi, 291, 295, 303, 305
Miner, Earl, 189, 194, 303, 304, 305, 312, 319, 320
Mishima Yukio, 41, 143, 144, 242, 283–284, 289; *Kamen no kokuhaku*, 105
Miura Tetsuo, 108, 109, 260, 269, 271, 292, 293, 315; "Gentōgashū," 255; "Haji no fu," 254; "Kikyō," 254–255; *Shinobugawa* (book), 105; "Shinobugawa" (short story), 247–256, 272, 289, 290; "Shoya," 254–255
Miyagi Otoya, 111, 221–222, 257, 273, 291, 293, 295
Miyagi Tatsurō, 256
Miyake Setsurei, 18
Miyamoto Yuriko, 100
Miyauchi Yutaka, 92
Miyazaki Sōhei, 304
Miyoshi Masao, xv, 122, 128, 143
Miyoshi Yukio, 77, 98, 99, 104, 105,

Miyoshi Yukio *(continued)* 124, 125, 126, 143, 255–256, 260, 314, 320, 326
Mizuno Yōshū, 61, 62
Mochizuki, Narae G., 121, 128
Moore, Charles A., 319
Moran, Chihoko, 326
Moran, Joseph, 326
Mori Ōgai, 18, 21, 28, 33, 63, 64, 89, 100, 112, 140, 144, 178; "Maihime," 54, 112, 133–134, 135, 138, 143; *Seinen*, 144, 145; *Vita sexualis*, 139, 144
Morikawa Tatsuya, 8, 98, 105, 106, 124, 164, 170, 192, 260, 267, 293
Morishige, Alyce Hisae, 246, 259
Morris, Ivan, 143, 307–308, 319
Motoori Norinaga, 137, 144; *Genji monogatari tama no ogushi*, 144, 189, 193
Müller, Klaus-Detlef, 193, 257, 304, 305
Murakami Ryū: *Kagirinaku tōmei ni chikai burū*, 105
Muramatsu Sadataka, 128, 167
Murasaki Shikibu: *Genji monogatari*, 110, 137, 188–189, 315
Mushakōji Saneatsu, 93, 140, 219
Mushanokōji. *See* Mushakōji

Nagai Kafū, 23–24, 26, 29, 89; *Jigoku no hana*, 24–25
Nakai Yoshiyuki, 144
Nakajima Makoto, xviii, 123
Nakamura Hajime, 319
Nakamura Kogetsu, 309
Nakamura Mitsuo, 8, 25, 29, 30, 41, 47, 50–51, 54, 57, 61, 67, 69, 74, 86–89, 91, 92, 96, 97, 102, 109, 114, 117–119, 124, 126, 145, 156, 158, 159, 162, 164, 235, 258
Nakamura Murao, 95, 141, 152–153, 154, 158
Nakamura Seiko, 61, 141
Nakamura Shin'ichirō, 105, 253, 259, 260
Nakamura Yū, 98, 141, 144, 145, 257, 258

Nakane Chie, 7, 326
Nakano Hideichirō, 303–304, 305
Nakano Shigeharu, 99
Nanbu Shūtarō, 257
Natsume, Sōseki, 33, 63, 64, 100, 109, 178, 224–227, 293; *Meian*, 224; *Wagahai wa neko de aru*, 162
Neumann, Bernd, 192, 304
Nietzsche, Friedrich, 18, 27, 28, 36, 153, 203
Niizeki Ryōzō, 308, 317, 319, 320
Nishida Kitarō, 109
Nishida Masayoshi, ix, 119, 128
Niwa Fumio, 88
Nomura Seiichi, 299–300, 304
Nosaka Akiyuki, xi
Novák, Miroslav, 127–128

Ōba Shunsuke, 166–167, 168
O'Brien, James A., 238, 242, 246, 259
Odagiri Hideo, 67, 69, 77, 98, 105, 108, 126, 220, 257
Ōe Kenzaburō, xi, 108, 123, 290, 291–292, 293, 295
Ōgai. *See* Mori Ōgai
Ogasawara Masaru, 80, 92, 96, 98, 110–111, 127, 135, 143, 144, 145, 159, 258
Ogata Akiko, 54, 57, 61, 62, 101
Ogawa Kunio, 105, 125, 326
Oguri Fūyō, 26, 51, 58, 61; *Koizame*, 66; *Seishun*, 50–51
Ogyū Sorai. *See* Sorai
Okada Michiyo, 44, 53, 89
Okada, Richard Hideki, 128
Okakura Tenshin (Kakuzō), 18
Okaya Kōji, 112
Okazaki Yoshie, 54, 69
Oketani Hideaki, 109, 114, 115, 127, 273, 293
Ōkubo Tadatoshi, 247, 259
Ōkubo Tsuneo, 30, 98, 208, 210, 256
Okuno Takeo, 237, 238, 239, 249, 251–252, 253, 255, 259, 260, 272, 287, 290, 295
Ōmori Morikazu, xviii
Ōmori Sumio, 117, 119, 144, 257

Ōnishi Tadao, 41
Ōnishi Takijirō, 310
Osanai Kaoru, 176
Ōta Seiichi, 111, 127
Ōtomo no Yakamochi, 193
Ozaki Kazuo, 108, 271, 276, 287, 293, 302; *Atami yuki*, 270
Ozaki Kōyō, 19, 21, 28, 32, 143; *Aobudō*, 68, 135, 138; *Konjiki yasha*, 24, 281

Passin, Herbert, 18
Petersen, Julius, 168
Piaget, Jean, 222
Poe, Edgar Allan, 33
Pontalis, J. B., 293
Posner, Roland, 127
Pouillon, J., 53
Powell, Irena, 92, 157
Power, J. B., 103, 127, 145
Proust, Marcel, 81, 82; *A la recherche du temps perdu*, 257
Pyle, Kenneth B., 20

Reed, Barbara Mito, 121
Richter, Frederick, 38, 42
Rimer, J. Thomas, 143
Robert, Marthe, 126
Rod, Édouard, 33
Rousseau, Jean-Jacques, 27, 36, 41, 116; *Confessions*, 25, 51, 79
Ryan, Marleigh G., 20, 30, 75, 77, 126

Saegusa Hiroto, 109, 267
Saegusa Yasutaka, 104, 258
Saeki Kazumi, xviii
Saeki Shōichi, xviii, 106, 117, 119, 127, 164, 267, 320
Saikaku, 18–19, 32, 110, 190; *Shoen ōkagami*, 20
Saitō Akira, 128
Saitō Kiyoe, 109, 168
Sakagami Hiroichi, 19
Sakai Toshihiko, 148
Sakita Susumu, 105
Sako Jun'ichirō, 287, 294
Sakurai Yoshio, 294

Sasabuchi, Tomoichi, 33, 40, 54, 67, 69
Sasaki Kiichi, 85, 92, 104, 126, 127, 164
Sasaki Mitsuzō, 230
Sata Ineko: "Kurenai," 124
Satō Etsuko, 97, 124
Satō Haruo, 112, 158, 304
Satō Kōichi, 112, 127
Satō Masaru, 98
Satō Yasumasa, 99, 105, 125
Satomi Ton, 149, 226; "Kimi to watakushi to," 226
Schamoni, Wolfgang, 143, 157
Schmidt, Siegfried J., 19, 192
Schnitzler, Arthur, 234
Schopenhauer, Arthur, 203
Schulte-Sasse, Jochen, 8, 326
Seidensticker, Edward, 29, 92, 96, 157, 159, 304
Senancour, Étienne Pivert de: *Oberman*, 79–80
Senuma Shigeki, 9, 75, 77, 96, 124, 144, 305, 319
Setouchi Harumi, xi
Shakespeare, William, 153
Shea, G. T., 157
Shiba Shirō. *See* Tōkai Sanshi
Shibata Shō, 324
Shiga Naoya, 81, 93, 100, 101, 102, 103–104, 111, 116, 120, 121, 125, 140, 162, 184, 221, 224, 241, 254, 258, 270, 272, 273, 274–275, 285, 303, 309, 313–314, 319; *An'ya kōro*, 104, 120, 180–181, 182, 226, 254, 275, 279–280, 284, 314; "Kinosaki nite," 257; "Kugenuma yuki," 288–289; "Kuniko," 226; "Moderu no fufuku," 226; "Nakamura Shin'ichirō kun no gimon ni tsuite," 280, 320; "Ōtsu Junkichi," 257; "Sōsaku yodan," 258, 288–289; "Wakai," 212–220, 236, 257, 274, 281; "Yuki no hi," 229; "Zoku sōsaku yodan," 214, 260, 320; "Zokuzoku sōsaku yodan," 320
Shimamura Hōgetsu, 26, 30, 32, 58, 61, 62
Shimamura Toshimasa, 109, 308
Shimao Toshio, 120; *Shi no toge*, 105

Shimazaki Toshiki, 259
Shimazaki Tōson, 18, 26, 27, 30, 33, 45, 48, 89, 101, 109, 176, 177; *Hakai*, 25, 45, 50–51, 58–59, 63, 67, 81, 87, 116, 267; *Haru*, 67, 102; *Kyūshujin*, 24; "Namiki," 51–52; *Shinsei*, 116, 141; *Suisai gaka*, 51, 69; *Wakanashū*, 18
Shinoda Hajime, x, xviii, 13, 19, 107, 123
Shirai Kōji, 112
Shōno Junzō, 105, 108
Shūkō. *See* Chikamatsu Shūkō
Sibley, William F., 29, 30, 104, 120, 126, 193, 257, 275, 293
Sienkiewicz, Henryk, 33
Sloterdijk, Peter, 193, 304
Sōma Gyofū, 61, 62
Sōma Tsuneo, 69, 98
Sorai, 136
Spae, Joseph, 318, 319, 320
Sparling, Kathryn, 120
Staiger, Emil, 167, 189, 194
Stanzel, Franz, 173
Stinchecum, Amanda Mayer, 128
Strindberg, August, 33, 116
Strohschneider-Kohrs, Ingrid, 200, 305
Strong, Kenneth, 109, 266–267
Sudermann, Hermann, 33; *Katzensteg*, 35
Sugimori Hisahide, 259
Sugiura Minpei, 108, 324, 326
Suzuki Daisetz, 319
Swedenborg, Emanuel, 26, 203

Tachibana no Narisue, 312
Tachibana Yutaka, 247, 259
Tadokoro Hitoshi, 110, 299, 304
Tagawa Suihō, 289
Taine, Hippolyte, 38
Takada Hanpō (Sanae), 132
Takahashi Hideo, 9, 77, 103, 104, 105, 107, 113, 118, 119, 126, 127, 237, 259, 291, 295, 300, 302, 305
Takami Jun, 97, 99, 109, 271, 305
Takayama Chogyū, 18, 28, 35
Takeda Rintarō, 88

Takeuchi Yoshimi, 109, 126, 324, 324, 326
Takii Kōsaku, 102, 248, 302, 305, 320
Tamai Kōsuke, 304
Tamiya Torahiko, 324, 326
Tanaka Hidemitsu, 126, 276
Tanaka Komimasa: "Sakana-uchi," 117
Tanikawa Tetsuzō, 257
Tanizaki Jun'ichirō, 109, 140, 155–156, 229
Tanizawa Eiichi, 244, 259
Tayama Katai, 23, 26, 27, 30, 31–69, 89, 110, 136, 158, 176, 177, 202, 208, 299, 315, 319; "Aki no yūbe", 32; *Daingun jūsei nikki*, 54; *En*, 63; "Futon," 3, 14, 31, 25, 39, 43–69, 81, 86, 87, 89–90, 101, 116, 131, 132, 139, 201, 205, 206, 208, 211; "Jūemon no saigo," 35, 38; *Makoku*, 49; *Meiji no shōsetsu: Shizenshugi to shajitsushugi*, 41; *No no hana*, 23, 34, 41; "Onna kyōshi," 41, 48, 49, 59; "Rokotsunaru byōsha," 27, 42, 49, 61; *Sei*, 63, 64; "*Sei* ni okeru kokoromi*," 64, 69; "Seika yokō," 33, 36; "Shōgatsu zuihitsu," 40; "Shōjobyō," 49, 117; "Shōsetsu sahō," 69; "Shōshijin," 32; "Sōshun," 304; "Tera no aki," 32; *Tōkyō no sanjūnen*, 34; *Tsuma*, 63; "Uribatake," 32; "Watakushi no Anna Mâru," 47; *Yamaga no mizu*, 32; "Yodan," 54; *Zansetsu*, 140–141
Terada Tōru, 80, 92, 95, 96, 97, 102, 124, 131, 164, 170, 192, 228, 258
Teruoka Yasutaka, 96
Thibaudet, Albert, 126
Tieghem, Paul van, 168
Todorov, Tzvetan, xii, 19, 53, 121, 193
Togawa Shūkotsu, 52
Tōkai Sanshi (Shiba Shirō), 132, 142–143; *Kajin no kigū*, 132–133, 137, 138, 142–143
Tokuda Shūkō. *See* Chikamatsu Shūkō
Tokuda Shūsei, 26, 102, 106; *Arakure*, 81; *Kabi*, 139, 186; *Shukuzu*, 102
Tokunaga Sunao, 108, 326

Tokutomi Roka, 19, 24, 111; *Hototogisu*, 24, 25; *Shinshun*, 141
Tolstoy, Lev N., 27, 33, 203, 234; *Anna Karenina*, 153; *War and Peace*, 153
Torii Kunio, 98, 99, 105, 124, 125
Tōson. *See* Shimazaki Tōson
Toyama Shigehiko, 111, 286, 287, 290, 291, 292, 294, 295, 318, 320
Toyoda Minoru, x
Tsuboi Sakae, 234
Tsuboi Shigeji, 234
Tsubouchi Shōyō, 15, 16–17, 28, 144, 156; *Shōsetsu shinzui*, 15, 17, 19, 27, 133, 137
Tsurumi Kazuko, 240, 259
Tsuruta Kin'ya, 102–103, 125, 127, 319
Tsushima Shūji. *See* Dazai Osamu
Tsushima Yūko, x
Turgenev, Ivan S., 26, 27, 66, 67; *First Love*, 35; *Rudin*, 50; "Svidaniye" (*Aibiki*), 32, 40; *Zapiski okhotnika*, 40
Tynjanov, Jurij, 200

Uchimura Kanzō, 18
Ueda Bin, 225
Ueda Makoto, 144, 157, 320
Ueda Miyoji, x, xviii
Uno Kōji, 103, 118, 154, 158, 174–175, 176, 220, 247, 256, 257, 286, 294, 308; "Amaki yo no hanashi," 141, 151, 174–175, 178; *Ku no sekai*, 103
Usui Yoshimi, 1, 8, 96, 104, 105, 126, 219, 247, 257, 258, 285, 294

Verhaeren, Émile, 33
Viëtor, Karl, 172

Wada Kingo, 32, 69, 77, 95, 110, 201
Wagatsuma Hiroshi, 259, 319
Wagner, Richard, 33, 36

Wakizaka Mitsuru, 82, 92
Waldmann, Günter, 265, 267
Walker, Janet, xv, 115–116, 120, 128
Warren, Austin, 311, 319
Watsuji Tetsurō, 84, 292, 295
Wechselblatt, Stephen, 120, 128
Weisstein, Ulrich, 35, 41
Wellek, René, 311, 319
Werner, Renate, 8, 326
Wordsworth, William, 26, 27

Yagi Yoshinori, 109, 270, 276, 289, 290, 294, 309, 316, 317
Yahagi Katsumi, 164
Yakushiji Noriaki, 99
Yamada Bimyō, 28
Yamagata Aritomo, 143
Yamagata Hiroshi, 97, 98, 113, 124, 127
Yamaguchi Toratarō, 134
Yamamoto Kenkichi, ix, 74, 102, 103, 107, 108, 118, 119, 125, 127, 128, 144, 222, 257, 274, 293, 305, 319
Yanagida Izumi, 40
Yanagida Kunio, 19
Yasuoka Shōtarō, 105, 109, 116, 124, 128, 181, 193, 257, 258
Yazaki Dan, 109, 119, 267
Yokomitsu Riichi, 88, 97, 156, 285
Yoshida Hiroo, 92, 96
Yoshida Seiichi, 22–23, 29, 30, 32, 35, 40, 41, 53, 54, 61, 62, 66, 68, 69, 97, 109, 110, 124, 135, 143, 145, 158, 162, 175, 186, 192, 200, 211, 256, 293, 301, 304, 305, 319
Yoshitake Yoshinori, 47, 54
Yoshiyuki Junnosuke, 105

Zimmermann, Hans-Dieter, 193, 194, 326
Zola, Émile, 21, 22–23, 24, 30, 33, 35, 37; *Nana*, 21, 23; *Roman expérimental*, 22, 24

Subject Index

aestheticism, 22, 140, 148, 251–253
affective schema, 190–191, 284
akirame, 304, 318
Akutagawa Prize, 247–248
allegory, 303
amae, 264, 273–274, 281, 303
anchorite. *See inja*
appreciation. *See kanshō*
archaism, 134, 251
art, concept of, 308–309
artist-bourgeois problem, 89
artistic character (of Japanese literary studies), 115
Asahi shinbun (newspaper), 65, 140, 145, 158
authenticity, 58, 59, 128, 135, 177, 271, 277, 288–290, 313–314
author, 46, 51, 52, 75, 99, 104, 111, 120, 132, 136, 140, 151, 152–153, 174–176, 179, 185, 187, 199, 208, 228, 237–238, 239, 253–254, 265, 266, 269–278, 301, 312, 314. *See also* writer
author-reader homology, 265, 273, 287
autobiographical, 44–46, 52, 53, 63–64, 89, 105, 112, 132, 134, 135, 140, 150–151, 162–163, 181, 185, 209, 229, 298, 312
autobiography, 32, 80, 112, 117, 118, 134, 152, 153, 163, 164, 176, 182, 192, 193, 237, 287, 304
automatic text (*écriture automatique*), 271–272, 280, 312
autonomy (of literature), 137, 148
aware. See mono no aware

bibliography, 73–74, 76–77
biographical approach, 3, 55, 228, 239, 264
biographism, 14, 311. *See also* biographical approach
biography, 193, 240, 242, 254, 311
Buddhism, 116, 190, 193, 311, 318
bundan ("literary world"), 29, 32, 33, 44, 52–53, 63, 83–84, 90, 97, 122, 139, 141, 142, 147, 150, 157, 177–179, 222, 223–227
bundan kōyūroku (records of *bundan* friendships), 140, 223
bungaku, 155, 157. *See also junbungaku*
Bungakukai (magazine/literary circle), 18, 27, 33, 67
Bungei kōza (magazine), 153
bungeigaku, 74
Bunshō sekai (magazine), 145

cataphoric, 244
catharsis, 180, 274, 292, 295

cathetic, 304
characteristics (of shishōsetsu), 2, 47, 161–164, 172, 192, 201
chōhen shōsetsu, xv, 208, 254
chōnin (townspeople), 136, 143
chōwa (harmony), 292
Christianity, 17, 19, 27, 28, 111, 240
Chūgai (magazine), 293
chūhen shōsetsu, xv, 208, 254
Chūō gakujutsu zasshi (magazine), 132
Chūō kōron (magazine), 141, 273
classical literature, Japanese. See tradition, literary
code, cultural, 6–7, 264, 283, 289, 298, 302, 307–320, 323
communication, literary, 5, 174–176, 177, 184, 197, 263–326
communicative function, 263, 269–295
confessional novel, 80, 230. See also kokuhaku shōsetsu
Confucianism, 17, 136, 137
content, level of, 244
context: historical and cultural, 13–19, 25, 53, 263; historical and social/socio-cultural, 37, 53, 68, 84, 109, 263, 307, 323, 325; individual, 37; literary, 171, 307
"conversion literature." See tenkō bungaku
cultural anthropology, 7, 302

dai san no shinjin ("third new generation"), 99, 105
Darwinism, 30
decadence, 36, 39, 201–204, 208
deep structure, 197
definition (of genre), 5, 76, 91, 93, 112, 161–194, 298
denki bungaku (biographical literature), 163
diary, 229, 230–232, 243, 264, 269, 270–271, 302, 304. See also nikki
dichotomy intellect vs. feeling, 271, 314–315
dilettantism, 149, 159, 308–309
discourse, 37, 75, 85, 91, 113–115, 317, 325

disillusionment, 28, 30
dō, 319
drama, 165, 166

écriture automatique. See automatic text
Edo (period), 15, 297
emotion, 218–219, 314–315, 324
empiricism, 264, 310–312, 322
enlightenment. See keimō
epistolary novel, 80
essay, 140
evolution, literary, 98–99, 197–200

factuality, 173, 174–179, 185, 193, 209, 224, 228, 230, 253, 263, 288, 289, 290, 310
fatalism, 218, 220, 303, 314–319
feudalism, 25, 304
fiction, 91, 103, 113, 133, 134, 161–162, 215, 217; Japanese, 15, 29; light, 153, 156, 227, 272
fictionality, 88, 89–90, 99, 215, 227, 237, 251–256, 288, 297, 308
field, semantic-semiotic, 6
film, 279
first-person form/narration, 2, 36, 66, 98, 112, 122, 132, 133, 135, 136, 142–143, 152, 153, 162, 174–175, 181–181, 201, 233, 242, 248, 301–302
first-person novel (I-novel), 80, 112, 116, 118, 131, 134, 154, 301–302
flashback, 43, 211, 214–215, 216
focus figure, 173, 175, 177, 179–192, 201, 224, 230–231, 245, 246, 273, 278, 279, 314
formalist approach, 3, 6
formalization. See hōhōka
frame/framing story, 65, 133, 184, 242, 244–247
"friendship novel." See bundan kōyūroku, tomodachi shōsetsu, yūjin shōsetsu
fūfu shōsetsu (novel about marriage), 166
fūkei shōsetsu ("landscape novel"), 302, 303
functional literature, 229–230, 269
fūryū, 110

fūzoku shōsetsu (novel of manners), 87–88

gakuya shōsetsu (backstage stories), 140
gakuyaochi shōsetsu (insider novel), 144
gei (art), 149, 301, 308–309
genbun itchi (unity of the spoken and written language), 17
Genji monogatari, 110, 137, 188–189, 315
genre, 33, 65, 75, 79, 83, 91, 95, 111–112, 117, 122–123, 126, 128, 190, 221, 224, 237, 253, 255, 271, 276, 298, 301, 307, 324
genre history, 5–6, 95–99, 167, 197–200
genre theory, 5, 6, 95–99, 100, 102, 131–194
Genroku (period), 110
gesaku, 15, 136–138, 155–156
gikyoku (drama), 166
giri (obligation), 304
gunki monogatari (war tales), 166

haikai, 301
haiku, 110, 152, 153, 183, 189, 190, 248, 300–301, 303, 308, 309
Heian (period), 121, 297, 298
Heike monogatari, 194
heimen byōsha ("flat description"), 26, 52, 64
hero. *See* protagonist
hōhōka (formalization), 99, 255–256
Hōjōki, 189, 300
honkaku shōsetsu (genuine novel), 133, 152–154, 220, 299
horizon of expectation, 4, 53, 57, 59, 126, 131
hyōron, 91

ichigen byōsha (one-dimensional description), 201
ichininshō shōsetsu, 131
Ich-Roman, 112, 127
identity, 7, 17, 28, 53, 192
individual, 34, 128, 270, 284, 308
individualism, 16, 27–28, 29, 35, 36, 41, 53, 266
individuality, 84, 283
influence, 3, 8, 32, 35–42, 46–48, 57, 116, 234, 297, 299
inja (anchorite), 84, 303
I-novel. *See* first-person novel
innovation, 4, 15, 28, 39, 57, 60; as renovation, 39–40, 60, 114, 298
intellectual, Japanese, 7, 16, 18–19, 27, 28, 45, 46, 48, 50, 51, 53, 59, 65, 85, 139, 208, 240, 246, 314, 319, 322
intertextuality, 209–211, 239, 255
irrationalism, 314–319

janru, 165, 167. *See also* genre
Japanology, xii-xiv, 119–123, 267, 325; German, xiv-xv, 7
jiden shōsetsu (autobiographical novel), 76
Jiji shinpō (magazine), 141, 157, 158
jijitsu (fact), 34, 68, 237, 271
jitsu, 136–138, 155, 161–162, 177, 307, 310
Jiyū bundan (magazine), 144
joji bungaku (prose), 166
jojō bungaku (poetry), 166
junbungaku ("pure" literature), x, 96, 97, 125, 137, 156–157, 163, 229, 248
Jūsannin (magazine), 117

Kagerō (no) nikki, 110, 297, 304
Kaishaku to kanshō (magazine), 326
Kaizō (magazine), 148, 156, 158
Kamakura (period), 298, 312
kanshi (poem in the Chinese style), 32
kanshō (appreciation), 107
kanzen chōaku (promotion of virtue and chastisement of vice), 15, 136, 137
katei shōsetsu (family novel), 166
keimō (enlightenment), 15, 16
Keizai ōrai (magazine), 79
kenkyū (academic studies), 91
Ken'yūsha, 19, 32, 35, 49, 59
kikō bungaku (travel literature), 298
Kin to gin (magazine), 117

kindai jiga (modern ego), xiii, 109, 266–267
kindaika. See modernization
kiyoshi (pure), 309
kodai (antiquity), 300
Kokin wakashū, 315
Kokon chomonjū, 312
kokoro (feeling), 314, 315, 316, 320
Kokuchō (magazine), 212
kokuhaku shōsetsu (confessional novel), 76, 140, 141, 142, 145
Kokumin no tomo (magazine), 133
kokutai, 17
Kozakura odoshi (magazine), 33
kūkyo no sedai ("generation of emptiness"), 105
kyakkansei. See objectivity
kyo (empty), 136–138, 155

language, Japanese, 86, 113–114, 121, 181
lexical-semantic level, 187
literary criticism, Japanese, x, xii, 1, 4, 76, 78, 85, 118, 151, 181, 183, 184, 199, 316, 323
literary historiography, Japanese, 4, 47, 57, 68, 86, 88
literary history, Japanese, 2–3, 131–138, 169, 170
literary studies: Japanese, xii, 4–5, 7–8, 13, 26, 31, 74–75, 95–119, 156, 161–168, 228, 239, 241, 252, 254, 255, 267, 272, 299–300, 311, 325; Western, xii–xiii, 5, 7–8, 13–14, 75, 119–123, 165, 167, 172–173, 267, 311
literary theory, 6, 7, 14, 83, 96, 114, 144, 147, 150, 154, 183, 230, 248, 263, 307
literature: Chinese, 297; comparative, 311; European, 26, 27, 33–34, 35–42, 46–48, 51, 66, 80, 84, 87, 91, 111, 151, 165, 167, 171, 176–177, 193, 203, 297, 316; French, 86, 91, 116; German, 193; Russian, 16, 20, 69, 153
lyrical capacity, 163

lyricism, 248–251, 264, 300–302. *See also* poetry

Mainichi shinbun (newspaper), 223
makoto, 136, 155, 161, 177, 274, 289, 307, 310, 313. *See also jitsu*
makoto principle, 264, 307–310, 312–313, 314, 322
Man'yōshū, 110, 193, 297
Marxism, 81–82, 86, 88, 150, 154, 240, 323. *See also* proletarian literature
mass literature. *See taishū bungaku*
mass media, Japanese, 285–286
Meiji (period), 3, 6, 14–19, 40, 63–64, 85, 132, 136, 156, 169, 277, 281, 314
Meiji restoration, 31, 137, 297, 324
memoirs, 176, 192
metacriticism, 5, 8, 114–115, 118
metaphor, 254
method, 4–5, 77, 172–173, 255–256
mi-no-ue-banashi (story about one's own life), 140, 300
miscellany literature. *See zuihitsu*
Mita bungaku (magazine), 257
modernization, 16, 17, 137, 266, 324
moderu shōsetsu (model novel), 140, 150, 223
mono no aware, 110, 116, 137, 188–191, 253, 264, 298, 302, 304, 315
monogatari, 297, 300
motif, 24, 75
muga (lack of ego), 292, 295, 303, 318. *See also mushi*
mujō(kan) (ephemerality), 188–191, 194, 235, 253, 264, 284, 298, 302, 318
Muromachi (period), 298
mushi (selflessness), 113, 127, 292, 295, 318
Myōjō (magazine), 19
mysticism, 36, 41, 140–141. *See also* nature mysticism

naikō no sedai ("introverted generation"), 92, 105, 125, 323
narcissism, 240, 241, 273–274, 276, 281

Subject Index

narrated time, 214
narrative focus, 52, 121
narrative literature, 165
narrative perspective (point of view), 43, 52, 64, 120–121, 179–182, 184, 187, 191, 201, 213–216, 224, 244, 278–280
narrative prose, Japanese, 64, 131, 137, 298
narrative rule, 231
narratology, 121–122
narrator, 179, 184, 185, 187–188, 191, 209, 213, 218, 228, 242–245, 278–285, 325; authorial, 52, 180, 280; unreliable, 246
naturalism: European, 21–24, 27, 28, 38, 41; Japanese (see *shizenshugi*)
nature mysticism, 264, 302–304
nature, 22–23, 34, 36, 38, 41, 50, 81, 82, 110, 113, 185, 189–190, 235, 250, 302–304, 322
newspaper, novel serialized in, 63
nihilism, 50
Nihon kaiki ("return to Japan"), 85
Nihon shōsetsu (magazine), 230
Nihonjinron, xi
nikki (*bungaku*: diary literature), 110, 138, 190, 192, 229, 297–300, 301, 304
ninjō (human emotions), 88, 137, 144, 304, 316
No, 110, 190
nouveau roman, 320
novella, 134, 143
Nyonin geijutsu (magazine), 230

objectivity, 22, 26, 28, 34, 38–39, 50, 60, 64, 177, 181, 245–246, 278–285

paradigms, change of, 137
parody, 66
pattern of behavior, cultural, 191, 264, 284, 302, 307
philology. *See* literary studies
plot, 24, 38, 66, 67, 138, 140, 155, 249, 283; level of, 185–187, 200
poeticity, 253

poetics, Japanese, 8, 60, 137–138, 155, 289, 315
poetry, 28, 29, 33, 136, 155, 157, 165, 166, 186, 189, 302, 312. *See also haiku, haikai*, lyricism, *shintaishi, tanka, waka*
premise, methodological, 4
production aesthetics, 6
proletarian literature, 82, 86, 91, 98, 148, 154–155, 294, 324. *See also* Marxism
prose literature, 163, 166; Japanese, 171, 297
protagonist (hero), 46, 51, 52, 65, 66, 89, 104, 120, 121, 140, 175, 179, 180, 207, 224, 228, 233, 246, 265, 278–285, 311
psychoanalysis, 104, 111, 126, 221–222, 272
psychological novel, 80, 88
psychology, 270–271, 273–274, 291
psychotherapy, 270–271, 284
public, Japanese, 33, 50, 83, 111, 142, 207, 239, 253, 277, 285–292
puroretaria bungaku. *See* proletarian literature

reader, 59, 63, 107, 139, 151, 174–176, 178–179, 182, 187–188, 199, 204, 209, 214–215, 238–239, 246, 264, 265, 275, 280–281, 285–292, 301, 325; identification with shishōsetsu hero, 188, 235–237, 287; implicit, 266; letter from, 151, 235, 326
realism, 17, 27, 29, 30, 54, 87, 289
reality, 161–162, 174–176, 178–179, 184, 186, 209, 226, 253, 264, 280–281, 288
rearisumu, 30. *See also* realism
reception, 54, 57–69, 131, 132, 136, 197, 207, 216, 238–239, 302, 312, 324
reception aesthetics, 6, 126
religion, 311
research (on shishōsetsu), 4, 73–128, 325
riariti (genuineness), 98, 177, 209–211, 310, 311

riarizumu, 30, 260, 283–284. *See also* realism
ritual, 7
rokotsunaru byōsha (unadorned description), 26, 38–39, 49, 52
roman de moeurs, 87
roman personnel, 112, 116, 118
roman-à-clef, 134, 224
romantic movement, 18, 27, 33
romanticism: European, 80, 127; Japanese (*see* romantic movement)

sakka, 116, 127
sakkaron (studies on authors), 100, 107–108
sakuhinron (studies on works), 100
sakusha, 113, 127
sararîman shōsetsu (novel about employees), 166
satori, 284, 318
secondary literature, 5, 73–128, 147, 161–168, 170, 264, 266, 308
seiji shōsetsu (political novel), 132, 137
self-reflection, 113
sentimentality, 24, 65, 188, 189, 191, 193, 220, 222, 232, 234–235, 264
series (of literary works), 31, 50, 170, 209–210, 256
setsuwa (*bungaku*), 166, 312
shajitsushugi, 30. *See also* realism
shasei (reproduced true to nature), 26, 183
Shigarami zōshi (magazine), 134
Shinchō (magazine), 154, 158, 230, 247
shinkankakuha (neoperceptionists), 82, 88
shinkyō shōsetsu (state-of-mind fiction), 76, 90, 91, 152–154, 220, 299, 300
shinpen zakki shōsetsu (pieces in note form on the immediate surroundings), 140
shinpenmono (stories on the immediate surroundings), 131, 135–136, 138
shinpiteki hanjūshugi ("mystic semi-animalism"), 26
Shinsei (magazine), 62

Shinshōsetsu (magazine), 43, 45, 152, 201, 208
shintaishi (free style poetry), 18
Shintaishi shō (Selection of Poetry in the New Style), 18
Shinto, 17, 18, 309
Shirakaba (magazine), 93
Shirakaba group, 90, 93, 98, 99, 140, 141, 142, 148
Shishōsetsu meisakusen (anthology), x, 117
shizen. *See* nature
shizenshugi (Japanese naturalism), 3, 14, 21–30, 31, 33–42, 45, 52–53, 57–58, 73, 80, 81, 82, 90, 93, 98, 99, 136, 138, 157, 177–178, 201, 266
shōsetsu, 8, 19–20, 122, 132–133, 135, 138, 154, 156, 162, 166, 223. *See also chōhen, chūhen, tanpen shōsetsu*
Shōwa (period), 88, 139, 156
social criticism, 24, 25, 26, 116, 157
socialism, 17, 19
society, 7, 34, 81, 82–83, 109, 148, 150, 154 155, 164, 239, 240, 246, 277–278, 318, 322, 323; Japanese, 7, 25, 85, 270, 273, 323
socio-psychological, 6, 7
soragoto, 136, 300
structural model, hypothetical, 5, 6, 172–173, 174–192, 197, 230, 253, 263
style, 18–19, 32, 82, 85–86, 113, 134, 165, 231, 247, 269
subject matter, 51, 75, 149, 298
subjectivism, 24, 109, 133, 140
subjectivity, 34, 36, 64, 163, 201, 278–285
superstructure, 197
surrealism, 105
symbol, 253, 303, 318

Tagebuch-Lyrik, 134
Taiheiyō (magazine), 41
Taishō (period), 96, 99, 147, 148, 156
taishū bungaku (mass literature), 97, 125, 137, 156
Taiyō (magazine), 33, 41, 42
tanbiha. *See* aestheticism

Tanemaku hito (magazine), 157
tanka, 110, 153, 300–301
tanpen shōsetsu, xv, 208, 254
taxonomy, native, 122, 123
Teikoku bungaku (magazine), 59, 62
teleologic, 198, 199
temporal structure, 182–185, 213–216, 280, 282–283
Tenbō (magazine), 237, 238
tenkō bungaku ("conversion literature"), 98, 277, 294
terminology, xv-xvi; Japanese, 1–2, 8, 19–20, 68, 75, 80–81, 91, 106–108, 113–115, 144, 165–168, 169, 183, 298; Western, 8, 80, 112
"third new generation." See *dai san no shinjin*
third-person form/narration, 2, 43, 122, 152, 162, 181–182, 301–302
tomodachi shōsetsu ("friendship novel"), 140, 223
Tosa nikki, 298, 315
tradition, literary, 6, 24, 39, 59, 60, 85, 110, 113, 138, 183, 188–192, 235, 263, 264, 297–305
Tsurezuregusa, 300
tsūzoku shōsetsu (light fiction), 156

uso (lie), 155, 283, 289. See also *kyo*

value, artistic, 176–177, 217–218, 241, 251, 255, 263, 289, 310, 311

wagamama shōsetsu (egocentric stories), 140
waka, 110, 189, 301
Waseda Bungaku (magazine), 54, 58, 141, 220
watakushishōsetsu, 1–2, 80, 133, 138–142
woman, 25, 43, 46, 47, 204–206, 210
working-class literature, 157
world literature, 167
World War I, 18
World War II, 96, 98, 154, 256, 310, 319, 323
writer, 89, 97, 107, 114, 117, 125, 151, 182, 224, 240–242, 313, 323. See also author

Yomiuri shinbun (newspaper), 63, 145
yōshiki (genre, style), 165
Yūben (magazine), 319
yūjin shōsetsu ("friendship novel"), 140, 223

zadankai (round-table talk), 97, 164
Zolaism, 22
zuihitsu (miscellanies), 83, 110, 138, 188, 192, 229, 297–300

Harvard East Asian Monographs

1. Liang Fang-chung, *The Single-Whip Method of Taxation in China*
2. Harold C. Hinton, *The Grain Tribute System of China, 1845–1911*
3. Ellsworth C. Carlson, *The Kaiping Mines, 1877–1912*
4. Chao Kuo-chün, *Agrarian Policies of Mainland China: A Documentary Study, 1949–1956*
5. Edgar Snow, *Random Notes on Red China, 1936–1945*
6. Edwin George Beal, Jr., *The Origin of Likin, 1835–1864*
7. Chao Kuo-chün, *Economic Planning and Organization in Mainland China: A Documentary Study, 1949–1957*
8. John K. Fairbank, *Ch'ing Documents: An Introductory Syllabus*
9. Helen Yin and Yi-chang Yin, *Economic Statistics of Mainland China, 1949–1957*
10. Wolfgang Franke, *The Reform and Abolition of the Traditional Chinese Examination System*
11. Albert Feuerwerker and S. Cheng, *Chinese Communist Studies of Modern Chinese History*
12. C. John Stanley, *Late Ch'ing Finance: Hu Kuang-yung as an Innovator*
13. S. M. Meng, *The Tsungli Yamen: Its Organization and Functions*
14. Ssu-yü Teng, *Historiography of the Taiping Rebellion*
15. Chun-Jo Liu, *Controversies in Modern Chinese Intellectual History: An Analytic Bibliography of Periodical Articles, Mainly of the May Fourth and Post-May Fourth Era*
16. Edward J. M. Rhoads, *The Chinese Red Army, 1927–1963: An Annotated Bibliography*
17. Andrew J. Nathan, *A History of the China International Famine Relief Commission*
18. Frank H. H. King (ed.) and Prescott Clarke, *A Research Guide to China-Coast Newspapers, 1822–1911*
19. Ellis Joffe, *Party and Army: Professionalism and Political Control in the Chinese Officer Corps, 1949–1964*

20. Toshio G. Tsukahira, *Feudal Control in Tokugawa Japan: The Sankin Kōtai System*
21. Kwang-Ching Liu, ed., *American Missionaries in China: Papers from Harvard Seminars*
22. George Moseley, *A Sino-Soviet Cultural Frontier: The Ili Kazakh Autonomous Chou*
23. Carl F. Nathan, *Plague Prevention and Politics in Manchuria, 1910–1931*
24. Adrian Arthur Bennett, *John Fryer: The Introduction of Western Science and Technology into Nineteenth-Century China*
25. Donald J. Friedman, *The Road from Isolation: The Campaign of the American Committee for Non-Participation in Japanese Aggression, 1938–1941*
26. Edward LeFevour, *Western Enterprise in Late Ch'ing China: A Selective Survey of Jardine, Matheson and Company's Operations, 1842–1895*
27. Charles Neuhauser, *Third World Politics: China and the Afro-Asian People's Solidarity Organization, 1957–1967*
28. Kungtu C. Sun, assisted by Ralph W. Huenemann, *The Economic Development of Manchuria in the First Half of the Twentieth Century*
29. Shahid Javed Burki, *A Study of Chinese Communes, 1965*
30. John Carter Vincent, *The Extraterritorial System in China: Final Phase*
31. Madeleine Chi, *China Diplomacy, 1914–1918*
32. Clifton Jackson Phillips, *Protestant America and the Pagan World: The First Half Century of the American Board of Commissioners for Foreign Missions, 1810–1860*
33. James Pusey, *Wu Han: Attacking the Present through the Past*
34. Ying-wan Cheng, *Postal Communication in China and Its Modernization, 1860–1896*
35. Tuvia Blumenthal, *Saving in Postwar Japan*
36. Peter Frost, *The Bakumatsu Currency Crisis*
37. Stephen C. Lockwood, *Augustine Heard and Company, 1858–1862*
38. Robert R. Campbell, *James Duncan Campbell: A Memoir by His Son*
39. Jerome Alan Cohen, ed., *The Dynamics of China's Foreign Relations*
40. V. V. Vishnyakova-Akimova, *Two Years in Revolutionary China, 1925–1927*, tr. Steven I. Levine
41. Meron Medzini, *French Policy in Japan during the Closing Years of the Tokugawa Regime*
42. *The Cultural Revolution in the Provinces*
43. Sidney A. Forsythe, *An American Missionary Community in China, 1895–1905*
44. Benjamin I. Schwartz, ed., *Reflections on the May Fourth Movement: A Symposium*
45. Ching Young Choe, *The Rule of the Taewŏn'gun, 1864–1873: Restoration in Yi Korea*

46. W. P. J. Hall, *A Bibliographical Guide to Japanese Research on the Chinese Economy, 1958–1970*
47. Jack J. Gerson, *Horatio Nelson Lay and Sino-British Relations, 1854–1864*
48. Paul Richard Bohr, *Famine and the Missionary: Timothy Richard as Relief Administrator and Advocate of National Reform*
49. Endymion Wilkinson, *The History of Imperial China: A Research Guide*
50. Britten Dean, *China and Great Britain: The Diplomacy of Commercial Relations, 1860–1864*
51. Ellsworth C. Carlson, *The Foochow Missionaries, 1847–1880*
52. Yeh-chien Wang, *An Estimate of the Land-Tax Collection in China, 1753 and 1908*
53. Richard M. Pfeffer, *Understanding Business Contracts in China, 1949–1963*
54. Han-sheng Chuan and Richard Kraus, *Mid-Ch'ing Rice Markets and Trade: An Essay in Price History*
55. Ranbir Vohra, *Lao She and the Chinese Revolution*
56. Liang-lin Hsiao, *China's Foreign Trade Statistics, 1864–1949*
57. Lee-hsia Hsu Ting, *Government Control of the Press in Modern China, 1900–1949*
58. Edward W. Wagner, *The Literati Purges: Political Conflict in Early Yi Korea*
59. Joungwon A. Kim, *Divided Korea: The Politics of Development, 1945–1972*
60. Noriko Kamachi, John K. Fairbank, and Chūzō Ichiko, *Japanese Studies of Modern China Since 1953: A Bibliographical Guide to Historical and Social-Science Research on the Nineteenth and Twentieth Centuries, Supplementary Volume for 1953–1969*
61. Donald A. Gibbs and Yun-chen Li, *A Bibliography of Studies and Translations of Modern Chinese Literature, 1918–1942*
62. Robert H. Silin, *Leadership and Values: The Organization of Large-Scale Taiwanese Enterprises*
63. David Pong, *A Critical Guide to the Kwangtung Provincial Archives Deposited at the Public Record Office of London*
64. Fred W. Drake, *China Charts the World: Hsu Chi-yü and His Geography of 1848*
65. William A. Brown and Urgunge Onon, translators and annotators, *History of the Mongolian People's Republic*
66. Edward L. Farmer, *Early Ming Government: The Evolution of Dual Capitals*
67. Ralph C. Croizier, *Koxinga and Chinese Nationalism: History, Myth, and the Hero*
68. William J. Tyler, tr., *The Psychological World of Natsume Sōseki*, by Doi Takeo

69. Eric Widmer, *The Russian Ecclesiastical Mission in Peking during the Eighteenth Century*
70. Charlton M. Lewis, *Prologue to the Chinese Revolution: The Transformation of Ideas and Institutions in Hunan Province, 1891–1907*
71. Preston Torbert, *The Ch'ing Imperial Household Department: A Study of its Organization and Principal Functions, 1662–1796*
72. Paul A. Cohen and John E. Schrecker, eds., *Reform in Nineteenth-Century China*
73. Jon Sigurdson, *Rural Industrialism in China*
74. Kang Chao, *The Development of Cotton Textile Production in China*
75. Valentin Rabe, *The Home Base of American China Missions, 1880–1920*
76. Sarasin Viraphol, *Tribute and Profit: Sino-Siamese Trade, 1652–1853*
77. Ch'i-ch'ing Hsiao, *The Military Establishment of the Yuan Dynasty*
78. Meishi Tsai, *Contemporary Chinese Novels and Short Stories, 1949–1974: An Annotated Bibliography*
79. Wellington K. K. Chan, *Merchants, Mandarins and Modern Enterprise in Late Ch'ing China*
80. Endymion Wilkinson, *Landlord and Labor in Late Imperial China: Case Studies from Shandong by Jing Su and Luo Lun*
81. Barry Keenan, *The Dewey Experiment in China: Educational Reform and Political Power in the Early Republic*
82. George A. Hayden, *Crime and Punishment in Medieval Chinese Drama: Three Judge Pao Plays*
83. Sang-Chul Suh, *Growth and Structural Changes in the Korean Economy, 1910–1940*
84. J. W. Dower, *Empire and Aftermath: Yoshida Shigeru and the Japanese Experience, 1878–1954*
85. Martin Collcutt, *Five Mountains: The Rinzai Zen Monastic Institution in Medieval Japan*
86. Kwang Suk Kim and Michael Roemer, *Growth and Structural Transformation*
87. Anne O. Krueger, *The Developmental Role of the Foreign Sector and Aid*
88. Edwin S. Mills and Byung-Nak Song, *Urbanization and Urban Problems*
89. Sung Hwan Ban, Pal Yong Moon, and Dwight H. Perkins, *Rural Development*
90. Noel F. McGinn, Donald R. Snodgrass, Yung Bong Kim, Shin-Bok Kim, and Quee-Young Kim, *Education and Development in Korea*
91. Leroy P. Jones and Il SaKong, *Government, Business, and Entrepreneurship in Economic Development: The Korean Case*
92. Edward S. Mason, Dwight H. Perkins, Kwang Suk Kim, David C. Cole, Mahn Je Kim, et al., *The Economic and Social Modernization of the Republic of Korea*

93. Robert Repetto, Tai Hwan Kwon, Son-Ung Kim, Dae Young Kim, John E. Sloboda, and Peter J. Donaldson, *Economic Development, Population Policy, and Demographic Transition in the Republic of Korea*
94. Parks M. Coble, Jr., *The Shanghai Capitalists and the Nationalist Government, 1927–1937*
95. Noriko Kamachi, *Reform in China: Huang Tsun-hsien and the Japanese Model*
96. Richard Wich, *Sino-Soviet Crisis Politics: A Study of Political Change and Communication*
97. Lillian M. Li, *China's Silk Trade: Traditional Industry in the Modern World, 1842–1937*
98. R. David Arkush, *Fei Xiaotong and Sociology in Revolutionary China*
99. Kenneth Alan Grossberg, *Japan's Renaissance: The Politics of the Muromachi Bakufu*
100. James Reeve Pusey, *China and Charles Darwin*
101. Hoyt Cleveland Tillman, *Utilitarian Confucianism: Ch'en Liang's Challenge to Chu Hsi*
102. Thomas A. Stanley, *Ōsugi Sakae, Anarchist in Taishō Japan: The Creativity of the Ego*
103. Jonathan K. Ocko, *Bureaucratic Reform in Provincial China: Ting Jih-ch'ang in Restoration Kiangsu, 1867–1870*
104. James Reed, *The Missionary Mind and American East Asia Policy, 1911–1915*
105. Neil L. Waters, *Japan's Local Pragmatists: The Transition from Bakumatsu to Meiji in the Kawasaki Region*
106. David C. Cole and Yung Chul Park, *Financial Development in Korea, 1945–1978*
107. Roy Bahl, Chuk Kyo Kim, and Chong Kee Park, *Public Finances during the Korean Modernization Process*
108. William D. Wray, *Mitsubishi and the N.Y.K., 1870–1914: Business Strategy in the Japanese Shipping Industry*
109. Ralph William Huenemann, *The Dragon and the Iron Horse: The Economics of Railroads in China, 1876–1937*
110. Benjamin A. Elman, *From Philosophy to Philology: Intellectual and Social Aspects of Change in Late Imperial China*
111. Jane Kate Leonard, *Wei Yuan and China's Rediscovery of the Maritime World*
112. Luke S. K. Kwong, *A Mosaic of the Hundred Days: Personalities, Politics, and Ideas of 1898*
113. John E. Wills, Jr., *Embassies and Illusions: Dutch and Portuguese Envoys to K'ang-hsi, 1666–1687*
114. Joshua A. Fogel, *Politics and Sinology: The Case of Naitō Konan (1866–1934)*

115. Jeffrey C. Kinkley, ed., *After Mao: Chinese Literature and Society, 1978–1981*
116. C. Andrew Gerstle, *Circles of Fantasy: Convention in the Plays of Chikamatsu*
117. Andrew Gordon, *The Evolution of Labor Relations in Japan: Heavy Industry, 1853–1955*
118. Daniel K. Gardner, *Chu Hsi and the* Ta Hsueh: *Neo-Confucian Reflection on the Confucian Canon*
119. Christine Guth Kanda, *Shinzō: Hachiman Imagery and its Development*
120. Robert Borgen, *Sugawara no Michizane and the Early Heian Court*
121. Chang-tai Hung, *Going to the People: Chinese Intellectual and Folk Literature, 1918–1937*
122. Michael A. Cusumano, *The Japanese Automobile Industry: Technology and Management at Nissan and Toyota*
123. Richard von Glahn, *The Country of Streams and Grottoes: Expansion, Settlement, and the Civilizing of the Sichuan Frontier in Song Times*
124. Steven D. Carter, *The Road to Komatsubara: A Classical Reading of the Renga Hyakuin*
125. Katherine F. Bruner, John K. Fairbank, and Richard T. Smith, *Entering China's Service: Robert Hart's Journals, 1854–1863*
126. Bob Tadashi Wakabayashi, *Anti-Foreignism and Western Learning in Early-Modern Japan: The New Theses of 1825*
127. Atsuko Hirai, *Individualism and Socialism: The Life and Thought of Kawai Eijirō (1891–1944)*
128. Ellen Widmer, *The Margins of Utopia:* Shui-hu hou-chuan *and the Literature of Ming Loyalism*
129. R. Kent Guy, *The Emperor's Four Treasuries: Scholars and the State in the Late Ch'ien-lung Era*
130. Peter C. Perdue, *Exhausting the Earth: State and Peasant in Hunan, 1500–1850*
131. Susan Chan Egan, *A Latterday Confucian: Reminiscences of William Hung (1893–1980)*
132. James T. C. Liu, *China Turning Inward: Intellectual-Political Changes in the Early Twelfth Century*
133. Paul A. Cohen, *Between Tradition and Modernity: Wang T'ao and Reform in Late Ch'ing China*
134. Kate Wildman Nakai, *Shogunal Politics: Arai Hakuseki and the Premises of Tokugawa Rule*
135. Parks M. Coble, *Facing Japan: Chinese Politics and Japanese Imperialism, 1931–1937*
136. Jon L. Saari, *Legacies of Childhood: Growing Up Chinese in a Time of Crisis, 1890–1920*
137. Susan Downing Videen, *Tales of Heichū*

138. Heinz Morioka and Miyoko Sasaki, *Rakugo: The Popular Narrative Art of Japan*
139. Joshua A. Fogel, *Nakae Ushikichi in China: The Mourning of Spirit*
140. Alexander Barton Woodside, *Vietnam and the Chinese Model: A Comparative Study of Vietnamese and Chinese Government in the First Half of the Nineteenth Century*
141. George Elison, *Deus Destroyed: The Image of Christianity in Early Modern Japan*
142. William D. Wray, ed., *Managing Industrial Enterprise: Cases from Japan's Prewar Experience*
143. T'ung-tsu Ch'ü, *Local Government in China under the Ch'ing*
144. Marie Anchordoguy, *Computers, Inc.: Japan's Challenge to IBM*
145. Barbara Molony, *Technology and Investment: The Prewar Japanese Chemical Industry*
146. Mary Elizabeth Berry, *Hideyoshi*
147. Laura E. Hein, *Fueling Growth: The Energy Revolution and Economic Policy in Postwar Japan*
148. Wen-hsin Yeh, *The Alienated Academy: Culture and Politics in Republican China, 1919–1937*
149. Dru C. Gladney, *Muslim Chinese: Ethnic Nationalism in the People's Republic*
150. Merle Goldman and Paul A. Cohen, eds., *Ideas Across Cultures: Essays on Chinese Thought in Honor of Benjamin I. Schwartz*
151. James Polachek, *The Inner Opium War*
152. Gail Lee Bernstein, *Japanese Marxist: A Portrait of Kawakami Hajime, 1879–1946*
153. Lloyd E. Eastman, *The Abortive Revolution: China under Nationalist Rule, 1927–1937*
154. Mark Mason, *American Multinationals and Japan: The Political Economy of Japanese Capital Controls, 1899–1980*
155. Richard J. Smith, John K. Fairbank, and Katherine F. Bruner, *Robert Hart and China's Early Modernization: His Journals, 1863–1866*
156. George J. Tanabe, Jr., *Myōe the Dreamkeeper: Fantasy and Knowledge in Kamakura Buddhism*
157. William Wayne Farris, *Heavenly Warriors: The Evolution of Japan's Military, 500–1300*
158. Yu-ming Shaw, *An American Missionary in China: John Leighton Stuart and Chinese-American Relations*
159. James B. Palais, *Politics and Policy in Traditional Korea*
160. Douglas Reynolds, *China, 1898–1912: The Xinzheng Revolution and Japan*
161. Roger Thompson, *China's Local Councils in the Age of Constitutional Reform*

162. William Johnston, *The Modern Epidemic: History of Tuberculosis in Japan*
163. Constantine Nomikos Vaporis, *Breaking Barriers: Travel and the State in Early Modern Japan*
164. Irmela Hijiya-Kirschnereit, *Rituals of Self-Revelation: Shishōsetsu as Literary Genre and Socio-Cultural Phenomenon*
165. James C. Baxter, *The Meiji Unification through the Lens of Ishikawa Prefecture*
166. Thomas R. H. Havens, *Architects of Affluence: The Tsutsumi Family and the Seibu-Saison Enterprises in Twentieth-Century Japan*
167. Anthony Hood Chambers, *The Secret Window: Ideal Worlds in Tanizaki's Fiction*
168. Steven J. Ericson, *The Sound of the Whistle: Railroads and the State in Meiji Japan*

'Futon' Tayama Katai
'The Drifting Cloud' Futabatei Shimei
'Comparing Heights' Higuchi Ichiyō (F)